Constructivism in International Relations

Maja Zehfuss' book offers a fundamental critique of constructivism, focusing on the work of Wendt, Onuf and Kratochwil. Using Germany's shift towards participation in international military operations as an illustration, she demonstrates why each version of constructivism fails in its own project and comes apart on the basis of its own assumptions. Inspired by Derridean thought, this book highlights the political consequences of constructivist representations of reality. Each critique concludes that constructivist notions of key concepts are impossible, and that this is not merely a question of theoretical inconsistency, but of politics. The book is premised on the notion that the 'empirical' and the 'theoretical' are less separate than is acknowledged in international relations, and must be read as intertwined. Zehfuss examines the scholars' role in international relations, worrying that, by looking to constructivism as the future, they will be severely curtailing their ability to act responsibly in this area.

MAJA ZEHFUSS is Lecturer in International Relations at the University of Warwick. She has contributed articles to *Zeitschrift für Internationale Beziehungen* and the *European Journal of International Relations*.

CAMBRIDGE STUDIES IN INTERNATIONAL RELATIONS: 83

Constructivism in International Relations

CAMBRIDGE STUDIES IN INTERNATIONAL RELATIONS

Constructivism in International Relations

The politics of reality

Maja Zehfuss

University of Warwick

CAMBRIDGE
UNIVERSITY PRESS

PUBLISHED BY THE PRESS SYNDICATE OF THE UNIVERSITY OF CAMBRIDGE
The Pitt Building, Trumpington Street, Cambridge, United Kingdom

CAMBRIDGE UNIVERSITY PRESS
The Edinburgh Building, Cambridge CB2 2RU, UK
40 West 20th Street, New York, NY 10011-4211, USA
477 Williamstown Road, Port Melbourne, VIC 3207, Australia
Ruiz de Alarcón 13, 28014 Madrid, Spain
Dock House, The Waterfront, Cape Town 8001, South Africa

http://www.cambridge.org

First published 2002

Printed in the United Kingdom at the University Press, Cambridge

Typeface Palatino 10/12.5 pt   *System* LATEX 2$_\varepsilon$ [TB]

A catalogue record for this book is available from the British Library

ISBN 0 521 81544 4 hardback
ISBN 0 521 89466 2 paperback

For Gertrud Wagner

Contents

Contents

x

Acknowledgements

The urge to write about the politics of reality stems to some extent from experiences before and beyond IR. In this sense I owe a hidden debt especially to the Germain family, Andrzej Sulima, Cornelius Görres and Mischa Wagenknecht.

The book has profited from discussions too numerous to recall, especially with those involved in the Aberystwyth Post International Group and CRIPT (Contemporary Research in International Political Theory). The Department of International Politics in Aberystwyth provided a congenial and supportive atmosphere during my time there and my thanks go to everyone who contributed to making it so.

I would like to thank those who have read, in part or in whole, various versions of this book or of work towards it and who have offered incisive comments: Ian Clark, Stuart Elden, Daniela Kroslak, Debbie Lisle, Richard Little, Nick Wheeler and an anonymous reader for Cambridge University Press. Friedrich Kratochwil, Nicholas Onuf and Alexander Wendt have all commented on my work and, although they obviously disagree with my argument to a greater or lesser extent, supported this project in various ways. I am particularly grateful to Nick Onuf for his detailed comments on the entire manuscript. Special thanks are due to Roger Tooze for inspiration on chapter 2 and to Horst Zehfuß for research support. I would also like to thank John Haslam at CUP for his support and Karen Anderson Howes for her work at the copy-editing stage. She impressed me with both her eye for detail and her respect for my text.

My greatest debt is to Jenny Edkins and Steve Smith. Their intellectual generosity, challenging queries and continuing support have not only made this a better book; their spirit and humour have also made me enjoy writing it.

The research for this book was supported by the University of Wales, Aberystwyth and the Economic and Social Research Council. It was completed whilst at the University of Warwick. My thanks go to all these institutions.

Material especially from chapters 2 and 3 has previously been published as 'Constructivism and Identity: A Dangerous Liaison', *European Journal of International Relations* 7 (2001), 315–48, and is reprinted by permission of Sage Publications Ltd (© Sage Publications and ECPR). Earlier versions of my introductions to constructivisms and the argument about Wendt and language have appeared as 'Sprachlosigkeit schränkt ein. Zur Bedeutung von Sprache in konstruktivistischen Theorien', *Zeitschrift für Internationale Beziehungen* 5 (1998), 109–37, and 'Constructivisms in International Relations: Wendt, Onuf, and Kratochwil', in Karin M. Fierke and Knud Erik Jørgensen (eds.), *Constructing International Relations: The Next Generation* (Armonk, NY: M. E. Sharpe, 2001), pp. 54–75. I gratefully acknowledge permission from Nomos Verlagsgesellschaft and M. E. Sharpe to reprint this material here.

Finally, the book could not have been written without the support of Edith, Horst and Ulrich Zehfuß. Gertrud Wagner, who should have been an academic and, but for a particular kind of the politics of reality, surely would have been, will always refuse to believe how much her unceasing support means to me. I dedicate this book to her.

Abbreviations

A	Wendt, 'Anarchy Is What States Make of It'
AMF	Allied Command Europe Mobile Force
AWACS	Airborne Warning and Control System
BMV	Bundesministerium der Verteidigung (Ministry of Defence)
C	Onuf, 'Constructivism: A User's Manual'
CDU	Christlich Demokratische Union (Christian Democratic Union)
CIS	Onuf, 'The Constitution of International Society'
CM	Onuf, 'A Constructivist Manifesto'
CSCE	Conference for Security and Cooperation in Europe
CSU	Christlich-Soziale Union (Christian-Social Union)
ECR	electronic combat and reconnaissance
FAZ	*Frankfurter Allgemeine Zeitung*
FDP	Freie Demokratische Partei (Free Democratic Party)
FoL	Derrida, 'Force of Law'
FR	*Frankfurter Rundschau*
FRG	Federal Republic of Germany
GDR	German Democratic Republic
IFOR	Implementation Force
IR	International Relations
ISC	Wendt, 'Identity and Structural Change'
LI	Derrida, *Limited Inc*.
LL	Linke Liste (List of the Left)
NATO	North Atlantic Treaty Organization
OG	Derrida, *Of Grammatology*
OH	Derrida, *The Other Heading*
P	Derrida, *Positions*

PDS	Partei des Demokratischen Sozialismus (Party of Democratic Socialism)
RND	Kratochwil, *Rules, Norms, and Decisions*
RNV	Kratochwil, 'Rules, Norms, Values'
SACEUR	Supreme Allied Commander Europe
SED	Sozialistische Einheitspartei Deutschlands (Socialist Unity Party of Germany)
SFOR	Stabilisation Force
SPD	Sozialdemokratische Partei Deutschlands (Social Democratic Party of Germany)
STIP	Wendt, *Social Theory of International Politics*
SZ	*Süddeutsche Zeitung*
THW	Technisches Hilfwerk (Technical Relief Organisation)
UNHCR	United Nations High Commissioner for Refugees
UNOSOM	United Nations Operation in Somalia
UNPROFOR	United Nations Protection Force in the Former Yugoslavia
UNTAC	United Nations Transitional Authority in Cambodia
WEU	Western European Union
WOM	Onuf, *World of Our Making*

1   Introduction

Celebrated by some and dismissed or even regarded as dangerous by others, constructivism has acquired considerable significance in International Relations.[1] Whilst judgements on the value and validity of constructivism differ widely, it seems all but impossible not to have an opinion. As a consequence, it is important to provide a critique that engages the claims of constructivism in detail. However, there is debate not only about whether constructivism is good for us but also, given the intellectual diversity of work labelled constructivist, about what it is in the first place. This poses a serious problem for the possibility of critique. This book focuses on the work of three key scholars; it does not aim to explore the whole range of constructivist work. And yet my critique is, I will argue, relevant to constructivism more broadly.

My critique works through careful readings of the work of Alexander Wendt, Friedrich Kratochwil and Nicholas Onuf, which are, in each case, related to the shift of the Federal Republic of Germany (FRG) towards using the military instrument in the international realm after the end of the Cold War. This allows me to offer a critique that is of relevance to experts in the area, but is at the same time accessible to those with only a passing familiarity with the matter at issue. In order to contextualise my argument, the introduction starts by visiting the literature on what constructivism is and why it matters. The second section of the chapter introduces the work of Wendt, Kratochwil and Onuf and the third provides some background knowledge on German military involvement abroad. Different readers may find that they wish to skip one or other of these sections, which chiefly aim to provide an introduction to the material

---

[1] In this book, International Relations or IR refers to the discipline, and international relations to what is construed as its empirical subject matter.

used throughout the book. The final section of the introduction provides a plan of the book together with a brief preview of the overall argument.

Constructivism in International Relations

The significance of constructivism is established more easily than its identity. Constructivism as a phenomenon has become inescapable. Conference panels concerning the social construction of concepts involved in the study of international relations and of actors involved in their making proliferate. A growing number of scholars claim to be studying international phenomena in a constructivist vein.[2] Workshops are even held to discuss the merits of constructivism for the study of international issues as such.[3] The significance of constructivism within IR is underlined by the claim, made repeatedly, that 'the debate' between rationalists and constructivists either currently is, or is about to become, the most significant one in the discipline.[4] In an alternative representation, constructivism is thought to occupy 'the middle ground' between rationalism and more radical approaches, often called reflectivist or relativist. It is no surprise, then, that the field has been described as undergoing or having undergone a 'constructivist turn'.[5] Interestingly, in

[2] See, for example, Emanuel Adler and Michael Barnett (eds.), *Security Communities* (Cambridge University Press, 1998); Peter J. Katzenstein (ed.), *The Culture of National Security: Norms and Identity in World Politics* (New York: Columbia University Press, 1996); Martha Finnemore, *National Interests in International Society* (Ithaca and London: Cornell University Press, 1996); Audie Klotz, *Norms in International Relations: The Struggle Against Apartheid* (Ithaca and London: Cornell University Press, 1995); Thomas Risse-Kappen, 'Democratic Peace – Warlike Democracies? A Social Constructivist Interpretation of the Liberal Argument', *European Journal of International Relations* 1 (1995), 491–517; Kurt Burch and Robert A. Denemark (eds.), *Constituting International Political Economy* (Boulder and London: Lynne Rienner Publishers, 1997); Jutta Weldes, Mark Laffey, Hugh Gusterson and Raymond Duvall (eds.), *Cultures of Insecurity: States, Communities, and the Production of Danger* (Minneapolis and London: University of Minnesota Press, 1999).
[3] See Knud Erik Jørgensen (ed.), *The Aarhus–Norsminde Papers: Constructivism, International Relations and European Studies* (Aarhus University, 1997).
[4] Richard Price and Christian Reus-Smit, 'Dangerous Liaisons? Critical International Theory and Constructivism', *European Journal of International Relations* 4 (1998), 263; Peter J. Katzenstein, Robert O. Keohane and Stephen Krasner, 'International Organization and the Study of World Politics', *International Organization* 52 (1998), 646; John Gerard Ruggie, *Constructing the World Polity: Essays on International Institutionalization* (London and New York: Routledge, 1998), p. 4; K. M. Fierke and Knud Erik Jørgensen, 'Introduction', in Karin M. Fierke and Knud Erik Jørgensen, *Constructing International Relations: The Next Generation* (Armonk, NY and London: M. E. Sharpe, 2001), p. 3.
[5] Jeffrey T. Checkel, 'The Constructivist Turn in International Relations Theory', *World Politics* 50 (1998), 324–48; Price and Reus-Smit, 'Dangerous Liaisons?', 263; Torbjørn L. Knutsen, *A History of International Relations Theory*, 2nd edn (Manchester University Press, 1997), p. 279.

terms of indicating an increasing acceptance of the approach, constructivism has ceased to be a matter only for the theoretically minded scholar. Textbooks targeted at undergraduate students introduce the approach at least in passing[6] and we are informed by a journal aimed at an audience beyond academia that constructivism is one of the three standard ways of analysing international politics.[7] A 'constructivist turn' could therefore be said to have occurred beyond the confines of theoretical debate.

Despite this unmistakable surge of constructivism, it remains difficult to identify its key claims uncontroversially. Thus I start by exploring the different assessments of constructivism's position in the discipline, which are based on different understandings of what constructivism is. In the first view, which opposes constructivism to rationalism, traditional or 'mainstream' approaches, such as Neorealism and Neoliberalism, are construed as rationalist. Although so-called rationalists typically share a range of assumptions about the nature of international politics, such as the notion that state actors are unitary and rational, their attitude towards what counts as reliable knowledge is key.[8] Rationalists subscribe to the tenets of what Steve Smith outlines as positivism. They believe that social phenomena may be explained in the same way as the natural world and that facts and values may be clearly separated. Their goal is to uncover regularities. Scientific enquiry, in their view, must rely on empirical validation or falsification.[9] The upshot of the rationalist position is therefore that actors and concepts are exogenously given. Actors act in this pregiven world according to the demands of instrumental reason. This assumption of instrumental rationality is crucial,[10] hence the term 'rationalism'.

Constructivism, as the supposedly polar opposite in this debating constellation, challenges the assumptions of rationalism, particularly

---

[6] Charles W. Kegley jr and Eugene R. Wittkopf, *World Politics: Trend and Transformation*, 7th edn (New York: St. Martin's, 1999), p. 39; Paul R. Viotti and Mark V. Kauppi, *International Relations Theory: Realism, Pluralism, Globalism and Beyond*, 3rd edn (Boston: Allyn and Bacon, 1999), pp. 217–18 and 429–30; more substantially John Baylis and Steve Smith (eds.), *The Globalization of World Politics* (Oxford University Press, 1997), pp. 183–7 and 204–5.

[7] Stephen M. Walt, 'International Relations: One World, Many Theories', *Foreign Policy* 110 (1998), 38.

[8] Steve Smith, 'The Discipline of International Relations: Still an American Social Science?', *British Journal of Politics and International Relations* 2 (2000), 382–3. Checkel claims the opposite: that the constructivists' debate with the mainstream is about ontology (Checkel, 'Constructivist Turn', 327).

[9] Steve Smith, 'Positivism and Beyond', in Steve Smith, Ken Booth and Marysia Zalewski (eds.), *International Theory: Positivism and Beyond* (Cambridge University Press, 1996), p. 16.

[10] Katzenstein, Keohane and Krasner, '*International Organization*', 679.

the notion of an unchanging reality of international politics. Anarchy is not an unavoidable feature of international reality; it is, in Wendt's famous words, 'what states make of it' (A). As a result of recognising that practice influences outcome, the social world is seen as constructed, not given. States may be self-interested but they continuously (re)define what that means. Their identities may change. Norms help define situations and hence influence international practice in a significant way. In order to appreciate this influence of identities and/or norms it is necessary to explore intersubjective meaning. Thus the positivist conception of the social world and knowledge about it is challenged. Interpreting meaning and grasping the influence of changing practice, rather than empirically validating explanations of independent mechanisms, become central. Thus constructivism is seen as pitched against rationalism. This debate is then the main site of contention in IR theory.

This notion of the rationalist–constructivist debate is problematic. For a start, whilst German scholars have indeed discussed the merits of rational choice versus constructivist approaches at length,[11] there is little evidence of a *debate* in the Anglo-Saxon context. In surveys of the state of the discipline in general and of constructivism in particular we are told time and again that this debate is happening and that it is crucially important. And yet we do not find exchanges between rationalist and

---

[11] Harald Müller, 'Internationale Beziehungen als kommunikatives Handeln. Zur Kritik der utilitaristischen Handlungstheorien', *Zeitschrift für Internationale Beziehungen* 1 (1994), 15–44; Harald Müller, 'Spielen hilft nicht immer. Die Grenzen des Rational-Choice-Ansatzes und der Platz der Theorie des kommunikativen Handelns in der Analyse internationaler Beziehungen', *Zeitschrift für Internationale Beziehungen* 2 (1995), 371–91; Gerald Schneider, 'Rational Choice und kommunikatives Handeln. Eine Replik auf Harald Müller', *Zeitschrift für Internationale Beziehungen* 1 (1994), 357–66; Otto Keck, 'Rationales kommunikatives Handeln in den internationalen Beziehungen. Ist eine Verbindung von Rational-Choice-Theorie und Habermas' Theorie des kommunikativen Handelns möglich?', *Zeitschrift für Internationale Beziehungen* 2 (1995), 5–48; Otto Keck, 'Zur sozialen Konstruktion des Rational-Choice-Ansatzes. Einige Klarstellungen zur Rationalismus-Konstruktivismus-Debatte', *Zeitschrift für Internationale Beziehungen* 4 (1997), 139–51; Thomas Risse-Kappen, 'Reden ist nicht billig. Zur Debatte um Kommunikation und Rationalität', *Zeitschrift für Internationale Beziehungen* 2 (1995), 171–84; Rainer Schmalz-Bruns, 'Die Theorie kommunikativen Handelns – eine Flaschenpost? Anmerkungen zur jüngsten Debatte in den internationalen Beziehungen', *Zeitschrift für Internationale Beziehungen* 2 (1995), 347–70; Volker von Prittwitz, 'Verständigung über die Verständigung. Anmerkungen und Ergänzungen zur Debatte über Rationalität und Kommunikation in den Internationalen Beziehungen', *Zeitschrift für Internationale Beziehungen* 3 (1996), 133–47; Bernhard Zangl and Michael Zürn, 'Argumentatives Handeln bei internationalen Verhandlungen. Moderate Anmerkungen zur post-realistischen Debatte', *Zeitschrift für Internationale Beziehungen* 3 (1996), 341–66; Michael Müller, 'Vom Dissensrisiko zur Ordnung der internationalen Staatenwelt. Zum Projekt einer normativ gehaltvollen Theorie', *Zeitschrift für Internationale Beziehungen* 3 (1996), 367–79.

constructivist scholars in key journals. However, the emphasis on this non-existent debate is interesting in itself; for the idea of the rationalist–constructivist debate as a crucial site for cutting-edge IR theory establishes not only the importance of constructivism but also the continued significance of rationalism.

In another popular representation constructivism can 'build a bridge'[12] between different approaches, provide a 'via media'[13] or occupy 'the middle ground'.[14] This is again as interesting as it is problematic. As I argue in chapter 2, it is not clear that the so-called middle ground is possible. Even if it is, the notion of 'middle ground' envisages constructivists as situated between, and able to engage in conversation with, rationalists and those deemed more radical than the constructivists. The emphasis on the constructivist–rationalist debate as the centre of attention, however, is more appropriate insofar as constructivists seem markedly more interested in conducting a conversation with one side than the other. Contrast the superficial and often caricatured treatment of other 'reflectivists' and their claims[15] with the careful reasoning vis-à-vis Realists and other rationalists.[16] Jeffrey Checkel even wants to 'synthesize' constructivism and rationalism, as does Wendt in the final pages of his *Social Theory of International Politics*.[17] In that sense, the invention of the rationalist–constructivist debate as the centre of action in IR theory underlines that the so-called middle ground is much closer to rationalism than to the other side.

Interestingly, the rhetoric of the middle has normative overtones which are not addressed.[18] It is portrayed, at least implicitly, as more reasonable than the position of those who, as they are not in the middle ground, must be on the fringe. Paradoxically, this implication is again underscored by the description revolving around a rationalist–constructivist

[12] A 394; Emanuel Adler, 'Seizing the Middle Ground: Constructivism in World Politics', *European Journal of International Relations* 3 (1997), 323.
[13] Steve Smith, 'New Approaches to International Theory', in Baylis and Smith, *Globalization of World Politics*, p. 188.
[14] Adler, 'Seizing the Middle Ground'; Viotti and Kauppi, *International Relations Theory*, p. 217.
[15] For example, Adler, 'Seizing the Middle Ground', 321 and 332–4.
[16] For example, *STIP passim*.
[17] Jeffrey Checkel, 'International Norms and Domestic Politics: Bridging the Rationalist–Constructivist Divide', *European Journal of International Relations* 3 (1997), 488; *STIP* 367. See also Alexander Wendt, 'On the Via Media: A Response to the Critics', *Review of International Studies* 26 (2000), 179–80.
[18] See Zangl and Zürn, 'Argumentatives Handeln', esp. 343–4, who promote a 'moderate constructivism' occupying a 'middle position' without explaining why this is desirable. See also Adler, 'Seizing the Middle Ground', 348.

debate. In this representation any approach that challenges the rationalist assumption of unchanging facts is subsumed under the category of constructivism. This covers a range of approaches and therefore the constructivist category is then often subdivided, for example into modernist and postmodern, or conventional, critical and postmodern. Of these, only the modernist or conventional variant is really understood to be in debate with rationalism. Hence, even in the representation that appears to include all critical approaches under the constructivist label, only the 'middle-ground' constructivists are proper constructivists. In contrast, so-called postmodernists are beyond the pale, as they are seen to consider social science impossible and to lack the willingness to debate rationalists in a scholarly way.[19] Hence, Nalini Persram objects to what she calls the 'strategic use of social constructivism',[20] which is part and parcel of the acceptance of constructivism. Representing it as the most significant 'radical' approach makes an engagement with (other) critical approaches seem superfluous and thus effectively marginalises them. This is confirmed by portrayals of the theoretical landscape which see Realism at one end of the spectrum and constructivism at the other,[21] leaving no room for (other) critical thinking. Either it will be subsumed under the constructivist label or it will be entirely dismissed. In both cases it disappears from sight, and thinking space is closed down. Thus constructivism is significant not only because it is considered central but also because of the possibility of deploying it strategically to exclude more radical perspectives from consideration. This in particular makes critique necessary.

Thus, constructivism is clearly significant to IR (theory) and its future development. However, we still lack clarity on what constructivism is. Critique usually starts with a clear delineation of its target. Although constructivism has been defined, explained, assessed and positioned,[22] there is little agreement about what it is. Some subsume any non-mainstream and hence non-rationalist approach under the constructivist label, whilst others want to reserve the term more specifically for

---

[19] Katzenstein, Keohane and Krasner, *'International Organization'*, 677.
[20] Nalini Persram, 'Coda: Sovereignty, Subjectivity, Strategy', in Jenny Edkins, Nalini Persram and Véronique Pin-Fat (eds.), *Sovereignty and Subjectivity* (Boulder and London: Lynne Rienner Publishers, 1999), p. 164.
[21] For example, Emanuel Adler and Michael Barnett, 'Security Communities in Theoretical Perspective', in Adler and Barnett, *Security Communities*, p. 10.
[22] Adler, 'Seizing the Middle Ground'; Checkel, 'Constructivist Turn'; Ted Hopf, 'The Promise of Constructivism in International Relations Theory', *International Security* 23 (1998), 171–200; Price and Reus-Smit, 'Dangerous Liaisons?'

a group of closely related approaches. The first classification usually involves identifying several different strands of constructivism, such as conventional, critical and postmodern.[23] This is in tension with those who offer a specific definition of constructivism, such as Adler who informs us that constructivism 'is the view that *the manner in which the material world shapes and is shaped by human action and interaction depends on dynamic normative and epistemic interpretations of the material world'*.[24] Such attempts at definition draw attention to an interesting point, the role of the material world in social construction, but they cannot obscure the intellectual diversity of constructivist work and the resulting lack of agreement on what constructivism is. Some reserve the term exclusively to label Wendt's approach.[25] More usually, however, constructivism is thought to include a range of distinct varieties.[26] Thus, one could say that constructivism provides the 'general rubric' under which a range of approaches are subsumed.[27]

The definitional problem of what constructivism is is not just a matter of whether different scholars claiming the constructivist label are engaged in the same project, of how diverse the constructivist camp is. It is very much about who is in it in the first place. For example, some argue for the need clearly to distinguish constructivism from poststructuralism or postmodernism.[28] Others, however, include a postmodernist variant.[29] Poststructuralists, such as Roxanne Lynn Doty and David Campbell, are sometimes mentioned in references to constructivism.[30]

[23] See Katzenstein, Keohane and Krasner, *'International Organization'*, 675.
[24] Adler, 'Seizing the Middle Ground', 322. All italics in quotations are as in the original unless otherwise noted.
[25] Andreas Hasenclever, Peter Mayer and Volker Rittberger, *Theories of International Regimes* (Cambridge University Press, 1997), p. 188; also Kegley and Wittkopf, *World Politics*, p. 39.
[26] See, for example, Adler, 'Seizing the Middle Ground', 335–6; Hans-Martin Jaeger, 'Konstruktionsfehler des Konstruktivismus in den Internationalen Beziehungen', *Zeitschrift für Internationale Beziehungen* 3 (1996), 315; STIP 1; and Knutsen, *History of IR Theory*, p. 279.
[27] Thomas U. Berger, 'The Past in the Present: Historical Memory and German National Security Policy', *German Politics* 6 (1997), 43.
[28] Adler, 'Seizing the Middle Ground', 320–1; Adler and Barnett, 'Security Communities', p. 12; Katzenstein, Keohane and Krasner, *'International Organization'*, 648 and 677–8; Vendulka Kubálková, Nicholas Onuf and Paul Kowert, 'Constructing Constructivism', in Vendulka Kubálková, Nicholas Onuf and Paul Kowert (eds.), *International Relations in a Constructed World* (Armonk, NY and London: M. E. Sharpe, 1998), p. 4.
[29] Ruggie, *Constructing the World Polity*, p. 35; Price and Reus-Smit, 'Dangerous Liaisons?', 269; Knutsen, *History of IR Theory*, p. 280.
[30] Michael C. Williams and Keith Krause, 'Preface: Towards Critical Security Studies', in Keith Krause and Michael C. Williams (eds.), *Critical Security Studies: Concepts and Cases* (London: UCL Press, 1997), p. xxi, n. 10; STIP 4.

Yet they are likely to reject any inclusion into the constructivist camp,[31] especially when it comes together with a definition of the position, such as Adler's, that excludes them intellectually.

Quite apart from the argument over whose work is appropriately classified as constructivist, there is also discussion about whether constructivism is properly to be seen as a theory of IR or rather as a philosophical category, a meta-theory or a method for empirical research, or whether it is indeed an approach relevant at several levels.[32] Despite all this, one would assume there to be minimum requirements for being a member of the club. In this context, Kratochwil's assertion that the 'issue is not whether somebody says or believes that she or he is a constructivist, but whether or not such a (self-)identification makes sense in view of some of the tenets defining constructivism'[33] is relevant, but he fails to spell out the tenets he has in mind.[34]

Even if the application of the label 'constructivist' is limited to those who claim it themselves, there is still a tremendous variety of work left. Some are interested in the significance of norms and identity for the construction of reality.[35] Others make norms defined as shared expectations about appropriate behaviour central to their argument.[36] There are contributions to the question of community building in relation to security issues,[37] explorations of the construction of national interests,[38]

---

[31] See David Campbell, 'Epilogue: The Disciplinary Politics of Theorizing Identity', in David Campbell, *Writing Security: United States Foreign Policy and the Politics of Identity*, revised edn (Manchester University Press, 1998), pp. 218–21; David Campbell, *National Deconstruction: Violence, Identity, and Justice in Bosnia* (Minneapolis and London: University of Minnesota Press, 1998), pp. 24–5; Roxanne Lynn Doty, *Imperial Encounters: The Politics of Representation in North–South Relations* (Minneapolis and London: University of Minnesota Press, 1996), 163–71.

[32] See Knud Erik Jørgensen, 'Four Levels and a Discipline', in Fierke and Jørgensen, *Constructing International Relations*, pp. 36–53; Friedrich V. Kratochwil, 'Constructivism as an Approach to Interdisciplinary Study', in Fierke and Jørgensen, *Constructing International Relations*, pp. 13–35; Checkel, 'Constructivist Turn', 325.

[33] Friedrich Kratochwil, 'Constructing a New Orthodoxy? Wendt's "Social Theory of International Politics" and the Constructivist Challenge', *Millennium: Journal of International Studies* 29 (2000), 89.

[34] He is somewhat more explicit in Kratochwil, 'Constructivism as an Approach', esp. pp. 16–19.

[35] Katzenstein, *Culture of National Security*.

[36] Finnemore, *National Interests in International Society*; Audie Klotz, 'Norms Reconstituting Interests: Global Racial Equality and US Sanctions Against South Africa', *International Organization* 49 (1995), 451–78; Klotz, *Norms in International Relations*.

[37] Adler and Barnett, *Security Communities*.

[38] Jutta Weldes, 'Constructing National Interests', *European Journal of International Relations* 2 (1996), 275–318; Jutta Weldes, *Constructing National Interests: The United States and the Cuban Missile Crisis* (Minneapolis and London: University of Minnesota Press, 1999).

analyses of language games.[39] This diversity is not merely about putting different concepts at the centre of the analysis but stems from relying on different intellectual traditions, ranging from various strands of sociology to Wittgensteinian thought. The intellectual diverseness of work that is represented as constructivist, either by its author or by others, makes it difficult to critique the approach at all, as it is not clear that there are claims and assumptions which are shared across the spectrum.

It is not surprising, then, that a sustained critical engagement with constructivist claims is lacking in the literature. Those who fashion themselves as constructivists have preferred to get on with empirical work and sometimes to explain to the uninitiated what constructivism is really all about. On the other hand, those who are critical of the approach understandably do not want to go beyond a discussion of constructivist assumptions with which they disagree from the start.[40] Hence, for all the hype surrounding it, it is tempting to argue that constructivism has not been taken seriously, either by its supporters or by its critics.

The impossibility of precisely delineating 'the' constructivist position must not mean, however, that we may only speechlessly watch the spectacle of the constructivist 'success story',[41] unable to pin it down for long enough to offer a well-founded critique. The significance of constructivism in IR, especially in its role as critical but acceptable alternative to the mainstream,[42] is such that critique is necessary. Its possibility is a more complex matter due to the lack of agreement on what this constructivism, which is thought to have such an impact on the discipline, actually is. To make the necessary critique possible, my strategy is to confine my critique to the work of three key constructivist scholars, Wendt, Kratochwil and Onuf, who have all had a part in making constructivism, and to draw wider conclusions only after having considered their arguments in detail. The next section will introduce their work to provide the background for an analysis that integrates theoretical arguments and empirical material. Beforehand, it is useful briefly to outline key elements of my approach.

---

[39] K. M. Fierke, 'Multiple Identities, Interfacing Games: The Social Construction of Western Action in Bosnia', *European Journal of International Relations* 2 (1996), 467–97; K. M. Fierke, *Changing Games, Changing Strategies: Critical Investigations in Security* (Manchester University Press, 1998).

[40] For example, Campbell, 'Epilogue'; Persram, 'Coda'.

[41] Stefano Guzzini, 'A Reconstruction of Constructivism in International Relations', *European Journal of International Relations* 6 (2000), 147.

[42] See Guzzini, 'Reconstruction', 147–8.

Although there is no agreed definition of constructivism, and I do not offer one, my analysis throughout the book will show that the constructivisms under consideration agree on the assumption of limited construction. That is, when their constructivist analysis starts, some reality has already been made and is taken as given. Constructivist work stresses the significance of meaning but assumes, at the same time, the existence of an *a priori* reality. This places it, intentionally or not, in a middle-ground position which is problematic but central to constructivism. Wendt's, Kratochwil's and Onuf's work thus reflect different ways in which the middle ground can be taken.

My argument is inspired by Jacques Derrida's thought, although it is not written only for those steeped in Continental philosophy. The Derridean commitment, which is laid out in detail in chapter 5, is significant for my analysis from the start. Accordingly, it seeks to reveal not what the constructivists in question *intend* to do, but what their theories do do, that is, how their own assumptions undermine their stated purpose and make their theories unravel. In the same spirit, the 'application' of the different theories to the case of German military involvement abroad, deliberately often using the same material and indeed the same quotations in the different theoretical contexts, does not aim to test the theories by holding them up against a supposed reality, but clarifies and illustrates how each theory's assumptions undermine it, make it 'deconstruct'. This strategy of bringing together without distinction what are called theoretical arguments and what is seen as empirical material is based on my interpretation of Derrida's claim that 'there is nothing outside of the text' presented in chapter 5. The crucial point for the moment is that it is the interplay between 'theory' and 'empirical material' which is relevant. Before my analytical strategy and its implications can be explained more fully in the final section of this introduction, it is necessary to outline the three constructivisms and the issues involved in the FRG's shift towards participation in international military operations.

Three constructivisms

Onuf first introduced the term 'constructivism' to IR and both Kratochwil and Wendt refer to this fact.[43] With *World of Our Making*,

---

[43] *WOM*; Rey Koslowski and Friedrich V. Kratochwil, 'Understanding Change in International Politics: The Soviet Empire's Demise and the International System', *International Organization* 48 (1994), 216, n. 3; A 393; and *STIP* 1.

Onuf presented the first constructivist theory of international relations in 1989. This ambitious and dense book was an unlikely candidate for reshaping the way IR scholars think. Indeed, the significance accorded to constructivism today is surprising in view of the limited impact this first formulation had. Yet it provided the label, taken up by Wendt in his 1992 article 'Anarchy Is What States Make of It', which has since proved attractive to many. Hence Wendt is credited with popularising the approach.[44] The reception of Wendt's book, which has been hailed as extremely important,[45] underscores the significance constructivism is attributed in IR today. Kratochwil, finally, who is also identified as a key constructivist,[46] co-authored an article with John Ruggie[47] early on which established the significance of intersubjectivity, a central constructivist concept. This is further developed in his *Rules, Norms, and Decisions* which is regularly referred to by scholars working in the constructivist vein.[48]

Hence, all three not only played an important part in setting off the constructivist project but also continue to influence it. Their work, although distinct, is of significance to constructivism in IR more broadly. The centrality of especially Wendt's work in relation to wider debates about constructivism is often noted, but Kratochwil and Onuf have also played a significant role in the construction of constructivism. Even if other sources are offered for their arguments, constructivists doing

[44] Steve Smith, 'New Approaches', p. 183; Ole Wæver, 'Figures of International Thought: Introducing Persons Instead of Paradigms', in Iver B. Neumann and Ole Wæver (eds.), *The Future of International Relations: Masters in the Making?* (London and New York: Routledge, 1997), p. 4.

[45] 'Forum on *Social Theory of International Politics*', *Review of International Studies* 26 (2000), 123; Robert O. Keohane, 'Ideas Part-Way Down', *Review of International Studies* 26 (2000), 125; Hayward E. Alker, 'On Learning from Wendt', *Review of International Studies* 26 (2000), 141; Steve Smith, 'Wendt's World', *Review of International Studies* 26 (2000), 151.

[46] Alexander Wendt, 'Constructing International Politics', *International Security* 20 (1995), 71; *STIP* 3, 31–2 and 84; Steve Smith, 'New Approaches', p. 183; Wæver, 'Figures', p. 24; Knutsen, *History of IR Theory*, p. 281; Martha Finnemore and Kathryn Sikkink, 'International Norms Dynamics and Political Change', *International Organization* 52 (1998), 890; Steve Smith, 'Wendt's World', 159.

[47] Ruggie is increasingly recognised as another key constructivist. However, although Ruggie claims to have done constructivist work since 1975, he, unlike Wendt, Kratochwil and Onuf, does not contend that he developed a new way of investigating international politics. See Ruggie, *Constructing the World Polity*, esp. p. 3 and ch. 1; John Gerard Ruggie, 'What Makes the World Hang Together? Neo-Utilitarianism and the Social Constructivist Challenge', *International Organization* 52 (1998), 855–85; Katzenstein, Keohane and Krasner, '*International Organization*', 660.

[48] Friedrich Kratochwil and John Gerard Ruggie, 'International Organization: A State of the Art on the Art of the State', *International Organization* 40 (1986), 753–75; *RND*.

empirical work often refer to Wendt, Kratochwil and Onuf.[49] Bizarrely, Wendt is sometimes quoted and hence implicitly credited with ideas, such as the claim that people act towards objects on the basis of the meaning these have for them, that should more appropriately be attributed to his source, Herbert Blumer's key work on symbolic interactionism.[50] As a result, and I further develop this in the conclusion, my critique is relevant beyond the work of Wendt, Kratochwil and Onuf, even if not all the issues I raise are pertinent to every piece of constructivist work; for I proceed by way of a careful reading of their work (and their work only) which I will now briefly introduce.

Wendt's constructivism

Wendt argues that the way international politics is conducted is made, not given, because identities and interests are constructed and supported by intersubjective practice.[51] The approach revolves around identity, which is construed as more basic than interests. Notions of self and the environment shape interactions and are shaped by interactions. Thereby social reality is created. Thus, the existing competitive international system could be reshaped. This claim develops from an engagement with realism[52] and structuration theory.[53]

Wendt's engagement with Anthony Giddens' structuration theory is significant in two respects. Firstly, Wendt follows Giddens in his solution to the agent–structure problem.[54] Hence, he conceptualises agents and structures as mutually constitutive entities with 'equal ontological status'.[55] As far as this implies that social reality develops in interaction,

---

[49] Finnemore, *National Interests in International Society*, pp. 4, 15 and 32; Thomas Risse-Kappen, 'Collective Identity in a Democratic Community: The Case of NATO', in Katzenstein, *Culture of National Security*, pp. 396 and 371; Michael N. Barnett, 'Identity and Alliances in the Middle East', in Katzenstein, *Culture of National Security*, pp. 407–8; Thomas U. Berger, 'Past in Present', 43; Weldes, 'Constructing National Interests', 279–80.

[50] Jutta Weldes, Mark Laffey, Hugh Gusterson and Raymond Duvall, 'Introduction: Constructing Insecurity', in Weldes et al., *Cultures of Insecurity*, p. 13. See Herbert Blumer, *Symbolic Interactionism: Perspective and Method* (Englewood Cliffs, NJ: Prentice-Hall, 1969), p. 2.

[51] Alexander Wendt, 'Levels of Analysis vs. Agents and Structures: Part III', *Review of International Studies* 18 (1992), 183. See also ISC 48; *STIP* 1.

[52] In this book 'realism' refers to the philosophical position and 'Realism' to the approach in IR.

[53] Alexander E. Wendt, 'The Agent–Structure Problem in International Relations Theory', *International Organization* 41 (1987), 335–70; Ian Shapiro and Alexander Wendt, 'The Difference That Realism Makes: Social Science and the Politics of Consent', *Politics and Society* 20 (1992), 197–223.

[54] See Anthony Giddens, *The Constitution of Society: Outline of the Theory of Structuration* (Cambridge: Polity Press, 1984).

[55] Wendt, 'Agent–Structure Problem', 339. See also *STIP* 180.

this prepares the ground for his constructivist argument. Secondly, the notion that structures 'really' exist is incompatible with empiricism. Wendt licences this claim by introducing scientific realism as the philosophical foundation of structuration theory.[56] In an article co-authored with Ian Shapiro, he explains that scientific realism consists in the belief that both the world of everyday objects and such unobservable entities and causal mechanisms as are posited by scientific theories exist independently of the mind.[57] The existence of unobservables is supported by the so-called miracle or ultimate argument. Successful manipulation of the world through scientific practice would be a miracle if science was not based on an existing causal structure of the world.[58] Significantly, Wendt assumes the existence of a reality independent of mind in terms of not only the material but also the social world. As a result, he argues that scientific explanation consisting in the identification of causal mechanisms is applicable to the social sciences.[59] In other words, there is a social reality 'out there', independent of our thoughts, and Wendt wants to explain it.[60]

Structuration theory calls for a focus on the study of social practices.[61] Wendt takes this further in 'Anarchy Is What States Make of It', in which he develops his constructivist approach. He starts by locating his position in relation to liberal and Realist theories of international politics. The point is to take into account the transformation of identities and interests, that is, of entities which are, because of their shared commitment to rationalism, taken as exogenously given by both Realists and liberals. However, Wendt claims an affinity to 'strong' liberal scholarship which addresses complex learning and therefore changes of identities and interests (A 393). He aims 'to build a bridge' between the liberal and the constructivist tradition and as a consequence 'between the realist–liberal and rationalist–reflectivist debates' (A 394). Thus Wendt positions his work *between* rationalist and reflective approaches as defined by Robert Keohane.[62] More recently, he speaks of finding a 'via media' between the 'mainstream' and 'postmodern' approaches (*STIP* 40 and 47).

---

[56] Wendt, 'The Agent–Structure Problem', 350. See also *STIP* ch. 2.
[57] Shapiro and Wendt, 'Difference That Realism Makes', 210.
[58] Shapiro and Wendt, 'Difference That Realism Makes', 211. See also *STIP* 63–7.
[59] Wendt, 'Agent–Structure Problem', 355.
[60] See also Alexander Wendt, 'Bridging the Theory/Meta-Theory Gap in International Relations', *Review of International Studies* 17 (1991), 391.
[61] Giddens, *Constitution of Society*, p. 2.
[62] Robert O. Keohane, 'International Institutions: Two Approaches', in Robert O. Keohane, *International Institutions and State Power: Essays in International Relations Theory* (Boulder: Westview Press, 1989), pp. 158–79.

Wendt develops his argument against the background of (Neo)-Realism, specifically Kenneth Waltz's work.[63] Like Waltz, Wendt proposes a state-centric structural theory.[64] His point *contra* Waltz is that the way international relations are conducted is socially constructed rather than transhistorically given. In Wendt's conceptualisation, structure does not exist apart from process, that is, the practices of actors (A 395; *STIP* 12 and 185). Although Wendt agrees with (Neo)Realists that the international system is characterised by anarchy and self-help, he argues against their claim that self-help is a necessary feature of anarchy (A 394; see also *STIP* 249). Rather it is an institution developed and sustained through process.

Using symbolic interactionist and structurationist sociology, Wendt presents an argument designed to show how self-help and power politics are socially constructed in a condition of anarchy. The claim is based on two principles of constructivism taken from symbolic interactionism.[65] Firstly, people act on the basis of meanings that objects and other actors have for them (A 396–7). And, secondly, these meanings are not inherent in the world but develop in interaction (A 403). Wendt develops his constructivist argument in relation to the claim that conceptions of security under conditions of anarchy do not have to be self-interested. Behaviour, according to Wendt, is influenced by intersubjective rather than material structures. It is based on collective meanings (A 397) through which actors acquire identities, that is, 'relatively stable, role-specific understandings and expectations about self' (A 397). Identities provide the basis for interests which are defined in the process of conceptualising situations (A 398; *STIP* 122). Identities are not only developed and maintained in interaction with others (A 401; *STIP* 36); they also crucially determine what kind of anarchy or security environment will prevail (A 399–400).[66] A self-help situation need not arise from the interaction of actors seeking their own survival under the condition of structural anarchy (A 404–5).

Wendt has elaborated on his notion of identity and its relation to the security environment in later work. Specifically, he focuses on collective identity formation (ISC).[67] Whether identities can be seen as

---

[63] See, for example, Kenneth N. Waltz, *Theory of International Politics* (New York: McGraw-Hill, 1979).

[64] Alexander Wendt, 'Collective Identity Formation and the International State', *American Political Science Review* 88 (1994), 385; see also *STIP* 6, 8–10 and 193.

[65] See Blumer, *Symbolic Interactionism*, p. 2.   [66] See also *STIP* ch. 6.

[67] An earlier version of this chapter appeared as 'Collective Identity Formation'.

collective depends on how interests are defined. What matters is whether and how far 'social identities involve an *identification* with the fate of the other' (ISC 52; see also *STIP* 106 and 229). The nature of identification in each situation shapes how boundaries of the self are drawn. If there is no positive identification, the other is relevant to the definition of interests only insofar as it may be used for the purposes of the self (ISC 52; *STIP* 240). This, Wendt argues, is the core of self-interest. Collective identity, on the other hand, refers to positive identification such that the other cognitively becomes a part of the self and its welfare is of concern (ISC 52). Actors who have such a collective identity define their interests on a higher level of aggregation, based on feelings of solidarity, community and loyalty. The point is not that self-interested identities will necessarily be replaced by collective ones but rather that cooperation may change actors' identities, rather than just their payoff structure (ISC 53–4), and hence the prevailing security environment.

Identity is, I would argue, the key to Wendt's approach. Research, according to Wendt, should focus on 'the relationship between what actors *do* and what they *are*' (A 424). Self-interested identities lie at the heart of the self-help system and identity change is the way to get out. Wendt's argument is presented in most detail in *Social Theory of International Politics* which, Wendt insists, is not an investigation into identity formation.[68] I do not take issue with this observation. What I claim and demonstrate in detail in chapter 2, however, is that Wendt's approach revolves around and hinges on his conception of identity.

Kratochwil's constructivism

Kratochwil's work is, on the one hand, a critique of the 'poverty of epistemology'[69] in IR and, on the other hand, an exploration of the role of rules and norms for political life and its analysis. Kratochwil criticises mainstream IR theory for a narrow conception of politics and human behaviour. Adopting a notion of rationality as instrumental leads, he argues, to excluding interesting questions about the ends sought from the analysis.[70] The normative character of politics must be denied in the name of 'science'.[71]

---

[68] *STIP* 11; Wendt, 'On the Via Media', 175.
[69] Friedrich Kratochwil, 'Errors Have Their Advantage', *International Organization* 38 (1984), 305.
[70] Kratochwil, 'Errors', 306 and 316–17; RNV 308.
[71] RNV 308; Friedrich Kratochwil, 'The Protagorean Quest: Community, Justice, and the "Oughts" and "Musts" of International Politics', *International Journal* 43 (1988), 212 and 218–22.

Positivist explanations, as they are common in IR, start from antecedent conditions, although intentionality and goal-directedness are important for human action.[72] In response Kratochwil focuses on everyday language and on the norms guiding human behaviour (*RND* 28–30). His analysis is indebted to linguistic philosophy, especially speech act theory, and practical philosophy, but also jurisprudential theories. Crucially, he asserts that international politics must be analysed in the context of norms properly understood (*RND* 10–12). The idea that norms influence all human conduct is turned into a more clearly constructivist approach when Kratochwil uses the metaphor of Wittgensteinian games defined by rules and norms as a starting point for analysis.[73]

Political interactions take place on the basis of partially shared, if contested, understandings which illuminate them for both actors and observers and thereby help analysis.[74] Any attempt to eliminate elements of appraisal and interpretation to make analyses more 'objective' leads to a misconceptualisation of praxis, as human beings use moral criteria and interpretation.[75] Kratochwil wants to move towards a conception of 'rationality' linked to common-sense understandings. The meaning of rationality should, following Jürgen Habermas' theory of communicative action, be seen as 'constituted by the *use* of the term' (RNV 310). Thus, an action or belief may be called 'rational' when it 'makes sense' to act that way. Significantly, this links in with normative considerations, as to 'call something rational means then to *endorse it* in terms of some norm or moral feeling that permits it' (RNV 311). Utilitarian calculation as depicted by an instrumental notion of rationality becomes possible only after an actor has already taken an attitude towards a situation (RNV 318).

Kratochwil's attempt to reintroduce the political dimension to IR theory relies on understanding 'political action in terms of meaningful, rather than purely instrumental, action'.[76] Based on a reading of Max Weber, he claims that action is meaningful if it can be placed in an intersubjectively shared context (*RND* 24). Kratochwil sees this context as based on and mediated by rules and norms. Consequently, norms are crucial to his discussion of political action. They shape decisions but also

---

[72] Kratochwil, 'Errors', 306.
[73] Koslowski and Kratochwil, 'Understanding Change', 216; Friedrich Kratochwil, 'The Embarrassment of Changes: Neo-realism as the Science of Realpolitik Without Politics', *Review of International Studies* 19 (1993), 75.
[74] Koslowski and Kratochwil, 'Understanding Change', 225.
[75] Kratochwil, 'Protagorean Quest', 206–7.   [76] Kratochwil, 'Embarrassment', 65.

give actions meaning and provide people with a medium through which they may communicate. Rules are speech acts which depend on successful communication (*RND* 34). They function only if they achieve the desired effect with the addressee; they are not independent of context. There are regulative and constitutive rules, and the latter cannot be reduced to the former. We cannot understand the role of norms in social life if we take regulative rules as paradigmatic,[77] because conceptualising norms as merely constraining is mistaken (*RND* 61). What Kratochwil calls 'practice-type' or 'institution-type' rules, for which promising and contracting are paradigmatic, are most important for his argument.[78] Following J. L. Austin, Kratochwil explains that these rules usually relate to performances in which the rule specifies the conditions under which an act counts as valid (*RND* 91–2).

Although rules and norms influence human behaviour fundamentally, they do not determine it. Therefore, processes of deliberation and interpretation must be analysed (*RND* 10–11).[79] As social problems do not have logically necessary solutions and social situations are necessarily indeterminate, analysis has to concentrate on how questions concerning validity claims are decided through discourse (*RND* 36). The interesting question is why decisions based on rules and norms which are not logically compelling receive support (*RND* 36). Instrumental explanations fail as rules 'often function "heteronomously", i.e., instruct us what interest of *others* we have to take into account while making our choices' (*RND* 95).[80] The key lies in realising that rule-following does not involve blind habit but argumentation (*RND* 97). Kratochwil explores legal reasoning because of its parallels with moral discourse. Both involve an element of heteronomy, that is, regard for the other. They are also based on a process of principled argumentation which leads to an equally principled application of the respective norms (*RND* 142 and 208).

It is necessary to investigate the reasons that are seen to be an acceptable justification for following a rule in specific circumstances.

---

[77] Friedrich Kratochwil, 'Norms Versus Numbers: Multilateralism and the Rationalist and Reflexivist Approaches to Institutions – a Unilateral Plea for Communicative Rationality', in John Gerard Ruggie (ed.), *Multilateralism Matters: The Theory and Praxis of an Institutional Form* (New York: Columbia University Press, 1993), p. 460. See also *RND* 28.

[78] See also Kratochwil, 'Protagorean Quest', 209.

[79] See also Friedrich V. Kratochwil, 'Thrasymmachos Revisited: On the Relevance of Norms for International Relations', *Journal of International Affairs* 37 (1984), 344 and 346.

[80] See also *RND* 130 and Friedrich V. Kratochwil, 'Is International Law "Proper" Law?', *Archiv für Rechts- und Sozialphilosophie* 69 (1983), 34.

Kratochwil argues that only the emergence of a 'moral point of view' can advance us towards a solution (*RND* 123). Norms provide the basis for a reasoning process in which some violations of the rules are classified as excusable, whilst others are not. For this process the identification of *relevant premises* (*RND* 37) is significant. Whether an action can obtain support depends on the definition of the situation, on what it is seen as an instance of. Therefore the justifications given for a particular course of action provide an important indication for its appraisal (*RND* 63).

As good reasons must be put forward for acts and decisions, the choice of a narrative becomes necessary and crucial (*RND* 213). Such narratives usually start from commonplaces or topoi. These, according to Kratochwil, locate the matters at issue with respect to common understandings which provide links in the argumentation (*RND* 219). Crucially, it is impossible to talk about human acts neutrally. A so-called objective fact is 'not the thing described but rather the intersubjective *validity* of a characterization upon which reasonable persons can agree' (*RND* 229).[81] Processes of reasoning do not lead to single best solutions even if some arguments are seen as more persuasive than others. Thus authoritative decisions are necessary (*RND* 142). This does not, however, mitigate the influence of norms and intersubjective context, as authoritative decisions that can be shown to be based on good reasons are different from arbitrary ones (*RND* 184).

Kratochwil thus argues that the role of rules and norms in social life must be 'radically reconceptualized'. The notion of game in the Wittgensteinian sense provides a useful starting point as

> rules and norms are not simply the distillation of individual utility calculations but rather the *antecedent conditions* for strategies and for the specification of criteria of rationality. Norms not only establish certain games and enable the players to pursue their goals within them, they also establish inter-subjective meanings that allow the actors to direct their actions towards each other, communicate with each other, appraise the quality of their actions, criticize claims and justify choices.[82]

Starting with the notion of game leads to a different conceptualisation of action and communication because we realise that 'language *does not*

---

[81] See also Friedrich Kratochwil, 'Is the Ship of Culture at Sea or Returning?', in Yosef Lapid and Friedrich Kratochwil (eds.), *The Return of Culture and Identity in IR Theory* (Boulder and London: Lynne Rienner Publishers, 1996), p. 219.

[82] Kratochwil, 'Embarrassment', 75–6. See also Friedrich Kratochwil, 'International Order and Individual Liberty: A Critical Examination of "Realism" as a Theory of International Politics', *Constitutional Political Economy* 3 (1992), 40.

mirror action by sticking a descriptive label on the activity: it *is* action'.[83] This conceptualisation of language, which involves the notion of construction and is related to rules and norms, is central to Kratochwil's constructivism. The context of rules and norms which provides the basis for intersubjectivity, and thus the possibility of understanding politics as involving meaningful action and normative questions, is crucial.

Onuf's constructivism

One of Onuf's key interests lies in the area where international relations and international law meet. He has extensively published on international law.[84] His constructivism links in with this focus insofar as it is based on an exploration of rules. *World of Our Making* is key in his formulation of a constructivist theory of international relations. This book is a complex exposition which advances by discussing and interpreting philosophy and social theory, that is, by 'a close reading of texts' (*WOM* 22), although Onuf has since provided briefer summaries of his constructivism (CM; C). His approach aims to do nothing less than create a new paradigm for International Relations which takes into account their political character. Onuf wants to make the study of international politics a contribution to social theory and locate it within an operative paradigm of political society (*WOM* 1; see also 22, 27 and 36). Significantly, this reshaping of the study of international politics would, following Onuf's thinking, have an effect on the social world; for the claims of social science and the projects following on from them are part of the practices creating the social world (*WOM* 15; see also 106).

Constructivism, according to Onuf, 'applies to all fields of social inquiry' and has the potential to bring together matters which at first seem unrelated (C 58). It starts from the belief that human beings are social.

---

[83] Kratochwil, 'Embarrassment', 76; Kratochwil, 'International Order', 40.

[84] Nicholas Greenwood Onuf, 'International Law-in-Action and the Numbers Game: A Comment', *International Studies Quarterly* 14 (1970), 325–33; Nicholas Greenwood Onuf, 'The Principle of Nonintervention, the United Nations, and the International System', *International Organization* 25 (1971), 209–27; Nicholas Greenwood Onuf, 'Law and Lawyers in International Crises', *International Organization* 29 (1975), 1035–53; Nicholas Greenwood Onuf, 'International Legal Order as an Idea', *American Journal of International Law* 73 (1979), 244–66; Nicholas Greenwood Onuf (ed.), *Law-Making in the Global Community* (Durham, NC: Carolina Academic Press, 1982); Nicholas Greenwood Onuf, 'Global Law-Making and Legal Thought', in Onuf, *Law-Making in the Global Community*, pp. 1–81; Nicholas Greenwood Onuf, 'International Codification: Interpreting the Last Half-Century', in Richard Falk, Friedrich Kratochwil and Saul H. Mendlovitz (eds.), *International Law: A Contemporary Perspective* (Boulder and London: Westview Press, 1985), pp. 264–79; Nicholas Onuf, 'The Constitution of International Society', *European Journal of International Law* 5 (1994), 1–19.

In other words, social relations make us human, construct us 'into the kind of beings that we are' (C 59). At the same time, through deeds and speaking, we use the raw materials of nature to make the world what it is (C 59). That is to say, constructivism is based on the notion that society and people make each other in an ongoing, two-way process. Deeds, which may consist in speech acts or physical actions, make the world (*WOM* 36). For deeds to be able to construct reality, they must have meaning. According to Onuf, meaning in human social relations depends on the existence of rules (*WOM* 21–2). Accordingly, his constructivism asserts the fundamental significance of rules for social reality and consequently for a constructivist social theory (*WOM* 66). Rules regulate aspects of the world but, from a constructivist point of view, they also always constitute situations in the first place (C 68; see also *WOM* 51).

Hence, any analysis of social life must start with rules. A rule, according to Onuf, 'is a statement that tells people *what* [they] *should* do' (C 59; see also *WOM* 51). Rules provide guidance for human behaviour and thereby make shared meaning possible. Moreover, they create the possibility of agency (CIS 6). People, as well as social constructs such as states, become agents in society only through rules. At the same time, rules provide agents with choices, most fundamentally with the choice of following or breaking them (C 59–60). Agents have goals in mind and 'they do the best they can to achieve their goals with the means that nature and society ... make available to them' (C 60). Agents act within an institutional context, that is, within the context of stable patterns of rules and related practices, but at the same time they act *on* this context. Thereby, they collectively change it but not according to their own choosing. Actions often have unintended consequences. Rules, institutions and unintended consequences form stable patterns called structures (C 61).

Onuf's conceptualisation of rules depends on speech acts. A speech act is the 'act of speaking in a form that gets someone else to act' (C 66). Thus language is performative, rather than merely descriptive (*WOM* 82). Speech acts follow the pattern: 'I (you, etc.) hereby assert (demand, promise) to anyone hearing me that some state of affairs exists or can be achieved' (C 66). Onuf classifies them into three categories, namely assertives, directives and commissives, depending on *how* the speaker intends to have an effect on the world. The success of speech acts depends on the addressee's response. They only work within a specific situation. If, however, a speech act is frequently repeated with comparable consequences, it turns into a convention (C 66). Once agents accept that they *should* do something they have repeatedly been doing, the convention becomes a rule. Rules retain the form of a speech act but generalise the relation between speaker and hearer. Finally, Onuf argues, 'agents recognize that they should follow the rules in question because they are rules and for no other reason' (C 67).

Rules are ubiquitous. Starting with rules, Onuf argues, leads to recognising that their existence automatically leads to an uneven distribution of benefits and hence a condition of rule (*WOM* 21–2; see also 128; C 62), in other words, 'a condition in which some agents use rules to exercise control and obtain advantages over other agents' (C 63). Agents respond to rules with the resources they have. Hence, some agents are able to 'exercise greater control over the content of those rules, and over their success in being followed, than other agents do' (C 75). Crucially, rules yield rule as a inescapable condition (C 63).

Rules turn human beings into agents who '*make* the material world a social reality for themselves as human beings' (C 64). Rules make agency possible but within limits. According to Onuf, many 'limits have a material component. We need air to breathe; we do not have wings to fly. No rule can readily make things otherwise, even though rules allow us, agents, to use resources to alter these limits, for example, by fashioning scuba gear and airplanes' (C 64–5). As a result, the 'freedom agents do have depends on their ability to recognize the material and social limits that apply to them' (C 65). Onuf thus construes the world as made up of a material and a social realm which are distinct but closely linked. The constructivism Onuf proposes 'does not draw a sharp distinction between material and social realities' (*WOM* 40) but stresses the role of what is socially made. Hence, deeds have to be related to both the social and the natural world correctly in order to produce the desired outcomes.[85] Therefore they, like language or speech, link the social and the material which Onuf conceptualises as distinct.

Unsurprisingly, given the significance he assigns to language, Onuf challenges positivist and empiricist but also realist[86] inclinations. There is, following his reasoning, no single truth. The truths we accept as such are inextricably linked to the arguments with which they are justified (*WOM* 35). Onuf claims that observers are unable to detach themselves from the matter investigated. They can never step outside the world

---

[85] See J. L. Austin, *How To Do Things With Words: The William James Lectures Delivered at Harvard University in 1955*, 2nd edn (Oxford: Clarendon Press, 1975).
[86] This refers to realism in the philosophy of science.

of constructions (*WOM* 43) to be neutral observers. This is crucial to Onuf's conception of knowledge. Ideas and events are not independent phenomena; rather, they necessarily interact.[87] Hence we can only know from within. We give certain concepts meaning. Other aspects of social reality become intelligible in relation to this starting point. Knowledge thus exists only in relation to a specific context (CM 7). Therefore, context is crucial. And context, because it is linguistically constituted, depends on rules. Rules and speech acts provide the link between 'word' and 'world'.

Given these brief summaries one might want to object that Onuf's and Kratochwil's work on the one hand and Wendt's on the other have little in common except the label. They largely build on different traditions and focus on different concepts and issues. Whilst Onuf and Kratochwil share a focus on rules and an affinity to speech act theory, Wendt draws on sociological traditions revolving around identity. Yet, on the other hand, they recognise each other as constructivists.[88] Both Kratochwil and Wendt refer to Onuf's introduction of the term 'constructivism' to IR scholarship.[89] Thus, despite the considerable differences between their approaches,[90] their projects could be considered similar.[91] This argument is taken up in chapter 5, after each scholar's specific claims and their implications have been analysed in detail.

My analysis does not discuss the tensions and shortcomings of these approaches only in the abstract but is related to a concrete development in contemporary international politics, which was perceived, by

---

[87] Nicholas Greenwood Onuf, 'Sovereignty: Outline of a Conceptual History', *Alternatives* 16 (1991), 426 and 429.

[88] *STIP* 1, 3, 32 and 84; Koslowski and Kratochwil, 'Understanding Change', 216, n. 3; Nicholas G. Onuf, 'The Politics of Constructivism', in Fierke and Jørgensen, *Constructing International Relations*, pp. 238 and 244; also Yosef Lapid and Friedrich Kratochwil, 'Revisiting the "National": Toward an Identity Agenda in Neorealism?', in Lapid and Kratochwil, *Return of Culture and Identity in IR Theory*, p. 121, but see also Kratochwil, 'Constructing a New Orthodoxy?', 89.

[89] *WOM* 36; Koslowski and Kratochwil, 'Understanding Change', 216, n. 3; A 393; and *STIP* 1.

[90] See Maja Zehfuß, 'Sprachlosigkeit schränkt ein. Zur Bedeutung von Sprache in konstruktivistischen Theorien', *Zeitschrift für Internationale Beziehungen* 5 (1998), 109–37; Maja Zehfuss, 'Constructivisms in International Relations: Wendt, Onuf, and Kratochwil', in Fierke and Jørgensen, *Constructing International Relations*, pp. 54–75.

[91] Hayward Alker, *Rediscoveries and Reformulations: Humanistic Methodologies for International Studies* (Cambridge University Press, 1996), pp. 408 and 412; Finnemore and Sikkink, 'International Norms Dynamics', 890; David Dessler, 'Constructivism Within a Positivist Social Science', *Review of International Studies* 25 (1999), 123.

politicians and academics, as involving a change in reality: German military involvement abroad after the end of the Cold War. Until the early 1990s, the FRG's armed forces, the Bundeswehr, had not been deployed beyond the state's borders other than for disaster relief in relation to floods, droughts and earthquakes. The notion that they should be used outside the FRG for military functions overturned what had seemed self-evident to many: that Germany could never again use force except for strictly defensive purposes. Nevertheless, military involvement abroad increasingly came to be seen as not only possible but inevitable. This shift in German military policy provides the background against which I discuss constructivist conceptualisations of reality. In the next section, I give an introduction to the problem of German military involvement abroad as portrayed in the literature.

German military involvement abroad

The conflict in the Persian Gulf region, arising when Iraq invaded Kuwait in 1990, drew attention to the FRG's refusal to use its military abroad. The failure to contribute to the multinational war effort against Iraq in 1991 generated a lot of interest both in politics and in academia, especially in terms of drawing conclusions about the FRG's future role in international politics. The Gulf War coincided with unification, which was seen to give Germany more weight and responsibility.[92] As a result, the country's 'new role' in international relations became an issue.[93] In this context, the crisis in the Gulf was construed as a 'test case'[94] or 'the catalyst for an eventual revision of previous German policy'.[95] The Gulf War, or so the argument went, had forced the question of Bundeswehr involvement abroad on to the agenda.[96] Nevertheless,

---

[92] Rudolf Scharping, 'Deutsche Außenpolitik muß berechenbar sein', *Internationale Politik* 50 (1995), 38–9; Harald Müller, 'German Foreign Policy After Unification', in Paul Stares (ed.), *The New Germany and the New Europe* (Washington, DC: Brookings Institution, 1992), p. 130.

[93] Joachim Bitterlich, 'La politique communautaire et occidentale de Bonn: un examen de passage pour l'Allemagne unie?', *Politique Etrangère* 56 (1991), 834.

[94] Thomas Kielinger, 'The Gulf War and the Consequences from the German Point of View', *Aussenpolitik*, 42/2 (1991), 243.

[95] Richard J. Evans, *Rereading German History: From Unification to Reunification 1800–1996* (London and New York: Routledge, 1997), p. 227.

[96] Thomas U. Berger, 'Past in Present', 54; Clay Clemens, 'Opportunity or Obligation? Redefining Germany's Military Role Outside of NATO', *Armed Forces and Society* 19 (1993), 232; Jeffrey S. Lantis, 'Rising to the Challenge: German Security Policy in the Post-Cold War Era', *German Politics and Society* 14 (1996), 23; Hilmar Linnenkamp, 'The Security Policy

the country did not contribute militarily to the operation in the Gulf. The government justified this refusal on constitutional grounds:[97] the Basic Law, the German constitution, ruled out the external use of force.

However, in the aftermath of the Gulf War, this interpretation of the constitution increasingly became contested. The constitutional regulations arguably could be read differently. Art. 87a (2) of the Basic Law, cited in support of the claim that military force could be used for defence only, also licences the use of force for other than defensive purposes if explicit permission can be found in the Basic Law. As Art. 24 of the Basic Law provides for the possibility of membership in a 'system of mutual collective defence', some argued that the use of force within the framework of the UN was permitted, if not required. On the other side of the debate were those who wanted to preserve the 'consensus on security policy', namely that Art. 87a (2) prohibited all deployments outside NATO territory.[98] Many arguably considered this the only valid reading of the constitution.[99] Due to this disagreement the question of the correct interpretation of the Basic Law became an important aspect of the debates about German military involvement abroad.[100]

The issue of constitutional constraints provided a starting point for the debates. Indeed, 'the constitutional angle assumed a central role'[101] at least until 1994 when the Federal Constitutional Court ruled that deployments in the context of such multilateral organisations as the UN, NATO or the WEU were legal. The long and complicated constitutional debate could have been avoided by changing the Basic Law. However, there was little agreement on *how* it should be changed,[102] and so all attempts to do so failed. This reflected the sensitivity of the matter in German politics. The literature on German post-Cold War security policy time and again refers to a reluctance on the part of the

of the New Germany', in Stares, *New Germany and New Europe*, p. 117; Harald Müller, 'German Foreign Policy', pp. 129–30 and 139; Wolfgang F. Schlör, 'German Security Policy: An Examination of the Trends in German Security Policy in a New European and Global Context', *Adelphi Paper* 277 (1993), 3.

[97] Harald Müller, 'German Foreign Policy', p. 136.
[98] See Kielinger, 'Gulf War', 244.
[99] Karl Kaiser and Klaus Becher, *Deutschland und der Irak-Konflikt. Internationale Sicherheitsverantwortung Deutschlands und Europas nach der deutschen Vereinigung* (Bonn: Europa Union Verlag, 1992), p. 11; Harald Müller, 'German Foreign Policy', p. 139.
[100] See, for example, Harald Müller, 'Military Intervention for European Security: The German Debate', in Lawrence Freedman (ed.), *Military Intervention in European Conflicts* (Oxford: Blackwell Publishers, 1994), pp. 128–9.
[101] Andrei S. Markovits and Simon Reich, *The German Predicament: Memory and Power in the New Europe* (Ithaca and London: Cornell University Press, 1997), p. 141.
[102] Harald Müller, 'German Foreign Policy', p. 140.

FRG, its political class and its general population to get involved in military operations beyond Germany's borders. Many commentators remark upon the aversion to all things military amongst the population, especially to a military role in international relations.[103] According to Thomas U. Berger, 'no other nations display as intense a sense of antimilitarism as do Germany and Japan'.[104] This view is confirmed by the reaction of the public to the Gulf War. Although the FRG did not participate, there were numerous demonstrations against it,[105] the number of conscientious objectors against military service rose sharply in January 1991[106] and, according to a poll taken at the same time, only one in four Germans was in favour of getting involved in international conflicts.[107] The concern of the German population about using force, once military involvement abroad was on the agenda, is also reflected in the number of publications on the topic aimed at the general public.[108]

This anti-militarism is often presented as an effect of post-Second World War socialisation. The non-violence and peacefulness required from the FRG after the war had become a matter of conviction.[109] The rejection of the use of force in international politics was thus seen as internalised. Jeffrey S. Lantis claims that restrictions on a more assertive military posture were 'deeply rooted in the public psyche'[110] and Jürgen

---

[103] Adrian Hyde-Price, '"Of Dragons and Snakes": Contemporary German Security Policy', in Gordon Smith, William E. Paterson and Stephen Padgett (eds.), *Developments in German Politics II* (Houndmills, Basingstoke and London: Macmillan, 1996), p. 177; Kaiser and Becher, *Deutschland und der Irak-Konflikt*, pp. 24 and 102; Franz-Josef Meiers, 'Germany: The Reluctant Power', *Survival* 37 (1995), 84–5; Schlör, 'German Security Policy', 5; Harald Müller, 'Military Intervention', p. 125.

[104] Thomas U. Berger, 'Norms, Identity, and National Security in Germany and Japan', in Katzenstein, *Culture of National Security*, p. 323.

[105] See, for example, Harald Müller, 'Military Intervention', p. 127; 'Demonstrationen gegen Golfkrieg in 75 Orten', *SZ*, 11 Jan. 1991, 2; 'Anti-Kriegsdemonstrationen gehen weiter', *SZ*, 17 Jan. 1991, 2; 'Demonstranten fordern: Kein Blut für Öl', *SZ*, 18 Jan. 1991, 8; 'Welle von Antikriegsdemonstrationen in Deutschland', *SZ*, 19–20 Jan. 1991, 7; 'Massenprotest gegen Golfkrieg', *SZ*, 28 Jan. 1991, 1.

[106] 'Drastischer Anstieg der Kriegsdienstverweigerung', *SZ*, 6 Feb. 1991, 1.

[107] 'Deutsche gegen Weltmachtrolle', *SZ*, 4 Jan. 1991, 1. See also Harald Müller, 'Military Intervention', pp. 139–40.

[108] For example, Stefan Brunner, *Deutsche Soldaten im Ausland. Fortsetzung der Außenpolitik mit militärischen Mitteln?* (Munich: Verlag C. H. Beck, 1993); Jürgen Grässlin, *Lizenz zum Töten? Wie die Bundeswehr zur internationalen Eingreiftruppe gemacht wird* (Munich: Knaur, 1997); Oskar Hoffmann, *Deutsche Blauhelme bei UN-Missionen. Politische Hintergründe und rechtliche Aspekte* (Munich: Verlag Bonn Aktuell, 1993); Dieter S. Lutz (ed.), *Deutsche Soldaten weltweit. Blauhelme, Eingreiftruppen, 'out of area' – Der Streit um unsere sicherheitspolitische Zukunft* (Reinbek: Rowohlt, 1993).

[109] Dieter Schröder, 'Deutsche an die Front?', *SZ*, 2–3 Feb. 1991, 4.

[110] Lantis, 'Rising to the Challenge', 19.

Habermas speaks of a 'historically well-grounded inhibition'.[111] The weariness about using force is attributed to history, namely the bitter experiences of the Second World War and the militarism of the Third Reich, which had lead to disaster. In Berger's words, there are 'few countries in the world where the past weighs more heavily on the present'.[112] Germany is considered different from other states as it always has to take into account its history in formulating its foreign policy.[113] The context of the Third Reich is also important because it, Berger argues, made for 'extreme sensitivity of military security issues'.[114] Michael E. Smith points out that the debate about military involvement abroad was 'emotionally charged'[115] and Robert H. Dorff speaks of it as taking place in 'an area fraught with so many emotional time bombs'.[116]

Traditionally, what Dorff calls the 'history argument'[117] had supported the claim that there were constitutional constraints: Germany could not use military force because of the legal situation and its past. Indeed, the constitutional restraints were thought to be based on historical reasons.[118] However, in the 1990s, the accepted lessons of the past became contested. The 'two-pronged motto "Never again war! Never again fascism!"',[119] considered to be ingrained in the thinking of the left but also confirmed as fundamental to the Basic Law by Chancellor Helmut Kohl,[120] came under tension; for, in relation to the Gulf War and especially Bosnia, it seemed that fascism and oppression could be ended

[111] Jürgen Habermas, *The Past as Future*, interviewed by Michael Haller, translated and edited by Max Pensky (Lincoln and London: University of Nebraska Press, 1994), p. 25.
[112] Thomas U. Berger, 'Past in Present', 39. See also William E. Paterson, 'Beyond Semi-Sovereignty: The New Germany in the New Europe', *German Politics* 5 (1996), 181.
[113] Franz H. U. Borkenhagen, *Außenpolitische Interessen Deutschlands. Rolle und Aufgaben der Bundeswehr* (Bonn and Berlin: Bouvier Verlag, 1997), pp. 10 and 68.
[114] Thomas U. Berger, 'Norms, Identity, and National Security', p. 355.
[115] Michael E. Smith, 'Sending the Bundeswehr to the Balkans: The Domestic Politics of Reflexive Multilateralism', *German Politics and Society* 14 (1996), 49.
[116] Robert H. Dorff, 'Normal Actor or Reluctant Power? The Future of German Security Policy', *European Security* 6 (1997), 60.
[117] Dorff, 'Normal Actor?', 58.
[118] Marie-Janine Calic, 'German Perspectives', in Alex Danchev and Thomas Halverson (eds.), *International Perspectives on the Yugoslav Conflict* (Houndmills and London: Macmillan, 1996), p. 72.
[119] Alice H. Cooper, 'When Just Causes Conflict with Acceptable Means: The German Peace Movement and Military Intervention in Bosnia', *German Politics and Society* 15 (1997), 100. See also Lothar Gutjahr, *German Foreign and Defence Policy After Unification* (London and New York: Pinter Publishers, 1994), p. 159.
[120] Helmut Kohl (chancellor) in Deutscher Bundestag, *Plenarprotokoll*, 11/228, 4 Oct. 1990, 18019.

only through war.[121] Hence, the two principles of 'never again war' and 'never again fascism' were increasingly perceived as contradictory rather than complementary. Thus, it was not clear whether Germany's past obliged the country to use military force to prevent aggression and ethnic cleansing, or whether military abstention was required, especially in the former Yugoslavia.[122]

Because of the history of the Third Reich, Germany's past is often conceptualised as a history of aberration. Unification could then provide the opportunity to achieve the 'normality' Germany had lacked in the past. As Andrei S. Markovits and Simon Reich put it, '[u]nification, in principle, made Germany a normal country.'[123] Thus 'Germany [wa]s called upon to be what it ha[d] never been: a "normal" state in the community of nations.'[124] There is, however, no consensus as to how 'normal' the FRG has become. Franz-Josef Meiers asserts that Germany is still far from normal,[125] whilst Lantis describes the normalisation of security policy as completed.[126] Whether it was claimed that Germany was already normal or that it should strive to become so, normality became an issue in the debates about the external use of force.[127] The idea that Germany should embark on the road of 'normalisation' was related to the notion of *Sonderweg*, that is, special path.[128] In the past Germany had diverged from the development of other countries – it had taken a special path – and this had led to disaster. Hence, any difference from other countries had to be avoided. Even the old FRG could be and was, as Stefan Berger points out, portrayed as having embarked on a *Sonderweg*.[129] The upshot of this argument, which suppresses all

---

[121] Cooper, 'Just Causes'.   [122] Calic, 'German Perspectives', p. 58.

[123] Markovits and Reich, *German Predicament*, p. 137.

[124] William Horsley, 'United Germany's Seven Cardinal Sins: A Critique of German Foreign Policy', *Millennium: Journal of International Studies* 21 (1992), 225.

[125] Meiers, 'Germany', 82.   [126] Lantis, 'Rising to the Challenge', 19.

[127] Clemens, 'Opportunity or Obligation?', 236; Catherine Kelleher and Cathleen Fisher, 'Germany', in Douglas J. Murray and Paul R. Viotti (eds.), *The Defense Policies of Nations: A Comparative Study*, 3rd edn (Baltimore and London: Johns Hopkins University Press, 1994), p. 169. See also Gunther Hellmann, 'Goodbye Bismarck? The Foreign Policy of Contemporary Germany', *Mershon International Studies Review* 40 (1996), 1–39, and Hanns W. Maull, 'Allemagne et Japon: deux pays à suivre', *Politique Etrangère* 60 (1995), 479.

[128] Christoph Bertram, 'The Power and the Past: Germany's New International Loneliness', in Arnulf Baring (ed.), *Germany's New Position in Europe: Problems and Perspectives* (Oxford and Providence, RI: Berg Publishers, 1994), p. 92. See also Thomas Banchoff, 'German Policy Towards the European Union: The Effects of Historical Memory', *German Politics* 6 (1997), 60–4.

[129] Stefan Berger, *The Search for Normality: National Identity and Historical Consciousness in Germany Since 1800* (Providence, RI, and Oxford: Berghahn Books, 1997), pp. 112 and 189.

difficulties of defining normality,[130] was that involvement in international military operations could not be avoided. 'Normal states have normal armies, which they use for normal purposes',[131] as Markovits and Reich put it.

This was related to the argument that 'the rest of the world' expected more involvement in crisis situations.[132] The shift towards participation in international military operations was then a response to expectations from abroad.[133] The FRG's involvement in the UN operation in Somalia, for instance, was attributed to 'international pressure'.[134] Membership in the Western alliance was considered significant in this context. The expectations and well-being of 'friends and partners' had to be taken into account.[135] Lothar Gutjahr speaks of an 'essential multilateralisation of Germany's security policy'.[136] Wolfgang F. Schlör calls it 'instinctive multilateralism'.[137] Some argue that multilateral integration had overriding significance for the German political establishment.[138] After all, it had made political rehabilitation possible.[139] The problem was that the FRG's 'policy of military abstinence no longer complement[ed] its commitment to multilateral security institutions';[140] for multilateralism, it was claimed, now required participating in multinational military operations.[141] The desire to acquire a permanent seat in the UN Security Council is also thought to have been a consideration.[142] German responsibility was seen as having grown as a result of unification.[143] In the debates on this 'new responsibility' the global military role was the key issue, Harald Müller claims.[144] Participation in international operations was portrayed as part of accepting responsibilities under the UN

[130] On the various meanings of normality, see Mary M. McKenzie, 'Competing Conceptions of Normality in the Post-Cold War Era: Germany, Europe, and Foreign Policy Change', *German Politics and Society* 14 (1996), esp. 2–4, and Thomas U. Berger, 'Past in Present', 41.
[131] Markovits and Reich, *German Predicament*, p. 137.
[132] Kielinger, 'Gulf War', 246.   [133] Clemens, 'Opportunity or Obligation?', 231.
[134] Lantis, 'Rising to the Challenge', 24.
[135] See, for example, Karsten Voigt, 'German Interest in Multilateralism', *Aussenpolitik* 47/2 (1996), 116; Hanns W. Maull, 'Germany in the Yugoslav Crisis', *Survival* 37 (1995/6), 127.
[136] Gutjahr, *German Foreign and Defence Policy*, p. 42.
[137] Schlör, 'German Security Policy', 6.
[138] Bertram, 'Power and Past'; Thomas U. Berger, 'Past in Present', 39–40.
[139] Banchoff, 'German Policy Towards the EU', 63.
[140] Schlör, 'German Security Policy', 4.   [141] McKenzie, 'Competing Conceptions', 4.
[142] Michael E. Smith, 'Sending the Bundeswehr', 59.
[143] Maull, 'Allemagne et Japon', 485; Scharping, 'Deutsche Außenpolitik', 38–9; Harald Müller, 'German Foreign Policy', p. 130.
[144] Harald Müller, 'German Foreign Policy', p. 139.

Charter.[145] Yet it was not only this 'new responsibility' which played a role in the debates. History, sometimes in combination with geographical location and economic power, provided a basis for the argument that the FRG had a special responsibility.[146] Germany had a duty to help people in distress because of the suffering it had caused in the past. These claims about responsibility supported the involvement in military operations.

Thus, whilst the debates about the constitution and the past, normality and responsibility carried on, the Bundeswehr was already being trained for UN missions, restructured to become more flexible and deployed abroad.[147] At first, deployments were, by not actually using force, carefully construed as legal under the Basic Law. Later they were arguably designed to test the limits of constitutional permissibility. Although the FRG did not participate in the Gulf War, some of the first deployments were related to it. Forces were sent to support the alliance partner Turkey. This was controversial but eventually accepted as within the remit of the NATO treaty.[148] The Bundeswehr also aided Kurdish refugees from Iraq in Turkey and Iran without much controversy being created.[149] Yet, these operations were already 'pushing the limits of what was possible under the consensus interpretation of the constitution'.[150] Minesweepers were sent to the Gulf, albeit only after an armistice had been reached. This also set a precedent, as it meant deploying soldiers outside the NATO area, if only on what was called a humanitarian mission.

In spring 1992 paramedics were sent to Cambodia.[151] In 1993, the Bundeswehr contributed to UNOSOM II in Somalia. From July 1992 the air force participated in the airlift to Sarajevo and from March 1993 in airdrops of supplies over East Bosnia. German soldiers were also part of the AWACS crews monitoring the flight ban over Bosnia. The navy contributed to Operation Sharp Guard, that is, NATO and WEU measures monitoring the UN embargo against the former Yugoslavia.[152] UN Resolution 816 of 31 March 1993 authorised the use of force to

---

[145] Gutjahr, *German Foreign and Defence Policy*, p. 101. See also Lantis, 'Rising to the Challenge', 25.

[146] Bitterlich, 'La politique communautaire et occidentale', 834; Scharping, 'Deutsche Außenpolitik', 38–9.

[147] Calic, 'German Perspectives', pp. 64–5.

[148] Harald Müller, 'German Foreign Policy', 137.

[149] Kaiser and Becher, *Deutschland und der Irak-Konflikt*, pp. 42–3; Kielinger, 'Gulf War', 247.

[150] Harald Müller, 'German Foreign Policy', pp. 131 and 142.

[151] Harald Müller, 'German Foreign Policy', p. 142.

[152] Calic, 'German Perspectives', p. 65; Lantis, 'Rising to the Challenge', 23–6.

enforce the flight ban over the former Yugoslavia, and in April NATO started the enforcement, employing its AWACS system. German soldiers constituted a significant proportion of AWACS crews and the government decided not to withdraw them despite concerns that participation in such an extended operation violated constitutional law. Both the SPD and the FDP appealed to the constitutional court to protest against the decision and clarify the legal situation.[153] The SPD also objected to the participation in the Somalia operation and in Operation Sharp Guard.[154] Interestingly, the government was in effect suing itself over the AWACS operation as the FDP was the junior coalition partner.[155]

On 12 July 1994 the Federal Constitutional Court ruled that military operations abroad in the context of membership in a 'system of mutual collective security', and thus all Bundeswehr missions under dispute, were legal.[156] In a special parliamentary meeting on 22 July, the ongoing operations were approved with the support of the SPD opposition.[157] Meiers argues that the court's ruling exposed the constitutional arguments as an 'excuse' previously used to avoid participation in international missions.[158] Yet the controversies surrounding the external use of the military continued. After all, the 'history argument' remained. As a result, the government was reluctant to define scenarios for troop deployments. It soon became necessary to consider these matters, however.

In December 1994 NATO requested Tornado fighters to help protect peace-keepers in Bosnia.[159] The government had portrayed a similar request in November as an 'unofficial enquiry' which did not require a response.[160] After some delay, the government promised aircraft and logistical assistance but no ground troops. The reluctance to commit troops to the Balkans was attributed to historical reasons, namely the role of the Wehrmacht in relation to the Serbs. It was feared that German soldiers would add to the problems in the region rather than help solve them.[161] On the other hand, many Germans also believed that, as Marie-Janine

---

[153] Maull, 'Germany in the Yugoslav Crisis', 109–10.

[154] Calic, 'German Perspectives', p. 65.

[155] Michael E. Smith, 'Sending the Bundeswehr', 57.

[156] Bundesverfassungsgericht, 'Urteil des Zweiten Senats vom 12. Juli 1994 aufgrund der mündlichen Verhandlung vom 19. und 20. April 1994', 12 Jul. 1994, E90, 286–394. See also Calic, 'German Perspectives', p. 65. All translations from German sources are, unless otherwise stated, my own.

[157] Calic, 'German Perspectives', p. 66.   [158] Meiers, 'Germany', 87.

[159] Calic, 'German Perspectives', p. 66.

[160] McKenzie, 'Competing Conceptions', 11; Meiers, 'Germany', 86.

[161] Calic, 'German Perspectives', p. 67.

Calic put it, 'inherited guilt obliged the Federal Republic to assume responsibility for the people in the former Yugoslavia'.[162]

The position that German soldiers could not be deployed to the former Yugoslavia because of the past, termed the 'Kohl doctrine',[163] was given up in the context of a possible hostile withdrawal of UNPROFOR which would have necessitated large-scale NATO intervention. In June 1995, the FRG decided to support NATO's rapid reaction force with troops and aircraft, although no ground troops were sent to Bosnia itself.[164] Fourteen Tornados were deployed to Italy and 500 soldiers to a field hospital in Croatia. This decision was controversial. Later in the same year, after the Dayton Accords, however, a similar deployment generated much less debate in parliament. The December 1995 decision to participate in IFOR – supported by the SPD opposition and opposed by the PDS whilst the Greens were split over the issue – marked, according to Mary M. McKenzie, the end of the argument that German soldiers could not be deployed in the same way as their European colleagues.[165]

Dorff remarks on the shift between the two parliamentary debates on 30 June and 6 December 1995 which suggests that the use of military force abroad had become much more politically acceptable within a few months. An overwhelming majority of parliamentarians supported the later deployment.[166] The willingness to take part in both operations was considered extremely significant. Michael E. Smith calls these decisions 'historic'.[167] Alice H. Cooper comments that contributing to the Bosnia mission was 'the biggest break with the past' as Germany, for the first time, sent troops 'to an area once occupied by the Wehrmacht'.[168] In December 1996, parliament decided to participate in SFOR, militarily securing the peace in Bosnia. Gregor Schöllgen claims this was the first time the Germans had been willing to risk soldiers' lives for a common cause and that, with this decision, parliament 'liquidated almost without a sound the remains of the political and military special role which Germany had played for half a century' on the basis of one argument: its history.[169] The shift towards 'normal' participation in international military operations could be considered complete at this stage.

[162] Calic, 'German Perspectives', p. 72.
[163] Maull, 'Germany in the Yugoslav Crisis', 112; McKenzie, 'Competing Conceptions', 11.
[164] Maull, 'Germany in the Yugoslav Crisis', 113.
[165] McKenzie, 'Competing Conceptions', 11.　　[166] Dorff, 'Normal Actor?', 56 and 65.
[167] Michael E. Smith, 'Sending the Bundeswehr', 49.　　[168] Cooper, 'Just Causes', 99.
[169] Gregor Schöllgen, 'Geschichte als Argument. Was kann und muß die deutsche Großmacht auf dem Weg ins 21. Jahrhundert tun?', *Internationale Politik* 52 (1997), 1.

Thus, in 1998, when NATO threatened air strikes against Yugoslavia because of attacks of Serbian security forces against the Albanian population in Kosovo, the FRG was immediately prepared to participate.[170] Although bombing another country was presented as entirely new for the Bundeswehr, as the first combat mission since the Second World War,[171] German fighter pilots had already carried out airstrikes against Bosnian Serb military positions in September 1995.[172] The novelty of the Kosovo operation for the Germans was arguably much like its novelty for other NATO countries.[173] Public debates and soul searching about being involved in 'war' notwithstanding, German participation in Operation Allied Force appears as the implementation and logical conclusion of a shift which had already taken place. Kosovo highlighted the consequences; the questions it posed had been answered beforehand.

As a result of these answers, Germany was seen to be leaving behind its non-military identity as an international actor. Some commentators worry about a remilitarisation of foreign policy. Stefan Berger speaks of 'mental remilitarisation'.[174] The reference to the Nazi past made this issue a moral question.[175] What is considered significant is that the use of military means outside NATO territory had not been considered a 'legitimate component' of the FRG's foreign policy before the end of the Cold War. This 'changed, and military options are now viewed by many political leaders as a *necessary* component of responsible German policy'.[176] Thus reality is perceived as having changed. What had been illegitimate and impossible is now necessary. This is where the shift in the FRG's practice links in with the problematic of constructivism; for, if anything at all is agreed about constructivism, it is that the approach deals with the construction of reality. The reality in the situation under discussion here was, moreover, seen to relate to issues of identity and norms, issues which my outline of Wendt's, Kratochwil's and Onuf's work showed to be central to constructivism.

---

[170] 'NATO droht Jugoslawien mit Luftangriffen', *SZ*, 12 Jun. 1998, 1; 'NATO nimmt weitere Ziele ins Visier', *SZ*, 23 Mar. 1999, 1.

[171] Kurt Kister, 'Der höchste Einsatz', *SZ*, 26 Mar. 1999, 4; Winfried Didzoleit et al., 'Ernstfall für Schröder', *Der Spiegel*, 13/53, 29 Mar. 1999, 22–30, here 23–4.

[172] Lantis, 'Rising to the Challenge', 19.

[173] See Renate Flottau et al., 'Alle Serben im Krieg', *Der Spiegel*, 13/53, 29 Mar. 1999, 194–213, here 196.

[174] Stefan Berger, *Search for Normality*, p. 186; see also p. 1.

[175] Kelleher and Fisher, 'Germany', p. 169. See also McKenzie, 'Competing Conceptions', 4.

[176] McKenzie, 'Competing Conceptions', 12.

Plan of the book

Having outlined both the key claims of the constructivist work under
consideration and some issues and events surrounding the German shift
towards military involvement abroad, I can now introduce the plan of
the book. Wendt's, Kratochwil's and Onuf's work allows me to rely
on extended theoretical arguments.[177] This is crucial for my enterprise,
which takes constructivist theories as seriously as possible and exposes
their flawed logic by drawing them together with a development in
international politics. Chapters 2, 3 and 4 critique the approaches of
Wendt, Kratochwil and Onuf in turn. Each of these chapters, which
can be read separately, focuses on concepts which are introduced as
central to the constructivist approach under discussion and explored in
relation to the issue of the FRG's participation in international military
operations. On this basis I argue that each approach fails in its own
project.

Chapter 2 starts with Wendt's constructivism and focuses on the question
of identity change. Wendt's key move lies in the argument that
actors' identities and interests are socially constructed. The possibility
of endogenous identity change is meant to set his conceptualisation
of international politics apart from rationalism. Using the redefinition of
the FRG's role in the international realm to include the possibility of

[177] In contrast, I make little use of their more empirical work which, in either remaining
abstract or not explicitly using constructivist insights, is of limited help to my enterprise. See Alexander Wendt and Daniel Friedheim, 'Hierarchy Under Anarchy: Informal
Empire and the East German State', *International Organization* 49 (1995), 689–721; this also
appeared in Thomas J. Biersteker and Cynthia Weber (eds.), *State Sovereignty as Social
Construct* (Cambridge University Press, 1996), pp. 240–77; Alexander Wendt and Michael
Barnett, 'Dependent State Formation and Third World Militarization', *Review of International Studies* 19 (1993), 321–47; Michael Barnett and Alexander Wendt, 'Systemic Sources
of Dependent Militarization', in Brian L. Job (ed.), *The Insecurity Dilemma: National Security
of Third World States* (Boulder and London: Lynne Rienner Publishers, 1992), pp. 97–119;
Friedrich Kratochwil, Paul Rohrlich and Harpreet Mahajan, *Peace and Sovereignty: Reflections on Conflict Over Territory* (Lanham, MD: University Press of America, 1985); Friedrich
Kratochwil, 'Of Systems, Boundaries, and Territoriality: An Inquiry into the Formation
of the State System', *World Politics* 34 (1986), 27–52; Friedrich Kratochwil, 'The Challenge of Security in a Changing World', *Journal of International Affairs* 43 (1989), 119–41;
Friedrich Kratochwil, 'The Limits of Contract', *European Journal of International Law* 5 (1994),
465–91; Friedrich V. Kratochwil, 'Politics, Norms and Peaceful Change', *Review of International Studies* 24 (1998), 193–218; Nicholas Greenwood Onuf and V. S. Peterson, 'Human
Rights from an International Regimes Perspective', *Journal of International Affairs* 37 (1984),
329–42; Onuf, 'Sovereignty'; Nicholas Onuf, 'Intervention for the Common Good', in Gene
M. Lyons and Michael Mastaduno (eds.), *Beyond Westphalia? State Sovereignty and International Intervention* (Baltimore and London: Johns Hopkins University Press, 1995),
pp. 43–58; Nicholas Onuf, 'Hegemony's Hegemony in IPE', in Burch and Denemark,
Constituting International Political Economy, pp. 91–110.

military involvement abroad, the chapter illustrates how identity matters in international politics in relation to Wendt's constructivism. I explain Wendt's identity move in relation to this shift in military policy, using especially his concept of collective identity. However, Wendt's move turns out to be limited because he does not take into account the dimension of language and excludes the domestic from consideration. This leads me to reconsider collective identity as a discursive phenomenon, exploring the idea of multilateralism in German politics. This shows a much more ambiguous situation which is, moreover, distinctly at odds with Wendt's claims. Finally, I show that Wendt's starting points make it impossible for him to think beyond the problematic concept of stable, circumscribable state identities which is necessary for his 'via media' between rationalism and 'postmodernism', and that this 'via media' is not a stable place.

Chapter 3 in some ways focuses on what Wendt omits. Kratochwil's approach suggests an analysis of domestic political debate and specifically of its normative aspects. As the argument about German military involvement abroad started as one about constitutional permissibility, the first section of the chapter presents the complex legal situation and its influence on the political debate. However, when Kratochwil speaks of rules and norms he means more than the law. Therefore, the chapter goes on to explore more broadly normative considerations, such as the rejection of war in principle. This analysis shows that people did indeed, as Kratochwil claims, refer to normative notions to explicate their positions. Further analysis taking into account how norms 'hang together', however, sheds doubt on the possibility of sharing meaning against the background of norms. Given the multiple possible understandings of the same norms, it seems doubtful whether the normative context can provide the basis for intersubjectivity. The possibility of intersubjectivity is fundamental to Kratochwil's approach, both for his substantive concerns and for his methodological commitments. The last section of the chapter argues that the reliance on intersubjectivity is itself political and that Kratochwil's treatment of norms misses at least part of the politics.

Chapter 4 again deals with rules, as Onuf's constructivism is based on them. Onuf's conceptualisation of rules, like Kratochwil's, relies on the idea of speech acts. However, the outcome is different. He is interested in how words create the world. The chapter explores the effect of practice on rules in relation to the constitutional situation. Increasing actual military involvement abroad and its contextualisation led to a changing interpretation of the rule structure. The chapter then goes on to explore why certain practices were more successful in shaping reality than others; in other words, it addresses the problem of the failure of speech acts. Specifically, it discusses Onuf's reliance on materiality as the limit of possible constructions. An analysis of the failure of alternatives and the material hindrances with respect to military involvement abroad suggests that materiality is not, in any simple way, a boundary of the possible. The last section of this chapter analyses the necessity, for Onuf's argument, of confirming the existence of separate social and material spheres and the impossibility of doing so at the same time. This raises the matter of invoking 'reality' to support arguments.

The politics of 'reality' is central to chapter 5, which takes up the points made in chapters 2, 3 and 4 and develops them further in relation to Derrida's work. After giving an introduction to Derrida's thought, it explores Wendt's, Kratochwil's and Onuf's work again, focusing on the 'reality' they invoke as a background to their claims. It shows how the notion of *différance* destabilises Wendt's position and his 'reality' of International Politics. It addresses how Derrida's critique of traditional conceptions of communication interferes with Kratochwil's concept of intersubjectivity, his everyday 'reality', and offers a critique of Kratochwil's conception of the normative from a Derridean perspective. The chapter then uses Derrida's claim that 'there is nothing outside of the text' to question Onuf's 'reality' of raw materials for construction. Finally, highlighting that each approach posits a 'reality' from which to start, it discusses the politics of constructivism, drawing attention to the similarities between the apparently different problems with each of the three constructivisms.

Constructivism addresses the issue of reality. Indeed, the question of what the reality of international politics is and how it came about is at the heart of the constructivist endeavour. However, the way in which constructivism addresses this issue is, in my view, deeply problematic. Although constructivism is about construction, it takes reality as in many ways given. In other words, constructivism purports to explain construction whilst still taking account of 'reality'. Throughout this book, it will become clear that this way of thinking has tremendous appeal to common sense. It is impossible to make this point plausible in a few sentences as 'common sense' typically dissolves under a critical gaze. However, the illustration of constructivist claims throughout this book with statements by politicians and the press shows an affinity between constructivist assumptions and widespread ways of talking about politics. They both start from certain givens, for instance. Whilst constructivists claim to take into account the effects of reality, politicians argue that they have no choice. The point is that the 'givens' with which this thinking starts are not politically innocent. Using Derrida's thought, I argue that the treatment of reality in constructivism and in politics are not two separate issues but rather two manifestations of the same problem.

What concerns me, and this will become clearer in chapters 5 and 6, is that reality cannot be known other than through our representations. Thus, whatever is asserted to be, the security of the 'is' is in question. Therefore, claiming a reality to start from, be it one of states, norms or natural raw materials, already involves a political act. Constructivists may agree that interpretation is involved, but typically, as I outline in chapter 5, see claiming a starting point as necessary. I worry that questions which concern these starting points are not asked and that the failure to ask them has implications for our ability to understand international relations. Moreover, it has an impact on which ways of thinking are thought to be relevant in the discipline; for the necessity to take reality into account circumscribes what we may think. It is this closing down of thinking space, in relation to both international relations and International Relations, that concerns me about constructivism. It is important to consider *why* constructivism works to limit the space for critical thinking. This argument is made more fully in the conclusion but the key issues can be outlined here. I will demonstrate that the constructivist theories under scrutiny appeal to reality and their ability to relate to it in order to support their claims. So did the politicians debating German military involvement abroad. This is a problematic move because there is no indisputable knowledge about what this 'reality' is. Neither the German politicians nor the constructivist scholars seem to reach agreement on what is nevertheless portrayed as self-evident. The effect of validating arguments against a supposed background reality is that positions which do not see this as a possibility look weak. They cannot provide the security of clear guidelines for political behaviour.

However, the 'insecurity' of thought which results from such positions can be understood as an opportunity; for responsibility towards the other in international relations becomes possible, or so I claim, only if the way things are is not attributed to a mysterious outside reality. The challenge is to overcome the boundaries of our thinking which make us believe that we are constrained by reality, rather than by our vocabulary, by our inability to think beyond what we construe as reality.

This challenge is difficult, not least because of the powerful hold the idea of reality has on our imagination. Obviously, questioning the supposedly clear distinction between representation and reality, and therefore the boundary which we believe reality imposes on us, will not automatically lead to a more responsible politics. The argument in this book does not offer this kind of answer or certainty. Neither does it aim to. However, it takes up the issue of why such a politics is necessary and why it is impossible unless we question the idea of reality as a limit, something constructivist approaches fail to do.

2   Identity change? Wendt's constructivism and German military involvement abroad

Alexander Wendt set out to show that (Neo)Realists are wrong: it is not an unchanging fact that the international realm is a self-help system. Rather, the international environment is created and recreated in processes of interaction. As the way states act may change, so can the international system. The key move in this argument is that actors' identities are not given but are developed and sustained or transformed in interaction (see ISC 48; A; *STIP*). This is, he argues, what sets a constructivist approach apart from the 'rationalism' of mainstream approaches to the study of international politics. Rationalists may admit that behaviour changes but they consider the properties of actors, such as their identity, external and prior to the process of international politics.[1] The concept of identity is employed to establish the difference from rationalism. The constructivist alternative presented by Wendt revolves around the construction of identity.

Wendt's work is addressed to the 'mainstream' (see A 397, n. 21; *STIP*). In his influential 'Anarchy Is What States Make of It', he locates his approach, with respect to the debate between Realists and liberals, where both sides share a commitment to rationalism and thus the assumption that agents' identities and interests are given. In Wendt's view, there is, however, a tradition of 'strong' liberal scholarship concerned with complex learning and thus changes in interests and identities (A 393). His objective is 'to build a bridge' between the liberal and the constructivist traditions and 'by extension, between the realist–liberal and rationalist–reflectivist debates' (A 394). Thus Wendt wants to position himself *between* the rationalist and the reflective camps[2] as defined by

---

[1] Wendt, 'Constructing International Politics', 71–2; *STIP* 27.
[2] He does not accept that there is a meta-theoretical split between the two (Wendt, 'Bridging the Theory/Meta-Theory Gap', 391).

38

Robert Keohane.[3] He aims to find a 'via media' between the mainstream and so-called postmodern approaches.[4] Although he claims the middle ground between what he considers polar opposites, his arguments are explicitly addressed to the (Neo)Realist side and his approach is thus constructed and positioned through an engagement with (Neo)Realist claims (*STIP passim*). This means that he clearly identifies where he differs with (Neo)Realism but also that he addresses its concerns. This was obvious when Wendt defined constructivism with reference to international politics:

> Constructivism is a structural theory of the international system that makes the following core claims: (1) states are the principal units of analysis for international political theory; (2) the key structures in the state system are intersubjective, rather than material; and (3) state identities and interests are in important part constructed by these social structures, rather than given exogenously to the system by human nature or domestic politics.[5]

Wendt subscribes to the notion that states are central and to the view that the structures of the international system are crucially important, both fundamental positions of (Neo)Realism. His move away from this position lies in emphasising intersubjectivity. Structure in Wendt's approach is different from the distribution of capabilities Kenneth Waltz is concerned with.[6] It exists only through process (A 395). And, significantly, process, i.e. what people do, is related to meaning. Wendt refers to two fundamental principles of constructivist social theory. Firstly, people's actions are based on meanings (A 396–7) and, secondly, meaning arises out of interaction (A 403). The significance of meaning rather than material structures encapsulates the move away from Realist claims and it hinges on the concept of identity. Identity makes possible the claim that international politics is constructed.

The identity move

Wendt argues that the way international relations are played out is not given but socially constructed. Briefly, a 'world in which identities and interests are learned and sustained by intersubjectively grounded

---

[3] Keohane, 'International Institutions'.   [4] *STIP* 40; see also *STIP* ch. 2.
[5] Wendt, 'Collective Identity Formation'. Wendt now defines constructivism separately from claims about international politics (*STIP* 1 and 193).
[6] Waltz, *Theory of International Politics*.

practice, by what states think and do, is one in which "anarchy is what states make of it". States may have made that system a competitive, self-help one in the past, but by the same token they might "unmake" those dynamics in the future.'[7] Wendt has much refined his argument since his influential 'Anarchy Is What States Make of It' but the claim that the way international relations are played out is not given but socially constructed remains central (*STIP* 70).

According to Wendt, it is the intersubjective, rather than the material, aspect of structures that influences behaviour. Intersubjective structures are constituted by collective meanings. Actors acquire identities, which Wendt defines as 'relatively stable, role-specific understandings and expectations about self' (A 397; see also *STIP* 21), by participating in collective meanings. Identity is 'a property of international actors that generates motivational and behavioral dispositions' (*STIP* 224). Thus identities are significant because they provide the basis for interests. Interests, in turn, develop in the process of defining situations (A 398; *STIP* 231 and 329–30).[8] An institution, such as self-help in the international realm, is a 'relatively stable set or "structure" of identities and interests' (A 397; see also *STIP* 160–1). Wendt discusses how different kinds of anarchy are constructed in interaction between states.[9] What kind of anarchy prevails depends, according to this argument, on the conceptions of security the actors have, on how they construe their identity in relation to others. Notions of security 'differ in the extent to which and the manner in which the self is identified cognitively with the other, and . . . it is upon this cognitive variation that the meaning of anarchy and the distribution of power depends' (A 399–400). Accordingly, positive identification with other states will lead to perceiving security threats not as a private matter for each state but as a responsibility of all. If the collective self is well developed between a group of states, security practices will be to some degree altruistic or prosocial (A 400–1). Wendt therefore discusses the identity problematic as one of whether and under which conditions identities are more collective or more egoistic (ISC; *STIP* esp. 336–69). Depending on where states fall on this continuum from positive to negative identification with other states, they will be more or less willing to engage in collective security practices. Crucially, conceptions of self and other, and consequently security interests, develop only in interaction (A 401; see also *STIP* 36). Therefore identity is the

---

[7] Wendt, 'Levels of Analysis', 183.   [8] See also *STIP* chs. 5 and 6.
[9] See esp. *STIP* ch. 6.

key to the development of different security environments or cultures of anarchy.

This argument puts identity at the core of the approach. The 'culture of anarchy' depends on how identity gets defined.[10] *Social Theory of International Politics* may not be an investigation into identity formation[11] but the concept of identity is crucial to Wendt's argument. According to Wendt, the 'daily life of international politics is an on-going process of states taking identities in relation to Others, casting them into corresponding counter-identities, and playing out the result' (*STIP* 21). The international system would not be played out in different cultures of anarchy were it not for different conceptualisations of identity. Hence, identity is the key to Wendt's *systemic* argument.

What is important is that the concept of identity integrates several crucial moves. Identity relates to the intersubjective aspect of structures and, therefore, its significance establishes the move away from a materialist argument (see *STIP* 23–4) and towards the claim that reality is constructed. The proposition that identities and not merely behaviour are shaped by structures or patterns of interaction is meant to set the approach apart from rationalism.[12] According to this argument, rationalists, such as game theorists, may admit that identities change but only prior to interaction, beyond the remit of their analysis (see *STIP* 315–16). Constructivists, on the other hand, are concerned to show that identities may change through interaction and that this matters. Moreover, the claim that definitions of identity, which are subject to change, influence security practices and ultimately the type of security environment states find themselves in establishes that the self-help system, although ingrained at this point in time, is not a given, unchanging fact. Identity provides a category which may change but which at the same time is 'relatively stable'. As Wendt puts it, 'identities may be hard to change, but they are not carved in stone' (*STIP* 21). Transforming definitions of self is more than altering behaviour and therefore a demanding process.

The key question is then how identities are constituted. After all, 'anarchy is what states make of it' because states' identities are made, not given. Wendt argues that conceptions of self and other arise from interaction between states. State actors, which always have an institutional legal order, the claim to a monopoly on the legitimate use of organised violence, sovereignty, a society and territory (*STIP* 202–14), exist prior

---

[10] *STIP* ch. 6.   [11] *STIP* 11; Wendt, 'On the Via Media', 175.
[12] Wendt, 'Constructing International Politics', 71–2; *STIP* 27, 35 and 44.

to interaction. Independent of social context, states have four 'national interests': to preserve and further their physical security, autonomy, economic well-being and collective self-esteem (*STIP* 235–7). Yet beyond this, reality develops through social interaction in which '[c]onceptions of self and interest tend to "mirror" the practices of significant others over time' (A 404; see also *STIP* 327 and 333–4). This process is illustrated in a story which is worth quoting at length:

> Consider two actors – ego and alter – encountering each other for the first time. Each wants to survive and has certain material capabilities, but neither actor has biological or domestic imperatives for power, glory, or conquest . . . and there is no history of security or insecurity between the two. What should they do? . . . [M]ost decisions are and should be made on the basis of probabilities, and these are produced by interaction, by what actors *do*.
>
> In the beginning is ego's gesture, which may consist, for example, of an advance, a retreat, a brandishing of arms, a laying down of arms, or an attack. For ego, this gesture represents the basis on which it is prepared to respond to alter. This basis is unknown to alter, however, and so it must make an inference or 'attribution' about ego's intentions and, in particular, given that this is anarchy, about whether ego is a threat . . . Alter may make an attributional 'error' in its inference about ego's intent, but there is no reason for it to assume a priori – before the gesture – that ego is threatening, since it is only through a process of signaling and interpreting that the costs and probabilities of being wrong can be determined. Social threats are constructed, not natural (A 404–5; see also *STIP* 328–35).

Wendt goes on to illustrate this process in a second story. If aliens were to contact the earth, we would, presumably, not immediately feel threatened. If 'they appear with one spaceship, saying what seems to be "we come in peace", we will feel "reassured" and will probably respond with a gesture intended to reassure them, even if this gesture is not necessarily interpreted by them as such' (A 405). Accordingly, whether a self-help situation ensues depends on social interaction. These stories illustrate how social acts are conceptualised in Wendt's work.[13] In *Social Theory* social acts are systematically broken down into four 'scenes'. Firstly, *ego*, based on its definition of the situation, engages in an act which signals to *alter* both which role *ego* is planning to take in the interaction and which corresponding role it envisages for *alter*. In the second

[13] In *Social Theory* Wendt no longer uses the example of an encounter with aliens (see also Kratochwil, 'Constructing a New Orthodoxy?', 76). However, the interaction between *ego* and *alter* is still used to conceptualise social action.

scene, *alter* interprets the meaning of *ego*'s action in relation to its own perception of the situation. *Alter*, on the basis of its interpretation, which may have involved learning, now engages in an action of its own. This constitutes a signal to *ego* in the same way in which *ego*'s action had been one to *alter*. Finally, in the fourth scene, *ego* responds. Thus Wendt describes social acts as processes of signalling, interpreting and responding, in which shared knowledge is created and social learning may occur (*STIP* 330–1).

Identities and interests are not only created in such interactions, they are also sustained that way. Through repeated interactive processes, what Peter L. Berger and Thomas Luckmann call 'reciprocal typifications'[14] and consequently stable identities and expectations about each other are developed. Thereby actors create and maintain social structures (A 405–6), which subsequently constrain choices. Once structures of identity and interests have been created, they are not easy to transform, because the social system becomes an objective social fact to the actors. Actors may have a stake in maintaining stable identities (A 411), due to external factors such as the incentives induced by established institutions and internal constraints such as commitment to established identities (*STIP* 339–40). In *Social Theory*, Wendt speaks of the logic of the self-fulfilling prophecy which sustains the identities and interests created in interaction (*STIP* 331; see also 184–9). Nevertheless, identity transformation is possible not only in first encounters, in which shared knowledge – or in Wendt's terminology 'culture' (*STIP* 141) – is created anew, as the illustrations may seem to suggest. Rather Wendt argues that this 'base model can be readily extended to situations in which culture already exists' (*STIP* 328),[15] such as the FRG's relationship with other countries.

If we use these conceptualisations to think about the issue of the FRG taking up military involvement abroad as a new practice after the end of the Cold War, we find that the FRG enters the stage as a unitary actor complete with intentions, beliefs and desires (see ISC 59; *STIP* 197). The FRG enters the interaction as an individual. It knows that it is 'the FRG',

---

[14] Peter L. Berger and Thomas Luckmann, *The Social Construction of Reality* (London: Allen Lane The Penguin Press, 1966), pp. 54–8 and 74.

[15] Culture is by definition shared in Wendt's approach. For a critique of the idea of first encounter in Wendt's earlier work, see Naeem Inayatullah and David L. Blaney, 'Knowing Encounters: Beyond Parochialism in International Relations Theory', in Lapid and Kratochwil, *Return of Culture and Identity in IR Theory*, pp. 65–84. Wendt now acknowledges that actors encountering 'the Other' for the first time already have ideas about self and other (*STIP* 141).

a state actor (cf. *STIP* 225). Its existence as a state actor is independent of the international system and – before engaging in any interaction at all – it is equipped with the desire to survive. This is part of its 'corporate identity' which refers to the 'intrinsic qualities that constitute actor individuality' (ISC 50). Actors' corporate identities 'are constituted by the self-organizing, homeostatic structures that make actors distinct entities' (*STIP* 224–5). In the case of state actors, this aspect of identity is based on domestic politics which Wendt considers 'ontologically prior to the states system' (ISC 51), 'exogenously given' (*STIP* 328; see also 246). As they are part of corporate identity, state actors enter the interaction having some pre-existing ideas about who they are even beyond their awareness of their individuality and their ability to act. At the time of the Gulf War the FRG represented itself as a non-military power in the international realm. In a government statement shortly before the end of the ultimatum against Iraq, the chancellor of the FRG spoke of solidarity with the Americans, the British and the French who carried the main burden in defending law and liberty in this case and of the financial burden for the FRG.[16] This implies that participation in a military operation in the Gulf simply was not at issue for the FRG at this stage.[17] Such behaviour would have interfered with the conception of self. Being non-military was part of the FRG's articulated identity.[18] Art. 87a (2) of the Basic Law was read to rule out the external use of military force for other than defensive purposes and armed forces were established only in the context of integration into the NATO command structure.[19] Government statements and international treaties affirmed that 'only peace w[ould] emanate from German soil'.[20] In the past, the FRG had

[16] Helmut Kohl (federal chancellor) in Deutscher Bundestag, *Plenarprotokoll*, 12/2, 14 Jan. 1991, 22.

[17] Witness the Bundestag debates on 14, 17 and 30 January 1991. There was, however, a brief discussion in August 1990 about a potential contribution to UN forces in the Gulf region and the possibility of sending minesweepers there. The government decided that this would be unconstitutional. See, for example, 'Streit um Bundeswehreinsatz am Golf', *SZ*, 10 Aug. 1990, 2; 'Uneinigkeit in der Bonner Koalition über einen Einsatz der Bundeswehr im Golf', *FAZ*, 16 Aug. 1990, 2; 'Kein Einsatz der Bundeswehr am Golf', *SZ*, 21 Aug. 1990, 2.

[18] For a commentary on how non-military German identity was thought to be, see Dieter Schröder, 'Deutsche an die Front?', *SZ*, 2–3 Feb. 1991, 4.

[19] See, for example, Bundesminister der Verteidigung, *Weißbuch 1985. Zur Lage und Entwicklung der Bundeswehr* (Bonn, 1985), p. 73, section 160.

[20] Hans-Dietrich Genscher, address of the foreign minister at the 45th General Assembly of the UN, in Presse- und Informationsamt der Bundesregierung, *Bulletin*, 115, 27 Sep. 1990, 1201; Helmut Kohl, message on the day of German unification on 3 October 1990 to all governments in the world, in Presse- und Informationsamt der Bundesregierung,

not participated in military operations abroad apart from disaster relief, and had explicitly rejected such a possibility at least in one case. In the 1980s, in the context of the Iran–Iraq war, the Americans had repeatedly demanded that the Europeans participate in interventions outside the NATO area.[21] At the time, the FRG refused to do more than deploy one destroyer, one frigate and one supply vessel to the Mediterranean, where they took over positions the US Navy had to abandon because of redeployments to the Gulf region.[22]

However, corporate identity which is exogenous to international politics represents only one aspect of a state's identity. It is the 'site' or 'platform' for other identities (*STIP* 225). In *Social Theory* Wendt distinguishes three other such identities: type, role and collective (*STIP* 224–30).[23] What is important to my argument is the distinction between one pregiven corporate identity and other aspects of identity, made through the process of relating to other actors, which can take 'multiple forms simultaneously within the same actor' (*STIP* 230). Thus I recall Wendt's earlier conceptualisation in which he opposed 'corporate identity' to 'social identity', which develops only through social interaction, a distinction he supported by referring to the concepts of 'I' and 'me' in George Herbert Mead's work.[24] Briefly, the process whereby a state defines its interests precisely and goes about satisfying them partially depends on its notion of self in relation to others, that is, social identities or roles. These are 'sets of meanings that an actor attributes to itself while taking the perspective of others – that is, as a social object' (ISC 51). Actors have several social identities but just one corporate identity. Social identities exist only in relation to others and thus provide a crucial connection for the mutually constitutive relationship between

---

Bulletin, 118, 5 Oct. 1990, 1227; 'Vertrag über die abschließende Regelung in bezug auf Deutschland', reprinted in *Grundgesetz für die Bundesrepublik Deutschland*, 51st revised edn (Munich: C. H. Beck'sche Verlagsbuchhandlung, 1993), Art. 2.

[21] Nina Philippi, *Bundeswehr-Auslandseinsätze als außen- und sicherheitspolitisches Problem des geeinten Deutschland* (Frankfurt am Main: Peter Lang, 1997), pp. 60–1. See also 'Bundesmarine: Germans to the front?', *Der Spiegel*, 49/41, 30 Nov. 1987, 19–21.

[22] 'Wir müssen erwachsen werden', *Der Spiegel*, 34/44, 20 Jul. 1990, 121–3, here 121–2; 'Drei Divisionen am Aufmarsch beteiligt', *FAZ*, 10 Aug. 1990, 5; 'Bonn schickt Marine ins Mittelmeer', *SZ*, 11–12 Aug. 1990, 1.

[23] Wendt claims that the latter is a distinct combination of the two former (*STIP* 229) and is, due to their fuzziness, himself unsure how to distinguish between the different categories (*STIP* 224).

[24] George H. Mead, *Mind, Self and Society: From the Standpoint of a Social Behaviourist* (University of Chicago Press, [1934] 1965), pp. 173–8. This reference to Mead may itself be problematic. See Ronen Palan, 'A World of Their Making: An Evaluation of the Constructivist Critique in International Relations', *Review of International Studies* 26 (2000), 575–98.

agents and structures. This type of identity is continuously (re)defined in processes of interaction. In some contexts social identities are relatively stable. This, however, is also a result of actors' practices, not a natural fact (ISC 51). Although interaction is usually aimed at satisfying interests, actors at the same time try to sustain their conception of themselves and others.[25] Sometimes identities are, however, transformed. Identity change requires social learning. Hence, the transformative potential is mediated through the interaction between *ego* and *alter* in which social learning occurs (*STIP* 326–35).[26]

One of the concrete mechanisms of identity transformation which Wendt considers is based on conscious efforts to change identity. Actors, he argues, are able to engage in critical self-reflection and they can transform or transcend roles. *Ego* may decide to engage in new practices. As the new behaviour affects the partner in interaction, this involves getting *alter* to behave in a new way as well. This process is not just about changing behaviour but about changing identity. As *alter*'s identity mirrors *ego*'s practices – or, more generally, the practices of significant others – changing *ego*'s practices influences *alter*'s conception of self. In a chapter co-authored with Ron Jepperson and Peter J. Katzenstein, Wendt explains that the

> concept of identity . . . functions as a crucial link between environmental structures and interests. The term comes from social psychology, where it refers to images of individuality and distinctiveness ('selfhood') held and projected by an actor and formed (and modified over time) through relations with significant 'others'. Thus the term (by convention) references mutually constructed and evolving images of self and other.[27]

When one partner in interaction presents the other with a new role definition, Wendt speaks of 'altercasting', that is, 'an attempt to induce alter to take on a new identity . . . by treating alter as if it already had that identity' (A 421).[28] This produces the desired effect only if the other takes up the new role.

As we have seen, at the time of the Gulf War the FRG displayed an identity which involved a definition of self as non-military, more precisely as a state which would use military force only for self-defence.

---

[25] See *STIP* ch. 7.
[26] See also Wendt's earlier explication of 'strategic practice' (ISC 56–8).
[27] Ronald L. Jepperson, Alexander Wendt and Peter J. Katzenstein, 'Norms, Identity, and Culture in National Security', in Katzenstein, *Culture of National Security*, p. 59.
[28] See also *STIP* ch. 7.

However, this presentation of self became contested by others. As role definitions by significant others are important, contestations may influence the FRG's definition of identity. Who is a *significant* other depends on power and dependency relationships (see *STIP* 327 and 331). Therefore, the United States should have this role vis-à-vis the FRG, but so should, probably, also those other countries which German politicians refer to when they speak of 'our friends and partners': the member states of NATO, the EU, the WEU and the UN.[29]

In August 1990 the United States requested military support for a possible intervention in the Gulf, at least the deployment of minesweepers to the eastern Mediterranean to protect the Suez Canal. The FRG was also asked to participate in a potential WEU operation in the Persian Gulf.[30] These requests implied a new representation of the FRG. They treated the FRG as if military involvement abroad was a type of behaviour compatible with its identity, as if the country contributed to international military operations, even though it had never done so before. This can be read as an attempt at 'altercasting' (see *STIP* 329 and 331). In other words, the United States and the WEU treated the FRG as if it already had a new role in the hope that the FRG would do what this new role, rather than the old one, demanded. The FRG did not, however, respond favourably to the attempt: it turned down the requests on constitutional grounds. It merely sent several ships to the Mediterranean in order to relieve the United States of NATO duties there, but these vessels had to stay within NATO territory.[31] They could neither go to the eastern Mediterranean to secure the Suez Canal nor to the Gulf region itself. The FRG also, reluctantly and on as low a level as possible, granted a request by NATO partner Turkey to deploy forces to its southern border in order to deter an Iraqi attack.[32]

---

[29] For references to Germany's 'friends and allies' or 'friends and partners', see, for example, Helmut Kohl (chancellor) in Deutscher Bundestag, *Plenarprotokoll*, 12/5, 30 Jan. 1991, 68 and 70; Bundesministerium der Verteidigung, *Weißbuch 1994. Weißbuch zur Sicherheit der Bundesrepublik Deutschland und zur Lage und Zukunft der Bundeswehr* (Bonn, 1994), p. 43, section 312; Klaus Kinkel (foreign minister) in Deutscher Bundestag, *Plenarprotokoll*, 12/240, 22 Jul. 1994, 21169. For Wendt on friendship in international politics, see *STIP* 298–9.

[30] 'Wir müssen erwachsen werden', *Der Spiegel*, 34/44, 20 Aug. 1990, 121–3, here 121; Kaiser and Becher, *Deutschland und der Irak-Konflikt*, p. 14. For more NATO demands, see 'Den Ernstfall nicht gewagt', *Der Spiegel*, 7/45, 11 Feb. 1991, 18–26, here 19.

[31] 'Bonn schickt Marine ins Mittelmeer', *SZ*, 11–12 Aug. 1990, 1; 'Die Deutschen an die Front', *Der Spiegel*, 6/45, 4 Feb. 1991, 18–22; 'Der Himmel schließt sich', *Der Spiegel*, 4/45, 21 Jan. 1991, 18–20, here 20. On the significance of NATO territory, see ch. 3.

[32] 'Der will schlicht überleben', *Der Spiegel*, 2/45, 7 Jan. 1991, 18–21, here 20; 'Bonn will keine Abstriche an UN-Entschließungen zulassen', *FAZ*, 5 Jan. 1991, 2; 'Bonn will "sorgfältig prüfen"', *FAZ*, 19 Jan. 1991, 5.

At the same time statements of German leaders suggested that the FRG *wanted* to take on the new role but considered it impossible. Reportedly, Chancellor Kohl felt in a dilemma during the Gulf crisis. On the one hand, he did not want to disappoint the Americans, who had unequivocally supported German unification. Yet, on the other hand, because of his reading of the constitution, he felt unable to accommodate their demands for military involvement.[33] He and the foreign minister repeatedly spoke of Germany's willingness to take on more international responsibility, including participation in international military operations, but also of its inability, due to constitutional restraints, to do so for the time being.[34] Wendt acknowledges the significance of such 'rhetorical practice' (ISC 57–8) or 'verbal communication' (*STIP* 346–7). However, *behaviour* is construed as the key to identity change. The interaction between *ego* and *alter* Wendt describes revolves around physical gestures. Wendt's actors do not speak. They only signal each other. A social act consists in sending a signal, interpreting it and responding on the basis of the interpretation (A 405; *STIP* 330). A 'conversation of gestures' develops.[35]

According to Mead, whom Wendt references, actors need reflective intelligence and consciousness for this process.[36] The problem is that, in order to be able to reflect and interpret, actors have to be capable of using language. Wendt does not investigate, or even mention, the role of language in this context.[37] In the literature on which Wendt relies the significance of language is mentioned time and again, without, however, its role being systematically conceptualised. Thus Mead understands language as part of the creation of the situation.[38] Berger and Luckmann point out that language 'objectivates . . . shared experiences',[39] which crucially makes shared conceptions of reality possible. We might assume that Wendt implies the actors' capacity to speak when he refers to signalling and interpreting. This reading of his argument is not convincing,

---

[33] 'Wir müssen erwachsen werden', *Der Spiegel*, 34/44, 20 Aug. 1990, 121–3, here 121.

[34] For examples, see Kaiser and Becher, *Deutschland und der Irak-Konflikt*, pp. 85–6. See also Hans-Dietrich Genscher, address of the foreign minister at the 46th General Assembly of the United Nations on 25 Sep. 1991 in New York, in Presse- und Informationsamt der Bundesregierung, *Bulletin*, 104, 26 Sep. 1991, 827.

[35] Mead, *Mind, Self and Society*, p. 77.

[36] Mead, *Mind, Self and Society*, pp. 77–81.

[37] Wendt has since recognised the significance of language (in a footnote) but it is not central to his approach (Jepperson, Wendt and Katzenstein, 'Norms, Identity, and Culture', p. 64, n. 98). See also n. 43 below.

[38] Mead, *Mind, Self and Society*, p. 78.

[39] Peter Berger and Luckmann, *Social Construction of Reality*, pp. 85–6.

though. His description of the development of relations between actors relies on gestures. In his story about *ego* and *alter*, *ego*'s first communicative action may consist of different activities such as 'an advance, a retreat, a brandishing of arms, a laying down of arms, or an attack' (A 404; see also *STIP* 326–35). If it may also consist of a declaration, a threat or an assertion, he fails to say so. I think in his story it may not, since it is about a 'first encounter'. *Ego* and *alter* meet in a state of nature; Wendt is careful not to attribute to these agents characteristics which they could acquire only by participating in a society (A 402; see also *STIP* 189 and 328). Hence, *ego* and *alter* are unlikely to share a language; this is particularly obvious when we think of the example of aliens landing on earth.

Thus, in Wendt's approach communication turns out to be similar to an exchange of moves in game theory. Reaching an interpretation of a situation consists in an exchange of moves where *ego* classifies *alter*'s gestures and responds to them on the basis of its – *ego*'s – experiences. The interpretation is unrelated to the meaning *alter* attributes to its gesture; it is therefore, as Jonathan Mercer points out, 'nothing but supposition, analogy or projection'.[40] A linguistic exchange in which these judgements and interpretations and the experiences on which they are based could be at issue does not take place. Reaching a shared interpretation of the situation, if it is possible, is based on trial and error. Using this approach, it seems impossible to analyse communication about the meaning of certain situations or actions.[41] Wendt's actors cannot communicate about their behaviour; they communicate *through* their behaviour.[42] In *Social Theory* Wendt occasionally comments on the significance of language and discourse.[43] However, his remarks on the issue remain scanty and he does not replace or amend the crucial mechanism of strategic interaction between *ego* and *alter*.[44] Therefore, physical behaviour remains at the centre of his approach. Thus, taking Wendt's approach seriously, analysis must focus on behaviour that can be grasped without a linguistic context.[45] Putting to one side for the moment doubts as to whether this is possible at all, two areas of political behaviour could be seen as

---

[40] Jonathan Mercer, 'Anarchy and Identity', *International Organization* 49 (1995), 248.
[41] See Harald Müller, 'Internationale Beziehungen als kommunikatives Handeln', 25; Harald Müller, 'Spielen hilft nicht immer', 375.
[42] See the analogous criticism of Realism in Kratochwil and Ruggie, 'International Organization', 765.
[43] *STIP* 57, 75, 88, 175–6, 210 and 346–7.   [44] *STIP* ch. 7, esp. 330–1.
[45] The above argument about the exclusion of language in Wendt's approach has already been made in Zehfuß, 'Sprachlosigkeit schränkt ein'; Zehfuss, 'Constructivisms in IR'.

communicating the willingness or otherwise of the FRG to take on the new role: participation in international military operations abroad after the Gulf War and the restructuring of the armed forces to make such participation possible.[46]

The interaction between the FRG and its significant others did not end with the FRG rejecting the new role it was presented with. Immediately after the Gulf War, the United States stated that German support for the mine-clearing operation in the Gulf would be 'desirable'.[47] A formal request was issued only after the German government had indicated that it would be able to comply. This deployment of minesweepers after the cease-fire[48] was considered humanitarian, akin to a disaster relief operation.[49] In 1992 the UN asked for a Bundeswehr deployment to its large peace-keeping operation in Cambodia. The request was for paramedic personnel with military training rather than for armed forces, so as 'not to embarrass the Germans',[50] claimed *Der Spiegel*. The FRG agreed to contribute to this operation, which again could be defined as a humanitarian mission and which therefore was not 'as military' as participating in the Gulf War would have been.[51] In other words, these operations required less ambitious identity changes than such participation would have done.

A series of requests for deployments followed. By 1995 the Bundeswehr was participating in UN missions in Cambodia, Somalia, Iraq, Bahrain, Georgia, the Adriatic Sea, Bosnia-Herzegovina and the former Yugoslavia, and contributed to airlifts to Rwanda, Sarajevo and East Bosnia.[52] Yet in many cases the FRG imposed some limitation on its involvement. In the monitoring of the embargo against the former Yugoslavia, German ships were allowed only to monitor, not to stop and

---

[46] One could also consider changing the constitution as a symbolic act signalling the willingness to take on the new role. However, it is unclear how domestic norms could figure in Wendt's approach.

[47] Quoted in 'USA wünschen deutsche Hilfe beim Minenräumen im Golf', *SZ*, 6 Mar. 1991, 2.

[48] Kaiser and Becher, *Deutschland und der Irak-Konflikt*, pp. 15–16.

[49] 'Bonn schickt fünf Minensucher in den Golf', *SZ*, 7 Mar. 1991, 1.

[50] 'Gewachsene Instinkte', *Der Spiegel*, 21/46, 18 May 1992, 27–30, here 27.

[51] Some SPD and FDP politicians criticised that the point of the deployment was not humanitarian aid to the population, as the Defence Ministry claimed, but medical care for the troops ('Rühe verabschiedet erste deutsche Blauhelme', *SZ*, 12 May 1992, 2).

[52] Bundesministerium der Verteidigung, official website of the Federal Ministry of Defence, http://www.bundeswehr.de/sicherheitspolitik/uno-missionen/einsaetze.htm (site last updated 14 September 1998); Reinhard Mutz, 'Die Bundeswehr steht am Ende ihrer Geschichte als Friedensarmee', *FR*, 16 Jul. 1993, 10.

search.[53] German surveillance aircraft carried no weapons.[54] In the UN mission to Somalia the Germans insisted on deploying the Bundeswehr only to a so-called secure environment.[55] Luftwaffe soldiers serving as part of AWACS crews were not allowed to enter Austrian or Hungarian airspace, that is, leave NATO airspace.[56] When the multinational crews operating AWACS reconnaissance aircraft as part of Operation Deny Flight were asked to pass on information to fighter aircraft enforcing the flight ban over Bosnia, a fierce debate ensued between the governing parties as to whether the German soldiers had to be withdrawn.[57] There were also restrictions, if gradually fewer, on direct involvement in the former Yugoslavia.

Although the FRG did not fully embrace the role suggested to it by its significant others, the gist of its responses suggested a willingness to move gradually away from its non-military role. This message was underpinned by aspects of its behaviour related to the FRG's capacity to engage in military operations. In the early 1990s the FRG started restructuring its armed forces. The soldiers of the East German army had to be integrated into the Bundeswehr and the overall number of troops reduced to comply with disarmament treaties.[58] Moreover, and crucially in this context, it was claimed that the armed forces had to prepare for new tasks. Inspector General[59] Dieter Wellershoff argued that the

[53] 'Angetreten zum Krieg', *Der Spiegel*, 31/46, 27 Jul. 1992, 29–30. This limitation was lifted in July 1994: 'Bundestag billigt mit großer Mehrheit Einsätze der Bundeswehr in der Adria und in AWACS-Flugzeugen', *SZ*, 23–4 Jul. 1994, 1.
[54] 'Wir können mit Farbbeuteln schmeißen', *Der Spiegel*, 32/46, 3 Aug. 1992, 36; 'Kabinett erweitert Einsatzmöglichkeit der Bundeswehr und erlaubt Gewalt gegen Blockadebrecher in der Adria', *SZ*, 16–17 Jul. 1994, 1.
[55] 'Rühe: Bundeswehr fliegt Anfang Juni nach Somalia', *SZ*, 16 Apr. 1993, 2; ' . . . morgen die ganze Welt', *Der Spiegel*, 16/47, 19 Apr. 1993, 18–22, here 21–2; 'Rühe und Kinkel suchen "Definitionen" des Somalia Einsatzes', *FAZ*, 20 Apr. 1993, 1–2.
[56] Eighteen AWACS planes were involved in monitoring the flight ban over Bosnia. One unit was flying over Austria and Hungary, the other over the Adriatic Sea. German soldiers could be part only of the latter. See Stefan Kornelius, 'Ein Drittel der Besatzung sind Deutsche', *SZ*, 14 Jan. 1993, p. 6. This limitation was lifted in July 1994: 'Bundestag billigt mit großer Mehrheit Einsätze der Bundeswehr in der Adria und in AWACS-Flugzeugen', *SZ*, 23–4 Jul. 1994, 1.
[57] 'Drohung aus Washington', *Der Spiegel*, 3/47, 18 Jan. 1993, 18–20; 'Kohl und Kinkel vor Gericht', *Der Spiegel*, 14/47, 5 Apr. 1993, 18–22; 'Unionsminister im Kabinett für AWACS-Kampfeinsatz', *SZ*, 3–4 Apr. 1993, 1; 'Gegen den Widerspruch der FDP-Minister beschließt das Kabinett deutsche AWACS-Einsätze', *FAZ*, 3 Apr. 1993, 1–2.
[58] See, for example, Sigurd Boysen, 'Sicherheitspolitik und Bundeswehr', *Österreichische Militärische Zeitschrift* 1 (1991), 30–5, and Geoffrey van Orden, 'The *Bundeswehr* in Transition', *Survival* 33 (1991), 352–70.
[59] The inspector general (*Generalinspekteur*) is the FRG's highest-ranking soldier but he lacks the powers of a commander-in-chief. His main function is to advise the government.

Bundeswehr needed mobile forces for the participation in international and multinational operations;[60] for, apart from legal obstacles to using force at the time of the Gulf War and unwillingness or inability to consider it, the FRG had simply been unable to do so. The Bundeswehr was neither trained nor equipped for such operations. As the new inspector general Klaus Naumann pointed out even in late 1991, it would have been 'irresponsible to send people to an operation ... for which they are not prepared. So far we have no soldiers who have been trained to be deployed to the desert or the jungle or somewhere.'[61] In May of the following year he still argued that the German armed forces were unable to take part in a large-scale peace operation.[62] Similarly, the defence minister contended that the forces were neither psychologically nor materially ready for combat missions.[63] The shortcomings were basic: for Cambodia the Bundeswehr had to buy uniforms for the tropical climate from the French.[64] Clearly, the armed forces had to be reorganised, equipped and trained to make participation in international missions possible at all.

The Bundeswehr started planning for international operations with 'confidential working papers' immediately after the Gulf War, even whilst the constitutional situation remained unclear.[65] In talks about the future structure of the Bundeswehr in early 1991, the governing parties agreed to create an intervention force and the defence minister demanded the acquisition of weaponry and equipment to increase mobility.[66] In January 1992 he and the leadership of the armed forces agreed to cuts in the defence budget which were mainly to affect tanks and heavy artillery. Flexibility was, in contrast, to be increased and equipment for rapid reaction forces to be acquired. At this point, these forces were expected to be available by 1995.[67] Inspector General Naumann justified a new armament programme with reference to worldwide operations of the Bundeswehr, as if parliament had changed

---

[60] 'Geschenk des Himmels', *Der Spiegel*, 42/44, 15 Oct. 1990, 26–30, here 30.
[61] 'Auf Atomwaffen angewiesen', interview with Inspector General Klaus Dieter Naumann, *Der Spiegel*, 42/45, 14 Oct. 1991, 76–9, here 79.
[62] 'Naumann: Bundeswehr ist bequem und überheblich geworden', *SZ*, 13 May 1992, 1.
[63] 'Rühe rechnet schon 1993 mit Blauhelmeinsätzen', *SZ*, 22 Jun. 1992, 2.
[64] 'Rühe: Bundeswehr fliegt Anfang Juni nach Somalia', *SZ*, 16 Apr. 1993, 2; 'CDU: Zukunft der Bundeswehr hat begonnen', *SZ*, 17 May 1993, 1.
[65] 'Wenn es die Führung will', *Der Spiegel*, 13/45, 25 Mar. 1991, 82–93, here 92.
[66] Ibid., 93; 'Die Deutschen an die Front', *Der Spiegel*, 6/45, 4 Feb. 1991, 18–22, here 22; 'Tolerant, charakterfest', *Der Spiegel*, 23/45, 3 Jun. 1991, 20–3, here 22–3.
[67] 'Bundeswehr will durch Verzicht auf neue Waffen 44 Milliarden Mark bis zum Jahr 2005 einsparen', *SZ*, 13 Jan. 1992, 1.

the Basic Law and as if the cabinet had adopted new guidelines for the armed forces.[68] Despite budgetary constraints, Naumann asked for money to prepare operations in regions 'where it is cold and mountainous or hot and flat'. He also wanted to familiarise military instructors with the danger of jungle warfare.[69] A few months later Bundeswehr participation in UN operations was to be possible by 1993.[70] Equipment had to be ordered in January to be able to fulfil the promise to have two battalions ready for UN operations by October 1993.[71] The military demanded the development of a multipurpose fighter helicopter which was to protect the envisaged rapid reaction forces.[72] Since the Transall had proved too small to transport air defence missiles during the Gulf War, the Bundeswehr also wanted new transport aircraft.[73] Acquiring equipment ranging from guns to amphibious reconnaissance vehicles was justified with the new range of tasks and the demands of deployments outside Europe.[74]

The planning clearly went beyond what the involvement in international operations at the time would have justified and what the government declared to be its position on the FRG's legal scope for manoeuvre. In March 1991 the head of the army Helge Hansen commissioned an internal inquiry into the demands on German forces if deployed as UN troops. Specific attention was paid to changes necessary if missions were broadened from peace-keeping to peace-enforcing in the event of mounting tension in the conflict region.[75] The army was planning multipurpose soldiers in rapid reaction forces whose tasks were to include the distribution of food in areas hit by drought; aid in case of accidents at a nuclear reactor, earthquakes and major fires; and helping refugees. They were to be ready to be deployed under extreme climatic conditions and able to fight guerrilla and terrorist attacks.[76] A Marines-style elite force for international operations was planned.[77]

---

[68] 'Risiken für Land und Volk', *Der Spiegel*, 4/46, 20 Jan. 1992, 33–5, here 33.
[69] Quoted in 'Größenwahn der Generäle', *Der Spiegel*, 15/46, 6 Apr. 1992, 18–21, here 20.
[70] 'Nahe dran am echten Krieg', *Der Spiegel*, 30/46, 20 Jul. 1992, 23–9, here 26; 'Rühe rechnet schon 1993 mit Blauhelmeinsätzen', *SZ*, 22 Jun. 1992, 2.
[71] '50 Prozent für die Witwe', *Der Spiegel*, 2/47, 11 Jan. 1993, 32–4, here 34; 'Rühe schafft Strukturen für internationale Einsätze', *SZ*, 16 Dec. 1992, 1.
[72] 'Das Rad neu erfinden', *Der Spiegel*, 36/46, 31 Aug. 1992, 99–103, here 102.
[73] 'Selber machen', *Der Spiegel*, 38/47, 20 Sep. 1993, 32; 'Mit Stolz', *Der Spiegel*, 29/45, 15 Jul. 1991, 26–8, here 28.
[74] 'Ich auch', *Der Spiegel*, 36/47, 6 Sep. 1993, 52–7, here 55.
[75] 'Gewachsene Instinkte', *Der Spiegel*, 21/46, 18 May 1992, 27–30, here 27.
[76] 'Viele bunte Smarties', *Der Spiegel*, 32/46, 3 Aug. 1992, 34–7, here 34.
[77] 'Einsatz ins Ungewisse', *Der Spiegel*, 5/49, 30 Jan. 1995, 68–79.

In September 1992, the army, under Hansen, was the first to move from thinking up scenarios and demanding equipment to creating crisis reaction forces. The Third Corps in Koblenz was immediately to start preparing and planning their deployment. From 1993 it would assume the command over army units deployed for UN or CSCE peace-keeping operations. Although Hansen's order mentioned peace-keeping only, it included instructions to focus especially on training for combat.[78] In November 1992 Defence Minister Rühe finally issued new guidelines for defence policy. The armed forces were not only to protect Germany and its citizens against external threats; they would also serve world peace and international security in accordance with the UN Charter, provide aid in emergency situations and support humanitarian missions.[79] The 1993 plan for the Bundeswehr and the 1994 White Paper on security show that the armed forces were to be restructured so as to make them far more mobile.[80] The White Paper mentions three capabilities the armed forces had to develop: to defend the FRG and the alliance; to participate in multinational crisis management in the framework of NATO and the WEU; and to participate appropriately in UN and CSCE operations.[81] Accordingly, the establishment of rapid reaction forces[82] and of headquarters for the coordination of UN 'blue helmet' operations was planned.[83] All this suggests that the FRG was planning to make military involvement abroad one of its standard practices.

Plans to increase the mobility of Bundeswehr forces and their capacity to operate abroad can be interpreted as a response to expectations from 'friends and partners'. *Der Spiegel* claimed that the United States and the UK were demanding military involvement in two roles. The Germans were to participate in rapid reaction forces within NATO, and in Gulf War-style operations in the framework of the UN.[84] In May 1991 the FRG agreed to a NATO reaction force which would also intervene outside the treaty area.[85] The restructuring of the Bundeswehr was in

---

[78] 'Transport von Gefallenen', *Der Spiegel*, 37/46, 7 Sep. 1992, 23–4.

[79] 'Feldjäger in die Wüste', *Der Spiegel*, 51/46, 14 Dec. 1992, 24–5; Bundesministerium der Verteidigung, 'Militärpolitische und militärstrategische Grundlagen und konzeptionelle Grundrichtung der Neugestaltung der Bundeswehr', reprinted in *FR*, 20 Feb. 1992, 21.

[80] Bundesminister der Verteidigung, *Die Bundeswehr der Zukunft – Bundeswehrplan '94* (Bonn, 1993); BMV, *Weißbuch 1994*, esp. ch. 5.

[81] BMV, *Weißbuch 1994*, p. 91, section 519.

[82] BMV, *Weißbuch 1994*, p. 93, section 527.

[83] 'Da müssen wir hin', *Der Spiegel*, 45/48, 7 Nov. 1994, 18–19, here 19.

[84] 'Den Ernstfall nicht gewagt', *Der Spiegel*, 7/45, 11 Feb. 1991, 18–26, here 23–5.

[85] 'Eine historische Entscheidung', *Der Spiegel*, 43/45, 21 Oct. 1991, 18–20, here 19; 'Tolerant, charakterfest', *Der Spiegel*, 23/45, 3 Jun. 1991, 20–3, here 23.

line with changes in NATO, particularly its new strategy[86] and its increasing reliance on multinational units, which were meant to deepen
the cohesion of the alliance.[87] Similarly, the German government supported the UN's move towards a more assertive military role and later
the UN secretary general's initiative to create 'standby' forces.[88]

The creation of multinational forces also expressed the FRG's
willingness to get more involved militarily.[89] In October 1991 Kohl and
Mitterrand proposed a European rapid reaction force. Europe was
to have 50,000 troops based on the already existing Franco-German
Corps.[90] The initiative developed into setting up what was called the
Eurokorps. It was to be ready to be deployed by 1995 and other EC
member states were invited to join. The tasks of the Eurokorps were to
include operations for the preservation and re-establishment of peace,
also outside NATO territory, but the treaty was linked to the regulations
of the UN Charter.[91]

This restructuring of the armed forces makes sense only if military
involvement abroad was to become a practice the FRG would repeatedly engage in. As we have seen, there was at the same time indeed
increasing involvement in international operations. Both can be read
as gestures signalling the FRG's willingness to accept the attempts by
its 'friends and partners' at 'altercasting' and gradually to take on the
new role. The Wendtian approach suggests that this reflects not merely
a change in behaviour but one in identity (see *STIP* 26). An actor's social
identity depends on relationships and indeed is thought to reflect the
behaviour of others towards it. Thus the new way in which its significant
others treated the FRG influenced its definition of self. The notion that
the FRG was undergoing a transformation of identity seems reasonable

---

[86] 'Wenn es die Führung will', *Der Spiegel*, 13/45, 25 Mar. 1991, 82–93, here 93. See
also Axel Sauder, *Souveränität und Integration. Französische und deutsche Konzeptionen europäischer Sicherheit nach dem Ende des Kalten Krieges (1990–1993)* (Baden-Baden:
Nomos Verlagsgesellschaft, 1995), p. 257, and NATO's 'New Strategic Concept', http://
www. nato.int/docu/comm/c911107a.htm (accessed 17 Nov. 1998), esp. sections 47 and 53.
[87] Sauder, *Souveränität und Integration*, p. 256; 'Deutsch–niederländisches Korps verein-
bart', *SZ*, 31 Mar. 1993, 6; 'Rühe: Neues Kapitel für das Bündnis', *SZ*, 23 Apr. 1993, 2; BMV,
Weißbuch 1994, pp. 58–9, sections 434 and 435.
[88] BMV, *Weißbuch 1994*, p. 68, section 463.
[89] See also Philip H. Gordon, *France, Germany, and the Western Alliance* (Boulder: Westview
Press, 1995), p. 45.
[90] 'Eine historische Entscheidung', *Der Spiegel*, 43/45, 21 Oct. 1991, 18–20; 'Eurokorps in
NATO eingebunden', *SZ*, 22 Jan. 1993, 2.
[91] 'Gewachsene Instinkte', *Der Spiegel*, 21/46, 18 May 1992, 27–30, here 30; 'Bonn und
Paris öffnen Armeekorps für andere Staaten', *SZ*, 13 May 1992, 2; 'Im Kriegsfall unter
NATO-Befehl', *SZ*, 22 May 1992, 1.

as repeated military deployments abroad and acquiring an intervention capacity were bound to interfere with the strongly non-military conception of self.

Collective identity

So far it is unclear, however, why the FRG moved away from its non-military identity at all. As Wendt reminds us, once stable identities are established, actors are likely to have a stake in maintaining them (A 411; *STIP* 339–40). Therefore, giving up a well-established and institutionalised identity such as the FRG's self-conception as a non-military power, if done intentionally, must be somehow motivated. The benefits of taking on the new identity must be expected to be greater than the likely costs of sticking with the old (A 419). Wendt hints that power relations affect whether role definitions become significant (*STIP* 327). This is not explored in detail and therefore remains unhelpful. In the case at hand it seems more promising to investigate the impact of what Wendt calls 'collective identity'. Whether identities can be viewed as collective depends on how interests are defined. Self-interest and collective interest are conceptualised 'as the effects of the extent to and manner in which social identities involve an *identification* with the fate of the other' (ISC 52; see also *STIP* 106 and 229). The nature of identification in each situation determines how the boundaries of the self are drawn. 'In the absence of positive identification interests will be defined without regard to the other, who will instead be viewed as an object to be manipulated for the gratification of the self' (ISC 52; see also *STIP* 240). This, Wendt argues, is the core of self-interest. Collective identity, on the other hand, a concept well developed in sociology, social psychology, philosophy and economics, refers to 'positive identification with the welfare of another, such that the other is seen as a cognitive extension of the Self rather than as independent' (ISC 52). Wendt expresses this even more strongly in his *Social Theory*:

> Collective identity takes the relationship between Self and Other to its logical conclusion, identification. Identification is a cognitive process in which the Self–Other distinction becomes blurred and at the limit transcended altogether. Self is 'categorized' *as* Other. Identification is usually issue-specific and rarely total (though may come close in love and patriotism), but always involves extending the boundaries of the Self to include the Other.[92]

---

[92] *STIP* 229 (footnotes deleted).

Actors who have a collective identity define their interests on a higher level of aggregation, based on feelings of solidarity, community and loyalty. They engage in diffuse reciprocity and are willing to bear costs without selective incentives, thereby making collective action easier (ISC 53). Collective identity then has 'the causal power to induce actors to define the welfare of the Other as part of that of the Self, to be "altruistic". Altruistic actors may still be rational, but the basis on which they calculate their interests is the group or "team".'[93] On the identity continuum actors will usually fall between the extremes of self-centred and solidaristic loyalties.

The point, Wendt argues, is not that self-interested identities will necessarily be replaced by collective ones but that identities are created in interaction. Cooperation thus may change actors' identities rather than just their payoff structure (ISC 53–4). In Wendt's words, the 'constructivist model is saying that the boundaries of the Self are at stake in and therefore may change in interaction, so that in cooperating states can form a collective identity' (*STIP* 317). If such a collective identity develops, states will consider the security of partners their responsibility. The security environment will be based on practices which are to some extent altruistic (A 400–1). When states accept the demands of the international rule structure as legitimate, Wendt speaks of a 'Kantian culture'. In his interpretation of the concept of legitimacy 'this means that states identify with each other, seeing each other's security not just as instrumentally related to their own, but as literally being their own. The cognitive boundaries of the Self are extended to include the Other.' This, he carries on to say, can be called many things, amongst them 'collective identity' and 'solidarity' (*STIP* 305; see also 337).

The behaviour of the FRG could be interpreted as reflecting such a collective identity. Restructuring was designed to enable the Bundeswehr to participate in multilateral operations as part of NATO or the WEU. Concrete operations such as the deployment of minesweepers to the Mediterranean or of troops to southern Turkey were portrayed as a contribution to the security of the alliance.[94] These efforts seem to show a concern with the welfare and security of others and therefore, following Wendt, an understanding of self which reaches beyond the boundary of the FRG. If Wendt is right, past cooperation might have led the FRG to understand its identity collectively and, as a result, to abandon the

[93] *STIP* 229 (footnotes deleted).
[94] 'Bonn schickt Minenräumer', *FAZ*, 11 Aug. 1990, 2. On the deployment to Turkey, see the next section of this chapter.

non-military self-conception which was increasingly out of tune with the concern for those others who were considered part of the self.

The FRG is frequently portrayed as keen on and adept at multilateral policies and integration.[95] Arguably, the pursuit of such policies reflects a more inclusive definition of identity. The claim that the FRG tends towards such a collective understanding of self is usually based on the idea that it benefited from postwar integration and multilateralism. The FRG, or so the story goes, was able to gain semi-sovereignty[96] through *Einbindung*, that is, integration with the West,[97] especially NATO. Even the first step of integration was bound up with the military. The idea that it was NATO and (military) integration, in particular the decreasing ability of European armed forces to act unilaterally, which ensured stability in Europe was and is widespread in Germany.[98] According to Chancellor Kohl, it was not the number of divisions that was significant but who had political control over them.[99] The NATO framework made it possible to shift political control over Germany's armed forces away from a purely national decision-making body without engaging in openly discriminatory policies against the country. This was reflected in the organisational set-up of the Bundeswehr. There was, for instance, no general staff, as most Bundeswehr forces were integrated into the NATO command structure.[100] The 1985 White Paper on security stated that the Bundeswehr was 'conceived of as an army in the alliance and not an instrument for the independent development of military power for the Federal Republic of Germany'.[101] Therefore, the FRG's military,

---

[95] See, for example, Bertram, 'Power and Past', p. 92; Gordon, *France, Germany*, p. 11.

[96] This term was coined by Peter J. Katzenstein. He did not base it on the foreign policy restrictions imposed on the FRG, for which it is often used. See his *Policy and Politics in West Germany: The Growth of a Semi-Sovereign State* (Philadelphia: Temple University Press, 1987). On the limitations of the FRG's sovereignty, see Gunther Hellmann, 'Die Westdeutschen, die Stationierungstruppen und die Vereinigung. Ein Lehrstück über "verantwortliche Machtpolitik"?', in Gunther Hellmann (ed.), *Alliierte Präsenz und deutsche Einheit. Die politischen Folgen militärischer Macht* (Baden-Baden: Nomos Verlagsgesellschaft, 1994), pp. 96–7.

[97] See Wolfram F. Hanrieder, *Germany, America, Europe: Forty Years of German Foreign Policy* (New Haven and London: Yale University Press, 1989), ch. 1.

[98] See Klaus Naumann, *Die Bundeswehr in einer Welt im Umbruch* (Berlin: Siedler Verlag, 1994), p. 138; Sauder, *Souveränität und Integration*, p. 160.

[99] Kohl, 'Ein geeintes Deutschland als Gewinn für Stabilität und Sicherheit in Europa', in Presse- und Informationsamt der Bundesregierung, *Bulletin*, 68, 29 May 1990, 587.

[100] Sauder, *Souveränität und Integration*, pp. 209 and 265; van Orden, '*Bundeswehr* in Transition', 354; Susanne Peters, 'Germany's Security Policy After Unification: Taking the Wrong Models', *European Security* 6 (1997), 24–5; Bundesminister der Verteidigung, *Weißbuch 1985*, p. 73, section 163.

[101] Bundesminister der Verteidigung, *Weißbuch 1985*, p. 73, section 160.

the very aspect of the state's capabilities often thought to represent its sovereignty,[102] was from the start integrated into a collective structure.

Integration at the same time provided the opportunity to gain influence, particularly in areas where the FRG's own possibilities were limited.[103] Arguably, the FRG's leaders supported this type of integration to secure some say, especially with respect to nuclear weapons which the FRG did not possess itself but which were stationed on its territory. This was thought to be possible only by contributing substantial conventional forces to NATO.[104] The principle of gearing defence policy towards the alliance became accepted by all successive governments.[105] Moreover, considering the country's position on the faultline of the East–West confrontation, German politicians were interested in developing frameworks of cooperation which also included the states of the Eastern bloc: for it had always been clear that unification would be possible only with the consent of Germany's European neighbours and the Allies, rather than against them.[106] This argument also relies on the belief that, without NATO and the Bundeswehr, peaceful change in Europe would not have come about.[107] Thus, the FRG favoured cooperative policies during the Cold War. Multilateralism was, however, to remain the basis of German security policy. As the 1994 White Paper states:

> Today Germany is embedded in a varied web of relationships which includes the alliances, the Euro-Atlantic institutions and the bilateral treaties with our neighbours. Integration and cooperation therefore not only remain the essential determining factors of German policy but at the same time become the central elements of a conception which aims for stability for the whole of Europe.[108]

Multilateral institutions such as the CSCE and NATO were seen as the basis of stability and therefore security.[109] Accordingly, Hanns W. Maull

---

[102] See, for example, Markovits and Reich, *German Predicament*, p. 137.
[103] See also Hanns W. Maull, 'A German Perspective', in Michael Brenner (ed.), *Multilateralism and Western Strategy* (London: Macmillan, 1995), pp. 42–76; Bertram, 'Power and Past', pp. 93–4.
[104] Sauder, *Souveränität und Integration*, p. 163; Naumann, *Bundeswehr*, p. 124.
[105] Sauder, *Souveränität und Integration*, p. 159.
[106] Hans-Dietrich Genscher, *Erinnerungen* (Munich: Goldmann, 1997). See also Chancellor Kohl's preface to the 1994 White Paper, BMV, *Weißbuch 1994*, VI, and Bertram, 'Power and Past', p. 93.
[107] Naumann, *Bundeswehr*, p. 125; Genscher, *Erinnerungen*.
[108] BMV, *Weißbuch 1994*, p. 13, section 107.
[109] BMV, *Weißbuch 1994*, pp. 44–5, section 318.

claims that the FRG has been socialised into a multilateralist foreign policy which involved substantial transfers of sovereignty and supranational integration within Europe.[110] Some even call integration with the West and specifically with NATO the FRG's 'reason of state'.[111] All this seems to reflect an understanding of self which included more than the FRG itself, in other words, a collective identity based, as Wendt suggests, on past cooperation. It is even said that Foreign Minister Klaus Kinkel often failed to set priorities and instead instructed ambassadors to NATO and the EU to endorse the opinion of the majority.[112] This latter point also shows a willingness to rely on others to make decisions beneficial to the self. As Wendt argues, 'collective identity implies giving over to the Other at least some responsibility for the care of the Self' (*STIP* 359).

In this interpretation the collective identity could lead the FRG to define its interests and then act taking into account not only the expectations but also the needs of others. This would have tangible effects. Arguably, the FRG not only started sending its military abroad but also restructured it fundamentally to be better able to do so. Or, to emphasise the point the approach is presumably designed to make, *contra* Realist claims: the FRG moved its troops around because it considered other states part of its identity, and for no other reason. Although this is a point worth making, it is made on the basis of the wrong reasons. It is not clear how we are supposed to investigate the existence or significance of such a collective identity and it is, in my view, impossible further to engage the issues raised by the notion of identity without going beyond Wendt's approach and ultimately leaving it behind. Some reasons for this are worth raising at this point.

The account is unsatisfactory as we get little sense of what exactly happens when identities, which Wendt considers to be 'relatively stable' (A 397; see also *STIP* 21), change. The centrality of physical gestures in Wendt's explication of social action renders it impossible to analyse identity formation as a discursive process. The recognition of 'rhetorical practice' (ISC 57) and 'verbal communication' (*STIP* 346–7) as significant is a step in the right direction but fails to address *how* discourse should be analysed. This omission is crucial because, as will be demonstrated in the final section of this chapter, the competing identity narratives

[110] Maull, 'German Perspective', p. 56.
[111] Sauder, *Souveränität und Integration*, p. 160; Volker Rühe (defence minister) in Deutscher Bundestag, *Plenarprotokoll*, 12/132, 15 Jan. 1993, 11484; Robert Gerald Livingston, 'United Germany: Bigger and Better', *Foreign Policy* 87 (1992), 171–2; Peters, 'Germany's Security Policy', 26.
[112] 'Damals als Beamter', *Der Spiegel*, 7/49, 13 Feb. 1995, 25–8, here 28.

highlighted by an exploration of the discursive constitution of identity endanger the assumption that states are pregiven, unitary actors. In
addressing the question of reality construction and identity formation
it is, as will be shown, problematic to take the referent of identity as
given *a priori*. In the situation under consideration here, for instance,
the assertion that the state was the relevant agent, and *qua* state was
identical with earlier German polities, pre-decided which avenues for
thought and practice were open and which were closed. This closure en-
forces a strict separation between the domestic and international realms.
The approach makes the domestic realm an exogenous problem, ignoring both domestic processes of identity formation and the interplay
of activities at the domestic and international levels. Although Wendt
acknowledges that something significant happens inside states (*STIP*
11, 21 and 27–8), these processes are treated as always already completed when international interaction takes place. They are, in Wendt's
words, 'ontologically prior to the states system' (ISC 51). Because states
confront the world as unitary actors, their corporate identity must be
established *a priori*. This restriction in Wendt's constructivism is reminiscent of his observation of a limit in rationalist game theory: identity
may change but only exogenously (*STIP* 315–16). In Wendt's approach,
corporate identity may change but this is separate from and prior to
any international interaction. In relation to the question of German military involvement abroad, intense contestations over identity took place
in the domestic realm. Yet these were clearly linked to perceptions of
what the 'abroad' demanded and only make sense in the context of the
changing international situation. When Bundeswehr soldiers were first
involved in combat as AWACS officers, it was not only *their* first time.
It was also the first combat mission NATO had been involved in as an
alliance.[113] The domestic and the international thus look less separate
than Wendt asserts. Moreover, ignoring domestic processes excludes a
central concern of other constructivisms: the consideration of the normative questions at issue, here the contestations over who the Germans/the
FRG/Germany *should* be.

Yet the important point is not that Wendt 'brackets' the domestic and
does not address normative issues, but the significance of this move for
his approach.[114] Structural change, a key focus of systemic theorising,

---

[113] 'NATO schießt vier Militärflugzeuge ab', *SZ*, 01 Mar. 1994, 1.
[114] Ted Hopf makes similar observations about Wendt's ambiguous attitude towards the
domestic without, however, drawing my conclusions: 'Constructivism All the Way Down',
International Politics 37 (2000), 372–3.

supervenes identity change (*STIP* 338). Thus identity transformation is crucial, even if not a *focus* of the theory. The exploration of German contestations over identity provides the material with which to demonstrate that Wendt's bracketing of domestic politics and his related failure to take seriously the discursive production of identity, of which normative questions are an inextricable part, is not an innocent methodological choice but a necessary move for his constructivist project.

Finally, there is the problem of disentangling identity and behaviour, because Wendt claims that it is not just behaviour but identity that changes. Yet it is unclear, with respect to an actual case such as the one considered here, what exactly sets apart a transformation of identity from a mere change in behaviour. Although Wendt's claim that the way in which others treat an actor will affect its conception of self rather than just its behaviour seems plausible, it is hard to pin down the qualitative difference between the two. After all, in his approach we are forced to infer actors' self-understandings from nothing but their behaviour. The FRG's identity may be recognised only by drawing conclusions from its behaviour. Increasing military involvement and the restructuring of the armed forces suggest a tangible move away from a non-military identity, particularly because they have 'material' effects. Yet this is precisely where the distinction between the material world of moving tanks or transferring economic resources and the less tangible realm of talk, meaning and beliefs, which is at least implicit in Wendt's approach,[115] creates problems. What an action means to someone depends on how they contextualise it. If an identity matters only in its realisation in certain types of behaviour, then it is difficult to see why we should call it 'identity' rather than 'behaviour'. Wendt claims identity to involve stable expectations about behaviour. Others have taken up the question of whether this is a good way to define identity.[116] Clearly, the idea of stability does not, in any case, solve the problem of telling apart identity and behaviour, because the possibility of identity transformation, of moving from one kind of anarchy to another, is crucial. Yet it needs to be solved if the distinction between constructivism and rationalism

---

[115] See esp. *STIP* ch. 3.
[116] See, for example, Iver B. Neumann, 'Self and Other in International Relations', *European Journal of International Relations* 2 (1996), 163–6; Sujata Chakrabarti Pasic, 'Culturing International Relations Theory: A Call for Extension', in Lapid and Kratochwil, *Return of Culture and Identity in IR Theory*, pp. 86 and 87–90.

is to be upheld;[117] for it relies on the claim that rationalists may be able to cope with changes in behaviour but not in identity.

The problem is that, to detect an identity change, it must be possible to identify the identity an actor 'has'. This possibility is implicit in the process Wendt describes. *Ego* presents *alter* with a new identity which *alter* either takes up or refuses. Contestation over the identity takes place only between *alter* and *ego*. Although there may be a gradual adjustment of the ideas about self and other on both sides, it is a contestation over two alternative but clearly identifiable notions of identity. How either the actors or the ideas about self and other get constituted in the first place is not part of the account.[118] This, in my view, misconceptualises identity construction. What is more, it is a necessary misconceptualisation for Wendt's approach. Identity is not only significant for Wendt's constructivism; it is also a problem for it.

Collective identity reconsidered

One of the problematic aspects of Wendt's treatment of identity is the question of how we would know when identity matters. The impact of identity must be inferred from behaviour. However, inferring identity from behaviour seems impossible. This can be illustrated with the FRG's reaction to Turkey's request for alliance support during the Gulf War. The operation in the Gulf itself was outside the remit of NATO. Therefore, in view of the claims about the constitution, 'friends and partners' were forced to accept that the FRG did not participate.[119] However, when Turkey requested assistance from NATO, the FRG's reliability as an ally became the focus of discussion in Germany.

On 2 January 1991 NATO's Defence Planning Committee decided to deploy the air component of the multinational Allied Mobile Force (AMF) to the southeast of Turkey in order to demonstrate the will of the alliance to defend the country in the event of an Iraqi attack. The FRG was reluctant to support the decision.[120] One of the chancellor's advisors claimed that Kohl and Foreign Minister Genscher had agreed to the resulting deployment of 18 Alpha Jets and 270 Bundeswehr soldiers to

---

[117] This distinction is crucial even in the hint towards a synthesis with 'rationalism for today and tomorrow, and constructivism for the *longue durée*' (*STIP* 367).

[118] Wendt might disagree with this as he claims that the international structure helps construct the actors (*STIP* 21).

[119] For the constitutional situation, see ch. 3.

[120] Kaiser and Becher, *Deutschland und der Irak-Konflikt*, p. 30.

Turkey only with the 'utmost reluctance'. According to *Der Spiegel*, they were worried about German soldiers being drawn into the Gulf War. The Alpha Jets, however, could not even be used to support ground troops or fight helicopters in Iraq from bases in Turkey because their range of 1000 km was too short.[121] Karl Kaiser and Klaus Becher claim that the theoretical possibility of getting embroiled in the war was less important than the worry that the stationing of NATO troops at the southern periphery of the Soviet Union might lead to adverse effects in that country. This was significant as the Two-Plus-Four Treaty about the external aspects of German unification had not yet been ratified.[122]

The FRG did deploy troops but the notion that this was done out of concern for the welfare of the other seems questionable in view of the discussion in Germany. Suspicions were voiced that the Turkish president Turgut Özal would attempt to provoke a security crisis to divert attention from domestic problems.[123] Andreas von Bülow of the SPD claimed that the Turkish government had ulterior motives with respect to Iraqi oilfields.[124] When German politicians discovered that US aircraft were flying missions against Iraq from Turkish bases, they started debating the exact circumstances under which assisting Turkey would be an alliance obligation. Many in the SPD leadership but also some members of the governing parties suggested that, in allowing US aircraft to operate from Turkish bases, Turkey was provoking Iraq. Therefore a potential Iraqi retaliation could not oblige the FRG to assist Turkey in accordance with Art. 5 of the NATO Treaty.[125] They considered German participation in the AMF deployment a mistake.[126] This is an amazing argument. Art. 5 speaks of 'an armed attack' against a member state in Europe or North America.[127] It does not differentiate between being an innocent victim of an attack and having provoked one. Nevertheless, even Chancellor Kohl stated that, should Turkey interfere in the Gulf

[121] 'Der will schlicht überleben', *Der Spiegel*, 2/45, 7 Jan. 1991, 18–21, here 20.
[122] Kaiser and Becher, *Deutschland und der Irak-Konflikt*, pp. 30–1. See also Genscher, *Erinnerungen*, pp. 901 and 907.
[123] 'Der Himmel schließt sich', *Der Spiegel*, 4/45, 21 Jan. 1991, 18–20, here 20; 'Schröder gegen Einsatz der Bundeswehr in der Türkei', *SZ*, 24 Jan. 1991, 2.
[124] 'Deutscher Einsatz verfassungswidrig', *SZ*, 1 Feb. 1991, 6.
[125] Kaiser and Becher, *Deutschland und der Irak-Konflikt*, p. 31; 'Vogel: Keine Mehrheit für Bundeswehr-Einsatz', *SZ*, 23 Jan. 1991, 2; 'Kinkel: Parlament nicht zuständig', *SZ*, 28 Jan. 1991, 6; 'SPD: Angriff des Irak auf die Türkei kein Bündnisfall', *SZ*, 31 Jan. 1991, 2.
[126] 'Eindringlicher Appell zur Rettung des Friedens', *SZ*, 15 Jan. 1991, 1; 'Schröder gegen Einsatz der Bundeswehr in der Türkei', *SZ*, 24 Jan. 1991, 2; 'SPD: Politische Fehlentscheidung', *SZ*, 6 Feb. 1991, 5.
[127] 'The North Atlantic Treaty', Washington, DC, 4 Apr. 1949, http://www.nato.int/docu/basictxt/treaty.htm.

War, this would not lead to any duties for the FRG arising from Art. 5. Moreover, there was debate on whether shelling on Turkish soil would be sufficient to count as an attack in terms of Art. 5 at all.[128] When what counts as an attack is linked to dubious legal arguments and thresholds of damage, it seems that, despite the ultimately supportive behaviour, the idea that there was solidarity or concern for the welfare of the other does not offer a good explanation. In Wendtian terms, Germany did not consider Turkey part of a collective identity with respect to this matter.

Kohl and Genscher argued that the deployment of the Alpha Jets was the 'utmost which c[ould] be demanded of the Germans'. According to a diplomat, the Germans were planning to fulfil NATO obligations 'at the lowest possible level'.[129] The situation took a new turn, however, when Özal argued in a German news programme in late January 1991 that Germany was responsible for Saddam's ability to threaten the use of biological and chemical weapons. Therefore the Germans should accept their responsibility and help the Turks. Kohl phoned Özal immediately to assure him that the FRG would lend military assistance in the event of an Iraqi attack on Turkey.[130] In February a further 530 troops and Hawk and Roland air defence missiles were deployed.[131] Özal's comments had apparently changed the situation. Arguably, they interfered with the representation of the newly unified Germany as responsible and reliable, in other words, with the representation of the FRG as defining its identity as part of a community of states. Hence, the evidence is mixed in terms of collective identity as Wendt describes it. On the one hand, the danger to an alliance partner who should have been considered part of the self should have ruled out the more narrowly self-interested arguments made against the deployment. On the other hand, the FRG did send the troops and therefore we might be justified in inferring that the collective identity led it to define its interests in terms of the alliance rather than the single state, that is, 'on a higher level of social aggregation' (ISC 53).

In the FRG the idea that interests have to be defined in relation to the welfare of others has some currency. When Foreign Minister Klaus Kinkel announced that, as Konrad Adenauer had already said, the best

---

[128] 'Der Himmel schließt sich', *Der Spiegel*, 4/45, 21 Jan. 1991, 18–20, here 20; 'Bonn hält deutschen Kriegseinsatz für unwahrscheinlich', *SZ*, 19–20 Jan. 1991, 1.

[129] Quoted in 'Der will schlicht überleben', *Der Spiegel*, 2/45, 7 Jan. 1991, 18–21, here 20.

[130] 'Das wird ein schwieriges Jahr', *Der Spiegel*, 5/45, 28 Jan. 1991, 16–23, here 16.

[131] 'Die Deutschen an die Front', *Der Spiegel*, 6/45, 4 Feb. 1991, 18–22, here 19; see also Kaiser and Becher, *Deutschland und der Irak-Konflikt*, p. 31; 'Neue Geldforderungen nicht ausgeschlossen', *SZ*, 9–10 Feb. 1991, 2.

foreign policy consisted in protecting one's own interest, he pointed out in the same breath that German interests were closely intertwined with those of its neighbours.[132] Therefore, they were not
self-interested interests, in Wendt's usage of the concept, as this definition of interest involved an element of regard for the other (ISC 52;
STIP 240). The idea that the welfare of others is important for the self is
reflected in the significance of the concept of multilateralism in German
politics. Multilateralism was often presented as a value which did not
require explanation or validation. On the eve of the end of the ultimatum against Iraq in January 1991 Chancellor Kohl, for instance, asserted
as a point in itself that the FRG had stayed in close cooperation with
the EC and NATO, especially with the United States.[133] He also argued
that the Germans had to be prepared to get more involved in order to
make a common foreign and security policy possible. This argument
was based on the idea that the conflict-prone developments after the
end of the Cold War made necessary a strong unified Europe, which
would provide stability.[134] According to Kohl, crises such as the one in
Yugoslavia could be dealt with only if there was a breakthrough in terms
of a common foreign and security policy.[135]

In the so-called Stoltenberg paper, the defence minister's memoran-
dum reflecting upon the future of the Bundeswehr in January 1992,
the first of the 'security interests' of the FRG mentioned is a 'collective security and defence policy in the Atlantic alliance'.[136] Foreign
Minister Kinkel argued that the 'system of collective security of the
United Nations and of regional agreements like the CSCE must be
made into a powerful instrument of the new world domestic politics.
This, however, demands sacrifices. One cannot have collective security
free of charge.'[137] In this view, Germany's insistence on being different
might lead to a renationalisation of politics in Europe and that could
be dangerous for Germany itself.[138] Werner Hoyer of the FDP agreed

---

[132] Klaus Kinkel, 'Kernfragen deutscher Außenpolitik', in Presse- und Informationsamt
der Bundesregierung, *Bulletin*, 82, 16 Oct. 1995, 800.
[133] Deutscher Bundestag, *Plenarprotokoll*, 12/2, 14 Jan. 1991, 22.
[134] Deutscher Bundestag, *Plenarprotokoll*, 12/5, 30 Jan. 1991, 84–5.
[135] Helmut Kohl, statement of the Federal Government in the Bundestag on 6 Nov. 1991,
in Presse- und Informationsamt der Bundesregierung, *Bulletin*, 124, 7 Nov. 1991, 986.
[136] BMV, 'Militärpolitische und militärstrategische Grundlagen', 21.
[137] Klaus Kinkel, address of the foreign minister at the 47th General Assembly of the
United Nations on 23 Sep. 1992, in Presse- und Informationsamt der Bundesregierung,
Bulletin, 101, 25 Sep. 1992, 950. See also Klaus Kinkel, 'Verantwortung, Realismus,
Zukunftssicherung', *FAZ*, 19 Mar. 1993, 8.
[138] Naumann, *Bundeswehr*, p. 217.

that a renationalisation of German foreign policy would be the worst outcome.[139] Karsten Voigt of the SPD claimed that the multilateral integration of German foreign and security policy was 'the logic not only of our history but also of our geography'.[140] His party colleague Peter Glotz argued that it had to be the top priority for Germans to integrate into a supranational Europe in which there would be no states any more which could fight each other.[141] Moreover, according to Kinkel, German unification was a direct result of a cooperative politics. This constituted an obligation for Germany to promote such a politics.[142] NATO membership had paved the way for the FRG to be accepted again in international politics. According to Rühe, '[o]nly the unswerving reliability and solidarity ha[d] made possible Germany's return to the community of peoples after the catastrophe of the Second World War.'[143] All these points underlined the significance of the FRG's integration into a 'community' of states. Being recognised as part of a collective identity, especially in NATO, was considered crucial. Rühe argued that it was important that German soldiers were not isolated in NATO.[144] Hans-Ulrich Klose of the SPD, who, as opposed to his party, supported international military operations from early on, was concerned that Germany had to remain 'partnerfähig', that is, capable of being a partner. This involved more than just being able to be in an alliance. Rather it included 'the willingness to work together also in the difficult cases in which there is no full agreement between all partners but in which acting is nevertheless necessary'.[145]

The ability to be a partner became salient in the controversy surrounding the participation in AWACS flights over Bosnia. As the crews in the planes were multinational, there was a strong sense that leaving those integrated units would constitute a betrayal. Arguably, AWACS could not have functioned properly for a prolonged period of time without the Germans, although the Ministry of Defence at first asserted that NATO's surveillance of air space would not be brought to a halt if the German crews were recalled.[146] NATO secretary general Manfred Wörner claimed in the German court case about AWACS that

---

[139] Deutscher Bundestag, *Plenarprotokoll*, 12/240, 22 Jul. 1994, 21194.
[140] Deutscher Bundestag, *Plenarprotokoll*, 12/219, 14 Apr. 1994, 18922.
[141] Peter Glotz, 'Neue deutsche Ideologie', *Der Spiegel*, 40/45, 30 Sep. 1991, 62.
[142] Kinkel, address to the 47th UN General Assembly, 953.
[143] Volker Rühe (defence minister) in Deutscher Bundestag, *Plenarprotokoll*, 12/151, 21 Apr. 1993, 12947–8.
[144] 'Koalition und SPD begrüßen das Karlsruher Urteil', *SZ*, 13 Jul. 1994, 2.
[145] Hans-Ulrich Klose, 'Die Deutschen und der Krieg am Golf', *FAZ*, 25 Jan. 1991, 6.
[146] 'Beharrliche Lockrufe von der Brücke', *SZ*, 14 Jan. 1993, 9.

the operation would suffer if the Germans pulled out.[147] Kohl was convinced that Germany's ability to be part of an alliance was at risk. Therefore, despite potential constitutional problems, German troops were to stay aboard the AWACS aircraft even if the mandate was changed to enforcing rather than monitoring the flight ban.[148] Defence Minister Rühe even argued that pulling the Germans out would be the first step towards leaving NATO.[149] Christian Schmidt of the CSU portrayed withdrawing the soldiers as pushing the FRG towards isolation.[150] The situation was difficult. The lawyer Kinkel argued that 'the Germans had to get out of the NATO planes because of the constitutional situation', whilst Foreign Minister Kinkel feared 'terrible damage in terms of foreign policy'.[151] Karl Lamers agreed that getting out of the AWACS operation would have damaged the reputation of the FRG as an alliance partner.[152] Rühe added that when 'the UN makes decisions and asks NATO for help, Germany cannot paralyse the AWACS planes'.[153]

In the Bundestag debate about the participation in the AWACS operation and the UN mission in Somalia, Kinkel defined the key question as follows: 'Do we, as a unified and sovereign Germany after the end of the bipolar world of the East–West conflict, arrive at a new consensus on foreign and security policy, which makes us a partner of the world community who, in a changed situation in the world, is able to act and is aware of its responsibility?'[154] The question, he said, was whether the Germans were ready to take up the 'tasks for peace' which the world community expected them to fulfil.[155] If the constitutional situation was not resolved, the Germans would find themselves on the political margins in NATO, the EC and the UN. Their partners had provided security for over forty years. If they left those partners on their own with the new tasks, the Germans would no longer be capable of being part of an alliance.[156] Kinkel justified the unconventional procedure of referring the decision to the constitutional court with its significance: 'What was

---

[147] 'Bis an die Schmerzgrenze', *Der Spiegel*, 15/47, 12 Apr. 1993, 22–5, here 23.
[148] 'Drohung aus Washington', *Der Spiegel*, 3/47, 18 Jan. 1993, 18–20, here 19.
[149] 'AWACS-Besatzung im Golfkrieg', *SZ*, 21 Jan. 1993, 1.
[150] 'Neue Koalitionskrise wegen AWACS', *SZ*, 22 Mar. 1993, 6.
[151] Quoted in '50 Prozent für die Witwe', *Der Spiegel*, 2/47, 11 Jan. 1993, 32–4, here 34.
[152] Karl Lamers (CDU/CSU) in Deutscher Bundestag, *Plenarprotokoll*, 12/150, 26 Mar. 1993, 12867.
[153] 'Raus aus dem Dilemma', interview with Volker Rühe, *Der Spiegel*, 52/46, 21 Dec. 1992, 21–3, here 21.
[154] Deutscher Bundestag, *Plenarprotokoll*, 12/151, 21 Apr. 1993, 12925.
[155] Ibid.   [156] Ibid., 12928.

at stake . . . was our calculability as an alliance partner.'[157] Participation in international military operations beyond traditional peace-keeping, which was all the SPD was prepared to accept, was necessary because an 'isolation of Germany in the community of states' had to be prevented.[158] Kinkel claimed that what was at issue was being ready for the future.[159]

Wolfgang Schäuble, the chairman of the CDU/CSU parliamentary group, made the same type of argument. He stressed that the alliance had kept peace and freedom 'for almost the whole lifetime of [his] generation'. This had been possible only with a contribution from the FRG, but the Germans had never been able to preserve peace and freedom on their own, and would not be able to do so in the future. This is why the FRG had to remain part of European and Atlantic integration and had to contribute to the preservation of peace through the framework of the UN.[160] He urged that the FRG needed to remain able to be a NATO partner.[161] There was, he argued, no better way to secure peace and freedom in the future. Therefore, the Germans had to continue never to act alone. According to Schäuble, the proposal for clarification of the Basic Law presented by the governing coalition was meant to ensure that the FRG could never again act militarily on its own.[162] The aims of the specific operation, such as enforcing the flight ban over Bosnia or protecting civilians from air raids, did not figure in this reasoning at all. Rather, the Germans and their relationship to their partners was at issue. The CSU chairman, Theo Waigel, argued that those who wanted to prevent German participation in the military implementation of the flight ban against Serbian aircraft did not do justice to German interests. He said that this was 'not just about reliability, but about Germany's ability to be part of an alliance and therefore our ability to survive'.[163]

The idea that the FRG had to ensure that it remained able to be a partner draws attention to the dual character seen to be attached to being part of a collective. On the one hand, the arrangement was to benefit the FRG mainly in terms of security. On the other hand, there seemed to be a degree of consideration for the other. For instance, when Belgian paratroopers brought German citizens to safety from the Rwandan civil

[157] Ibid.   [158] Ibid., 12929.
[159] Klaus Kinkel, 'Die transatlantische Partnerschaft als Fundament der Außenpolitik', in Presse- und Informationsamt der Bundesregierung, *Bulletin*, 36, 8 May 1993, 312.
[160] Deutscher Bundestag, *Plenarprotokoll*, 12/151, 21 Apr. 1993, 12935.
[161] 'Die Deutschen an die Front', *Der Spiegel*, 6/45, 4 Feb. 1991, 18–22, here 20.
[162] Deutscher Bundestag, *Plenarprotokoll*, 12/151, 21 Apr. 1993, 12935.
[163] Quoted in 'Waigel wirft der FDP Scheinheiligkeit vor', *SZ*, 29 Mar. 1993, 2.

war, Günther Friedrich Nolting of the FDP criticised Germany for rely-ing with great casualness on its alliance partners without it being clear what would happen if they in turn relied on Germany.[164] Acting in mul-tilateral frameworks was considered a safeguard against catastrophes. As Rühe put it: 'If we act together with others we can never be wrong.'[165] In his speech in the Bundestag debate about the governing parties' pro-posal for changing the constitution, Rühe contextualised this idea with the notions of responsibility and solidarity. He claimed that Germany was now confronted with the task of taking on 'the same responsibility as its neighbours in a new and changed international system'.[166] Solidarity had to be a two-way street. Germany had profited most from changes in Europe and the world. He claimed that '[i]nternational teamwork and the ability to be part of an alliance are an indispensable part of the rea-sons of state of Germany.'[167] This required responsibility. He claimed that if the Germans 'had always behaved in the past in such a way as to only do what [their] neighbours also consider[ed] right [they] would have spared [them]selves quite a bit, if not everything'.[168] If the FRG was not going to use its military, it was in danger of becoming an inter-national outsider. Crucially, 'Germany w[ould] never act on its own, but always together with allies and partners. Each individual case w[ould] be considered against the background of [its] values, [its] interests and in the awareness of [its] responsibility to history.'[169] This reasoning not only makes the claim that military involvement abroad is a reflection of responsibility and solidarity; it also asserts that acting together with oth-ers ensures that one does not do the wrong thing and therefore does not endanger either the self or the other. This 'never alone' principle was also pointed out and supported by Schäuble and Lamers of the CDU/CSU and Hoyer of the FDP.[170] After the ruling of the constitutional court lifted the perceived restrictions on military involvement abroad, Kinkel reaf-firmed that Germany would never act alone.[171] Whatever the *behaviour* may have been, German politicians of all persuasions portrayed the

---

[164] 'Kinkel: Deutschland wird auch in Zukunft öfter nein als ja sagen', *FAZ*, 18 Apr. 1994, 2.
[165] 'Das ist keine Drohgebärde', interview with Defence Minister Volker Rühe, *Der Spiegel*, 30/46, 20 Jul. 1992, 32–5, here 34.
[166] Volker Rühe (defence minister) in Deutscher Bundestag, *Plenarprotokoll*, 12/132, 15 Jan. 1993, 11483.
[167] Ibid., 11484.   [168] Ibid.   [169] Ibid., 11485.
[170] Wolfgang Schäuble (CDU/CSU) in Deutscher Bundestag, *Plenarprotokoll*, 12/132, 15 Jan. 1993, 11464; 'Ghali für volle Teilnahme Bonns an UNO-Einsätzen', *SZ*, 12 Jan. 1993, 1; Werner Hoyer (FDP) in Deutscher Bundestag, *Plenarprotokoll*, 12/132, 15 Jan. 1993, 11469.
[171] 'Koalition und SPD begrüßen das Karlsruher Urteil', *SZ*, 13 Jul. 1994, 2; Claus Gennrich, 'Kinkel: Jetzt sind wir frei – wenn der Sicherheitsrat zustimmt', *FAZ*, 14 Jul. 1993, 3; 'Ein

FRG as a team player, as taking seriously the welfare and concerns of others. Rühe stated that the FRG 'conceives of itself as part of a bigger community and an alliance partner'.[172] The protection of the self could very well be understood as coterminous with protection of the other.

Whether the claim that the FRG conceived of itself as part of a bigger whole was 'true' or not, or whether this 'caused' the FRG to behave in certain ways rather than others, it clearly created the opportunity to contextualise military involvement abroad in a particular way. The governing parties argued that there was pressure from abroad on the government to get militarily involved.[173] Arguably, the allies were tired of having to operate without active German support.[174] The 'pressure from abroad' argument had two important implications. Firstly, it allowed the government to claim that the idea of military involvement, which was, after all, unpopular within Germany, had not been theirs but that of the FRG's 'friends and partners' or even the 'community of peoples'. Secondly, because 'friends and partners' were demanding involvement, something more than the lives of Somalis or Bosnians was at stake. The issue was rather portrayed as one of the FRG's status as an ally or even its ability to be an ally at all. As Josef Joffe put it in relation to one specific conflict, this was 'not about the Balkans but about the alliance'.[175] And Robert Leicht commented about the deployment of a destroyer to the Adriatic: 'Our ship is not going along in order to move apart the parties in the Yugoslavian civil war, but at best so the NATO partners will stay together.'[176]

When the Somalia operation came on the agenda in late 1992, Kinkel and Rühe claimed that the international pressure to deploy combat troops to UN operations was increasing.[177] Kinkel spoke of 'terrible pressure' from abroad.[178] That Rühe felt under pressure seems apparent in a speech he gave in London in March 1993. He assured the audience that he was aware of the need for constitutional change and explained

Spagat zwischen Geld und Moral', interview with Foreign Minister Klaus Kinkel, *SZ*, 16–17 Jul. 1994, 12.
[172] Volker Rühe, 'Es geht nicht um Eroberungskriege, es geht um Hilfe', *FAZ*, 10 Sep. 1993, 12.
[173] For example, Christian Schmidt (CDU/CSU) in Deutscher Bundestag, *Plenarprotokoll*, 12/150, 26 Mar. 1993, 12880.
[174] Dieter Schröder, 'Am Ende eines Sonderweges', *SZ*, 13 Apr. 1993, 4.
[175] Josef Joffe, 'Abschied von der "Kohl-Doktrin"', *SZ*, 16 Dec. 1994, 4.
[176] Robert Leicht, 'Mit Volldampf in den Verfassungsstreit', *Die Zeit*, 24 Jul. 1992, 3.
[177] 'Feldjäger in die Wüste', *Der Spiegel*, 51/46, 14 Dec. 1992, 24–5, here 24.
[178] Quoted in 'Eine regelrechte Psychose', *Der Spiegel*, 52/46, 21 Dec. 1992, 18–20, here 19. See also Helmut Kerscher, 'Karlsruher Fernaufklärung', *SZ*, 8–9 Apr. 1993, 3.

that the Federal Government had therefore introduced a bill in parliament but that it was unlikely to get the required two-thirds majority. However, he would continue to work hard for a consensus.[179] Both Rühe and Kohl appealed to international audiences to understand that change takes time. At the 1994 Conference on Security Policy in Munich, Kohl asked for understanding as the Germans were unable to overturn their attitudes 'overnight'.[180] Rühe also asserted that any change would take time as the 'grown instincts of the people in Germany [could] not be commanded away just like that'.[181]

Yet it seems implausible to claim that the Federal Government was an innocent victim of foreign bullying. With respect to the fast adjustment of operational rules for German troops involved in international missions after the court ruling, NATO allies explicitly rejected the government's assertion that they had pressured the FRG.[182] Especially during the Gulf War, members of the government had repeatedly hinted that the FRG would rapidly change its constitution to make participation in military operations possible. Foreign Minister Genscher had even declared in front of the UN Assembly that German forces would participate in UN operations before there was a majority supporting this move in the Bundestag.[183] In the summer of 1992 Foreign Minister Kinkel kept calling for threatening gestures from the West in relation to Sarajevo. Kinkel went on to claim, with respect to a potential WEU mission to monitor the embargo against the former Yugoslavia in the Adriatic Sea, that the external pressure for German participation was increasing.[184] He was being asked all the time, he said, when the Germans would finally join in. Moreover, he explicitly stated that the operation had not been the German government's idea.[185] His calls for threatening gestures, however, may have been interpreted as a willingness to follow them up. As US secretary of defense Richard Cheney pointed out, to go down that route would make sense only if one was also ready to go to war.[186] The

---

[179] Volker Rühe, 'Gestaltung euro-atlantischer Politik – eine "Grand Strategy" für eine neue Zeit', in Presse- und Informationsamt der Bundesregierung, *Bulletin*, 27, 1 Apr. 1993, 230.
[180] Helmut Kohl, 'Europäische Sicherheit und die Rolle Deutschlands', in Presse- und Informationsamt der Bundesregierung, *Bulletin*, 15, 16 Feb. 1994, 134.
[181] Quoted in 'Gewachsene Instinkte', *Der Spiegel*, 21/46, 18 May 1992, 27–30, here 27; 'Langfristig auch Kampfeinsätze', *SZ*, 15 May 1992, 1.
[182] 'NATO-Partner bestreiten Drängen auf Sondersitzung', *SZ*, 19 Jul. 1994, 2.
[183] 'Grundlage entzogen', *Der Spiegel*, 41/45, 7 Oct. 1991, 45.
[184] 'Toter Vogel', *Der Spiegel*, 29/46, 13 Jul. 1992, 22–3, here 23.
[185] 'Nahe dran am echten Krieg', *Der Spiegel*, 30/46, 20 Jul. 1992, 22–9, here 23.
[186] 'Toter Vogel', *Der Spiegel*, 29/46, 13 Jul. 1992, 22–3, here 23.

government's rhetoric certainly suggested that it was about to create the preconditions for military operations, and the 'pressure' from outside Germany has to be viewed in this context.

This issue is illustrated by the events surrounding NATO's request for Tornados to be deployed to Bosnia. On 30 November 1994 SACEUR General George Joulwan approached the German government with a request to deploy Electronic Combat Reconnaissance-Tornados to protect a potential withdrawal of peace-keeping troops from Bosnia. Joulwan wrote that he would be 'extremely grateful if Germany could offer forces to the operation "Deny Flight"'; he added that 'six to eight ECR-Tornados especially, would be most useful'.[187] ECR-Tornados recognise the radar of air defence missiles and destroy the position using missiles which find their target by following the radar rays to their source. Only the United States and the FRG had such planes at the time. When the Federal Government received the request, it had not yet made basic policy decisions on appropriate future deployments. Therefore, in a creative move it classified Joulwan's request as an 'informal enquiry' on the grounds that it had not been discussed by the NATO Council. As the SACEUR may not issue orders but only ask whether Bundesluftwaffe aircraft may be deployed for a combat mission outside NATO territory, the government reasoned that Joulwan's telex could not have been a request. Consequently, the government merely let it be known that the issue would be examined.[188]

On 6 December the government had still got no further than agreeing on a first meeting about the matter for the following day. It insisted that it was not pressured to come to a quick decision as no deadline for a response was specified.[189] The meeting on 7 December led to a three-point declaration. Firstly, it stated that SACEUR had sent a 'preliminary enquiry' to the Defence Ministry asking whether the FRG could provide Tornados for the enforcement of the flight ban over Bosnia-Herzegovina. Secondly, it made clear that there had not been a formal or official request. This had in the meantime been confirmed in a letter by NATO secretary general Willy Claes to the Federal Government.

---

[187] Quoted in 'Ganz verbindlich', *Der Spiegel*, 50/48, 12 Dec. 1994, 22–6, here 22.
[188] Meiers, 'Germany', 85–6; 'Bonn reagiert zurückhaltend auf die Anfrage der NATO', *FAZ*, 3 Dec. 1994, 1–2; 'Bonn will einen Einsatz deutscher Kampfflugzeuge in Ex-Jugoslawien ohne Gesichtsverlust vermeiden', *SZ*, 3–4 Dec. 1994, 1; Martin Winter, 'Was Tornados mit Sardinen zu tun haben', *FR*, 7 Dec. 1994, 3; 'Wie in Somalia', *Der Spiegel*, 49/48, 5 Dec. 1994, 18–21, here 18; 'Ganz verbindlich', *Der Spiegel*, 50/48, 12 Dec. 1994, 22–6, here 22.
[189] 'Gegen deutsche Blauhelme im Kaukasus', *SZ*, 7 Dec. 1994, 7.

Thirdly, the government therefore saw no reason to reach a decision.[190] Udo Bergdoll commented in the *Süddeutsche Zeitung* that the government must have been in a deep mess to have invented such an elegant excuse: 'No request, no reply. Therefore nothing has happened.'[191] According to *Der Spiegel*, Kinkel had asked for Claes' letter.[192] Claes had been kind enough to support this face-saving operation and claimed the military staff had not recognised how sensitive the issue would be for Germany.[193]

On 12 December the Federal Government received an official request, this time based on a NATO Council decision, inquiring what member states would be willing to contribute if the UN Security Council asked NATO to protect a potential withdrawal of UNPROFOR troops.[194] On 20 December the Federal Government decided that it would send paramedics and sea and air forces. This would also involve deploying ECR-Tornados.[195] So, eventually, the government decided to make Tornado fighters available for a potential withdrawal. For technical reasons, there was, according to Kohl, 'no substitute' for German Tornados. He referred to obligations in the NATO alliance, to which Germany owed its peace and liberty, and said: 'We cannot claim rights in the community of peoples and shirk when it comes to the duties.'[196] However, Kohl did not specify how support for a withdrawal of UN peace-keepers would constitute a NATO obligation or indeed what rights and duties 'in the community of peoples' he was talking about. Just before officially receiving the new request, he had started saying that a deployment might be necessary for example to protect 'the soldiers of . . . friends' in the event of a withdrawal,[197] that the Germans could not 'let down [their] friends'.[198] Klose of the SPD agreed that in such a situation the Germans

[190] 'Deutsche "Tornados" nicht nach Bosnien', *SZ*, 8 Dec. 1994, 1; Martin Winter, 'Bonn läßt Frage nach Tornados unbeantwortet', *FR*, 8 Dec. 1994, 1.
[191] Udo Bergdoll, 'Aus Bonn ein vernebeltes Nein', *SZ*, 8 Dec. 1994, 4.
[192] 'Ganz verbindlich', *Der Spiegel*, 50/48, 12 Dec. 1994, 22–6, here 22.
[193] Udo Bergdoll, 'Aus Bonn ein vernebeltes Nein', *SZ*, 8 Dec. 1994, 4; anon. (WTR), 'Unehrliche Debatte', *FR*, 8 Dec. 1994, 3.
[194] 'Bonn will Blauhelmen helfen', *SZ*, 13 Dec. 1994, 1; 'Die Nato fragt nach deutschen Bodentruppen für Bosnien', *FAZ*, 13 Dec. 1994, 1–2, here 1. See also Meiers, 'Germany', 87.
[195] 'Bonner Hilfezusage für Blauhelm-Abzug aus Bosnien', *SZ*, 21 Dec. 1994, 2; 'Rühe: Keine deutschen Bodentruppen', *FAZ*, 21 Dec. 1994, 2.
[196] Quoted in 'SPD streitet über Bundeswehr-Einsatz in Bosnien', *FAZ*, 19 Dec. 1994, 1–2, here 1.
[197] Quoted in 'Bonn will Blauhelmen helfen', *SZ*, 13 Dec. 1994, 1; 'Die Nato fragt nach deutschen Bodentruppen für Bosnien', *FAZ*, 13 Dec. 1994, 1–2, here 1.
[198] Quoted in 'Kein Hurra geschrien', *Der Spiegel*, 51/48, 19 Dec. 1994, 18–21, here 18.

could not refuse to help.[199] *Der Spiegel* insinuated that the allies had threatened to hold the chancellor publicly responsible if one of their transport aircraft was shot down by Serb missiles because they lacked protection by ECR-Tornados.[200] Franz-Josef Meiers suggests that the decision was, rather, based on the expectation that a withdrawal would not take place in the foreseeable future.[201] The mission for the Tornado fighters was radically limited, excluding participation both in NATO Operation Deny Flight and in punitive strikes against the warring parties on behalf of UNPROFOR, arguably to make it more likely that they would not fly.[202]

This episode could be read to support the view that external pressure forced the FRG to abandon its non-military policy. After all, before receiving the enquiry or request from NATO in November the government had apparently not even looked into criteria for approving operations. However, *Der Spiegel* claimed that Inspector General Naumann had stopped an earlier request in September by making it clear to Joulwan that it was unhelpful directly before a general election.[203] Kofi Annan, then UN deputy secretary general for peace-keeping operations, confirmed that the Federal Government had asked that the topic of Bundeswehr involvement only be raised after the 1994 elections.[204] Naumann also supposedly encouraged Joulwan's second request six weeks after the election.[205] As the military leadership had classified the first communication as a clear *request*, the Chancellor's office and the Foreign Office suspected that they had encouraged it to make a decision inevitable.[206] The *Frankfurter Rundschau* also reported speculations that German generals had ordered the NATO enquiry in order to force the government to abandon the position that German soldiers could be deployed to the Balkans only for humanitarian missions.[207] Rudolf Scharping of the SPD and Joschka Fischer of the Greens, too, claimed that the military leadership had pushed for a deployment. Naumann

---

[199] 'Drohpotential muß sein', interview with Hans-Ulrich Klose, *Der Spiegel*, 50/48, 12 Dec. 1994, 24.
[200] 'Ganz verbindlich', *Der Spiegel*, 50/48, 12 Dec. 1994, 22–6, here 26.
[201] Meiers, 'Germany', 87. See also 'Luft und Wasser', *Der Spiegel*, 52/48, 26 Dec. 1994, 22–5, here 23.
[202] 'Dabeisein ist alles', *Der Spiegel*, 26/49, 26 Jun. 1995, 22–5, here 24.
[203] 'Einsatz ins Ungewisse', *Der Spiegel*, 5/49, 30 Jan. 1995, 68–79, here 78.
[204] 'Da müssen wir hin', *Der Spiegel*, 45/48, 7 Nov. 1994, 18–19, here 18.
[205] 'Einsatz ins Ungewisse', *Der Spiegel*, 5/49, 30 Jan. 1995, 68–79, here 78; 'Kein Hurra geschrien', *Der Spiegel*, 51/48, 19 Dec. 1994, 18–21, here 19.
[206] 'Ganz verbindlich', *Der Spiegel*, 50/48, 12 Dec. 1994, 22–6, here 24.
[207] Martin Winter, 'Was Tornados mit Sardinen zu tun haben', *FR*, 7 Dec. 1994, 3.

rejected these allegations. He revealed that the NATO Council had instructed the military side with 'immediate emergency planning' for a potential withdrawal in September. Yet it remained unclear why NATO, in the face of urgency, had waited until December to ask the member states for contributions.[208] Scharping thus claimed that the political pressure from abroad which was 'politically being suspected' did not exist.[209]

Later the allies demanded that the Germans not only participate in a possible withdrawal scenario but also help protect the deployment of reinforcement forces and the movement of dispersed UN troops to 'safe areas'.[210] An evacuation of UN soldiers could have meant the involvement of German ground troops in combat. The SACEUR was planning to send the multinational NATO rapid reaction forces for this task. These units allegedly could not function without German helicopters, engineers and transport forces.[211] Yet again this appeared to be related to German promises. *Der Spiegel*, at least, claimed that '[w]eek by week the Federal Government ha[d] increasingly committed itself to military participation with its promises in the NATO Council'[212] and commented, when the Bundeswehr was finally sent to the Balkans, that the main aim of its activity in Croatia was to impress NATO allies.[213]

Whatever the precise sequence of events, they suggest that the claim that it was the others who wanted the FRG to get involved is, at least, dubious. And they show that the assumption on which this claim is based, namely that the domestic and international realms are separate, has a lot to answer for. An approach like Wendt's which ignores the interconnectedness of these spheres is not only unable to describe or analyse events such as these. It also supports the logic of thought sustained by this separation and thereby makes possible claims such as the government's assertion that the responsibility for the shift towards military involvement lay elsewhere, namely in the international realm. The approach therefore supports a particular political construction of reality.

This particular construction of reality is interesting insofar as it is arguably also at odds with Wendt's claims on behalf of collective identity. The development of collective identity is thought to lead to a more

---

[208] 'Bonn sagt der NATO Unterstützung zu', *SZ*, 17–18 Dec. 1994, 1.
[209] 'Rühe: Keine deutschen Bodentruppen', *FAZ*, 21 Dec. 1994, 2.
[210] 'Nur noch Gewalt', *Der Spiegel*, 23/49, 5 Jun. 1995, 30–1, here 30.
[211] 'Wie in Somalia', *Der Spiegel*, 49/48, 5 Dec. 1994, 18–21, here 18.
[212] 'Nur noch Gewalt', *Der Spiegel*, 23/49, 5 Jun. 1995, 30–1, here 31.
[213] 'Warten auf Kundschaft', *Der Spiegel*, 33/49, 14 Aug. 1995, 37–8, here 38.

peaceful, benign security environment and ultimately to an 'international state' or 'Kantian culture'.[214] In such a culture, internal disputes are settled non-violently and defence against external security threats is provided as a team (*STIP* 299). The reference to Immanuel Kant and his *Perpetual Peace* (*STIP* 297) suggests that this would be a more peaceful, less military world. This is also the idea behind what is discussed as 'multilateralism' in Germany. In the 1994 White Paper the government expressed the expectation that a cooperative security order would specifically guard against the use of military force.[215] An important outcome of increasing integration and multilateralism was seen to be reassurance for neighbouring countries that the FRG could not engage in aggressive, militarist policies. As the overwhelming part of the Bundeswehr was integrated into NATO structures, the FRG simply could not make any use of its armed forces its alliance partners did not approve of. During the Cold War this meant that the Bundeswehr could be used only to defend the FRG or NATO allies. After its end both the FRG's normative commitment to NATO and the related practical integration of its forces into the alliance's command structure continued to ensure that the Bundeswehr would only be used for collectively supported purposes. However, the outcome of this arrangement suddenly became the reverse of what had been expected. It seemed to require the FRG to take up arms, if against those outside the collective identity and hence, it seems, outside the 'Kantian culture'.

The need to take up arms prompted fears in relation to further military integration. Critics worried that 'through the Eurokorps the Germans could be forced into worldwide military adventures of their allies', although the actual deployment of troops would be based on each state's decision. It was unclear how the German government should be able to resist if its partners wanted to use the forces and were dependent on German contingents.[216] In parliament, Lamers accused Voigt of implying that European partners might draw the FRG into adventures: 'do you really not see that this is actually a perversion of the fundamental maxim of German and Western postwar politics as such?'[217] Yet, paradoxically, an arrangement that was to stop the use of German armed

---

[214] Wendt, 'Collective Identity Formation'; *STIP*, ch. 6.

[215] BMV, *Weißbuch 1994*, p. 32, section 234.

[216] 'Gewachsene Instinkte', *Der Spiegel*, 21/46, 18 May 1992, 27–30, here 30; see also Rudolph Chimelli, 'Euro-Korps steht allen Staaten der EG offen', *SZ*, 23–4 May 1992, 2.

[217] Karl Lamers (CDU/CSU) in Deutscher Bundestag, *Plenarprotokoll*, 12/132, 15 Jan. 1993, 11482.

force now suggested or even required it. The fear that the Eurokorps might lead to further entanglement with violent conflict was not unfounded. The French foreign minister Hervé de Charette wanted to send the Eurokorps to the Balkans.[218]

German politicians viewed the Eurokorps as an opportunity to institutionalise and advance a common identity in Europe. Kohl saw it as a symbolical step towards European union. A Kohl confidant claimed that its true significance was the 'political symbolical content'.[219] Rühe also argued that it was necessary to work towards a political union of Europe with a common defence identity, and that the Eurokorps represented a step towards this aim.[220] Similarly, Naumann claimed that the Bundeswehr had to support the establishment of a multinational armed force in order to make a 'clearly recognisable contribution to the integration of Europe'.[221] The problem with these assessments of the integrationist thrust of the Eurokorps was that, according to *Der Spiegel*, it was precisely that issue 'which the Germans and the French judge[d] completely differently'.[222] The interesting point is that, for the Germans, it was no longer a situation in which integration made possible certain arrangements with respect to the armed forces which would foster security, but rather in which the organisation of armed forces was to be a further step towards deeper integration. In other words, the means–ends relationship was seen as having been turned around. The 1994 White Paper bluntly stated that the Bundeswehr 'fosters ... the integration of Europe'.[223] 'The integration', commented *Der Spiegel*, 'is to be pushed forward militarily in the era after the Cold War, of all times.'[224] This is interesting because it reverses the logic of the arrangement. It may also be worrying because this new logic may lead to uses of armed force for reasons unrelated to the specific conflict in which it is being employed.

This is illustrated well by the first UN mission the Bundeswehr participated in with more than paramedic personnel. In relation to the Somalia operation, the *Süddeutsche Zeitung* referred to both German politicians and the UN secretary general Boutros Boutros Ghali as 'regretting' that

[218] 'Länger verheddern', *Der Spiegel*, 40/49, 2 Oct. 1995, 36–8, here 37–8.
[219] Quoted in 'Spaltpilz in der Allianz', *Der Spiegel*, 23/46, 1 Jun. 1992, 22–4, here 23.
[220] Rühe, 'Gestaltung euro-atlantischer Politik', 230–1.
[221] Naumann, *Bundeswehr*, p. 139.
[222] 'Spaltpilz in der Allianz', *Der Spiegel*, 23/46, 1 Jun. 1992, 22–4, here 23; see also 'Kinkel verteidigt das Europakorps', *SZ*, 2 Jul. 1992, 8.
[223] BMV, *Weißbuch 1994*, p. 89, section 515.
[224] 'Eine historische Entscheidung', *Der Spiegel*, 43/45, 21 Oct. 1991, 18–20, here 20.

the FRG was not part of it.[225] Boutros Ghali supported German participation in UN peace missions.[226] However, *Der Spiegel* claimed that the
international pressure, to which Kinkel, Kohl and Rühe were continually referring, did not really exist. Boutros Ghali was not concerned
with German infantry. What he had been asking for in a confidential
telex before Christmas 1992 was for the FRG to transport a field hospital to Somalia and to assist in building up a central police force.[227] The
Süddeutsche Zeitung reported that the government considered making
an offer of a field hospital to the UN without mentioning any request
from the UN.[228]

Later Kinkel supposedly encouraged Boutros Ghali to ask publicly
for as much support from Germany as he wanted.[229] So Boutros Ghali
declared that 'Germany's full participation in peace-keeping and peace-
making operations of the United Nations' was needed.[230] He claimed
that, without German involvement, the UN would be unable to fulfil
its new role.[231] This is important because, as Michael Berndt points out,
the Federal Government had been trying to present the whole process
of moving towards military operations abroad as not only started, but
also dominated, from abroad.[232] It also serves to illustrate a further diffi-
culty with the constructivist approach under consideration. In Wendt's
description of 'altercasting', *ego* sets out to make *alter* change its identity
in accordance with *ego*'s identity design for *alter*. Whilst *alter* has an input
into the process, it is more passive than *ego*'s: it can accept or reject the
new identity. It is therefore crucial to know who is *ego* and who is *alter*. In
other words: who started the interaction? Was the FRG merely responding to role suggestions by others or had the government increasingly
become trapped by its own promises with respect to Somalia, as the
opposition claimed?

In December 1992 the government had promised 1,500 troops to the
UN to hand out supplies, repair roads and bridges and build a telephone

[225] 'Fehlen von deutschen Soldaten bedauert', *SZ*, 7 Dec. 1992, 1.
[226] 'Streit um Bundeswehreinsätze dauert an', *SZ*, 7 Dec. 1992, 6.
[227] '50 Prozent für die Witwe', *Der Spiegel*, 2/47, 11 Jan. 1993, 32–4, here 32.
[228] 'Kinkel strebt breites Bündnis an', *SZ*, 10 Dec. 1992, 1; 'Bonn will sofort helfen', *SZ*, 12–13 Dec. 1992, 9.
[229] 'Drohung aus Washington', *Der Spiegel*, 3/47, 18 Jan. 1993, 18–20, here 18.
[230] Quoted in 'Ghali für volle Teilnahme Bonns an UNO-Einsätzen', *SZ*, 12 Jan. 1993, 1; 'Drohung aus Washington', *Der Spiegel*, 3/47, 18 Jan. 1993, 18–20, here 18.
[231] 'Ghali für volle Teilnahme Bonns an UNO-Einsätzen', *SZ*, 12 Jan. 1993, 1.
[232] Michael Berndt, *Deutsche Militärpolitik in der 'neuen Weltunordnung'. Zwischen nationalen Interessen und globalen Entwicklungen* (Münster: Agenda Verlag, 1997), p. 181.

system. They were to be lightly armed for self-defence.[233] In April 1993 the German government received a request from the UN secretary general, referring to Security Council Resolution 814, for logistical support in 'secure environments' in Somalia. The *Süddeutsche Zeitung* described this request as a reaction to the Federal Government's decision of December 1992.[234] In mid-April 1993, the government admitted that the UN was requesting deployments 'different' from those offered in late 1992.[235] In Wendt's approach it would be important to know who set off the interaction as the initiative rests with that actor throughout. Ascertaining this, however, seems difficult.

The problem with the envisaged operation was that the government had been unable to change the constitution as it had planned at the time the commitment had been made and therefore, unless it was a purely humanitarian and consequently 'un-military' mission, many believed the deployment to be unconstitutional. *Der Spiegel* claimed that the closer the Somalia operation got, the more it became clear that it was not about humanitarian aid. Whilst it was unclear where exactly the troops would go and what they would do, it was certain that even the first forty soldiers would be accompanied by press officers to market the operation in the media. The Bundeswehr refused the management of the port in Mogadishu and the transportation of and care for refugees, as well as classic engineering tasks, because those tasks were not considered 'attractive'.[236] Even the Foreign Office criticised the Ministry of Defence for being interested in a deployment to Somalia only if it was going to improve its image.[237]

The point of German participation in the mission, other than publicity, remained unclear. The mix of soldiers deployed suggested that aiding the Somali population was not the main concern. Of the 1,640 troops, only about 700 were directly or indirectly to help the Somalis. The rest were for the use of the Bundeswehr itself.[238] Moreover, it was

---

[233] 'Eine regelrechte Psychose', *Der Spiegel*, 52/46, 21 Dec. 1992, 18–20, here 18–19; 'Bonn entsendet bewaffnete Soldaten nach Somalia', *SZ*, 18 Dec. 1992, 1.

[234] 'SPD droht Regierung bei Einsatz der Bundeswehr in Somalia mit einer weiteren Klage in Karlsruhe', *SZ*, 15 Apr. 1993, 1; ' . . . morgen die ganze Welt', *Der Spiegel*, 16/47, 19 Apr. 1993, 18–22, here 21.

[235] Quoted in 'FDP befürchtet Kampfeinsatz', *SZ*, 19 Apr. 1993, 1.

[236] 'Massive Vorwürfe gegen Verteidigungsministerium', *SZ*, 21 Apr. 1993, 1; 'Wo fliegen wir hin?' , *Der Spiegel*, 18/47, 3 May 1993, 23–6, here 23.

[237] 'Schritt für Schritt in den Krieg', *Der Spiegel*, 17/47, 26 Apr. 1993, 18–27, here 23; see also 'Massive Vorwürfe gegen Verteidigungsministerium', *SZ*, 21 Apr. 1993, 1; Stefan Kornelius, 'Wir werden keinen Luftballon bunt anmalen', *SZ*, 22 Apr. 1993, 6.

[238] 'Wo fliegen wir hin?', *Der Spiegel*, 18/47, 3 May 1993, 23–6, here 23.

controversial whether the kind of help that armed forces provided was at this stage still needed in Somalia.[239] The drilling of wells and laying of pipelines, originally supposed to be the task of the German soldiers, was in the meantime being done by Africa specialists of the Technisches Hilfswerk (THW).[240] By the time the Bundeswehr mission got under way, *Der Spiegel* argued, its focus was not humanitarian any more.[241] The UN had changed plans so that the Indian soldiers whom the Germans were to support logistically were sent to a different area of Somalia.[242] Only 3 of the 4,700 Indian soldiers had arrived by October. Since the German troops were, as a result, useless for military matters, they had time to build wells, fix dams and roads and provide medical services to Somalis.[243] *Der Spiegel* commented: 'The German soldiers in Somalia are not needed – now they pass the time with good deeds.'[244] Foreign Minister Kinkel complained to Boutros Ghali that 1,700 Germans were deployed to support 3 Indians. They had been waiting for the Indian troops for three months. Kinkel wanted Boutros Ghali to give a useful task to the Germans, whilst Defence Minister Rühe preferred to pull the Bundeswehr out. As Rühe said: 'Waiting for the Indians is like waiting for Godot.'[245] In early 1994 the Bundeswehr withdrew from Somalia.[246] It does not seem that German participation in the operation was particularly useful.

According to Kinkel, however, the operation had improved the FRG's 'international standing' and had the effect of a 'stamp of quality' with the UN. Even though the Germans had been deployed abroad for the first time, their peace-keeping had been 'professional'.[247] When the cabinet had decided in 1993 to send soldiers to Somalia, Kinkel had already claimed that this decision was popular abroad.[248] This conveniently ignores that Germany had been 'not an easy partner' because of the

[239] Ibid., 25; 'SPD droht Regierung bei Einsatz der Bundeswehr in Somalia mit einer weiteren Klage in Karlsruhe', *SZ*, 15 Apr. 1993, 1.
[240] 'Wo fliegen wir hin?', *Der Spiegel*, 18/47, 3 May 1993, 23–6, here 26. The THW is a relief organisation which gives technical aid in emergency situations.
[241] 'Auch Verluste', *Der Spiegel*, 24/47, 14 Jun. 1993, 33.
[242] 'Im Wettlauf raus', *Der Spiegel*, 40/47, 4 Oct. 1993, 32–4, here 32; 'Somalia-Einsatz angelaufen', *SZ*, 13 May 1993, 1; 'Kohl und Kinkel weisen Scharpings Angebot zurück', *SZ*, 16 Aug. 1993, 2.
[243] 'Helden an der Patsche', *Der Spiegel*, 43/47, 25 Oct. 1993, 31–2; 'Kohl und Kinkel weisen Scharpings Angebot zurück', *SZ*, 16 Aug. 1993, 2.
[244] 'Helden an der Patsche', *Der Spiegel*, 43/47, 25 Oct. 1993, 31–2, here 31.
[245] Quoted in 'Krieg der Worte', *Der Spiegel*, 47/47, 22 Nov. 1993, 37–8, here 38.
[246] 'Ja, Menschlichkeit', *Der Spiegel*, 4/48, 24 Jan. 1994, 40–1.
[247] Quoted in 'Ja, Tapferkeit', *Der Spiegel*, 10/48, 7 Mar. 1994, 27–8, here 28.
[248] Deutscher Bundestag, *Plenarprotokoll*, 12/151, 21 Apr. 1993, 12929.

uncertain legal situation and its inexperience.[249] There had been a lot of back and forth about the involvement, particularly in relation to where the Germans were actually prepared to go.[250] Because of the unclear legal situation, the Bundeswehr reconnaissance team had to be protected first by Canadian, then Nigerian troops.[251] *Der Spiegel* also lists many obvious mistakes the Germans made. The army's pallets did not fit into the aircraft. Therefore, the air force repacked and transported material which belonged together in different planes, creating time-consuming unpacking and re-sorting tasks. Some equipment for engineering tasks was missing altogether. Besides, the troops lacked cash to pay for material and services on site. Finally, it had not been a good idea to mix troops – who were moreover mentally insufficiently prepared – from more than 200 units.[252] FDP defence policy expert Jürgen Koppelin had pointed out even before the operation was undertaken that the Bundeswehr was not equipped for the mission.[253]

Rühe later claimed that the benchmark for participation in UN operations was whether the Bundeswehr could really help.[254] This would have suggested that the FRG get involved in mine-clearing operations, for instance, as the German navy had special equipment.[255] Yet, the government was apparently interested in high-publicity operations which would illustrate the Germans' willingness to take their commitment to their partners seriously without, however, endangering German soldiers. The impression that the Somalia operation, for instance, had been decided on for domestic and alliance political reasons was hard to avoid.[256] Given the events and problems recounted, it certainly seems implausible to claim that it was undertaken because, as Rühe's criterion required, the Bundeswehr could really help.

This exploration of notions of collective identity, solidarity or multilateralism highlights limitations of and problems with Wendt's approach which excludes such consideration of collective identity as it externalises

---

[249] Stefan Kornelius, 'Deutsche Blauhelme brauchen ein Korsett', *SZ*, 10 May 1993, 4.

[250] See, for example, Stefan Kornelius, 'Wir werden keinen Luftballon bunt anmalen', *SZ*, 22 Apr. 1993, 6; 'Probleme vor Somalia-Einsatz', *SZ*, 10 May 1993, 1.

[251] 'Nigerianer schützen deutsche Soldaten', *SZ*, 26 May 1993, 8.

[252] 'Ja, Tapferkeit', *Der Spiegel*, 10/48, 7 Mar. 1994, 27–8, here 28. See also 'Rühe: Für Wehrpflichtige ändert sich nichts', *SZ*, 14 Jul. 1994, 1; 'Kinkel und Scharping deuten das Bundeswehr-Urteil', *FAZ*, 14 Jul. 1994, 1.

[253] 'Rühe: Bundeswehr fliegt Anfang Juni nach Somalia', *SZ*, 16 Apr. 1993, 2.

[254] 'Rühe: UNO-Mandat Voraussetzung für Auslandseinsatz', *SZ*, 25 Nov. 1994, 2.

[255] 'Bonn schickt fünf Minensuchboote in den Golf', *SZ*, 7 Mar. 1991, 1; 'Bonn schickt Marine ins Mittelmeer', *SZ*, 11–12 Aug. 1990, 1.

[256] Stefan Kornelius, 'Ein mehrfach ungewisses Abenteuer', *SZ*, 18 May 1993, 4.

'domestic' discussions and fails to take into account the effects of dis-course. The episodes recounted show that collective identity was re-ferred to, but it will have to be left to other approaches to tell us how this matters. Clearly, it would be difficult to claim that collective iden-tity 'caused' the FRG to behave in particular ways. Firstly, this would discount the significance of the forces which worked *against* taking up a pattern of behaviour more in tune with collective identity. Secondly, there is an implication that there must have been a competition between a self-interested identity and a collective identity (see *STIP* 337). Yet the FRG's reluctance to get involved militarily was arguably as much (or as little) based on consideration for the welfare of others as was the deci-sion to participate in military operations. Thirdly, in Wendt's usage of causality, it seems problematic to claim that collective identity causes more peaceful behaviour. Wendt's argument drives towards the notion that more collective definitions of identity lead to more peaceful dispo-sitions, if strictly speaking only internally. The case at hand, however, showed the FRG becoming potentially less peaceful as it left behind a non-military pattern of behaviour and took up arms. Mercer has argued that each collective identity will always also be defined against someone else and therefore may lead to aggressive behaviour externally.[257] This is not what I am concerned with here. It is not that collective identity may lead actors to make war *against* others but that it may lead them to make war *for* others.

The important question is then: for whom was the FRG going to war? It could, of course, be argued that the military operations undertaken were for those in need, the Somalis, Bosnians and Kosovars, and that they were therefore good. However, the lack of consideration for what the Bundeswehr was actually able to do and the failure to explicate how any of the operations were supposed to help these people suggest that there were other reasons. It seems more likely that the FRG went to war for its allies and for itself as one of them. The collective identity was with the other Western countries, not with those in need. If this collective identity can lead the FRG to go elsewhere and make war, Wendt's suggestion that 'a new international political culture has emerged in the West within which non-violence and team play are the norm' (*STIP* 297) seems at least debatable; for this international political culture appears to have discouraged a non-military German identity in favour of one which was at least capable of violence against others. Even if Wendt is referring

[257] Mercer, 'Anarchy and Identity'.

here only to non-violence within the collective identity of the West, this development sits uneasily with his claims.

The identity of identity

The value assigned to multilateralism in the German discourse on military policy was based on understandings of history. In this vein, the integration of the armed forces into NATO structures was to guard against German aggression. The fear of a *return* to a violent politics was evident in many statements, in particular the accusation that the government was remilitarising German foreign policy. How interpretations of history became significant in the discourse on German military involvement abroad will be addressed in chapter 3. Here this historical linkage interests me only insofar as it betrays a specific understanding of identity. Crucially, the notion that 'the FRG' must refrain from using its military abroad relies on equating 'the FRG', 'Germany' and 'the Germans'. In other words, it is based on the idea that the FRG is the contemporary expression of the entity which was the Third Reich from 1933 until 1945, and that 'the FRG' is the relevant actor.

The FRG represents itself and is represented by others as the successor of the Nazi state. In a conceptualisation which takes states as given it cannot be otherwise. On the other hand, the FRG is at the same time portrayed in many ways as the negation of the Nazi state. It is constitutionally committed to the equality of men and women from all backgrounds, for instance. One of the defining characteristics of the FRG as *different* from the Third Reich used to be its renunciation of the use of military force other than for (collective) self-defence. Art. 87a (2) of the Basic Law, which was thought to rule out military operations beyond defence, had been portrayed as the product of the lessons of the Second World War. Government statements and international treaties affirmed that 'only peace w[ould] emanate from German soil'.[258] Hence the equation of 'Germany' and 'the FRG' is more problematic than it would at first seem. At the same time, the rejection of armed force makes sense only in the context of the history of the Third Reich and thus relies on this very equation. In the debates on military involvement abroad it was never disputed that the Germans and the FRG had to define their identity in relation to the Third Reich, although the concrete expression of

---

[258] See, for example, Genscher, address at the 45th UN General Assembly, 1201; Kohl, message on the day of German unification, 1227; 'Vertrag über die abschließende Regelung', Art. 2.

this relationship was very much at issue. As will be shown in chapter 3, this dual relationship of attachment and rejection or identity and difference became particularly obvious in the argument over whether the FRG had to abstain from war altogether.

Although the Third Reich can be represented as a powerful source of German identity, the relationship between the Nazi state and the FRG or the Germans is hardly linear or logical. Arguably, the Nazi past instead represents the other within the self. The confidence with which the Nazi past was claimed as the origin providing the relevant context in which to deliver judgement on the issue of military involvement abroad worked to hide the tension in telling German identity, the 'difference *with itself*' without which cultural identity is not possible (*OH* 9–10 [16]);[259] for the issue of using the military abroad launched the Germans into the heart of a contradiction in the way they understood who they were. On the one hand, the issue was seen as explosive because of the Nazi past. On the other hand, it was the integration with the West, seen as the overcoming of the Nazi past, that seemed to make military involvement inevitable now. Either option – taking part in international military operations in the context of international institutions or (partially) withdrawing from multilateralist settings in order not to have to use the military – involved establishing a relationship of both identity and difference with the Nazi past.

Moreover, German military involvement abroad was construed as *both* problematic *and* necessary because of the history of the Third Reich. The *problematic* aspect becomes obvious in the claim that the Bundeswehr should not go where the Wehrmacht had caused havoc during the Second World War.[260] It is also implicit in the fear that any Bundeswehr deployment abroad would lead to a remilitarisation of German foreign policy.[261] On the other hand, the idea that participation in international operations was *necessary* to live up to the historical responsibility[262] was also at least partially based on Germany's

---

[259] In references to Derrida's work, numbers in brackets refer to the location in the French originals listed in the bibliography.

[260] This has been termed the 'Kohl' doctrine (Josef Joffe, 'Abschied von der "Kohl-Doktrin"', *SZ*, 16 Dec. 1994, 4), but was also subscribed to by others. See, for example, Klaus Kinkel, 'Peacekeeping Missions: Germany Can Now Play Its Part', *NATO Review* 42/5 (1994), 7 and Joschka Fischer (Bündnis90/Die Grünen) in Deutscher Bundestag, *Plenarprotokoll*, 13/48, 30 Jun. 1995, 3975.

[261] For example, Peter Glotz (SPD) in Deutscher Bundestag, *Plenarprotokoll*, 12/151, 21 Apr. 1993, 12970.

[262] Klaus Kinkel (foreign minister) in Deutscher Bundestag, *Plenarprotokoll*, 12/240, 22 Jul. 1994, 21166.

responsibility for the Second World War and the Holocaust. The difference from the Nazi past was as fundamental to this argument as the identity with the Nazi state. This representation of identity thus always already involved a 'difference *with itself*' (*OH* 9–10 [16]). If the relationship between the Nazi state and the FRG had been one of identity *only*, the idea of sending its troops abroad would certainly not have found the support of European neighbours.

The difference of the FRG with Germany's past – despite the representation of the FRG as 'Germany' and therefore as sharing an identity with the Third Reich – was established not only through its non-military character but crucially also through integration with the West. The acceptance of Western values through integration into Western institutions is represented as the key difference between the dark Germanies of the past and the enlightened, responsible Germany of today.[263] Integration was seen as the precondition for political rehabilitation.[264] In his speech justifying the deployment of German troops to support NATO's rapid reaction forces in the former Yugoslavia, Foreign Minister Kinkel put this decision into the context of a series of historical decisions which, with the exception of *Ostpolitik*, were all represented as instances in which the seriousness of the FRG's commitment to Western integration was seen to be at issue: rearmament, joining NATO, the renunciation of nuclear weapons and the implementation of NATO's twin-track decision.[265] Part of the problem was then that the contradiction between the commitment to military abstention and the commitment to Western integration – which together established the desirable difference from that other, darker Germany – were in tension; for the partners in NATO demanded a military contribution, and military integration worked to involve the Bundeswehr in international operations more or less automatically. This was the case, for instance, with the deployment of NATO's rapid reaction force to the former Yugoslavia.[266] It is important to note that, even though this tension was resolved in favour of discarding military abstention, the narrative on identity, though presented as referring to a

[263] See, for example, Jürgen Habermas, 'A Kind of Settlement of Damages: The Apologetic Tendencies in German History Writing', in *Forever Under the Shadow of Hitler? Original Documents of the Historikerstreit, the Controversy Concerning the Singularity of the Holocaust*, translated by James Knowlton and Truett Cates (Atlantic Highlands, NJ: Humanities Press, 1993), (reprinted from *Die Zeit*, 11 Jul. 1986), pp. 43–4.

[264] Kielinger, 'Gulf War', 244–5.

[265] Klaus Kinkel (foreign minister) in Deutscher Bundestag, *Plenarprotokoll*, 13/48, 30 Jun. 1995, 3955.

[266] 'Wie in Somalia', *Der Spiegel*, 49/48, 5 Dec. 1994, 18–21, here 18. Note also the controversy surrounding the AWACS mission in 1993.

coherent entity, still relies on both the special responsibility derived from the FRG's identity with the Nazi state and its ability to deliver a better future to the people in the former Yugoslavia through military intervention, which is based on the FRG's difference from the Nazi state.

The necessary multiplicity of origins referred to in telling identity puts into question the naturalness of the succession of German states – Third Reich, old FRG, new FRG – which is used as the basis for claiming a special responsibility. This seemingly natural narrative of identity also denies the history of the German Democratic Republic (GDR). Kinkel argued that the Allies had liberated the Germans and made a democratic beginning possible. Moreover, 'Germany' had been protected by the Western allies during the Cold War and therefore they could now legitimately expect solidarity from the Germans.[267] This erases the existence of the other Germany which was anything but protected by those Western allies and claims the solidarity of those Germans who did not enjoy this protection but now, as citizens of the FRG, have become part of the collective telling of identity. The slippage between 'Germany', 'the FRG' and 'the Germans', sometimes even when reference is clearly made only to the old FRG, works to obscure the making of identity through discourse. The equation of the FRG with Germany and earlier German states seems to be in accordance with common sense. Recognising that any representation of the FRG involves incorporating a number of different sources of identity, even if one is ostensibly prioritised over the other, exposes the non-natural character of the identity which provided the basis for the justification of German military involvement abroad. Things were much less clear than some wanted to claim. The Nazi past meant both that the FRG should use the military and that it could not use it. Moreover, the FRG had to intervene to prove its membership of the Western community but its interventions were good only because it was already considered part of the West.

The contingency and even inherently contradictory character of these expressions of identity is not only invisible through Wendt's framework, but also in tension with his conceptualisation of identity. The illustration suggests that it is impossible to circumscribe 'the identity' the FRG 'has' or to list the characteristics which 'having' a certain identity entails. Identities depend on concrete articulations. Whether the FRG is thought to be different from or identical with the Third Reich in any

[267] Klaus Kinkel (foreign minister) in Deutscher Bundestag, *Plenarprotokoll*, 13/48, 30 Jun. 1995, 3956–7.

given situation is not clear *a priori*. In Wendt's framework, however, that identity of both is assumed. When, in his theoretical argument for the constructedness of anarchy, Wendt asks us to assume two actors, *ego* and *alter*, this starting point is presented as innocent and relatively free of prior assumptions (see A 404–5; *STIP* 328),[268] and indeed as necessary. Actors, according to Wendt, have to be identified '[b]efore we can be constructivist about anything' (*STIP* 7). For a systemic theory of international politics, more specifically, states must be treated as given (*STIP* 244). This 'essentialist' (*STIP* 198) claim seems problematic for a 'constructivist' theory.[269] Taking state actors as given presupposes the identity between 'the FRG' and 'Germany'. It is therefore impossible for this approach to appreciate the ambiguity involved in construing the identity of 'the FRG' with 'Germany' and therefore 'the Third Reich'. This identity is taken as given, presumably on the basis of the (limited) spatial continuity.

Wendt informs us that '[w]hat makes . . . Germany "Germany" is primarily the discourse and agency of those who call themselves Germans, not the agency and discourse of outsiders' (*STIP* 74). The identity of the state as Germany is therefore not created in social interaction. It is, as corporate identity (*STIP* 328), prior to international politics. Wendt's starting point obscures that this representation is neither necessary nor innocent. The identity between different German polities, as far as it exists, is an accomplishment of discourse. The argument that solidarity with the West is necessary as a repayment of protection during the Cold War makes sense only if 'Germany' can be construed as being identical with 'the FRG', excluding the GDR. The shift towards using the military abroad relied on this problematic equation. The exclusion of the consideration of the relevant self, which is reflected in the discourse on German military involvement abroad and in Wendt's approach to the analysis of international politics, is a political move in that it establishes a non-natural relationship as given and unchangeable.

---

[268] David Campbell also takes issue with this. See Campbell, 'Political Prosaics, Transversal Politics, and the Anarchical World', in Michael J. Shapiro and Hayward R. Alker (eds.), *Challenging Boundaries* (Minneapolis: University of Minnesota Press, 1996), pp. 12–13; Campbell, 'Epilogue', pp. 219–22. This point also has been raised as problematic from a different perspective: Inayatullah and Blaney, 'Knowing Encounters', p. 73; Pasic, 'Culturing IR Theory', pp. 87–90. For a more abstract critique of the problem with the identity of state identity, see Jens Bartelson, 'Second Natures: Is the State Identical with Itself?', *European Journal of International Relations* 4 (1998), 305–12.

[269] See also Roxanne Lynn Doty, 'Desire All the Way Down', *Review of International Studies* 26 (2000), 137–9, and Kratochwil, 'Constructing a New Orthodoxy?', 75 and 91.

Wendt defends at length his belief that state agents have essential properties (*STIP* 198–214). These are meant to set them apart from 'dogs, trees, football teams, universities, and so on' (*STIP* 213–14). Wendt does not consider the constitution of states as subjects in the first place.[270] It is important to recall here that Wendt asks us to assume two actors, *ego* and *alter*, who come to interact only after we have imagined them on their own. This starting point, he tells us, is an 'interactionist convention' (*STIP* 328). Analogously, we have to imagine states as prior to and independent from social context. Wendt seems to have no problem with this move, which has already been criticised by Pasic in relation to his earlier work.[271] Wendt even knows what the actors are like before they come to be part of a context: he defends an anthropomorphic conception of the state (A 397, n. 21; *STIP* 10 and 215). What I want to draw attention to here is that the assumption of unity connected to this anthropomorphic conception of the state leads to a specific understanding of identity which seems problematic in relation to the issues raised by the debates on German military involvement abroad.[272] It cannot deal with the complexity and contingency of identity and ultimately restricts identity to a question of boundaries.

Excluding the process of the construction of the state as a bearer of identity and of domestic processes of articulating state identity are part of the problem. This reduces identity to something negotiable between states. It is not surprising, given this starting point, that Wendt is mainly concerned with the *boundaries* of, rather than the content of theories about, the self.[273] Wendt addresses identity as the question of who is considered part of the self. If other states are considered part of the self, that is, if the boundary of the self gets pushed outward beyond the boundary of the state, Wendt argues that there exists a collective rather than egoistic definition of identity (ISC 52–3; *STIP* 229). He informs us that the 'constructivist model is saying that the boundaries of the Self are at stake in and therefore may change in interaction, so that in cooperating states can form a collective identity' (*STIP* 317). The question of who is considered part of the self is certainly an important one. Yet the particular way in which it is posed does not allow for a consideration

---

[270] See also Campbell, 'Epilogue', pp. 220–1.
[271] Pasic, 'Culturing IR Theory', pp. 86–90.
[272] On the assumption of unity and the consequence of identity, see also Pasic, 'Culturing IR Theory', p. 100.
[273] *STIP* 229, 241–2, 243, 305 and 317. It could be argued that the discussion of 'type' and 'role' identities addresses content (see *STIP* 225–8).

of the significant process of constructing 'Germany' or any other state as a subject and the relevant agent in the first place.

My 'Wendtian' reading of the shift towards German military involvement abroad hence excluded intriguing aspects of identity representation. Clearly, the problem is not that Wendt's framework fails to address the specifics of German identity construction. It is more fundamental. Wendt's anthropomorphic concept of the state cannot cope with identities which are unstable in themselves. Identity change is merely about shifting from one relatively stable identity to another. States are unitary actors with minds, desires and intentions. Wendt's recognition that domestic politics influences state behaviour and state identity fails to address the complexity of the issue at hand (*STIP* 264 and 364). Viewed in the context of Wendt's framework, the issue considered here must be construed around *a state with an identifiable identity*, what is denoted by 'Germany'. The insecurity of the German state's identity can thus at best be considered a curiosity. Although Wendt claims that '[h]istory matters' (*STIP* 109), multiple histories do not. 'Germany' makes an appearance only as a unified entity. Considering identity, in this setting, does not make thinking more problematic. There is no space for contemplating Jacques Derrida's claim that 'difference to itself [*différence à soi*], that which differs and diverges from itself, of itself' is always part of cultural identity (*OH* 10 [16]). Rather, as David Campbell points out, '"identity" is rendered in essentialist ways as a variable that can be inserted into already existing theoretical commitments'.[274]

Excluding consideration of the genesis of the actor is not the only problem. Wendt argues that what he calls 'ideas' have both constitutive and causal effects.[275] Although he is more concerned with making a case for the significance of constitution, based on his commitment to scientific realism he also considers identity a causal category which helps explain international politics.[276] Wendt's reliance on scientific realism is related to his earlier criticism regarding the unsophisticated treatment of the so-called agent–structure problem in Neorealism and World Systems Theory.[277] Wendt claimed that both agents and structures

---

[274] Campbell, 'Epilogue', p. 218.

[275] Alexander Wendt, 'On Constitution and Causation in International Relations', *Review of International Studies*, special issue 24 (1998), 101–17; *STIP*, ch. 3.

[276] Wendt, 'On Constitution and Causation', 107; *STIP* 93 and 229. Steve Smith claims that Wendt's constitutive theory is basically a form of causal theory: 'Wendt's World', 157. On Wendt's commitment to scientific realism and its problems, see also Kratochwil, 'Constructing a New Orthodoxy?'

[277] Wendt, 'Agent–Structure Problem'; Wendt, 'Levels of Analysis'.

are significant for explaining the social world but that there is no obvious way to conceive of their relationship.[278] The solution, he argued, could be found in Giddens' structuration theory, specifically the claim that 'the structural properties of social systems are both the medium and outcome of the practices which constitute those systems'.[279] Structuration theory was attractive for Wendt's project because it 'conceptualizes agents and structures as mutually constitutive yet ontologically distinct entities' and gives 'equal ontological status'[280] to both agents and structures. Operating within the discipline of IR with its implicit commitment to positivism,[281] Wendt had to license his talk about unobservable structures having ontological status. He introduced scientific realism as the philosophical foundation of structuration theory.[282] 'Commonsense realism is the belief that the world of everyday objects exists independently of the mind... Scientific realism is the additional conviction that the unobservable entities and causal mechanisms often posited by scientific theories exist.'[283] According to scientific realism, it makes sense to assume the existence of unobservable entities if they can 'bring about changes in material things'.[284] Scientific realists observe that scientific practice usually operates on realist assumptions and that this practice appears successful in manipulating the world. The best explanation for both, they contend, is 'that science provides at least partly true descriptions of the causal structure of the world. Were this not the case, the ability of science to get us to the moon would be an inexplicable miracle.'[285] What is important is that 'the basic realist idea that scientific explanation consists in the identification of underlying causal mechanisms... *does apply to the social sciences*'.[286] In other words, there is a social reality out there, independent of our thoughts about it, and

[278] Wendt, 'Agent–Structure Problem', 338.

[279] Anthony Giddens, *Central Problems in Social Theory: Action, Structure and Contradiction in Social Analysis* (London: Macmillan, 1979), p. 69, quoted in Wendt, 'Agent–Structure problem', 361. See also Giddens, *Constitution of Society*, pp. 16–28, and Roy Bhaskar, *The Possibility of Naturalism. A Philosophical Critique of the Contemporary Human Sciences* (Brighton: Harvester Press, 1979), pp. 43–4. More recently, Wendt uses the concept of supervenience, wherein macro-structures depend on micro-structures but cannot be reduced to them, to explicate the relationship between structures and agents (see ISC 48–51; *STIP* 155–6, 338 and 371–2).

[280] Wendt, 'Agent–Structure problem', 360 and 339.

[281] Steve Smith, 'Positivism and Beyond', pp. 16–17 and 32.

[282] Wendt, 'Agent–Structure Problem', 350.

[283] Shapiro and Wendt, 'Difference That Realism Makes', 210.

[284] Bhaskar, *Possibility of Naturalism*, p. 16.

[285] Shapiro and Wendt, 'Difference That Realism Makes', 211.

[286] Wendt, 'Agent–Structure Problem', 355 (italics added).

Wendt is committed to explaining it.[287] His constructivism 'endorses a scientific approach to social inquiry'.[288]

This creates further problems. The illustration in this chapter shows that identities as they are defined in discourse fail to be logically bounded entities. Identities are continuously articulated, re-articulated and contested, which makes them hard to pin down as explanatory categories. The stories we tell about ourselves are not necessarily coherent. If identity is to 'cause' anything, however, it must be an antecedent condition for a subsequent effect and as such distinguishable from what it causes.[289] At one point, Wendt tells us that, as part of his argument, he is advancing 'a simple causal theory of collective identity formation' (*STIP* 317). On the other hand, structure is supposed to have causal effects on identity (*STIP* 144). Here, identity is effect rather than cause but the requirement of clear separation remains.[290] Wendt's treatment of identity as something which is attached to and negotiated between pre-existing anthropomorphic actors and which *explains* (or is explained) requires conceptualising identity as a unitary, circumscribable concept. It makes necessary the identity of identity.

In sum, although Wendt argues that the world is constructed, there are certain aspects of the world which, based on a defence of scientific realism,[291] he takes as given. As Doty puts it, Wendt 'seems to suggest that one should go with social construction when it is convenient and reify when it is not'.[292] What is particularly telling is that it is precisely with respect to the key move of identity (trans)formation that Wendt evades the implications of the argument that what we call reality is constructed rather than given. Acknowledging that identities do not exist apart from articulation and contextualisation, have no clear bounds and fail to be logically coherent, as the illustration suggests, would threaten the premises of the approach.

The threat is fundamental as it endangers the project. Wendt tells us that he is seeking a '"via media" through the Third Debate' (*STIP* 40

---

[287] See also Wendt, 'Bridging the Theory/Meta-Theory Gap', 391, and his insistence that most postpositivists are 'tacit realists' because they are 'guided by the desire to make their theories correspond to how the world works': Wendt, 'On Constitution and Causation', 107; also 116.

[288] *STIP* 1; see also 39, 77, 374 and 378.

[289] Wendt, 'On Constitution and Causation', 105; *STIP* 25, 79 and 167.

[290] Doty also comments on the need to categorise, define and distinguish for what Wendt wants to do and the impossibility of this task: Doty, 'Desire', 137–8.

[291] See Shapiro and Wendt, 'Difference That Realism Makes'; *STIP*, ch. 2.

[292] Doty, 'Desire', 138.

and 47). This via media entails addressing social construction, or what Wendt calls 'an idealist and holist ontology', whilst 'maintaining a commitment to science' (*STIP* 47).[293] Wendt discusses the philosophical grounding which he claims for this middle way in great detail in chapter 2 of *Social Theory*. In terms of International Relations he is claiming a departure from rationalism[294] which does not force him to give up science as he understands it, which does not, in other words, force him to subscribe to 'postmodernism'. The claim that 'anarchy is what states make of it' revolves around the idea that identities are socially constructed and may be changed, even if such identity transformation is not easy. This is crucial to establishing constructivism as fundamentally different from rationalist 'mainstream' theorising. Although Wendt, in his *Social Theory*, argues that 'there is no contradiction between rationalist and constructivist models of the social process' (*STIP* 366–7), he upholds a difference in analytical focus between the two. Constructivist models will be most useful, he tells us, when we have reason to think that identities and interests will change (*STIP* 367). Thus, as before, the possibility of identity change establishes the difference between rationalism and constructivism.[295] Yet, at the same time, identity must not be as malleable, contingent and elusive as the illustration in this chapter suggests; for acknowledging that identity is 'never given, received or attained'[296] would entail a move in a direction Wendt seems to fancy even less than the rationalism of the 'mainstream'. In a collection of 'constructivist' contributions to the study of national security, the authors of the chapter explicating the analytical framework, one of whom was Wendt, felt it necessary to point out that their usage of the term 'identity' did not signal a 'commitment to some exotic (presumably Parisian) social theory'.[297] This may have been a flippant remark. However, if thinking through the claim that identity is constructed makes it necessary to accept that the subjects themselves do not exist apart from context, then Wendt, and some other constructivists, have a problem with the space they are attempting to carve out for themselves. The 'via media' (*STIP* 40 and 47) or 'middle ground', where Wendt clearly aims to locate his approach, may, if it exists at all, not be as stable a place as he thinks.

---

[293] On the problematic of the via media and science, see also Kratochwil, 'Constructing a New Orthodoxy?', and Smith, 'Wendt's World'. See also Wendt, 'On the Via Media'.
[294] Wendt, 'Constructing International Politics', 71–2; *STIP* 27 and 35.
[295] See n. 117.
[296] Jacques Derrida, *Monolingualism of the Other; or, The Prothesis of Origin*, translated by Patrick Mensah (Stanford University Press, 1998), p. 28 [p. 53].
[297] Jepperson, Wendt and Katzenstein, 'Norms, Identity, and Culture', p. 34.

3   Intersubjectivity and the normative: Kratochwil's constructivism and German military involvement abroad

Friedrich Kratochwil makes a complex argument about the role of rules and reasoning in international relations in order to bring the normative back in.[1] His constructivism develops out of two related but nevertheless distinct strands. On the one hand, Kratochwil expresses dissatisfaction with the epistemological stance in (traditional) IR theory. Its reliance on positivism and resulting conception of objective science, he argues, exclude consideration of the normative character of politics. On the other hand, and flowing from this, is his preoccupation with the role of rules and norms in political life and its analysis. His key claim can be seen to lie in the assertion that international politics must be analysed in the context of norms properly understood.

Kratochwil's constructivist position is explicitly stated in 'Understanding Change in International Politics', an article he co-authored with Rey Koslowski. They see constructivism as centring on practices which are based on rules and norms.[2] According to Koslowski and Kratochwil, all political systems are remade or changed through actors' practices. Thus, '[f]undamental change of the international system occurs when actors, through their practices, change the rules and norms constitutive of international interaction.'[3] As practices on the international level depend on practices on the domestic level, such changes 'occur when beliefs and identities of domestic actors are altered thereby also altering rules and norms that are constitutive of their political practices'.[4]

---

[1] This desire to bring the normative back in is already evident in Friedrich V. Kratochwil, 'The Humean Perspective on International Relations', *World Order Studies Program*, Occasional Paper No. 9 (1981), 1.

[2] Koslowski and Kratochwil, 'Understanding Change', 226.

[3] Koslowski and Kratochwil, 'Understanding Change', 216.

[4] Koslowski and Kratochwil, 'Understanding Change', 216.

Koslowski and Kratochwil argue strongly against the elimination of the domestic level from international analysis.[5] According to them, we cannot know *a priori* whether domestic or international structures will be more significant for international change. 'Rather, what is important is the way in which changed practices arising from new conceptions of identity and political community are adopted by individuals and the way in which the interactions among states are thereby altered or vice versa.'[6] This constructivist approach, articulated in response to Neorealism's inability to explain the end of the Cold War, claims to focus on the problem of change.[7] The emphasis on the domestic dimension of identity change and the consequences for behaviour in the international realm resonate with those aspects of the German shift towards military activity in the international realm that the Wendtian account did not consider. 'Understanding Change in International Politics', though an explicit formulation of his constructivism, is not one of Kratochwil's most intriguing pieces, if only because little space is devoted there to an exposition of his complex arguments. Therefore, the claims remain general. Hence it is more promising to follow up his arguments about the poverty of epistemology and the significance of norms for the analysis of politics to see how he arrives at a position which, although not at first labelled 'constructivist', draws attention to how parties in interaction 'constantly renegotiate the reality in which they operate' (*RND* 102).

The significance of the normative

Like Wendt, Kratochwil presents his arguments as a critique of (Neo)Realism.[8] However, he seems less concerned with facilitating a conversation. Much of his work is a polemic against the 'poverty of epistemology' in IR.[9] This shortcoming is fundamentally important, Kratochwil claims, as our understanding of human action depends on our view of knowledge (*RND* 21). He argues forcefully that the positivist approach employed by much of IR scholarship is inadequate for the problem of politics. Politics is inextricably linked to what it is to

---

[5] Koslowski and Kratochwil, 'Understanding Change', 217.
[6] Koslowski and Kratochwil, 'Understanding Change', 224.
[7] Kratochwil, 'International Order'; Kratochwil, 'Embarrassment'; and esp. Koslowski and Kratochwil, 'Understanding Change'.
[8] See esp. Kratochwil, 'Embarrassment'; *RND*; and Koslowski and Kratochwil, 'Understanding Change'.
[9] Kratochwil, 'Errors', 305.

be human, that is, interpreting oneself and one's surroundings.[10] Positivist explanations, which proceed in terms of antecedent conditions rather than by reference to an aim towards which an act is meant to contribute, make it difficult to understand human action. Referring to practical philosophy, Kratochwil argues that 'intentionality and goal-directedness'[11] need to be considered in analyses of human action. Accordingly, an action has to be located in an intersubjective context to grasp its meaning because to 'have explained an action often means to have made intelligible the goals for the purpose of which it was undertaken'.[12]

This poses some problems as errors of interpretation may occur when elucidating the meaning of behaviour in this way. However, the interpretative nature of the analysis is unavoidable because it is inherent in human action itself. To ignore actors' understandings of their behaviour amounts to ignoring a crucial aspect of that behaviour. Moreover, taking them into account is possible, Kratochwil argues, because it is fundamentally different from trying to get into the head of an actor. Understanding action in terms of meaning is an act of interpretation, not of empathy,[13] because meaning exists only in relation to an intersubjective context. This is reminiscent of Wittgenstein's refusal to consider meaning that is not communicated to others to be meaning at all.[14] Interpretation must be related to the intersubjective context, which, according to Kratochwil, is based on norms and rules. There is, consequently, nothing idiosyncratic about the meaning of behaviour.

Different actors will, to be sure, disagree on how actions are to be classified. However, the ability of actors to engage in a debate about what an action *is* indicates that there is some agreement on what it *could be*. It 'is the contested, but nevertheless partially shared understandings that illuminate ... interactions and help us in our analysis'.[15] In other words, actors refer to the context of norms and rules to give their actions meaning and this same context enables the analyst to, at least partially, understand what is going on. The observer must not only consider the facts of overt behaviour; 'beyond that lies the realm of intersubjective rules which are constitutive of social practice, and which an interpretive

---

[10] Kratochwil, 'Protagorean Quest'.   [11] Kratochwil, 'Errors', 306.
[12] Kratochwil, 'Errors', 317, and also *RND* 24.
[13] Kratochwil, 'Ship of Culture', pp. 217–18.
[14] Ludwig Wittgenstein, *Philosophical Investigations*, translated by G. E. M. Anscombe (Oxford: Basil Blackwell, 1974), §§ 262–75.
[15] Koslowski and Kratochwil, 'Understanding Change', 225.

epistemology has to uncover'.[16] This 'intersubjectivity' is not the same as consensus. In describing a fact or situation, 'no unanimity might actually be achieved. Nevertheless, this observation does not detract from the fact that it is only on the basis of the presumption that such intersubjective characterizations *are* possible and that they can, at least in principle, be reasonably debated, that we can communicate about practical matters and attribute praise or blame' (*RND* 229). This presumption, he claims, makes interpretative analysis feasible. Opting out of the admittedly precarious operation of interpretation is, moreover, impossible because eliminating the elements of appraisal and interpretation to make the analysis 'objective' leads to a misconception of the problem of praxis.[17] Analyses must address the normative aspect of social institutions and questions of morality.[18] It is important to realise that humans, as a matter of fact, use moral criteria. They do not merely make predictions about future conduct on the basis of probabilities; rather, they take into account questions of right and wrong. As a result, a 'moral point of view' emerges in human interaction, based both on the reasoning process related to obligations and on our emotions regarding ourselves and our way of life.[19] Assessing responsibility or ascribing praise with reference to norms is therefore part of explaining an action. Hence, the 'explanation' is significantly shaped by moral and pragmatic considerations (*RND* 100); for

> the characterization of actions whether in the legal or practical discourse is not a description at all, but rather an *appraisal*; it is an evaluation of 'facts' in terms of some normative considerations. We might take issue with a specific characterization, bracket the implicit evaluation, or make it the explicit topic of our dispute; but what does not seem possible – unless we leave the practical discourse – is the reduction of the characterization to a description in the language of pure observation. On the contrary, what acquires here the status of an 'objective' fact is not the thing described but rather the intersubjective *validity* of a characterization upon which reasonable persons can agree.[20]

As there are no value-free descriptions, the exclusion of normative considerations in analyses of politics renders it impossible to grasp what is going on. What is more, it allows us to disown any relationship with the situation at hand. Hence, by misrepresenting human action in the

---

[16] Friedrich Kratochwil, 'Regimes, Interpretation and the "Science" of Politics: A Reappraisal', *Millennium: Journal of International Studies* 17 (1988), 277.
[17] Kratochwil, 'Protagorean Quest', 206.   [18] Kratochwil, 'Protagorean Quest', 214.
[19] Kratochwil, 'Protagorean Quest', 207.   [20] *RND* 229 (footnote deleted).

positivist way we are 'most likely to misunderstand ourselves and our task in shaping our destiny'.[21] Thus, apart from making social life unintelligible, positivist explanations define away the normative dimension and thus the problem of responsibility.

In order to overcome this discrepancy between what is important to humans in their social interactions and the ways in which these interactions are being explained, Kratochwil focuses on the role of norms in politics. More precisely he investigates why actors have recourse to norms (*RND* 5). He sees the intersubjective context which enables actors to makes sense of the world as based on and mediated by rules and norms. Therefore, he starts his discussion of political action with three assumptions. Firstly, he supposes 'that it is useful to study the role of norms in shaping decisions from the baseline of an abstract initial situation which is defined, more or less, in public choice terms' (*RND* 10). In other words, rules and norms serve to reduce the complexity of situations and impose a certain rationality on actors. Relatedly, Kratochwil assumes that human action is rule-governed. Rules give action meaning (*RND* 10–11). They do so in a variety of ways, not only by providing guidance; they are 'also the means which allow people to pursue goals, share meanings, communicate with each other, criticize assertions, and justify actions' (*RND* 11). For instance, in the case of disputes they 'structure the antagonism between the parties and regulate the pursuit of their respective interests' (*RND* 181). Yet, rules and norms do not determine human behaviour. Accordingly, Kratochwil's third assumption is that the reasoning process and therefore processes of deliberation and interpretation are important and must be analysed (*RND* 11).

To make his argument, it is important for Kratochwil appropriately to conceptualise what rules and norms are. He claims that, 'while all rules are norms, not all norms exhibit rule-like characteristics' (*RND* 10). He does not explain why this is the case and draws no clear distinction between the two categories in his discussion of different types of rules and norms.[22] Indeed, Nicholas Onuf complains that in Kratochwil's approach '[p]rinciples and rules of high specificity are treated as analytically separable, then conflated in order to create a uniformly operative model of law' (*WOM* 77). Therefore, my discussion of these concepts does not treat them as separate.

---

[21] Kratochwil, 'Errors', 319.
[22] See *RND*, esp. chs. 3 and 4. See also Friedrich Kratochwil, 'The Force of Prescriptions', *International Organization* 38 (1984), 685–708.

To regard rules and norms as merely constraining or as causes of human behaviour is, Kratochwil claims, unhelpful (*RND* 5 and 61). He argues that 'we have to understand how the social world is intrinsically linked to language and how language, because it is a rule-governed activity, can provide us with a point of departure for our inquiry into the function of norms in social life' (*RND* 6). According to Kratochwil, norms are speech acts and they depend upon successful communication. Their perlocutionary effect (*RND* 34), that is, the impact they have on the hearer, is significant (*RND* 8). They always apply generally to similar situations. Although rules need not come in explicit verbal form, formality provides several advantages. Explicit rules can be communicated to actors with different historic and cultural backgrounds, they allow for greater precision and they may enable actors to break out of a deadlock over the choice between equally desirable ways of cooperating (*RND* 78–9 and 53–6). Communication about tacit understandings becomes necessary when they are violated. In such a situation, actors may either deny the existence of tacit rules and hence any potential violation of a rule, or acknowledge the rule but argue that it was not applicable or that their deviant behaviour should be excused on specific grounds. The former is completely different from the latter, Kratochwil argues, as it questions the normality of the actor who relied on the rule; for, by '"denying the experience" of the other, one also implies that the other person's understanding of the relationship, as well as of the common social world, is faulty or mistaken' (*RND* 82).[23]

Rules and norms 'link individual autonomy to sociality' (*RND* 70) by providing guidance and acting as a problem-solving device. They do so in three ways. They may rule out certain forms of behaviour. They may create schemes or schedules for coordinating the enjoyment of scarce resources. And they provide the basis for a discourse in which the parties discuss grievances, negotiate solutions and ask for third-party mediation (*RND* 70). This means that rules 'simplify choice-situations by drawing attention to factors which an actor has to take into account' (*RND* 72). Yet, whilst rules have some common characteristics, it is important to recognise their different functions.

'Instruction-type' rules, such as 'do not plant tomatoes before 15 April', encapsulate experiential knowledge about a means–end relationship. Thus they apply only if the goal that is meant to be achieved

---

[23] On the significance of formality, see also Friedrich Kratochwil, 'Contract and Regimes: Do Issue Specificity and Variations of Formality Matter?', in Volker Rittberger (ed.), *Regime Theory and International Relations* (Oxford: Clarendon Press, 1993), pp. 84–92.

by following the rule is sought (*RND* 73). 'Practice-type' or 'institution-type' rules, for which promising and contracting are paradigmatic,[24] are most important for Kratochwil's argument, however. In this case, there is a logical rather than empirical relationship between following the rule and achieving its objective. If, for instance, I say that I promise something I will automatically have done so. Following J. L. Austin's reasoning about speech acts,[25] Kratochwil claims that these rules usually relate to performances in which the rule specifies the conditions under which an act will be considered valid. In many cases, one has to follow certain prescribed procedures in order properly to execute a speech act in accordance with a practice-type rule, as, for instance, in lifting the hand when taking an oath (*RND* 91–2). This serves to 'objectify the subjective aspects of the situation' (*RND* 92). At least in legal proceedings, this makes it possible to infer intentions from empirical facts such as the use of certain words, rather than to second-guess the state of mind of a person. The practices defined by institution-type rules are part of a wider normative context set by precepts, a further rule-type. Precepts, such as 'do not lie', are 'prescriptions of the highest generality which try to overcome the dilemmas between self-interested and socially desirable actions' (*RND* 92). They are based on a universal claim to validity and provide the support for specific validity-claims of practices, whilst practice-type rules define the practices as such (*RND* 93).

If we use these conceptualisations to think about the issue of the FRG taking up military involvement abroad as a new practice after the end of the Cold War, the recourse to norms in the process becomes significant. In order to elucidate the significance of rules and their function in communication, it is crucial to take into account the actual political discourse.[26] The Federal Government invoked rules as important when it declined on constitutional grounds the first post-Cold War request for a deployment of its military abroad, a US demand for military support in a potential operation in the Gulf or at least the deployment of minesweepers to the eastern Mediterranean. It merely sent several ships to the western Mediterranean to relieve US vessels of NATO duties. These ships

---

[24] See Kratochwil, 'Protagorean Quest', 209, but also Kratochwil, 'Limits of Contract'.

[25] Austin, *How to Do Things with Words*. See also John R. Searle, *Speech Acts: An Essay in the Philosophy of Language* (Cambridge University Press, 1969).

[26] Friedrich V. Kratochwil, 'On the Notion of Interest in International Relations', *International Organization* 30 (1982), 9; Friedrich Kratochwil, 'Sovereignty as *Dominium*: Is There a Right of Humanitarian Intervention?', in Lyons and Mastanduno, *Beyond Westphalia?*, p. 21.

had to remain within the NATO region.[27] Thus, the first response to the possibility of deploying the German navy to a conflict region abroad consisted in claims about the legality of such a move.[28] This reaction is difficult to understand or even represent without recourse to norms.

Bundeswehr deployments in relation to the Gulf War and later as part of a number of UN missions were construed as problematic on the basis of the belief that the constitution restricted the external use of force to defence. In order to explore whether these rules were significant in the way Kratochwil suggests, it is first necessary to explicate them in some detail. In the Basic Law, there is one clear limitation on the use of force: 'Any activities apt or intended to disturb peaceful international relations, especially preparations for military aggression, shall be unconstitutional.'[29] This states an accepted position of international law and cannot therefore be construed as a special restriction on the FRG. Beyond this, it is Art. 87a (2) which can be thought to constrain the use of the military: 'Other than for defence purposes the Armed Forces may only be employed to the extent explicitly permitted by this Basic Law.'[30] This may seem like a straightforward prohibition against using the military other than for defensive operations unless the Basic Law specifically provides for an alternative use, but the scope of application, meaning and effect of this regulation were all contentious.

The first problem concerns the scope of Art. 87a (2). Because of the position of the norm within the constitution and the historical context of its addition to the Basic Law, it is possible to argue that it is not applicable to the external use of force at all. Rather, it is addressed to using the military within the FRG itself. Art. 87a forms part of Chapter VIII of the constitution which addresses the implementation of federal law and the federal administration, i.e. domestic matters. It was added to the Basic Law in 1968 as part of legislation on the state of emergency and replaced the former Art. 143, which had explicitly regulated the

---

[27] 'Bonn schickt Marine ins Mittelmeer', *SZ*, 11–12 Aug. 1990, 1; 'Wir müssen erwachsen werden', *Der Spiegel*, 34/44, 20 Aug. 1990, 121–3, here 121; 'Der Himmel schließt sich', *Der Spiegel*, 4/45, 21 Jan. 1991, 18–20, here 20.
[28] See, for example, 'Uneinigkeit in Bonner Koalition über einen Einsatz der Bundeswehr im Golf', *FAZ*, 16 Aug. 1990, 2.
[29] Art. 26 (1), *Basic Law for the Federal Republic of Germany*, promulgated by the Parliamentary Council on 23 May 1949 (version in effect since 15 November 1994), official translation (Bonn: Press and Information Office of the Federal Government, 1995).
[30] Art. 87a (2) of the Basic Law. The German word 'einsetzen', used in the original text, should in my view be translated as 'to deploy' rather than 'to employ'. This is important because there was debate about what constitutes a 'deployment' of the armed forces. See *Grundgesetz für die Bundesrepublik Deutschland*.

internal use of the military. It is therefore conceivable that the legislators did not intend to address the external use of the armed forces with this norm at all or did not even think about it, especially since in 1968 there was little reason to legislate for Bundeswehr deployments outside German territory. In the event of escalation in the East–West confrontation, the fighting was expected to take place on German soil anyway, and the norm could not have been aimed at UN operations, as the Federal Republic was not a member at the time.[31] The point is that, if this regulation is addressed only to a potential internal use of the army, there would be no limitation to external use apart from the general restrictions of international law[32] and the prohibition against wars of aggression. However, this view was contested. The wording gives no indication that the norm is meant to be limited to internal Bundeswehr deployments. Moreover, historical documents show that a comprehensive regulation for all uses of the armed forces was intended. The Legal Committee of the Bundestag stated its intention to use Art. 87a 'also' to legislate for the internal use of the military.[33] Because of these semantic and historical arguments, the 'prevailing opinion'[34] among experts on constitutional law held that Art. 87a was applicable to the question of external deployments of the Bundeswehr,[35] although there were a number of dissenters.

If it is granted that the norm is applicable, its meaning, and therefore the meaning of the key terms used in the norm, must be determined in more detail. There are three interpretations of what constitutes an 'employment' or rather 'deployment'.[36] The first makes the usage of arms the central criterion. The second defines any use of the military as a 'deployment'. The third considers it an action which is not neutral in terms of force, i.e. an action which constitutes an element of the use of force on behalf of the state. On the last, and most widespread, interpretation, UN peacekeeping, as well as any form of individual or collective self-defence are covered by the regulation whilst support of UN operations

---

[31] Philippi, *Bundeswehr-Auslandseinsätze*, pp. 35–6. Khan and Zöckler argue, in contrast, that German accession to the UN was discussed at the time and that therefore participation in UN operations was a realistic possibility: Daniel-Erasmus Khan and Markus Zöckler, 'Germans to the Front? Or Le malade imaginaire', *European Journal of International Law* 3 (1992), 168.

[32] The general rules of international law form part of German law and override domestic laws: Art. 25 of the Basic Law.

[33] Deutscher Bundestag, *Drucksache*, 5/2873, 1968.

[34] This is a literal translation of a technical term in German legal discourse referring to the interpretation subscribed to by a majority of prominent legal experts and judges.

[35] Philippi, *Bundeswehr-Auslandseinsätze*, p. 37.   [36] See n. 30 above.

through payment in kind, transporting of troops or logistical support are not.[37]

Any action exceeding this kind of support is then constitutional only if it is taken 'for defence', if the Basic Law 'explicitly permits' it or if Art. 87a is overruled in principle by a regulation which requires military action. With respect to the question of what constitutes 'defence', there are again three different positions. The first equates it to any form of defence against aggression permissible under international law, that is, individual and collective self-defence according to Art. 51 of the UN Charter. The second takes defence to mean territorial defence. The third links it to the defence of the existing state order, that is, the state order which reflects the spirit of the Basic Law. As the latter may include legitimate alliance politics, collective defence in the framework of NATO or the WEU would be constitutional. The participation in other operations of these organisations or the UN, on the other hand, would require explicit permission by the Basic Law.[38]

A military deployment which cannot be construed as defence but which falls within the scope of Art. 87a (2) is still constitutional if the Basic Law explicitly permits it. The only norm in the Basic Law which could constitute express permission is Art. 24 (2): 'With a view to maintaining peace the Federation may become a party to a system of [mutual] collective security; in doing so it shall consent to such limitations upon its sovereign powers as will bring about and secure a peaceful and lasting order in Europe and among the nations of the world.'[39] As such systems work only if their members are willing and able in principle to use force, this can be read as an explicit permission to use force within the framework of a 'system of mutual collective security', such as the UN. However, a competing interpretation emphasises that express permission in legal discourse refers to permission given *expressis verbis*. As Art. 24 (2) does not mention 'Bundeswehr', 'armed forces', 'peacekeeping' or such like, it cannot constitute the required

---

[37] Philippi, *Bundeswehr-Auslandseinsätze*, pp. 37–9; for a slightly different account of this aspect, see Khan and Zöckler, 'Germans to the Front?', 171–3.

[38] Philippi, *Bundeswehr-Auslandseinsätze*, pp. 40–1; Khan and Zöckler, 'Germans to the Front?', 170–1. For a somewhat different interpretation, see Brunner, *Deutsche Soldaten im Ausland*, pp. 36–42.

[39] Official translation; my addition. The official translation excludes an important term. The German text speaks of a 'system of *mutual* collective defence' (italics added). The original reads: 'Der Bund kann sich zur Wahrung des Friedens einem System gegenseitiger kollektiver Sicherheit einordnen; er wird hierbei in die Beschränkungen seiner Hoheitsrechte einwilligen, die eine friedliche und dauerhafte Ordnung in Europa und zwischen den Völkern der Welt herbeiführen und sichern.'

permission. Accordingly, Bundeswehr participation in UN operations would be unconstitutional.[40]

Yet, even if Art. 24 (2) does not constitute express permission, it may nevertheless take precedence over Art. 87a (2). The latter was added to the Basic Law only in 1968 and cannot have changed the scope and effect of the already existing Art. 24 (2); for, according to Art. 79 (1), existing regulations of the constitution can be changed only by a law which expressly states this intent. Therefore, what is permitted by Art. 24 (2), that is, participation in arrangements of 'mutual collective security', cannot be ruled out by Art. 87a (2). This must include the possibility of taking on such duties as are typically part of such arrangements, that is, using the military to restore and enforce peace.

This brief overview makes it possible to investigate in more detail how these constitutional norms may be seen to have provided an inter-subjective context and how this context may have invested the Federal Government's refusal to send minesweepers anywhere other than the western Mediterranean with meaning. According to Kratochwil, norms tell us which aspects of a situation we have to take into account (*RND* 10). This argument can be supported in relation to three aspects of the envis-aged international operations which became significant – the location of the deployment, the character of the operation and the framework for the operation – and which take on importance with reference to the constitution.

On 20 August 1990, following the US request for support, Chancel-lor Helmut Kohl, Foreign Minister Hans-Dietrich Genscher and Defence Minister Gerhard Stoltenberg reached an understanding to the effect that the Bundeswehr would not be sent to the Gulf and that such a deploy-ment would be unconstitutional. The constitution was to be changed, however, to make participation in UN peace missions beyond NATO ter-ritory possible in the future.[41] Whether a deployment was to take place within NATO territory or beyond its southern limit was considered a decisive criterion for its legality. Given that the Basic Law does not men-tion NATO territory[42] or its southern limit, the Tropic of Cancer,[43] this may be a strange place to start in order to demonstrate the significance

---

[40] Philippi, *Bundeswehr-Auslandseinsätze*, pp. 42–4; Khan and Zöckler, 'Germans to the Front?', 169 and 173.

[41] 'Kein Einsatz der Bundeswehr am Golf', *SZ*, 21 Aug. 1990, 2.

[42] Philippi, *Bundeswehr-Auslandseinsätze*, p. 29, n. 120. Strangely Hans-Georg Franzke im-plies that it is relevant, without advancing any reasons: 'Art. 24 II als Rechtsgrundlage für den Außeneinsatz der Bundeswehr?', *Neue Juristische Wochenschrift* 45 (1992), 3075.

[43] Brunner, *Deutsche Soldaten im Ausland*, p. 38.

of the context of constitutional norms. Yet, despite the wording of the Basic Law, the public, even the informed public, was obviously under the impression that the Tropic of Cancer was relevant in terms of constitutionality. This is illustrated by claims in the press that a deployment outside NATO territory was considered unconstitutional by a majority of experts on constitutional law.[44] Although this is an unlikely claim because constitutional lawyers should know that NATO territory is not mentioned in the Basic Law, it is not wholly beside the point. One of the interpretations of the licence, in Art. 87a (2), to defend the country takes it to include legitimate alliance politics, such as membership in NATO. In the context of this interpretation, the idea that military activity within the NATO area but not beyond counts as defensive is not implausible. Moreover, this idea had been amalgamated into a 'consensus on security policy',[45] to which the major parties subscribed during the Cold War. According to this consensus, using military force other than in self-defence was impossible for West Germany.

In 1982 the 'consensus on security policy' was developed into a *legal* position.[46] In the 1980s, in the context of the Iran–Iraq war, the Americans repeatedly demanded that Europeans participate in interventions outside the NATO area. A report commissioned by the then chancellor Helmut Schmidt exploring the legality of Bundeswehr deployments abroad argued that they were legal in the event of an armed attack on the FRG or of self-defence or assistance in the context of NATO or the WEU. Preserving economic interests militarily, however, was unconstitutional. On the issue which was to become the major point of contention in the 1990s, namely participation in UN operations, it was vague and indicated that the ministries involved had come to differing conclusions. The report became the basis for two decisions of the Federal Security Council[47] which turned the 'consensus on security policy' into a legal position.[48] In September and November 1982, in other words before

---

[44] 'Streit um Bundeswehreinsatz am Golf', *SZ*, 10 Aug. 1990, 2.

[45] Werner Hoyer (FDP) refers to this notion in Deutscher Bundestag, *Plenarprotokoll*, 12/132, 15 Jan. 1993, 11468. See also Philippi, *Bundeswehr-Auslandseinsätze*, p. 61.

[46] In 1967 a legal examination found no obstacles to participation in UN peace-keeping in Israel: Philippi, *Bundeswehr-Auslandseinsätze*, p. 60, n. 298; 'Weder Grundgesetzänderung noch Entsendegesetz', *FAZ*, 25 Nov. 1992, 1–2, here 2. This may be less interesting in terms of the legal situation than Philippi suggests, as the potentially restrictive Art. 87a (2) was added to the Basic Law only in 1968.

[47] The Federal Security Council is a cabinet institution which discusses issues in foreign and security policy.

[48] Philippi, *Bundeswehr-Auslandseinsätze*, pp. 60–1. See also Kaiser and Becher, *Deutschland und der Irak-Konflikt*, p. 85.

and after the change in government from a coalition of SPD and FDP to one of CDU/CSU and FDP, the Federal Security Council stated that the military forces of the FRG, due to constitutional constraints, could on no account help out in crisis situations outside NATO territory.[49]

This established the link between the constitutional permissibility of operations and the location of the deployment. From then on this restrictive interpretation of the Basic Law came to be seen as binding. From a legal point of view it is strange that the question of *where* troops were to be deployed became significant. The Basic Law makes no reference to geography; rather it refers to *what* the armed forces can and cannot do. Therefore sending the Bundeswehr beyond NATO territory to defend the FRG or its NATO partners should have been legal, whilst a deployment within NATO territory in the pursuit of economic interests should have been ruled out. However, deployments within the North Atlantic area were conceptualised to be 'for defence', those 'out of area', as it was called, were taken to be not defensive.[50] As Kratochwil argues, 'rules and norms constitute a practice within which certain acts or utterances "count" as something' (*RND* 7). Thus, the discussion about the location of the deployment in some way functioned as a discussion about the character of the deployment, and therefore about its acceptability in terms of Art. 87a (2).

The consensus on security policy repeatedly came under threat in the late 1980s as Conservative politicians increasingly supported the view that Art. 87a (2) was not at all applicable to the external use of the Bundeswehr.[51] However, the consensus nevertheless seemed to influence thinking in relation to the 1990–1 Gulf War.[52] The potential deployment of minesweepers was construed as a problem precisely because of the suggestion that the vessels should leave NATO territory. Thus, the issue of sending minesweepers to the Gulf was discussed in terms of the possibility of a Bundeswehr mission in a conflict region outside NATO territory. As no agreement was reached on the constitutionality of such a deployment, German minesweepers could start aiding

---

[49] Philippi, *Bundeswehr-Auslandseinsätze*, p. 61; Kielinger, 'Gulf War', 244; 'Vor die Wand', *Der Spiegel*, 31/43, 31 Jul. 1989, 22–3, here 23; Leicht, 'Mit Volldampf', 3. Kielinger dates the second decision to December.
[50] Calic implies this: 'German Perspectives', p. 62.
[51] 'Bundesmarine: Germans to the front?', *Der Spiegel*, 49/41, 30 Nov. 1987, 19–21; 'Wir müssen erwachsen werden', *Der Spiegel*, 34/44, 20 Jul. 1990, 121–3, here 121–2; Philippi, *Bundeswehr-Auslandseinsätze*, p. 62; 'Vor die Wand', *Der Spiegel*, 31/43, 31 Jul. 1989, 22–3.
[52] See also Leicht, 'Mit Volldampf', 3.

the multinational efforts to clear the Persian Gulf of sea mines only in March 1991, after an armistice had been reached.[53] The geographic criterion continued to define the problem in relation to Operation Deny Flight. German soldiers were not allowed to enter Austria or Hungary: AWACS aircraft operated by crews including German nationals could patrol the skies only from within NATO airspace.[54]

Although leaving NATO territory was construed as a problem, the Bundeswehr was, as a matter of fact, deployed to other places. For instance, in 1992 the Bundeswehr gave medical aid to UNTAC and the civilian population in Cambodia. Clearly, Cambodia is not located in the North Atlantic region. Nevertheless, and despite initial concern amongst the SPD that such an operation would be unconstitutional,[55] there seems to have been little controversy surrounding this use of the Bundeswehr.[56] Similarly, the airlift transporting supplies to Kurdish refugees in Iraq (and Turkey) in August 1991 was ignored in terms of the discussion about military involvement abroad.[57] Moreover, the Bundesluftwaffe was involved in an airlift to Sarajevo from July 1992 and in air drops of supplies over East Bosnia from March 1993.[58] Although the airlift to Sarajevo was arguably one of the more dangerous missions the German armed forces had participated in thus far,[59] there was little debate about it. If the decisive criterion for the legality of any use of the Bundeswehr had indeed been geographical, these operations should have been just as controversial as sending minesweepers to the Gulf or engineers to Somalia. Arguably, they did not generate as much debate because they were perceived as legal on the grounds that the use of the armed forces remained below the threshold of a 'deployment'. In two of the three common interpretations of Art. 87a(2) of the Basic Law the use of arms is significant. Airlifts and the provision of medical aid by Bundeswehr personnel therefore fall short of a deployment. Hence they are not unconstitutional.

[53] Kaiser and Becher, *Deutschland und der Irak-Konflikt*, pp. 15–16.
[54] Stefan Kornelius, 'Ein Drittel der Besatzung sind Deutsche', *SZ*, 14 Jan. 1993, p. 6.
[55] 'SPD: Für Blauhelmeinsatz Grundgesetz ändern', *SZ*, 20 May 1992, 2.
[56] There was criticism that the operation was not 'humanitarian' as the government claimed but doubts about its legality did not become a serious issue: 'Rühe verabschiedet erste deutsche Blauhelme', *SZ*, 12 May 1992, 2.
[57] Kaiser and Becher, *Deutschland und der Irak-Konflikt*, pp. 42–3; Kielinger, 'Gulf War', 247. For press reports, see 'Sozis in der Klemme', *Der Spiegel*, 20/45, 13 May 1991, 31–2, here 31; 'Hering in Senfsoße', *Der Spiegel*, 20/45, 13 May 1991, 32–3, here 32.
[58] 'Bundeswehr nimmt an Bosnien-Luftbrücke teil', *SZ*, 30 Mar. 1993, 1.
[59] '"Combat approach" auf Sarajevo', *Der Spiegel*, 38/46, 14 Sep. 1992, 174.

It is difficult, on the basis of press sources, to establish why these cases failed to be controversial. Although Kratochwil claims that rule-following does not involve blind habit but argumentation, none of the actors made any specific attempt to justify these operations. We can therefore, at best, guess that there was no need to do so as they were generally accepted to be in accordance with the relevant rules. Kratochwil's point becomes important when there is doubt about the legitimacy of action, and actors therefore resort to norms to explain and justify their behaviour. He argues that the prescriptive force of norms lies in 'a claim to validity which is mediated by language and which can be validated discursively' (*RND* 97). Therefore, investigating the process of reasoning in relation to norms can elucidate the normative power of prescriptions. In Kratochwil's words, 'it is through *analyzing the reasons which are specific to different rule-types that the intersubjective validity of norms and thus their "deontic status" can be established*' (*RND* 97). Rules and norms shape decisions through the reasoning process (*RND* 43). Norms can provide persuasive reasons for decisions which are not necessarily logically compelling (*RND* 36). They also influence who is admitted to the debate in the first place and which styles of reasoning are considered adequate (*RND* 34). Actors may moreover refer to well-institutionalised norms to explicate disappointments about others' conduct without thereby endangering or questioning the overall social relationship (*RND* 56).

Because norms have these functions, actors discuss actions in relation to them. In other words, they invoke norms to justify and legitimate behaviour. They may also plead and apologise in relation to norms in order to excuse behaviour seen to violate the rules. 'Because human actions need interpretation, the justifications and excuses are important yardsticks for appraising particular choices' (*RND* 63). This is significant because it brings the impact of norms out in the open, into the realm of what Kratochwil and other constructivists call intersubjectivity. It is therefore not merely the actor who must 'refer to rules and norms when he/she wants to make a choice'; rather 'the observer, as well, must understand the normative structure underlying the action, in order to interpret and appraise choices' (*RND* 11). The reasoning which goes along with rule-following or rule-violation indicates the meaning of behaviour both to other actors and to analysts.

As the legality of most operations in which the government wanted to take part was in doubt, justifications were given for their constitutionality, if not always explicitly. In relation to sending a destroyer to the Adriatic Sea to monitor the UN embargo against Serbia, the German government simply disputed that this was a 'deployment' according to the spirit of the Basic Law. Rather it was an 'employment' in accordance with a long-standing practice of the FRG. The usage of the military remained under the threshold of a 'deployment' as it had done in the cases of the Cambodia operation and the airlift to Sarajevo.[60] The government called sending minesweepers to the Gulf in March 1991 'humanitarian'.[61] What is significant is not whether there was indeed any benefit to mankind or element of aid to the other but again whether the operation was a deployment. On two of the interpretations of what constitutes a 'deployment' of the military, the use of force is the decisive criterion. Therefore, claiming that a mission was 'humanitarian' worked as an implicit claim that it was merely a relief effort by men in uniform, that is, not a proper deployment. Hence, it could not be ruled out by Art. 87a (2) of the Basic Law.

This argument recurs in relation to the Somalia operation. In January 1993 the defence minister mentioned doubts as to whether the mission was merely humanitarian. Because it would involve an element of fighting, the unclear constitutional situation prevented Bundeswehr participation, he argued.[62] Similarly, Karsten Voigt of the SPD disputed the legitimacy of the operation on the grounds that the soldiers would be carrying weapons for self-defence.[63] He thereby implicitly asserted that participation in the Somalia mission would constitute a 'deployment' and would therefore be illegal. Although politicians often failed to refer explicitly to the constitutional norms, one may assume that their conceptualisation of different potential operations as either problematic or not problematic was somehow based on interpretations of the rule structure. The question of whether a mission could be construed as humanitarian or not might make sense independently, but it acquired its special significance in terms of the constitutional situation.

Although the question of NATO territory and the character of the use of the Bundeswehr were the most prominent areas of contestation in relation to constitutional norms, the issue of the organisational framework was also significant. Chancellor Kohl at one point claimed in relation to a potential Bundeswehr deployment to the Gulf that if there was going to

---

[60] 'Bundeswehr-Einsatz verfassungskonform', *SZ*, 9–10 Jan. 1993, 2.
[61] 'Bonn schickt fünf Minensuchboote in den Golf', *SZ*, 07 Mar. 1991, 1; 'Eine regelrechte Psychose', *Der Spiegel*, 52/46, 21 Dec. 1992, 18–20, here 19–20.
[62] 'Bundeswehr-Einsatz wird fraglich', *SZ*, 21 Jan. 1993, 1.
[63] 'Kanzleramt korrigiert Mitteilung Rühes', *SZ*, 17–18 Apr. 1993, 2.

be a UN operation this would entail 'a different situation'[64] with respect to constitutionality. It seems at first mysterious why UN involvement should change the regulations under the Basic Law. The legal advisor of the CDU/CSU parliamentary group, Langner, was more explicit. He claimed that such a deployment would be possible because of Art. 24 (2) of the Basic Law, which provides for the possibility of being a part of a 'system of mutual collective defence'.[65] In other words, on this reading of the constitution, the Bundeswehr was allowed to intervene abroad as part of a 'system of mutual collective defence' and this would be the case if the UN was involved.

Clearly, norms can be interpreted as profoundly significant in relation to these issues. The situation was defined in terms of norms. The willingness to deploy the navy to the western but not the eastern Mediterranean makes sense only in reference to the normative role of NATO territory which in turn can be grasped only in relation to constitutional regulations. Thus, conceptualising the question of a minesweeper deployment and, more generally, of Bundeswehr deployments abroad as a matter of constitutional law meant that interpretations of the Basic Law influenced which aspects of the situation were considered relevant. Kratochwil argues that rules make situations intelligible by 'delineating the factors that a decision-maker has to take into account' (*RND* 10). The constitutional response defined the situation in a particular way. A different framing of the refusal to send minesweepers to the Gulf, such as the claim that it was not feasible whilst the country was in the midst of the process of unification, might have led to discussions about shortages of political resources at this difficult time, or about the complexities of merging two armies and the consequential inability to engage in new types of activities at this point. This was not the case. Rather, the significance of NATO territory, the use of weapons and the organisational framework were debated. This made sense only if one took the rule structure into account and was prepared to accept it as important. Karl Kaiser and Klaus Becher comment in their analysis of the Gulf War that, as a consequence of the government's justifications of their policy with reference to the Basic Law, many Germans had started to believe that the FRG should not get involved in any military conflicts apart from defence within the NATO alliance.[66] The debate was therefore a

---

[64] 'Kohl schließt Einsatz im Golf nicht aus', *FAZ*, 17 Aug. 1990, 4; 'Bonn sucht nach einer Einigung im Streit um Golfeinsatz', *FAZ*, 18 Aug. 1990, 4.
[65] 'Kohl schließt Einsatz im Golf nicht aus', *FAZ*, 17 Aug. 1990, 4.
[66] Kaiser and Becher, *Deutschland und der Irak-Konflikt*, p. 11.

serious discussion about important aspects of the state's legal order for the Germans. Foreign politicians, however, who may have been less familiar with the rule structure or at least not socialised into it, called the debate 'old and sterile'[67] or even 'ridiculous'.[68] The point is not that one side or other failed to understand what the situation really was. It is that, unlike the Germans amongst themselves, foreign politicians and Germans had difficulties engaging in a reasoned argument with each other because they did not share a context of norms.

It makes sense to understand the FRG's recourse to norms over the question of a potential military involvement in the Gulf as an attempt to justify the refusal. As Kratochwil points out, 'legal norms provide particularly powerful justifications for certain political choices' (*RND* 206). They are, therefore, an important part of attempts at legitimisation and delegitimisation (*RND* 206). However, the situation was complex. The FRG's refusal on constitutional grounds to deploy minesweepers to the Gulf region involved a degree of interpretation. This point was not lost on foreign commentators and politicians.[69] On 8 August 1990 President George Bush seemed to accept Kohl's constitutional argument. Yet the United States suggested only a few days later that the German navy should deploy its minesweepers to the eastern Mediterranean to protect the Suez Canal.[70] Kohl, accordingly, argued that abroad no one was convinced any more that the Germans' hands were tied by the constitution.[71] Josef Joffe complained that, when asked for a contribution to the preservation of peace in the Gulf, German politicians continually responded either that it was impossible because it was unconstitutional or that it would be possible only if the Basic Law was changed. He considered this merely an excuse.[72] Although

---

[67] US foreign secretary James Baker quoted in 'Der will schlicht überleben', *Der Spiegel*, 2/45, 7 Jan. 1991, 18–21, here 21.
[68] US diplomat quoted in 'Wie wir es wünschen', *Der Spiegel*, 13/45, 25 Mar. 1991, 20–1, here 21.
[69] 'Westeuropas militärischer Einsatz zu gering', *FAZ*, 31 Aug. 1990, 4; 'Bonn soll seinen Beitrag leisten', *Der Spiegel*, 38/44, 17 Sep. 1990, 21–2, here 21; 'Den Ernstfall nicht gewagt', *Der Spiegel*, 7/45, 11 Jul. 1991, 18–26, here 25.
[70] 'Wir müssen erwachsen werden', *Der Spiegel*, 34/44, 20 Aug. 1989, 121–3, here 121. Michael J. Inacker, member of the Defence Ministry planning staff in 1989/90, even claims that in a letter of 20 August US secretary of defense Richard Cheney suggested that the FRG should send combat troops: Michael J. Inacker, *Unter Ausschluß der Öffentlichkeit? Die Deutschen in der Golfallianz* (Bonn and Berlin: Bouvier Verlag, 1991), p. 84.
[71] 'Wir stehen vor einem gewaltigen Kraftakt', interview with Chancellor Helmut Kohl, *SZ*, 11 Oct. 1990, 13.
[72] Josef Joffe, 'Versteckspiel mit dem Grundgesetz', *SZ*, 14–15 Aug. 1990, 4. The CSU agreed with this view: 'CSU verlangt größere Rolle für Deutschland', *SZ*, 13 Jan. 1992, 1.

officially the FRG's partners 'welcomed' the plans for constitutional change, there was growing disappointment about its inaction. The *Frankfurter Allgemeine Zeitung* claimed that the partner countries were 'convinced that Bonn [was] hiding behind the Basic Law'.[73] The attempt to legitimise the refusal via the recourse to norms therefore seems to have failed, as it was not accepted any more that, because of the existence of the constitutional norms, the FRG had no choice but to decline.

Relying on constitutional norms portrayed the issue as one of law rather than politics, that is, of determination rather than choice. As Kratochwil points out, policies are changed, rules are violated (*RND* 207). Therefore basing one's position on constitutional norms entails an implicit assertion that change is not an option. Yet, whatever constitutional restraint there may have been against the external use of force, it could, according to Art. 79 (2) of the Basic Law, have been changed by a majority of two-thirds of the members of both houses of parliament. None of the regulations cited in support of the position that Germany was constrained in the way it could use its military, Art. 87a (2) in particular, forms part of the unalterable core of the Basic Law, as defined in Art. 79 (3). This aspect became increasingly important in the debates as proposals to change the constitution were put forward.[74] Strangely, although Kratochwil's constructivism supposedly focuses on change, there is not much in his extended argument which addresses the phenomenon of norm change. I do not, therefore, investigate the debates about changing the Basic Law here. This issue will be discussed in chapter 4. Suffice it to say that all efforts formally to amend, clarify or alter the constitution failed.

Nevertheless, the government involved the Bundeswehr in a series of international operations. Therefore, a case had to be made as to why they were in accordance with the existing regulations. The missions were portrayed as being below the threshold of a 'deployment' as relevant to Art. 87a (2). The SPD did not accept this representation and the SPD parliamentary group therefore appealed to the constitutional court in July 1992 over participation in Operation Sharp Guard, that is, NATO and WEU measures monitoring the UN embargo against the former Yugoslavia.[75]

---

[73] 'Westeuropas militärischer Einsatz zu gering', *FAZ*, 31 Aug. 1990, 4.

[74] See the different proposals: Deutscher Bundestag, *Drucksache*, 12/2896, 23 Jun. 1992 (SPD); Deutscher Bundestag, *Drucksache*, 12/3014, 2 Jul. 1992 (Bündnis90/Die Grünen); Deutscher Bundestag, *Drucksache*, 12/3055, 21 Jul. 1992 (PDS/Linke Liste); Deutscher Bundestag, *Drucksache*, 12/4135, 15 Jan. 1993 (CDU/CSU and FDP).

[75] 'Verstimmung im Kabinett über Adria-Einsatz der "Hamburg"', *FAZ*, 20 Nov. 1992, 1–2, here 2.

It was the participation in the AWACS contingent monitoring the flight ban over Bosnia and Herzegovina, however, that made the legal process significant. Due to the constitutional situation, German soldiers had had a special status from the start. Aircraft with Germans in their crews could fly only over NATO territory, not over Hungary or Austria. The decision to enforce, rather than just monitor the flight ban, created further problems. AWACS crews were to pass on communication between fighter pilots and their base. In terms of international law, this made them combatants. As a consequence, the FDP wanted to withdraw the German soldiers because such a mission was, in their view, not covered by the Basic Law. Yet, the situation was complicated. As *Der Spiegel* pointed out, as a lawyer, Kinkel argued that 'the Germans ha[d] to get out of the NATO planes because of the constitutional situation', whilst as the foreign minister he feared 'terrible damage in terms of foreign policy'.[76] Defence Minister Rühe claimed that pulling out amounted to sabotaging the mission because one-third of the AWACS crews were German.[77] In March the governing parties reached an agreement to the effect that if a decision by the cabinet became necessary – the UN Security Council had not yet extended the mandate to include enforcement of the flight ban – FDP ministers would abstain and the FDP parliamentary group would then appeal to the constitutional court.[78] This put the FDP in a contradictory position. In effect their ministers were going along with a government decision considered unconstitutional by the party. On 2 April 1993 the government decided not to withdraw German soldiers from the AWACS crews despite the UN's decision in Resolution 816 to enforce the flight ban over Bosnia militarily.[79] In response, the SPD parliamentary group introduced a motion to demand that the government take back its decision on the grounds that it was unconstitutional.[80]

More significantly, both the SPD and the FDP appealed to the constitutional court. Three separate Bundeswehr deployments were at issue

[76] Quoted in '50 Prozent für die Witwe', *Der Spiegel*, 2/47, 11 Jan. 1993, 32–4, here 34.
[77] 'Raus aus dem Dilemma', interview with Volker Rühe, *Der Spiegel*, 52/46, 21 Dec. 1992, 21–3, here 21–2.
[78] 'FDP will gegen CDU/CSU in Karlsruhe klagen', *SZ*, 25 Mar. 1993, 1; Stefan Kornelius und Udo Bergdoll, 'Selbstüberlistung – ein Fall fürs höchste Gericht', *SZ*, 26 Mar. 1993, 3; Josef Joffe, 'Die "peinlichste Kabinettssitzung des Jahres"', *SZ*, 2 Apr. 1993, 4; 'Unionsminister im Kabinett für AWACS-Kampfeinsatz', *SZ*, 3–4 Apr. 1993, 1.
[79] Bundesverfassungsgericht, 'Urteil des Zweiten Senats vom 8. April 1993 aufgrund der mündlichen Verhandlung vom 7. April 1993', 8 Apr. 1993, E88, 173 and 175. See also, 'AWACS-Streit bringt FDP in die Klemme', *SZ*, 7 Apr. 1993, 2.
[80] Deutscher Bundestag, *Drucksache*, 12/4710, 6 Apr. 1993.

in the final decision: the monitoring of the embargo against Serbia and Montenegro within the framework of NATO and the WEU; the involvement in the enforcement of the flight ban over Bosnia-Herzegovina by NATO forces on behalf of the UN; and the participation in UNOSOM II in Somalia.[81] In the final ruling, published only on 12 July 1994,[82] the court declared that all deployments were in accordance with the Basic Law. They were all based on a UN mandate. Their legal basis was Art. 24 (2) of the Basic Law which allowed for integration into a 'system of mutual collective security'. Art. 87a (2) did not overrule this provision.[83] The court argued that the licence to integrate the FRG into a system of mutual collective security included authorisation 'to take on such tasks as are typically linked to such a system and therefore also to use the Bundeswehr for operations which take place within the framework and according to the rules of such a system'.[84] A system of mutual collective security, the court argued, as a matter of rule, relies also on armed forces. Member states had to be prepared in principle to make them available to preserve or re-establish peace.[85] The Parliamentary Council, which drafted the Basic Law, had been aware of this.[86] The court went on to establish that a 'system of mutual collective security'

> constitutes, through a system of rules which ensure peace and through building up its own organisation, a status of restriction in terms of international law which mutually commits to the preservation of peace and grants security. It does not matter whether the system is thereby meant exclusively or mainly to guarantee peace among the member states or to oblige collective assistance in the event of an attack from outside.[87]

Therefore, alliances for collective self-defence can be 'systems of mutual collective security' if they are committed exclusively to the preservation of peace.[88] According to the court, both the UN and NATO satisfy these criteria.[89] As a result, all of the deployments were constitutional because

---

[81] Bundesverfassungsgericht, 'Urteil des Zweiten Senats', 12 Jul. 1994, E90, 305–13.
[82] For legal commentaries on the ruling see Georg Nolte, 'Bundeswehreinsätze in kollektiven Sicherheitssystemen. Zum Urteil des Bundesverfassungsgerichts vom 12. Juli 1994', *Zeitschrift für ausländisches öffentliches und Völkerrecht* 54 (1994), 652–85 and Manfred H. Wiegandt, 'Germany's International Integration: The Rulings of the German Federal Constitutional Court on the Maastricht Treaty and the Out-of-Area Deployment of German Troops', *The American University Journal of International Law and Policy* 10 (1995), 889–916.
[83] Bundesverfassungsgericht, 'Urteil des Zweiten Senats', 12 Jul. 1994, E90, 344.
[84] Ibid., 345.   [85] Ibid.   [86] Ibid., 346 and 291–2.   [87] Ibid., 349.   [88] Ibid.
[89] Ibid., 349–51.

they constituted a normal part of membership in systems of mutual collective security.[90]

The court refrained from pronouncing an opinion on the contentious issues of what is meant by 'defence' and 'deployment' in Art. 87a, as this was not necessary with respect to the questions at issue. Art. 87a could not, in any case, rule out the usage of the armed forces within a system as envisaged by Art. 24 (2) of the Basic Law. Art. 24 (2) had been part of the Basic Law from the beginning. There was no evidence that the legislators had aimed to limit the authorisation given by Art. 24 (2) with Art. 87a. The point of Art. 87a instead was to regulate the domestic use of the military in the event of a state of emergency. Beyond that there was no intention either to make new uses of the armed forces possible or to limit such uses as had already been authorised by the Basic Law.[91] The court also considered the historical context. Although the FRG did not have an army at the time the Basic Law was created – it did not even have an independent foreign policy – the Parliamentary Council did address the issue of military security. In particular, they were aware that membership in a system of collective security, as mentioned in Art. 24 (2) of the Basic Law, would entail certain commitments, also of a military nature.[92] This court ruling meant that any Bundeswehr deployment in the framework of a collective security system was constitutional. There were only two scenarios in which the legal situation was still in question: it remained open whether the German army might defend a country with which it was not linked in a collective security system and whether it might be used for such unilateral interventions as are permitted by international law.[93]

Several points are important in relation to Kratochwil's argument. Firstly, 'the law' had a noticeable impact on people's attitudes. A lot of heated argument vanished after the court's decision. The Bundestag approved the operations in the Adriatic and on AWACS reconnaissance planes in a special session on 22 July 1994 with the support of the SPD.[94] Although important substantive disagreements remained between politicians and parties, the assurance that the operations were in accordance with the law made a difference. Whether this is related to a specifically German way of dealing with political problems which relies on constitutional legitimation, as some claim, is a moot point.[95] The

---

[90] Ibid., 351–5.   [91] Ibid., 355–7.   [92] Ibid., 291–2.
[93] Nolte, 'Bundeswehreinsätze', 684.
[94] Deutscher Bundestag, *Plenarprotokoll*, 12/240, 22 Jul. 1994, 21208–9.
[95] Paterson, 'Beyond Semi-Sovereignty', 176; Linnenkamp, 'Security Policy', p. 118; Nolte, 'Bundeswehreinsätze', 653.

point is that what was perceived to be 'the law' mattered. As Kratochwil argues, '[o]ur attitudes towards the norms in a society are largely formed by the respect towards "the law" which was inculcated during socialization. Thus, while we may object to *this* or *that* law, compliance with norms is significantly shaped by our values, among which deference to "the law" is one of the most important' (*RND* 63–4). However, the authoritative decision could end only the legal debate. There was still a need to define justified behaviour within the area staked out by the court's ruling. This was partially due to the significance of procedural regulations for the legal realm. Clear regulations as to who could raise grievances with the constitutional court and what sorts of grievances could legitimately be raised meant that what was most controversial in the political domain could not be articulated before the court. Because of procedural regulations the main issue in the decision was not the legality of the external use of force as such, but the rights of the Bundestag in the related decision-making process. The SPD and FDP not only had to appeal as parliamentary groups rather than as parties in order to be able to make the necessary plea that *their* constitutional rights had been violated[96] – note Kratochwil's point on the rules determining who is allowed to speak (*RND* 34) – they were also unable to raise the issue of the legality of Bundeswehr deployments *as such*. On the rights of the Bundestag, the court concluded that 'the deployment of armed forces requires in principle the prior constitutive consent of the Bundestag'.[97]

It seems worth noting at this point that the claim that norms shape behaviour, even if they do not 'cause' it, presents us with some problems. Clearly, the constitutional norms were well institutionalised. They were formulated explicitly and specified the conditions of their applicability. Such explicit formulation, Kratochwil claims, allows for precision (*RND* 78–9 and 53–6). There was, at the start of the debates on German military involvement abroad, even a broadly consensual interpretation of the constitutional norms. Yet, despite these favourable conditions, there was both confusion and disagreement about what the norms meant for concrete cases. This is not surprising as 'at each turning-point a "practical judgment" is required as to how a certain factual situation is to be appraised' (*RND* 240). However, the worry is that even those who had to make the decision about potential Bundeswehr deployments did

---

[96] Art. 93 (1) of the Basic Law; anon. (KER), 'In Rechten und Pflichten verletzt sein', *SZ*, 3–4 Apr. 1993, 5.

[97] Bundesverfassungsgericht, 'Urteil des Zweiten Senats', 12 Jul. 1994, E90, 381; also 381–90.

not have a clear grasp of what the rules entailed. This is reflected in some of Chancellor Kohl's assertions about why sending minesweepers to the Gulf would be legal. On the one hand, reference was made to Art. 24, which allows for integration into a 'system of mutual collective defence'. On the other hand, the government expressed the view that the operation was also about the protection of 1,000 Germans prohibited from leaving Iraq.[98] As a legal argument, this is confused. If Art. 24 legalises the operation then it must be thought to take precedence over Art. 87a (2), in which case the obscure reference to German lives, presumably designed to satisfy the 'only for defence' criterion in Art. 87a (2), would be irrelevant.

Despite the explicit formulation of the rules, it was also possible to make diametrically opposed claims on behalf of the constitution. Former defence minister Rupert Scholz, a constitutional lawyer, argued that there was no restriction on operations outside the NATO area in the Basic Law, whilst Oskar Lafontaine, the SPD candidate for chancellor in the 1990 election, insisted that the Basic Law left no room even to discuss such a deployment.[99] It seems obvious that there was little agreement on what exactly the norms were and what they meant. Although, according to Genscher, the constitutional situation was 'completely clear',[100] the regulations in the Basic Law were also described as 'remarkably unclear'.[101] It is hard to see how the actors can be influenced in their reasoning and acting by the norms if they fail to understand them, or how the norms as such can be said to be influential if different actors view them fundamentally differently. Therefore, it seems problematic to argue that norms guided or constrained choices. Although this bears out Kratochwil's claim that it makes little sense to treat norms as causes (*RND* 5), this point, as discussed below, may also prove a problem for his approach.

Despite the lack of agreement on what the constitutional norms exactly meant, they were considered significant by all participants in the debates within Germany. Even those who held that the Basic Law did not rule out any deployments abroad, as Art. 87a (2), which contains the supposed restriction, is addressed to potential internal uses of the Bundeswehr only, referred to the constitutional regulations, thereby making them an agreed reference point for the debate. Many of them

---

[98] 'Wir müssen erwachsen werden', *Der Spiegel*, 34/44, 20 Aug. 1990, 121–3, here 121.
[99] 'Streit um Bundeswehreinsatz am Golf', *SZ*, 10 Aug. 1990, 2.
[100] 'Keine Mehrheit für Marine-Einsatz im Golf', *SZ*, 16 Aug. 1990, 1.
[101] Anon. (MES), 'An den Golf nur mit der UNO', *SZ*, 16 Aug. 1990, 4.

also suggested that the constitution should be amended to avoid the impression that the government was just changing the interpretation to suit itself.[102] Thus, the normative power of the interpretation was considered significant even by those who disagreed with it. The existence of the norms had an impact on how people were reasoning. *'The important issue for investigation then becomes under what circumstances which type of reasons serve as a sufficient justification for following a rule'* (*RND* 97). It is this reasoning process which will be explored in more detail now.

Norms as the basis of intersubjectivity

The court ruling could not answer the crucial question of whether the FRG *should* get involved in international military operations. Therefore, immediately after its publication, Rudolf Scharping, the SPD candidate for chancellor at the time, argued on behalf of his party that now the question of what future foreign policy should be like was open.[103] Although the debate had revolved around constitutionality, it had involved broader normative considerations from the start. As the 1994 White Paper states, 'joint responsibility and participation is *rightly* demanded of Germany'.[104] Legal norms are important in the attempt to legitimise or delegitimise certain political positions. They were used to support what politicians considered right in the context of more broadly moral considerations. The constitutional norms, as has been demonstrated, also helped constitute the issue as a problem in the first place. Yet normative considerations beyond the relatively clear rules of the legal system were used to justify, communicate and criticise certain options (cf. *RND* 11). The relevance of broader normative questions was asserted, for instance, when Chancellor Kohl pointed out that 'the people starving in Somalia [could] not wait until the German parties have finished their argument about the constitution'.[105] In other words, there

---

[102] Ulrich Irmer, 'SPD darf sich nicht länger verweigern', *Pressedienst der FDP Bundestagsfraktion*, 11 Jan. 1992, quoted in Philippi, *Bundeswehr-Auslandseinsätze*, p. 102; 'Kontroverse um Militärstrategie', *FR*, 20 Feb. 1992, 1; Leicht, 'Mit Volldampf', 3; 'Rühe ändert seine Ansicht zur Möglichkeit von Kampfeinsätzen', *FAZ*, 23 Nov. 1992, 1–2, here 2; Stefan Kornelius, 'Die Hüter der reinen Lehre bremsen die Interpretationskünstler', *SZ*, 21 Dec. 1992, 5; 'Regierung über Bundeswehr-Einsätze tief zerstritten', *SZ*, 8 Jan. 1993, 2.
[103] Deutscher Bundestag, *Plenarprotokoll*, 12/240, 22 Jul. 1994, 21170.
[104] BMV, *Weißbuch 1994*, p. 45, section 319 (italics added).
[105] Quoted in 'Eine regelrechte Psychose', *Der Spiegel*, 52/46, 21 Dec. 1992, 18–20, here 18. Rühe is attributed with a similar statement in 'Bonn will sofort helfen', *SZ*, 12–13 Dec. 1992, 9.

was something other, and arguably more important, than German constitutional law at stake. A similar point had long been made by Burkhard
Hirsch of the FDP who had argued that the constitutional debate covered up the real question which was – if the FRG was meant to take on
greater responsibility as everyone argued – 'how, why and with respect
to whom [it had to] accept this responsibility.'[106]

When Kratochwil speaks of rules and norms he refers to more than
the law. The reasoning process in moral discourse is similar to legal reasoning in several ways. Both involve an element of heteronomy, that
is, regard for the other. Moreover, both display a process of principled argumentation which leads to an equally principled application
of the respective norms (*RND* 142 and 208). Practical reasoning involves not just a statement of personal preferences. Claims cannot be
advanced on merely idiosyncratic grounds because the ' "logic" of arguing requires that our claims satisfy certain criteria' (*RND* 12). Therefore, good reasons have to be advanced not only in legal but also in
practical and moral disputes. Kratochwil points out that '[c]laims that
something *is* right, i.e., the right thing to do, make necessary the giving
of reasons and invites [*sic*] challenges on the basis of intersubjectively
shared standards' (*RND* 160). In situations where what is at stake is
'gaining adherence to an alternative in a situation in which no logically compelling solution is possible but a choice cannot be avoided'
(*RND* 210), rhetoric, which serves to strengthen the plausibility of one's
position, becomes significant. It is wrong, according to Kratochwil, to
understand rhetoric as merely dressing up appearances, for it 'is concerned with the problem of praxis, i.e. the necessity of choice in situations where no logically compelling solution is possible'.[107] This may
be the case in both legal and moral arguments. Nevertheless, the two
differ significantly. Firstly, actors themselves normally make distinctions between 'the prescriptive force of legal norms and imperatives
of "comity" or "morality"' (*RND* 36). Moreover, moral arguments are
often indeterminate whilst legal arguments must lead to a decision.
The possibility of coming to a definite decision at the end of a legal
disagreement is ensured by procedural rules, concerning, for example, what counts as evidence or under which circumstances certain
rules will come into effect. In contrast, moral arguments use wider
principles rather than more narrowly defined rules and the debate is

---

[106] Deutscher Bundestag, *Plenarprotokoll*, 12/132, 15 Jan. 1993, 11480.
[107] Kratochwil, 'Is International Law "Proper" Law?', 40.

likely to turn on whether certain principles were applicable at all (*RND* 207).

In a debate addressing the question of what should be done, such as whether the FRG should take part in international operations, we expect people not only to assert positions but to explain and justify them in a way accessible to others. The question is how shared understanding or intersubjectivity develops. As Kratochwil argues, '[c]ommon understandings can be arrived at through the stabilization and evocation of generally shared expectations among actors in a specific situation. The medium of understanding is then neither logical cogency or semantic truth, but rather *claims to the validity of norms* on the basis of which actors can communicate, coordinate their actions, and adjust their preferences' (*RND* 32). What is important in this process of communication and reasoning is not necessarily the coherence of the argument in strictly logical terms. After all, both legal and practical reasoning become relevant when a 'logical' solution is not available. They are about persuading others of choices which are not logically compelling. Kratochwil draws attention to the significance of the starting points of the argument (*RND* 38). The premises from which an argument starts are crucial for arriving at a decision (*RND* 37). Therefore, this kind of reasoning requires the choice of a 'narrative' which contextualises the argument (*RND* 213). Topoi or commonplaces are significant. A 'topos is . . . a *shared judgment* in a society that enables the respective actors to back their choices by means of accepted beliefs, rules of preference, or general classification schemes' (*RND* 218). Topoi are decisive for attaining assent to practical choices (*RND* 38).

> Topoi, or commonplaces, thus not only establish 'starting-points' for arguments, but locate the issues of a debate in a substantive set of common understandings that provide for the crucial connections within the structure of the argument. Precisely because topoi reflect our commonsense understandings, these general topoi are 'persuasive' and can easily be resorted to when technical knowledge about an issue is lacking or has become problematic. (*RND* 219–20)

Making a case for or against German participation in international military operations then involves appealing to principles and common understandings that are likely to be agreed upon by other people but that also contextualise them in a narrative in such a way that a particular position can be supported. To show whether this was the case requires a complex argument. My exploration will take two steps. Firstly, I will demonstrate how certain normative commitments, principles or commonplaces were shared amongst a number of people. This involves showing that both those arguing for participation in international operations and those who rejected this course of action alluded to some of the same norms. In order to do this, I will present together statements made in relation to different conflicts and at different points in time, according to the norms on which they are based. However, this leads to a 'decontextualised' presentation of the norms. Therefore, I will, secondly, analyse three key speeches in one particular Bundestag debate to investigate more closely the strategies of reasoning pursued by appealing to these norms.

In relation to the Gulf War, two normative principles immediately emerged in the political reasoning. The first was based on the idea that war had to be avoided, the second on the necessity of opposing dictatorship. Quite a few German politicians opposed war as an instrument of politics either in principle or for Germany specifically. Most prominently, Foreign Minister Genscher argued that war could under no circumstances be a means of politics. This view was influenced by his experiences of the Second World War.[108] Willi Hoss of Bündnis90/Die Grünen questioned the permissibility of war as a means of solving conflict in principle.[109] Heidemarie Wieczorek-Zeul of the SPD drew attention to the German people's aversion to war because of the past. They did not, according to her, want German soldiers to go to war forty-six years after the end of the Second World War.[110] Conservative politicians agreed that Germans were weary of war.[111] Gregor Gysi, the chairman of the PDS, argued that German history should lead to self-restraint such that the FRG would not engage in war unless it was attacked.[112] As a consequence, the PDS wanted to exclude participation in war altogether.[113] These points drive towards the rejection of war as a policy option, in particular for Germans.

Yet this was only one side of the story. One of the prominent narratives in relation to the Gulf War relied on drawing an analogy between Iraq

[108] 'Die Deutschen an die Front', *Der Spiegel*, 6/45, 4 Feb. 1991, 18–22, here 19.
[109] Deutscher Bundestag, *Plenarprotokoll*, 11/235, 15 Nov. 1990, 18849.
[110] Deutscher Bundestag, *Plenarprotokoll*, 12/2, 14 Jan. 1991, 41.
[111] Michaela Geiger (CDU/CSU) in Deutscher Bundestag, *Plenarprotokoll*, 11/235, 15 Nov. 1990, 18847; Helmut Kohl (chancellor) in Deutscher Bundestag, *Plenarprotokoll*, 12/2, 14 Jan. 1991, 23.
[112] Deutscher Bundestag, *Plenarprotokoll*, 12/2, 14 Jan. 1991, 35.
[113] Motion of PDS members of parliament in Deutscher Bundestag, *Drucksache*, 12/28, 11 Jan. 1991.

and Nazi Germany or, more specifically, Saddam Hussein and Adolf Hitler, and therefore suggested a different judgement as to what the situation was and what sort of response was required. Although Saddam was sometimes explicitly called the 'Hitler of the Middle East' or the 'Hitler of Arabia',[114] the comparison usually worked by implication. The point made through this comparison was that historical experience showed a policy of appeasement to be a mistake with terrible consequences. Chancellor Kohl, for instance, stated that the Federal Government had supported all resolutions of the UN Security Council with respect to the Gulf War in the conviction that law must never yield to injustice, that, as German history taught, aggressors must be stopped in time and that the preservation of law and peace in each region of the world was a matter of concern for the whole community of peoples.[115] The idea that aggressors had to be opposed decisively was voiced not only by the chancellor. Otto Graf Lambsdorff of the FDP argued that the Germans especially must not forget the potential consequences of not opposing an aggressor in time.[116] The point of these historical analogies was to portray the military operation of the Western allies against Iraq as decisive action against a dictator and therefore as justified. Hans-Ulrich Klose of the SPD supported military action, as well. He arrived at this conclusion, not shared by many in his party at the time, through the comparison between Saddam and Hitler. Calling Saddam a 'second Hitler', he predictably concluded that aggressors had to be stopped. Appeasement was, he argued, as history showed, not a viable option.[117] The analogy was therefore used to support German military involvement abroad.

Moreover, the Germans' horrible experiences with war and dictatorship not only induced a desire to avoid war in the future. They could also be construed as constituting a special responsibility. As Foreign Minister Kinkel put it: 'The experience of our most recent history, namely the period of the National-Socialist dictatorship with an inhuman and destructive regime and the regime of injustice of a different kind in the former

---

[114] Vera Wollenberger (Bündnis90/Die Grünen) in Deutscher Bundestag, *Plenarprotokoll*, 12/2, 14 Jan. 1991, 36; 'Der erste Schritt auf dem Marsch gegen Israel', *SZ*, 4–5 Aug. 1990, 4.
[115] Deutscher Bundestag, *Plenarprotokoll*, 12/2, 14 Jan. 1991, 22; Deutscher Bundestag, *Plenarprotokoll*, 12/3, 17 Jan. 1991, 47.
[116] Helmut Kohl (chancellor) in Deutscher Bundestag, *Plenarprotokoll*, 12/2, 14 Jan. 1991, 23; Graf Lambsdorff (FDP), ibid., 32; Graf Lambsdorff (FDP) in Deutscher Bundestag, *Plenarprotokoll*, 12/3, 17 Jan. 1991, 51.
[117] Klose, 'Die Deutschen und der Krieg am Golf', 6.

GDR, really establishes a special responsibility for German foreign policy, to actively promote peace and human rights in the international realm.'[118] According to Chancellor Kohl, this 'special responsibility' led to a second imperative, also considered a response to the Nazi past: never again fascism. 'Never again war! Never again dictatorship!'[119] This 'double oath' was often considered to be at the heart of German postwar identity, an expression of the lessons of the Second World War and the Third Reich. Kohl reconfirmed this twofold normative commitment on the eve of German unification and expressed his intention to use history as a guide to the future.[120]

Both war and fascism were evils which had to be opposed. Since they had come together in the past, the rejection of each was thought to reinforce the rejection of the other. Yet if Saddam was like Hitler, then the opposition to his dictatorship would, as the failure of appeasement in the 1930s showed, have to take the form of war. Hence, the two normative principles were now seen to be in tension. What was at issue was not preventing an oppressive regime coming to power in Germany but rather taking a stand against dictatorship and potentially genocide elsewhere, in Iraq and later the former Yugoslavia. Alice H. Cooper observed: 'Incipiently during the Gulf War and emphatically in Bosnia, parts of the left saw themselves confronted with a conflict between fundamental values that had been considered mutually reinforcing during the Cold War: between antifascism and pacifism; between internationalism and pacifism; and between collective security and antimilitarism.'[121] These tensions were a problem not only for 'the left' as the competing values were considered fundamental to German postwar culture.[122] According to Kohl, the Basic Law was based on them. Concretely, the question became whether the Nazi past obliged the FRG to prevent aggression and mass expulsion in the former Yugoslavia or whether it rather prohibited the country from militarily intervening in the region.[123]

The two themes of general opposition to war and the necessity of war in the face of aggression and oppression kept appearing in discussions

[118] Deutscher Bundestag, *Plenarprotokoll*, 12/101, 22 Jul. 1992, 8609.
[119] Helmut Kohl (chancellor) in Deutscher Bundestag, *Plenarprotokoll*, 11/228, 4 Oct. 1990, 18019.
[120] Ibid.
[121] Cooper, 'Just Causes', 103. See also Markovits and Reich, *German Predicament*, p. 146.
[122] See Cora Stephan, 'An der deutschen Heimatfront', *Der Spiegel*, 10/45, 4 Mar. 1991, 242.
[123] Calic, 'German Perspectives', p. 58.

about potential participation in different international operations. Obviously, those who opposed military involvement abroad referred to the 'never again war' principle. The Social Democrats, according to Peter Glotz, had a clear position on war: 'The Germans have led enough wars in this century. We are not available and pretty unsuited for the task of world policeman or assistant world policemen.'[124] Germans had killed millions in this century and millions of Germans had been killed. Therefore, Glotz claimed, the Germans had a right to say that they would help financially, logistically etc., but that they wanted to be left alone when it came to war.[125] According to Günter Verheugen, there was a tradition in German foreign policy, represented by the SPD, which argued that war could not be a means of politics.[126] Because of its history, Germany had always to stress the peaceful possibilities.[127] Wolfgang Ullmann of the Greens pointed out that the UN had developed because of what originated in Germany from 1939 onwards and that this challenge could not be met by 'irresponsible brandishing of arms'.[128] The PDS/Linke Liste parliamentary group argued that an 'awareness of German history' obliged Germany to exert the utmost restraint in military matters.[129] Clearly, those rejecting military involvement drew on a shared notion about the necessity of avoiding war and they displayed an awareness of doing so.

Indeed, some argued that this was or had until recently been a broader consensus. In opposition to one of the government's attempts to change the Basic Law in order to make participation in international operations possible, Verheugen of the SPD argued:

> With this change in the Basic Law you are entering a dangerous, slippery slope. You radically break with our previously shared conviction which we have learnt from German history: that war must not be a means of politics any more. Up to now this has belonged to the existential foundations of our understanding of the state and has held us together domestically.[130]

Uwe-Jens Heuer of the PDS/Linke Liste pointed out that, because of the historical experience, he would have considered the notion that

[124] Deutscher Bundestag, *Plenarprotokoll*, 12/151, 21 Apr. 1993, 12968.
[125] Ibid., 12969.
[126] Günter Verheugen (SPD), ibid., 12951.
[127] Rudolf Scharping (prime minister of Rhineland-Palatinate) in Deutscher Bundestag, *Plenarprotokoll*, 12/240, 22 Jul. 1994, 21174.
[128] Deutscher Bundestag, *Plenarprotokoll*, 12/150, 26 Mar. 1993, 12879.
[129] Deutscher Bundestag, *Drucksache*, 12/3055, 21 Jul. 1992.
[130] Deutscher Bundestag, *Plenarprotokoll*, 12/132, 15 Jan. 1993, 11479.

he would have to contribute to decisions about war deployments of German soldiers 'absurd' only a short time earlier.[131] His colleague Andrea Lederer claimed that a lesson drawn from the fact that two world wars had started in Germany had been the consensus for forty years: 'The consensus was: War must never again emanate from German soil.'[132] Now, however, one could see a militarisation of foreign policy expressed in the continuity of rearmament, nuclear upgrading and international deployments.[133] Lederer complained that '[a]ll parties, especially the SPD, have stated: Never again German soldiers in other countries! War must never again emanate from German soil! – I really ask myself seriously why this should have become different today.'[134]

This reliance on the 'never again war' principle to justify their position was an obvious move for those who opposed Bundeswehr deployments abroad. Interestingly, however, this rejection of war could also be found amongst those who were in principle in favour of participation in international military operations. It was framed as a 'culture of restraint' by the government. Defence Minister Rühe, referring also to Kohl's conviction on this matter, stated that the Germans should exercise restraint for historical reasons.[135] In the parliamentary debate about the ruling of the constitutional court, Foreign Minister Kinkel was at pains to make clear that the removal of perceived legal restrictions did not mean that German foreign policy would change decisively. The culture of restraint would remain. German participation in military operations would not be automatic. There would be no militarisation of German foreign policy.[136] In the same context, Günther Friedrich Nolting, on behalf of the FDP, stated continued support for the 'confidence-building foreign policy, the responsible restraint'.[137] Military involvement was, according to these arguments, permissible only because it would prevent war. As Wolfgang Schäuble put it, participation in AWACS and the deployment to Somalia were about 'securing the peace task of the Bundeswehr' which meant 'to avoid war at all costs'.[138] Thus, the 'never again war' principle was in some sense agreed across the political

---

[131] Deutscher Bundestag, *Plenarprotokoll*, 12/151, 21 Apr. 1993, 12954.
[132] Andrea Lederer (PDS/Linke Liste), ibid., 12942–3.   [133] Ibid., 12942.
[134] Deutscher Bundestag, *Plenarprotokoll*, 12/132, 15 Jan. 1993, 11472.
[135] Deutscher Bundestag, *Plenarprotokoll*, 12/151, 21 Apr. 1993, 12946.
[136] Deutscher Bundestag, *Plenarprotokoll*, 12/240, 22 Jul. 1994, 21167; Kinkel, 'Peacekeeping Missions', 4.
[137] Deutscher Bundestag, *Plenarprotokoll*, 12/240, 22 Jul. 1994, 21204.
[138] Wolfgang Schäuble (CDU/CSU) in Deutscher Bundestag, *Plenarprotokoll*, 12/151, 21 Apr. 1993, 12934.

spectrum. It was used by both sides to explicate and legitimate their positions.

Something similar can be said about the 'never again dictatorship' principle. Kinkel pointed out that the situation in Nazi Germany which had been a threat to global peace and human rights had been ended through the use of violence.[139] He declared that concerning the

> responsibility for peace and human rights no one may stand aside, not even [the Germans]. Precisely because Germany has broken the peace in the past, it is morally–ethically obliged to participate in the defence of peace with all its power now. If there is one lesson from the period of National Socialism which is quite inescapable, then it is that unfortunately violence sometimes can only be removed through counterviolence.[140]

Kinkel argued that those who, despite their opposition to war, were 'not willing to resist the war-monger militarily if necessary, [were] not able to create peace or protect human rights. They only pursue[d] a policy of words.'[141] This idea was repeatedly expressed by Conservative politicians. Christian Schmidt said that

> It is wrong to make up the historical argument, that we should never again be allowed to participate in the peaceful–humanitarian sense of the United Nations somewhere, because earlier on these instruments have been misused for aggression. On the contrary, from our historical responsibility flows the obligation to help end these violations of human rights in those places where violations of human rights originate.[142]

The same notion was taken up by Defence Minister Rühe when he argued that the 'concentration camps in Germany were closed solely by soldiers and not through resolutions...Therefore the use of the military can be morally very imperative.'[143] Freimut Duve of the SPD agreed. He argued that he had 'always understood the question of the singularity of Germany's genocide of the Jews as the task to prevent future genocide and also to ask questions when it starts and not only to ask questions when it has been carried out'.[144] His colleague Rudolf

---

[139] Deutscher Bundestag, *Plenarprotokoll*, 12/132, 15 Jan. 1993, 11474.
[140] Deutscher Bundestag, *Plenarprotokoll*, 12/240, 22 Jul. 1994, 21166.
[141] Ibid., 21167.
[142] Christian Schmidt (CDU/CSU) in Deutscher Bundestag, *Plenarprotokoll*, 12/132, 15 Jan. 1993, 11493.
[143] Ibid., 11484.
[144] Deutscher Bundestag, *Plenarprotokoll*, 12/151, 21 Apr. 1993, 12970.

Scharping claimed that the humanitarian situation and the Germans' own 'bitter experiences' put them under an obligation 'to stand up passionately for peace and freedom and also for being free from violence and hatred'.[145] So, again, there was a degree of common understanding with respect to the need to oppose oppression. The same point was also often framed with respect to responsibility. As Kinkel put it: 'we should consider the horrors of the past. But we especially have a special responsibility from this past to contribute towards the restoration of peace, non-violence and human rights.'[146] Kinkel also spoke of the FRG's growing responsibility.[147]

The question of international responsibility was a major issue in the debates[148] but further normative notions were also seen to be part of the relevant context. The demands of solidarity and multilateralism had to be taken into account. The significance of the latter has already been highlighted in chapter 2. It became important in relation to the debate because it was possible to argue, as Kinkel did, that 'a lesson from this history really can only be: Never again to step out of line of the community of Western peoples'.[149] Similarly, Defence Minister Rühe claimed that '[i]nternational teamwork and the ability to be part of an alliance [we]re an indispensable part of the reasons of state of Germany'.[150] As a consequence, Germans had to be willing to practise solidarity. Or, as he had put it earlier: 'If we act together with others we can never be wrong.'[151] Therefore, other norms had to be understood in relation to the requirements of cooperating with partners, neighbours and the international community. The notions of 'responsibility' and 'solidarity' were invoked so often that Verheugen accused the foreign minister of throwing around key terms like 'solidarity', 'reputation', 'credibility' and 'shirking responsibility' instead of adhering to the principle that German soldiers must not be endangered. Solidarity with the UN could also be shown by participating in peace missions in which there was no historical burden.[152] The important point is that Verheugen agrees

---

[145] Deutscher Bundestag, *Plenarprotokoll*, 13/48, 30 Jun. 1995, 3959.
[146] Deutscher Bundestag, *Plenarprotokoll*, 12/132, 15 Jan. 1993, 11474.
[147] 'Der europäische Weg ist absolut alternativlos', interview with Foreign Minister Klaus Kinkel, *SZ*, 19 May 1992, 8.
[148] See also Calic, 'German Perspectives', p. 53.
[149] Deutscher Bundestag, *Plenarprotokoll*, 12/151, 21 Apr. 1993, 12928.
[150] Deutscher Bundestag, *Plenarprotokoll*, 12/132, 15 Jan. 1993, 11484.
[151] 'Das ist keine Drohgebärde', interview with Defence Minister Volker Rühe, *Der Spiegel*, 30/46, 20 Jul. 1992, 32–5, here 34.
[152] Günter Verheugen (SPD) in Deutscher Bundestag, *Plenarprotokoll*, 13/48, 30 Jun. 1995, 3990.

with rather than questions the significance of these normative notions. Therefore, they may be seen as common reference points which make intersubjectivity and shared meaning possible.

These impressions from the discussions indicate that responsibility, solidarity and multilateralism as well as opposition to war and oppression were important underlying normative notions. However, they do not show how they were used in the reasoning process. This could be observed at any point in the discussions. To be able to analyse it in detail, I focus on one parliamentary debate, referring to other events to contextualise it. It should be noted that within Kratochwil's approach it is legitimate to focus on domestic debate to analyse what may be construed as international phenomena, for, if 'one understands both the international system and the state in terms of normatively constituted practices, international and domestic politics are not hermetically sealed within their own spheres'.[153]

On 16 June 1995 the UN Security Council issued the mandate for an additional rapid reaction force to protect and support UNPROFOR troops already stationed in the former Yugoslavia. On 26 June the Federal Government decided to contribute to the protection and support of this force[154] and on 30 June the Bundestag debated this decision. The government had made the following proposal for which it was seeking support:

> The Bundestag agrees to the deployment of armed troops . . . for the protection and support of the rapid reaction force, designed to enable the UN peace troops in the former Yugoslavia to fulfil their mandate. The aforementioned contribution, complemented by naval forces and additional personnel for international headquarters, is also available for a NATO operation supporting a potential withdrawal.[155]

The debate about this proposal is significant because it was the first time since the ruling of the constitutional court that a deployment of German troops to a 'dangerous international conflict'[156] was under discussion. The legal rules of the Basic Law could not be used any more to support or discredit specific positions. Hence it was necessary to resort to other argumentative strategies such as the appeal to broader normative

---

[153] Koslowski and Kratochwil, 'Understanding Change', 223.
[154] The cabinet decision is reprinted as 'Europäische Truppe schützen und stützen', *SZ*, 27 Jun. 1995, 5. See also 'Deutsche "Tornados" sollen in Bosnien zum Schutz der europäischen Eingreiftruppe eingesetzt werden', *SZ*, 27 Jun. 1995, 1.
[155] Deutscher Bundestag, *Drucksache*, 13/1802, 26 Jun. 1995.
[156] Klaus Kinkel (foreign minister) in Deutscher Bundestag, *Plenarprotokoll*, 13/48, 30 Jun. 1995, 3955.

principles. Moreover, the government had to overcome the normative power of its earlier claims. It had repeatedly stated that it would under no circumstances send soldiers to the Balkans, where Wehrmacht troops had caused havoc during the Second World War.[157] The following statement by Hermann-Otto Solms of the FDP captures the case which had been made:

> One thing must be clear... especially in view of deployments in the former Yugoslavia: There must not be under any circumstances any deployment of German troops in the area of the former Yugoslavia – neither on the water nor on the ground nor in the air. This is imperative if only for historical reasons. In any case, the FDP is fully convinced of that. We know that we share this conviction with the chancellor.[158]

This has been called the 'Kohl doctrine'.[159] The reasoning behind it was a fear of escalation and a concern for the safety of German soldiers,[160] but the argument had been problematic from the start. After all, as some duly pointed out, this ruled out pretty much all of Europe[161] and even beyond, and thereby made the commitment to military involvement abroad meaningless. Nevertheless, the 'Kohl doctrine' remained a shared position,[162] which did not come under real challenge until 1995.[163] Accepting the government's proposal on assistance for the rapid reaction force would arguably break with the Kohl doctrine, although Foreign Minister Kinkel insisted that it would not because no ground troops would be deployed.[164] To secure support for the government's decision, Kinkel justified it in terms of norms which he expected to be shared by others.

[157] See, for example, Volker Rühe (defence minister) in Deutscher Bundestag, *Plenarprotokoll*, 12/151, 21 Apr. 1993, 12947; Kinkel, 'Peacekeeping Missions', 7.
[158] Deutscher Bundestag, *Plenarprotokoll*, 12/151, 21 Apr. 1993, 12941.
[159] Josef Joffe, 'Abschied von der "Kohl-Doktrin"', *SZ*, 16 Dec. 1994, 4.
[160] Kinkel, 'Peacekeeping Missions', 7; 'Länger verheddern', *Der Spiegel*, 40/49, 2 Oct. 1995, 36–8, here 37; 'Wir haben eine neue Rolle übernommen', interview with Volker Rühe, *Der Spiegel*, 42/49, 16 Oct. 1995, 24–7, here 24.
[161] Josef Joffe, 'Abschied von der "Kohl-Doktrin"', *SZ*, 16 Dec. 1994, 4; Dorff, 'Normal Actor?', 58; Michael E. Smith, 'Sending the Bundeswehr', 54.
[162] See also, for example, Karsten Voigt (SPD) in Deutscher Bundestag, *Plenarprotokoll*, 12/240, 22 Jul. 1994, 21201; Wolfgang Ullmann (Bündnis90/Die Grünen) in Deutscher Bundestag, *Plenarprotokoll*, 12/150, 26 Mar. 1993, 12879; Andrea Lederer (PDS/Linke Liste) in Deutscher Bundestag, *Plenarprotokoll*, 12/151, 21 Apr. 1993, 12944.
[163] Unless participation in the AWACS mission from 1993 overturned the 'not to Yugoslavia' principle as the PDS/Linke Liste claimed. See Deutscher Bundestag, *Drucksache*, 12/4711, 5 Apr. 1993.
[164] Deutscher Bundestag, *Plenarprotokoll*, 13/48, 30 Jun. 1995, 3957.

Kinkel started his speech by assigning special historical significance to the decision the Bundestag was about to make, and invoked other political decisions which were seen to have set the direction of future policy: the establishment of the Bundeswehr, joining NATO, the renunciation of nuclear weapons, the implementation of NATO's twin-track decision and the policy of reconciliation with Eastern neighbours.[165] Thereby he made the matter at issue part of a series of decisions which not only were considered extremely significant but which also, with the exception of *Ostpolitik*, were often framed as demands of being part of the West. In choosing this starting point, Kinkel made clear that integration with the West was an underlying norm in terms of which he intended to explain and justify the government's decision. Integration with the West had, significantly, been considered a safeguard against a return to militarism and fascism.[166]

Membership in international institutions was an expression of this integration. In the international fora Germany had supported the creation of the rapid reaction force. Therefore, there was, according to Kinkel, only one possible course of action: 'We want to and have to show solidarity.'[167] The need to contribute to the military force in the former Yugoslavia was based, in Kinkel's argument, on the need to show solidarity with the countries which had been carrying the burden of the loss of lives of their citizens in an effort to help other human beings, in particular France and Great Britain, and with those 'innocent' people who were dying cruel deaths in the former Yugoslavia.[168] Germany had to show solidarity with its allies because it had received protection and solidarity with respect to security issues from its 'friends and partners' during the Cold War. According to Kinkel, solidarity was expected from Germany and this expectation was legitimate.[169] In this argument, helping the suffering people in the former Yugoslavia and participating in the actions of the Western partners, which seem to be two distinct ideas, were merged in the concept of solidarity.

The claim that solidarity necessitated participating in the military operation was embedded in an interpretation of the meaning of history. During the Cold War, Kinkel argued, Germany, in view of its history and the division of the country, had focused on territorial defence. This 'culture of restraint' had been good and accepted. Yet after the fall of the Iron Curtain, reunification and gaining full sovereignty, Germany

[165] Ibid., 3955.   [166] See ch. 2.
[167] Deutscher Bundestag, *Plenarprotokoll*, 13/48, 30 Jun. 1995, 3956.
[168] Ibid., 3955–6.   [169] Ibid., 3956.

was now expected 'actively to contribute towards the protection of the international order and of human rights, especially in Europe'.[170] Kinkel argued, then, that Germans had 'a political and moral obligation to help, also and particularly in view of our history'.[171] He noted that it had been the Allies who, using military force, had freed the Germans from Nazi dictatorship and made a new democratic beginning possible. This, he claimed, had been forgotten too quickly. The Germans had not liberated themselves from the regime.[172] This links the deployment to the duty to oppose oppression. Kinkel also claimed that the world was watching how the Bundestag decided this case, whether the Germans were reliable, capable of showing solidarity and being part of an alliance, whether they would contribute to giving the peace mission in Bosnia a last chance or whether the Germans would shirk whilst their friends and partners made a big additional effort. Those who wanted the peace-keepers to remain in Bosnia had to contribute to making it possible. A lowering of the threshold for military involvement was, according to Kinkel, not at issue. The decision was not about waging war but about preventing war.[173] This was a reference to the 'never again war' principle which was, however, located in the context of the competing normative commitments of solidarity and integration.

Kinkel reminded people that taking up more international responsibility was not always pleasant. Showing solidarity implied sharing burdens, risks and dangers. The deployment was a necessary but difficult step. Any other reaction would damage German credibility and isolate the country. However, this step implied risks and dangers. The soldiers' lives could be lost. Therefore, the soldiers had to know that the Bundestag supported them. Their mission was a humanitarian one to give people in the former Yugoslavia a chance of peace and survival. Germany's partners and friends should know that it was not merely paying lip-service to its increasing responsibility.[174] Saying 'without me', as the SPD had been accused of doing in the 1950s in discussions about rearmament,[175] or reacting ambiguously would be shirking responsibility. Kinkel finished his speech by asking the members of parliament, including the opposition, to show solidarity with 'our allies, our soldiers, but in particular with the people in a truly sorely afflicted country!'[176]

---

[170] Ibid., 3957.   [171] Ibid.   [172] Ibid.   [173] Ibid.   [174] Ibid., 3958.
[175] Donald Abenheim, *Reforging the Iron Cross: The Search for Tradition in the West German Armed Forces* (Princeton University Press, 1988), p. 43.
[176] Deutscher Bundestag, *Plenarprotokoll*, 13/48, 30 Jun. 1995, 3959.

Kinkel explained the need to send German forces to the former Yugoslavia in terms of solidarity and responsibility, more specifically the solidarity within the context of Western integration and the responsibility to oppose oppressive regimes. He also referred to the 'never again war' principle which, some would have argued, he was about to abandon. Kinkel referred to norms and principles in order to make sense of his position, communicate his ideas, justify his claims and criticise those of others (*RND* 11). Thereby he indicated the space in which he thought the issue was to be discussed.

Opposition to the government's proposal was couched in terms of some of the same norms. The leader of the SPD opposition Rudolf Scharping, for instance, argued that the humanitarian situation and the Germans' own 'bitter experiences' put them under an obligation 'to stand up passionately for peace and freedom and also for being free from violence and hatred'.[177] Thereby he referred to the opposition both to war and to oppression. He went on to argue that the only criterion for Germany's policy had to be how it would be possible to help the people in Bosnia-Herzegovina. Although Kinkel's case had been about the need to end oppressive violence and solidarity with people in distress, too, the aspect of how best to help people in Bosnia was not prominent in his considerations.

Scharping also referred to the significance of Western integration when he accused the government of having contributed towards the existing situation with its policy of rapidly recognising Croatia and Slovenia in 1991. He portrayed this as Germany having gone astray from the Western community,[178] something he considered problematic. However, he did not draw Kinkel's conclusion that this deployment was required to ensure that the FRG remained close to its partners.[179] Scharping supported the rapid reaction force as such but thought that the imperative not to send German soldiers to the Balkans due to historical reasons was more significant for this particular decision. The only military option the SPD was willing to consider was enforcing the embargo with troops under UN command.[180] This underlines the significance Scharping attributed to integration. If troops were not under German control, they could intervene abroad. In Scharping's argument, as in Kinkel's, integration could therefore overrule the imperative against war. He did not oppose the use of force as such. According to Scharping, the Social Democrats supported it insofar as it would help the

[177] Ibid.   [178] Ibid., 3960.   [179] See also ibid., 3964–5.   [180] Ibid., 3961.

population and as it would further a peaceful solution. However, the use of armed force had to be strictly limited to aiding a peaceful end to the conflict.[181] German participation was, he argued, likely to escalate the conflict. Scharping stated his respect for the foreign minister's decision to review his position in the light of new developments and a re-evaluation of arguments. Kinkel should, however, also respect those who, on the basis of his previous arguments and an evaluation of the facts, wanted to stick with a decision which used to represent a consensus.[182] Consequently, Scharping accepted the normative context in which Kinkel had presented his argument but rejected his conclusion.

Although Scharping used many references to history, as well, there did not seem to be an overall narrative comparable to Kinkel's. The beauty of Kinkel's story, in terms of supporting his position, was that it pushed those opposed to his view into a politically unappealing corner. By default, they were portrayed both as failing to show solidarity with people in distress and with those who had helped them in the past, and as rejecting their historical responsibility. Moreover, they were represented as denying the foundational moment of the FRG. Scharping's story was that, because of the disastrous history, the FRG must always stand up for peace and freedom and put people at the centre of its policy. What mattered were the people in Bosnia. The weakness of this story was that it failed to make clear why Scharping's approach would be more helpful for the people than any other. He also portrayed the government's policy of recognition in 1991 as having left the consensus of the Western community and therefore as at the root of the problem. Be that as it may, this argument seems to be beside the point. Moreover, Scharping established that the government's proposal constituted an about-turn in German foreign policy. The trouble with this was that most politicians were not disputing this in the first place. So, in order to get some mileage out of his claim, he would have had to establish why the FRG should *not*, in view of its considerably changed international position, change its foreign policy.

Although German history offers ample material on the less-than-desirable consequences of using the military externally, Scharping failed to produce a credible narrative to this effect. He did, however, offer two historically informed points on why the German military should not go to the former Yugoslavia: the danger of escalation and the danger for German soldiers who might, if captured, become the target of revenge

---

[181] Ibid., 3965.   [182] Ibid., 3961.

for Nazi crimes. Both these points should have been hard to oppose for the government, as it had used them itself only shortly before. They should have provided a potentially intersubjectively shared basis from which to develop a counternarrative. The problem was that Scharping was unable credibly to reject Kinkel's analogy between the Bundeswehr and the Allied liberators of the Second World War. Kratochwil suggests that a possible attack against this type of argument could consist in a 'denial of the appropriateness of the topical analogy' (*RND* 219). Scharping attempted no such thing and therefore was unable to dispel the power of the analogy. He also failed to assert a countertopos. According to Kratochwil, 'the finding of an appropriate countertopos, i.e., providing a different context, is more likely to be persuasive than arduous empirical proofs that the generalization upon which the above argument relies is not true most of the time' (*RND* 219). Scharping disagreed only with details and thus left Kinkel's narrative intact.

In his response to Kinkel's speech, Joschka Fischer, a leading politician of Bündnis90/Die Grünen, drew attention to the government's argument that the deployment was necessary in order to show solidarity in the alliance. If this was true, he argued, one had to ask why the government was limiting its involvement, why it was not sending ground troops. He pointed out that the government had always rejected this possibility for historical reasons. Fischer said that solidarity needed to be contextualised also with respect to what was possible in view of the past and what was therefore politically and morally responsible and justifiable.[183] He accused the government of arguing, in effect, that the FRG had not been capable of forming part of an alliance since 1949 just because it did not send soldiers all over the world.[184] Clearly, Fischer did not reject the idea that solidarity with the Western partners was important.

However, in his view this was not the most fundamental problem which had to be addressed. Rather, the key problem for him was the normative tension between the opposition to war and the opposition to oppression. What was at issue, according to Fischer, was weighing up what one had to do in order to end this horrible war. On the one hand, one might become guilty by not interfering; on the other hand, one might risk escalating the conflict by getting involved and thereby become guilty again.[185] Fischer admitted that the Bosnian conflict posed problems for the Greens as a pacifist party. The return of the most brutal forms of

[183] Ibid., 3972.   [184] Ibid., 3974.   [185] Ibid., 3971.

violence posed the greatest challenge to the basic pacifist position. As long as he was not sure, however, that the decision to deploy troops was going to help rather than lead to a disaster for which all Germans would have to pay, and some probably with their lives, he could not support it.[186] In other words, he was not persuaded that he should abandon his opposition to war in favour of any of the other relevant norms which he recognised to be in tension with this one.

All three politicians appealed to normative ideas and principles to make intelligible and to justify their position. They also all seem to refer to the same set of them. There was no disagreement about the validity of the norms as such. All agreed that war was bad, that people who were being oppressed should be helped, that Western integration was a good thing and so on. Therefore, it was possible to engage in a discussion in which each seemed to understand the other. It could be argued that it was possible for them to share meaning against the background of the norms. The norms could then provide the basis for a discourse in which solutions would be negotiated (*RND* 11 and 70). However, although they all three ostensibly referred to the same norms, each drew radically different conclusions from their adherence to them.

The politics of intersubjectivity and the normative

In order to discuss the issue of participation in international military operations, a number of norms were referred to. If the set of norms mentioned above was powerful in shaping responses to the question of military involvement abroad, then it seems important to look at how they 'hang together'; for what norms mean may depend on which other norms are thought to be related to them. On its own, 'never again war' suggests military abstention. Accordingly, the Basic Law was thought to restrict the external use of the military to collective self-defence. 'Never again war' was meant to ensure that 'only peace w[ould] emanate from German soil'.[187] This interpretation was championed by those, like Scharping and Fischer, who wanted to avoid change in military policy. However, they soon found themselves at odds with what came to be a new reading of the normative context. Whilst responsible practice for the FRG traditionally had been military abstention ensured through

---

[186] Ibid., 3975–6.
[187] Preamble of the Basic Law; 'Vertrag über die abschließende Regelung', Art. 2.

political and military integration in international institutions, taking responsibility increasingly referred to military involvement abroad within
the framework of international institutions. This interpretation relied
on according significance to multilateralism and solidarity with Western partners. In this context, it even became possible to define military
involvement abroad as an expression of the 'never again war' principle.

This shift in how the normative context hung together can be seen in
Kinkel's speech outlined above. He argued that Germany had 'a political and moral obligation to help, also and particularly in view of [its]
history'.[188] He stressed that the Allies had freed the Germans from Nazi
dictatorship *through the use of military force* and thereby had enabled
them to make a new democratic beginning. It was important to remember that the Germans had not accomplished liberation from the regime
themselves.[189] Thus Kinkel likened German military involvement in the
former Yugoslavia to the Allied intervention in the Second World War
and thereby created a new analogy. The Germans were shifted, in this
narrative, to the position of those who liberate, who constitute the hope
for 'innocent' people living and dying in conditions of war and oppression. This move makes the Bundeswehr similar to the heroic liberators
of the Second World War bringing peace and freedom, rather than to
Wehrmacht troops committing atrocities in the Balkans. The moral is
that taking responsibility now involved doing exactly what would have
been considered dangerous and irresponsible earlier. Kinkel thereby
provided a new connection in the 'logical' structure of the 'facts'. As
Kratochwil contends, 'the task of the orator is to point to new connections among "facts" which the audience has not grasped or understood'
(*RND* 217). The starting point for Kinkel's narrative which made sense
of the government's decision was still Germany's Nazi past and the responsibility flowing from it, but he reinterpreted it to constitute a duty to
intervene rather than an imperative to abstain from using military force.
Kinkel referred to the normative notions which had previously constituted the basis of the FRG's non-military identity, such as opposition
to oppression and taking responsibility. However, they now worked to
underpin a duty to use the military instrument.

Kinkel even invoked the 'never again war' imperative. He argued
that the decision to deploy the Bundeswehr to the former Yugoslavia
was not about waging war but about preventing war. The claim that

---

[188] Klaus Kinkel (Foreign Minister) in Deutscher Bundestag, *Plenarprotokoll*, 13/48, 30 Jun.
1995, 3957.
[189] Ibid.

the German Tornado fighters would wage war, he said, turned things on their head. In fact, they would act only in the event of an aggression against the rapid reaction force.[190] Kinkel claimed not to understand the policy of the opposition who were in favour of the UN remaining in Bosnia but refused to deploy ECR-Tornado fighters. He implied that this policy amounted to supporting UNPROFOR remaining in Bosnia to the last Frenchman or Briton.[191] The argument here seemed to be that someone had to do the fighting in order to stop the fighting. Therefore, the deployment would not itself constitute war but rather a prevention of war. It was then in accordance with the 'never again war' principle and not a violation of it, as the opposition claimed. Obviously, the meaning of the principle had shifted. However, Kinkel's case involved an inherent contradiction. In his account, war was defined as that which *the other* was doing. What the Bundeswehr would be doing was something different altogether. It would stop war. Yet Kinkel at the same time stressed that it was necessary to use force as the Allies had done in the Second World War.[192] Unless we are prepared to say that the Allies were not waging war at the time, the logic of Kinkel's argument drives towards an obligation for the FRG to engage in war, which is directly at odds with his claim that the Bundeswehr would only stop war but not itself get involved in any such thing. This contradiction did not, however, prevent this new reading of the normative context from becoming accepted.

Kinkel combined two key arguments in his case for deploying soldiers to the former Yugoslavia. The FRG had to do this to show solidarity with its Western partners and to help fellow human beings who were suffering. The government wanted to prove that it was a reliable ally because the Western allies had always been reliable partners during the Cold War. They had been prepared to defend the FRG when it was necessary; so now the FRG had to be at their side. This emphasis on solidarity with partners and people in distress worked to prioritise the opposition to dictatorship over the opposition to war. Crucially, none of the norms referred to by Kinkel and others can be understood in isolation. Opposition to war could mean not using military force or helping to end the conflict in the former Yugoslavia. What opposing oppression meant was likely to be shaped by how one interpreted the 'never again war' principle and so on. The context in which norms are articulated is therefore significant.

[190] Ibid., 3957–8.   [191] Ibid., 3957.   [192] Ibid.

The government prioritised multilateralism. Given the preferences of the FRG's 'partners and friends' the choice between opposing war and opposing fascism was relatively easy then, especially since the kind of war envisaged could be construed as an opposition to war. Kinkel also stressed that the FRG would not even exist had it not been for the Allied intervention in the Second World War, which ended the barbarity of the Nazi regime. For these reasons, intervention is at least sometimes good. This amounts to a rearticulation of the relationship between the norms against war and against oppression. The use of force was now necessary to prevent war and further suffering. It did not in itself constitute war, which, of course, the government did not want to get involved in. Accordingly, the government studiously avoided the term 'war'. Rather, it referred to 'peace-making measures', 'coping with a crisis situation', the 'last resort' or even 'energetic prevention'.[193] Or, as Ulrich Irmer of the FDP put it, what the German soldiers would participate in was a 'peace mission', not a 'war mission'.[194]

Hence, there was no simple case of norms being in contradiction. Rather a set of norms was in tension but at the same time served to contextualise each other. The contradictory prescriptions of what may be construed as shared norms were acknowledged a number of times. The tension was not only due to different people interpreting the same norms differently. Kinkel's position embraces normative tension within it. His rearticulation of the normative context leaves us with a conundrum if norms are to be significant. Given that Kinkel still referred to the norms which were significant traditionally but came to a different interpretation of them, had the normative context changed or was it still the same? Or, to look at this differently, if Kinkel could argue that the opposition to war required sending soldiers to the former Yugoslavia whereas others claimed that it simply meant not to fight, then one has to ask whether it makes sense to claim that norms were the basis for 'shared meaning'. Thus, if the normative context did provide the basis for intersubjectivity and therefore the space for political debate, it is not at all clear where this space was.

In order to understand this issue more clearly, it is necessary to consider how we determine what qualifies as a norm. The possibility of multiple interpretations of certain normative notions, and the related impossibility of clearly identifying the intersubjective space

---

[193] 'Einsatz ins Ungewisse', *Der Spiegel*, 5/49, 30 Jan. 1995, 68–79, here 71.
[194] Deutscher Bundestag, *Plenarprotokoll*, 13/76, 6 Dec. 1995, 6644.

for discussion they would delineate, might be due to the vagueness of such ideas as responsibility and solidarity or even the two 'never again' principles. Two points can be made. Firstly, although, as I observed earlier, Kratochwil claims that the distinction between norms, rules and values is important, he fails to present a credible criterion that might enable the analyst to separate them. He himself discusses norms and rules together, without clearly distinguishing one from the other.[195] He comments upon the greater generality of values as opposed to norms and their appeal to emotionality rather than rationality (*RND* 64).[196] However, whilst he cites 'good neighborliness' as a general value at one point (*RND* 108), he classifies 'love your neighbor' as a rule at another (*RND* 92–3). The latter seems hardly more specific than, say, 'act in solidarity with your partners'. Thus, my classification of the normative concepts I have discussed as 'norms' seems justified. It also seems unavoidable if extra-legal rules are to be taken into account, as Kratochwil's approach suggests. Secondly, the objection that generic values or broad principles cannot be treated as norms in Kratochwil's sense, even if it was justified, does not resolve the issue; for the question of whether meaning can be seen as shared in the case at hand does not go away if only clearly formulated rules are taken into account. The fascinating point about the constitutional norms is precisely that, although they played an important part in the reasoning process and in how reality was constructed, their meaning was overturned without the norms themselves having changed. The text of the constitution remained the same but its prescriptive force did not, and thus its meaning had arguably changed. In other words, the shift in the meaning of the legal norms was not much different from the shift in the meaning of the 'never again war' principle: on the surface the norms stayed the same but they were now taken to mean something different entirely.

The question is whether this is a problem for Kratochwil's approach at all. Is it indeed important to his analysis whether or not the speaker and the addressee share an understanding of the situation? After all, as the material presented from the debates in Germany suggests, actors did refer to norms in order to support their positions and communicate them to others. This would seem to prove Kratochwil's point. Yet, his argument hinges on the possibility of intersubjectivity. His profound critique of the positivist approach is based on its failure to consider

[195] *RND*, esp. chs. 3 and 4.
[196] See also Friedrich Kratochwil, 'Norms and Values: Rethinking the Domestic Analogy', *Ethics and International Affairs* 1 (1987), 154–8.

intersubjective meaning.[197] The point of exploring rules, norms and reasoning processes is to take into account the intersubjective context. The possibility of intersubjectively shared interpretations is necessary to Kratochwil's methodological claims. There is, he argues, nothing idiosyncratic about interpretations because meaning is shared.[198] Referring to the context of rules and norms is fundamentally different from imputing mental states or intentions (*RND* 100–1). This matters not only for actors; rather, it is, on the basis of intersubjective meaning, also possible to 'share' analyses of politics. Knowledge is related to 'non-idiosyncratic justification of judgements'.[199] Hence, Kratochwil believes that the 'unprejudiced assessment of the empirical evidence'[200] and the empirical testing of explanations[201] are possible. Significantly, this 'scientific' ethos is based on the possibility of intersubjectivity.

Intersubjectivity is also crucial for delineating what is to be considered in analyses and what may justifiably be excluded. This becomes clear in Kratochwil's discussion of the concept of rationality. He criticises the narrow conception of rationality adopted in IR, which excludes an analysis of aims. Such a perspective is unable to deal with how social and political identities are built and altered (RNV 304). Kratochwil contends that what appears rational to actors is less related to an objectively identifiable payoff structure, as rationalists would have it, than to their interpretation of the situation. The latter depends on attitudes based on social values (RNV 303)[202] and on the institutional structure of the situation.[203] If a notion of instrumental rationality is employed, methodology determines what constitutes acceptable knowledge, what are acceptable objects for our analyses. As a result, Kratochwil argues, the search for alternative ends and their justification is excluded. What is at issue is the effective functioning of a system, not whether the current system is to be desired (RNV 308).

ꞏ To escape this exclusion of thinking about goals, Kratochwil aims to develop an approach which 'is sensitive to the social conditioning of our actions' (RNV 304). Accordingly, he wants to move from a conception of rationality which defines it as an *a priori* specifiable property to one

---

[197] Kratochwil and Ruggie, 'International Organization', 764–5.
[198] Kratochwil, 'Ship of Culture', pp. 217–18.
[199] Friedrich Kratochwil, 'Changing Relations Between State, Market and Society, and the Problem of Knowledge', *Pacific Focus* 9 (1994), 47.
[200] Kratochwil, 'Thrasymmachos Revisited', 347.
[201] Kratochwil, 'Norms Versus Numbers', p. 462.
[202] See also Kratochwil, 'Norms Versus Numbers', p. 457.
[203] Kratochwil, 'Norms Versus Numbers', p. 471.

which relates to common-sense understandings of the term 'rational', referring to 'a structure of communication in which validity claims can be examined intersubjectively' (RNV 304). The appropriate theoretical model for understanding rationality, Kratochwil argues, can be found in Jürgen Habermas' theory of communicative action (RNV 304). The meaning of rationality should be seen 'to be constituted by the *use* of the term' (RNV 310).[204] An action or belief is commonly called 'rational' when it 'makes sense' to act in that way (RNV 310). The notion of rationality is, moreover, bound up with normative discourse as to 'call something rational means then to *endorse it* in terms of some norm or moral feeling that permits it' (RNV 311). Thus, rationality is determined by what people believe it to be.

Rationality is significant because it tells us what must be included in our analyses; for Kratochwil's reconceptualisation of rationality is designed to make the aspects of politics that are important to the actors themselves part of scientific inquiry. Kratochwil does not question the restriction of academic analysis to the rational, although he repeatedly alludes to the significance of the emotional, which he construes as not rational.[205] As intersubjective sharing determines the relevant meaning of 'rationality', 'sharedness' comes to determine appropriate objects of analysis. This bias in favour of the dominant, serious and literal has been criticised by Jacques Derrida in relation to speech act theory (*LI*), which is an important influence on Kratochwil's thought. The implications of this critique will be explored in chapter 5. Two points are, however, worth making here. Firstly, intersubjectivity is a central concept in Kratochwil's approach. It is worth noting that, as in Wendt's approach, we are faced with a central concept which is apparently more unstable than claimed but which serves to ensure the difference of the approach from poststructuralist thought. The intersubjective context, on which much of Kratochwil's argument is based, is more elusive than can be acknowledged within his framework. Secondly, the reliance on intersubjectivity is in itself political. In order to make this second point, I want to explore in more detail now how the focus on norms, although designed to reintroduce the genuinely normative and political character of human interaction into our analyses, works to separate the normative from the political and thereby obscures the politics of norms. Crucially,

---

[204] He refers to Pufendorf rather than Wittgenstein to support this point (*RND* 149).
[205] *RND* 64; Kratochwil, 'Protagorean Quest', 207; RNV 318 and esp. 326; also Friedrich Kratochwil, 'Citizenship: On the Border of Order', in Lapid and Kratochwil, *Return of Culture and Identity in IR Theory*, pp. 196–7; also in *Alternatives* 19 (1994), 485–506.

the claim that political debate becomes possible in relation to the normative context draws our attention away from the political character of the norms themselves and of appeals to them. Rather than engaging in an abstract argument as to why norms cannot rest on anything other than a *coup de force*,[206] I want to show how the reference to norms in the debates on German militarisation closed off potential areas of debate.

The significance of opposing war and oppression, of taking responsibility and of integration with the West was based on the role these were thought to play in dealing with Germany's Nazi past. The history of the Third Reich – which was sometimes referred to simply as 'the history'[207] – was considered the obvious starting point in discussing the external use of force in the FRG. As Detlef Kleinert put it, the 'root was after all 1945'.[208] This reference helped to establish the parameters of the debate in which the opposition to war was pitched against the opposition to fascism and what was at stake was the responsibility of the German state and its people. History was used as a context to give actions meaning. Germany had to help liberate the people in the former Yugoslavia from oppression as the Allies had liberated the Germans from the Nazi regime.[209] Moreover, because the Germans had brought so much suffering to other people in the past, they had to accept their responsibility by preventing such crimes now.[210]

This construction of the issue facing Germany is interesting in this context for two reasons. Firstly, the matter was construed as problematic in relation to a linear understanding of identity which equated 'the FRG', 'Germany' and 'the Germans' and therefore required a response from the current 'German' polity as successor of the Nazi state. The implications of and problems with this identity construction have been discussed in chapter 2. This means, secondly, that, despite claims to the contrary, military involvement abroad became an issue and a problem in relation to understandings of the self rather than to considerations of the needs or desires of others. In the dominant construction of the issue, the problem

[206] See FoL. See also ch. 5.
[207] Christian Schwarz-Schilling (CDU/CSU) in Deutscher Bundestag, *Plenarprotokoll*, 12/219, 14 Apr. 1994, 18923.
[208] Detlef Kleinert (FDP) in Deutscher Bundestag, *Plenarprotokoll*, 12/151, 21 Apr. 1993, 12952.
[209] Klaus Kinkel (foreign minister) in Deutscher Bundestag, *Plenarprotokoll*, 13/48, 30 Jun. 1995, 3957.
[210] Freimut Duve (SPD) in Deutscher Bundestag, *Plenarprotokoll*, 12/151, 21 Apr. 1993, 12970; Klaus Kinkel (foreign minister) in Deutscher Bundestag, *Plenarprotokoll*, 12/240, 22 Jul. 1994, 21166.

was therefore *not* the warring Somalis or the starving Bosnians but their significance for how 'the Germans' constructed their own identity. This point was raised a number of times. Marielouise Beck of Bündnis90/Die Grünen, for instance, complained that it was Germany's reputation that was being put at the centre of the debate rather than the question of how it was possible to help the people in Bosnia.[211] Similarly, Gregor Gysi of the PDS argued that it was not really the former Yugoslavia which was at issue in the debate but rather Germany itself.[212] Josef Joffe claimed that support for NATO's rapid reaction force was 'not about the Balkans but about the alliance'.[213] Even the deployment of a destroyer to the Adriatic became a question of identity. As Robert Leicht pointed out, at 'the centre of this controversy is not really the self-determination of the Bosnians but the self-definition of the Germans'.[214] The question of identity was prominent and sensitive because it was contextualised with the Nazi past. At issue was the appropriate way of dealing with the horrible heritage of the Third Reich rather than with the conflict in the former Yugoslavia.[215] One effect of this conceptualisation was that considering what might actually help the people in need at the centre of the conflicts was almost completely excluded from the debates. The people on whose behalf the military operations were to be undertaken were not at issue.

Contextualising potential military deployments with respect to the militarist history of the Third Reich also had an effect on how the issue was 'classified'. It was represented as a moral question of far-reaching significance. The problem was that the Nazi past was interpreted as supporting two different normative imperatives: that the FRG should use the military and that it must not use it. Verheugen contended that there were two possible lessons to be drawn from German history. Either German uniforms could never again be seen in places where the Wehrmacht and the Waffen-SS had been deployed during the Second World War or, alternatively, because the Germans went everywhere then, they could not turn down any calls for help now. The two positions were, according to Verheugen, morally incompatible.[216] This contradictory imperative was contextualised, by Kinkel and others, in relation to

---

[211] Deutscher Bundestag, *Plenarprotokoll*, 13/48, 30 Jun. 1995, 4009.
[212] Ibid., 3978.
[213] Josef Joffe, 'Abschied von der "Kohl-Doktrin"', *SZ*, 16 Dec. 1994, 4.
[214] Leicht, 'Mit Volldampf', 3.
[215] Witness the exchange between Vera Wollenberger, Peter Glotz and Freimut Duve in Deutscher Bundestag, *Plenarprotokoll*, 12/151, 21 Apr. 1993.
[216] Günter Verheugen (SPD) in Deutscher Bundestag, *Plenarprotokoll*, 13/48, 30 Jun. 1995, 3988.

the demands of multilateralism. 'Partners and friends' demanded that the Bundeswehr be deployed abroad. Therefore, whilst rejecting the use of force and Western integration had both been seen as ways to ensure the difference from the Third Reich, they now seemed to support different prescriptions. The significance of both, however, also relied on an identification with the Nazi state as the predecessor of the current German polity. This yielded a normatively complex situation where the rules did not in any simple way prescribe to 'do X if Y' or unambiguously clarify that 'A counts as B'. Although there was no obvious logic with which to address this problem the complexity was not acknowledged. Rather, the issue was closed by prioritising one interpretation over all others. Glotz of the SPD complained that the Germans thought they were not allowed to have differing opinions on whether to engage in war or not. They had to get involved militarily in order to live up to their responsibility and repay their debt to the Western allies.[217] He was concerned that this closed down the necessary space for discussion.

The clash over whether military involvement was an expression of responsibility or a dangerous first step towards a return to power politics relied on the contextualisation with respect to the Nazi past. It was understood as an argument over the relative importance of 'never again war' and 'never again fascism', framed within a competition between responsibility and irresponsibility. It was portrayed as a choice between the acceptance or rejection of abstract norms. The options were either the general willingness to send troops abroad and to risk one's soldiers' lives, or the principled refusal to get involved in any type of military operation beyond defence. The singular narrative which made war and genocide in other countries a problem for 'the FRG', framed as the morally purified heir to the Nazi regime, worked to construe the debate as a dichotomous choice of far-reaching moral significance. In this context, the endorsement of norms became more important than the potential outcome of any particular act. The question was not whether any particular deployment would be useful or right but whether the principle behind it was moral. This represented the choice as profoundly significant and potentially dangerous. Politicians accused each other of changing the nature of the FRG, militarising foreign policy and being irresponsible and short-sighted.[218] The emotionally charged nature of the debates suggested that more was at stake than was admitted.

[217] Peter Glotz, 'Der ungerechte Krieg', *Der Spiegel*, 9/45, 25 Feb. 1991, 39.
[218] See for example Günter Verheugen (SPD) in Deutscher Bundestag, *Plenarprotokoll*, 12/132, 15 Jan. 1993, 11480; Andrea Lederer (PDS/Linke Liste) in Deutscher Bundestag,

The fundamental issues raised by linking the political problem at hand with the Nazi past were hard to address openly. Timothy Garton Ash has observed that in making statements which would contextualise the Holocaust and thereby potentially doubt its uniqueness one enters a political minefield.[219] Something similar could be said about discussing anything at all which is thought to be related to the Holocaust and which might lead to a reinterpretation of its significance for contemporary politics. Because of the contextualisation with respect to the Third Reich, the discussion about German military involvement abroad was conducted in the language of morality, giving the air of significance to any matter involved. Yet, intuitively in contrast to this moral framing, there was a reluctance to address the question of responsibility as one of a relationship to others; rather a technical fix was offered. Military involvement abroad came to be seen as a solution to the problem of responsibility. In 1995 former foreign minister Genscher noted that Chancellor Kohl's idea that Germany had greater responsibility after unification implied that the Germans had been shirking so far and that, in this argument, 'new responsibility mean[t]: Bundeswehr deployments abroad'.[220]

This equation made it difficult to reject the use of force. However, Genscher's comment drew attention to the narrowness of this idea of what taking responsibility meant. He had always argued that the FRG needed to pursue a 'policy of responsibility' but using the military instrument had not been a part of this. According to Genscher, a policy of responsibility was based on recognising the problems of partners and attempting to solve them rather than pursuing unilateral gain.[221] Responsibility, in his view, was a responsibility towards future generations in terms of protecting the environment, preserving peace and creating a just world order.[222] Yet Genscher's stance did not indicate exactly how the unified Germany was going to work towards peace in the world and a better future for Europe. Consequently, *Der Spiegel*

Plenarprotokoll, 12/151, 21 Apr. 1993, 12942; Rudolf Scharping (SPD) in Deutscher Bundestag, *Plenarprotokoll*, 13/48, 30 Jun. 1995, 3960; Hermann-Otto Solms (FDP) in Deutscher Bundestag, *Plenarprotokoll*, 12/240, 22 Jul. 1994, 21180.
[219] Timothy Garton Ash, *In Europe's Name: Germany and the Divided Continent* (London: Vintage, 1993), p. 219.
[220] Quoted in 'Einsatz ins Ungewisse', *Der Spiegel*, 5/49, 30 Jan. 1995, 68–79, here 75.
[221] 'Nicht den Buchhaltern überlassen', interview with Foreign Minister Hans-Dietrich Genscher, *Der Spiegel*, 20/44, 14 May 1990, 28–30, here 28.
[222] 'Geheimnis des Genscherismus', interview with Foreign Minister Hans-Dietrich Genscher, *Der Spiegel*, 40/44, 1 Oct. 1990, 30–5, here 33–4.

complained that it was 'apart from verbose declarations of their foreign minister, unclear to the Bonners [that is, members of the Federal Government] what they should do with the "greater responsibility"'.[223] Participation in international military operations seemed to provide the practical answers Genscher's considerations lacked. As a result, alternative conceptions of how responsibility should be taken were not discussed. The controversy was narrowed down to one about military involvement abroad. This debate could, moreover, be conducted without addressing the problematic of identity and difference with the Nazi past.

Burkhard Hirsch of the FDP had, as we have seen, attempted to open up the discussion about taking responsibility. He was concerned that, by making military involvement abroad a constitutional issue, the real questions were being avoided: 'The discussion about the constitutional instruments must no longer cover up another question, namely – if we should take on a greater responsibility – how, for which aims and towards whom we must take this responsibility.'[224] What is interesting about this question, which apparently went unheard, is that it undermines the notion that the commitment to taking responsibility itself means anything. There was always going to be an issue of interpretation. Acting responsibly could mean a number of things, most obviously either intervening on behalf of people in distress or exercising restraint in relation to matters military. Hirsch's question seems, however, to drive at the more subversive point that the choice between different interpretations of the constitution and therefore different general rules was not about responsibility at all. Responsibility would only be at issue in a specific decision about how to relate to others.

Fischer pointed more openly to how flawed the reasoning was that one course of action with respect to the former Yugoslavia was more responsible than the other *in principle*. The problem was that, on the one hand, one might become guilty by not interfering; on the other hand, one might risk escalating the conflict by getting involved and thereby become guilty again.[225] For Fischer, there clearly was no given path with respect to the use of force (cf. *OH* 41 [43]). He explained that the core of his political identity was based on two 'never again' principles, 'never again war' and 'never again Auschwitz' but that the big contradiction was that it might not be possible to prevent Auschwitz without war. He specifically stated that this contradiction could not be resolved and

---

[223] 'Das wird ein schwieriges Jahr', *Der Spiegel*, 5/45, 28 Jan. 1991, 16–23, here 23.
[224] Deutscher Bundestag, *Plenarprotokoll*, 12/132, 15 Jan. 1993, 11480.
[225] Deutscher Bundestag, *Plenarprotokoll*, 13/48, 30 Jun. 1995, 3971.

therefore recommended that his party stand up for this contradiction rather than aim to resolve it in one way or another.[226]

Fischer's refusal to resolve the contradiction once and for all seems to recognise that responsibility does not lie in inventing a general rule but in the decision of what to do in a concrete situation, a decision which will not be fully responsible or just. In a debate in which all sides claim to have the recipe for responsible behaviour *in principle*, acknowledging the impossibility of setting out a programme, *and* acting ethically at the same time,[227] was not likely to be very popular. If ethics is seen to lie in a universally valid attitude, then acknowledging the contradictory demands inherent in each particular decision must look weak, as it cannot provide the desired guide to the future. This suggests that, although the discussion revolved around ethical issues, the reasoning process closed off an ethical approach to specific situations. The choice was between different rules thought to settle the issue in general. The problem of prioritising one normative commitment in principle, such as the imperative to act in solidarity with alliance partners, was addressed by Uta Zapf of the SPD: 'When Herr Lamers says that there will of course be a national decision in each case but basically means by this that this national decision is not open any more, because, you see, we must vote the same way as the alliance partners, then we can skip those sittings in which we as parliamentarians decide.'[228] In a sense, then, once the commitment to solidarity with Western partners had been made, politics had become superfluous.

The recourse to norms, at the same time as potentially creating the space for an ethical decision, also closes down the space for politics and ethics. Claiming that choosing a particular course of action is merely the expression of a general rule, rather than a decision, obscures the responsibility of the subject. German military involvement abroad was portrayed as an expression of anti-fascism and integration with the West. It was presented as the technical solution to the problem of the FRG's increasing responsibility. Both anti-militarism and anti-fascism were considered important norms by actors on all sides of the debate, but the belief was that it was necessary to come down on one side or

---

[226] 'Das wäre blutiger Zynismus', *Der Spiegel*, 34/49, 21 Aug. 1995, 27–9, here 29.
[227] See *OH* 44–5 [46]. See also ch. 5.
[228] Deutscher Bundestag, *Plenarprotokoll*, 12/240, 22 Jul. 1994, 21207. For Lamers' claim that Germany could not take a position on war and peace different from that of its partners because it was in a 'political marriage' with them, see Karl Lamers, 'Was die Friedensmissionen lehren', *Die politische Meinung* 39 (1994), 55.

other, and that the decision for one rule or other would set out the moral future course of action. The logic was the same on both sides. The commitment either to 'never again war' or to participating in military operations authorised by the 'international community' would constitute taking responsibility. Responsibility was seen to lie in adhering to a general rule rather than in confronting the ethico-political merits of a singular decision. This is reflected in the opposition's fear that sending a few uniformed men to operate a hospital in Croatia could lead to a fundamental remilitarisation of German foreign policy, that subscribing to this individual decision would mean accepting a rule, as well as in the governing parties' claim that changing the constitution would constitute a responsible decision.

The question arises whether this is related to Kratochwil's approach or merely reflects an idiosyncratic usage of norms in the particular debates studied. After all, Kratochwil draws our attention to the necessity of relating singular situations to the rule structure, that is, of judgement. Doing justice, for instance, 'involves, above all, the exercise of practical judgments in which abstract norms and concrete circumstances are fitted together' (*RND* 241). However, the rule structure, the norms to which actors may appeal in order to justify and clarify their positions are, in Kratochwil's approach, not questioned themselves. Kratochwil does not conceptualise norms themselves and their effects as political.[229] There seems to be a strange exclusion of power in his notion of politics. The idea that political and practical debate takes place within the space provided by a shared normative context conjures up the image of people sitting down and calmly talking it over. Arguments get presented and listened to and a solution is negotiated in relation to the normative context. The analogy between a legal discourse on grievances and political debate suggests the equality of speakers. I trust that Kratochwil does not intentionally assume such an equality in political discourse, but his analogy either obscures the power relations between actors or it is simply misplaced. In this conceptualisation normative reasoning, as a consequence, becomes detached from the question of power relations.

Kratochwil elucidates in great detail how norms can be used to support political positions. What he fails to analyse, though, is how the norms themselves are already part of political positions. He raises the issue when he argues that, 'because the constitution is "constitutive" of

---

[229] See, however, Friedrich Kratochwil, 'Of Law and Human Action: A Jurisprudential Plea for a World Order Perspective in International Legal Studies', in Falk, Kratochwil and Mendlovitz, *International Law*, p. 639.

the political system, the conventional taxonomy of "politics" and "law" hides rather than illuminates important conceptual dimensions' (*RND* 251). However, he does not seem to get a handle on the political significance of the constitutive function of norms. It is interesting, in this context, to explore how Kratochwil conceptualises politics. He objects to E. H. Carr's definition of politics which involves the idea that domestic politics is the realm of authority, whereas international politics is characterised by struggle and power:

> This is an odd conception of politics indeed. Gone is not only the notion that political associations are based on common notions of the good and the just, as Aristotle suggested. Gone is the classical conception of a community as an association under a common law. Gone is also the notion that politics depends on bargaining and negotiation and nonviolent attitudes towards fellow-citizens.[230]

In Kratochwil's view, politics is inextricably linked to being human; that is, it is related to the ability to interpret oneself and one's surroundings.[231] Emphasising the dimension of shared meaning and values, of communication, Kratochwil in turn excludes an explicit consideration of power. Whilst this is understandable as part of distancing his thinking from the dominant Realist mode of theorising, it has important consequences for his approach. His early interest in analysing the 'management of power',[232] which reflected one way of explicitly addressing an aspect of the phenomenon of power, seems to have all but disappeared, in favour of a concern with the normative, which, crucially, is strangely separated from the question of power.

Norms, in Kratochwil's conceptualisation, are linked to politics in that they make human association possible. Norms constitute practices (*RND* 7), they provide for the possibility of peacefully resolving conflicts (*RND* 181) and, crucially, they make communication possible in the first place. Shared meaning becomes possible against the background of norms (*RND* 32 and 61). Intersubjectivity is intrinsically linked to the existence of norms. Accordingly, Kratochwil discusses norms in the context of a consideration of language (*RND* 6). This conceptualisation, which makes them a medium of communication, draws the attention away from their political effects. Nevertheless, Kratochwil mentions

---

[230] Kratochwil, 'Politics, Norms and Peaceful Change', 199.
[231] Kratochwil, 'Protagorean Quest'.
[232] Friedrich Kratochwil, *International Order and Foreign Policy* (Boulder: Westview Press, 1978), 1.

consequences of norms which are in tension with the seemingly neutral status of a communication device. He claims that norms impact on which styles of reasoning are considered permissible and on who is allowed to take part in decision-making processes (*RND* 34). He points out that, through the reasoning process based on them, rules and norms mould decisions (*RND* 43). It is, he argues, precisely the 'common understandings buttressing norms' which make a reasoned decision different from an arbitrary one (*RND* 185). Hence, norms are bound up with the issue of legitimacy. In other words, norms are, unsurprisingly, normative. The upshot of this is, however, that, if intersubjectivity is based on norms and rules, it is anything but neutral. Shared meaning, in this conceptualisation, is inextricably linked to what is accepted as legitimate or good. Notions of rationality, which, as Kratochwil himself suggests, tell us what we may justifiably exclude from our analyses, are based on intersubjectivity. This is a powerful and fruitful argument, but not one that Kratochwil makes explicit or takes to its conclusion. What is problematic is that this normativity of intersubjectivity, that is, the unavoidable normative and political character of the concept of intersubjectivity so construed, is not acknowledged.

Analyses in terms of the normative are usually considered a step to reintroducing into IR what human interactions and politics are actually about.[233] What the argument in this chapter suggests is, however, that Kratochwil's analysis in relation to norms also misses at least part of the political. Blaming one's acts on norms constitutes precisely the escape from responsibility which those who want to reintroduce the normative dimension claim to be arguing against. Norms are construed as existing separately from politics, separately from the influence of power. Although aimed at reintroducing law and morality to analyses of politics, making norms the basis for debate, in Kratochwil's conceptualisation, implicitly separates the normative from the political. It obscures that the norms themselves are based on political decisions and that they perpetuate power structures. And this is significant, for such 'remarks are not merely of academic interest and they do not concern solely the relative advantages of modes of analysis. What is at stake is rather the understanding of social reality and, through practice, its reproduction' (*RND* 258).

---

[233] See, for example, Steve Smith, 'The Forty Years' Detour: The Resurgence of Normative Theory in International Relations', *Millennium: Journal of International Studies* 21 (1992), 489–506.

4   Words and world: Onuf's constructivism and German military involvement abroad

Nicholas Onuf's project is to 'reconstruct' the discipline of IR by analysing how people construct social reality (*WOM*). He questions its traditional boundaries and aims to create a new paradigm of international relations which takes account of their political character and makes them part of social theory (*WOM* 1; see also 22, 27 and 36). This reconceptualisation is more than an academic exercise since the social world is created by human practices and '[c]onstitutive claims on behalf of social science disciplines, and the projects they engender, are among these practices' (*WOM* 15; see also 106). Formulating a constructivist approach to international relations therefore at the same time represents a contribution to shaping international reality. Onuf's definition of a constructivist theory rests on the idea, developed in Anthony Giddens' structuration theory, that 'people *and* society construct, or constitute, each other' (*WOM* 36; see also C 59 and CM 7). The processes of construction and their institutionalisation are crucial to Onuf's conception of reality. In basic terms, human beings construct reality through their deeds. Crucially, these deeds may be speech acts. Speech acts in turn may, through repetition, be institutionalised into rules and thereby provide the context and basis for meaning of human action. This process is deeply political because rules distribute benefits unevenly. In other words, rules privilege some people over others. The effect is rule.

Onuf's constructivism revolves around the related concepts of speech acts, deeds and rules. It starts, he claims, with deeds: 'I begin with Goethe's aphorism, which for Wittgenstein seemed to express a philosophical position: In the beginning was the deed. I call this position constructivism' (*WOM* 36). Deeds may consist in physical actions or the speaking of words (*WOM* 36). Deeds are thus the starting point of Onuf's constructivism even if they cannot provide secure grounds;[1] for there cannot be a philosophical foundation for constructivism which does not itself develop from the construction of reality and therefore from human practice. Deeds establish social reality because they carry meaning. Onuf argues that meaning in human social relationships depends on the existence of rules (*WOM* 21–2). Accordingly, Onuf's constructivism asserts the fundamental significance of rules for social reality and consequently for a constructivist social theory (*WOM* 66). To see rules as aspects of *praxis* is 'the necessary starting point for a constructivist social theory' (*WOM* 63). This beginning is, however, not a separate place. Onuf contends that 'we must start in the middle, so to speak, because people and society, always having made each other, are already there and just about to change' (C 59). This means beginning with a consideration of rules, which Onuf considers a third element between people and society.

Rules, as Onuf conceptualises them, are essentially social. On the one hand, they provide guidance for human behaviour and thereby make shared meaning possible. On the other hand, they create the possibility of agency in the first place (CIS 6). Agency, in turn, influences rules because

> [e]very time agents choose to follow a rule, they *change* it – they strengthen it by making it more likely that they and others will follow the rule in the future. Every time agents choose not to follow a rule, they change the rule by weakening it, and in so doing they may well contribute to the constitution of some new rule.   (CIS 18)

Rules are, moreover, important because they are the basic ingredient of Onuf's definition of politics. According to Onuf, political society has two general properties. There are always rules which make human activity meaningful. Secondly, rules result in an uneven distribution of benefits. This leads to a condition of rule (*WOM* 21–2; see also 128). Politics therefore is always potentially about privilege and thus involves normative questions. Through the rules–rule nexus society and politics are closely linked. Society is based on rules; politics always deals with asymmetric social relations generated by rules, that is, rule (*WOM* 22). Crucially, what people do is not only inextricably linked to rules; it also constructs rules and, more generally, the world.

---

[1] Constructivism cannot be grounded (*WOM* 46). Yet elsewhere Onuf defends the possibility of grounds (CIS 4).

Words making the world

Onuf subscribes to the view that the social world is constructed by deeds which may consist in the speaking of words rather than some physical activity. This notion is developed in speech act theory. As Onuf argues, the 'distinctive claim of the theory of speech acts is that language is both representative and performative. People use words to represent deeds and they can use words, and words alone, to perform deeds' (*WOM* 82). Rules develop from speech acts and the theory of speech acts can therefore be employed to analyse them. Consequently, Onuf's understanding of rules is based on speech act theory which 'systematically relates speakers' (authors') intentions to linguistic activity' (*WOM* 81). Language is central in Onuf's analysis insofar as it enables people to construct their worlds. Language does not describe or represent reality; rather it creates reality, for the 'point of a speech act is to have an effect on some state of affairs' (*WOM* 98). Onuf argues that

> speech acts are social performances, that is, they have direct social consequences. Such acts take the generic form, I [verb such as declare, demand, promise] that [propositional content]. Because people respond to them with their own performances, not always spoken, the pattern of speech acts and related performances constitute those practices that make the material conditions and artifacts of human experience meaningful. More specifically, the pattern of speech acts endows practices with normativity; they give rise to rules which, in synopsizing that pattern, fix preferences and expectations and shape the future against the past.
> (*WOM* 183)

Therefore, talking may create normative constraints for actions. Speaking, in other words, 'is an activity with normative consequences'.[2] These vary according to the kind of speaking involved. Onuf postulates three types of speech acts which differ in how they link words and world. Assertives 'either reflect an existing words-to-world fit or propose a new one. They do not endeavor to change an existing arrangement.'[3] Directives 'fit world to words' because they '(set in train actions that) change the world' (*WOM* 93). Commissives, on the other hand, fit 'words to the world. To commit oneself is to project a desired state of affairs and bring it to bear on oneself' (*WOM* 93).

---

[2] Nicholas Onuf, 'Speaking of Policy', in Vendulka Kubálková (ed.), *Foreign Policy in a Constructed World* (Armonk, NY: M. E. Sharpe, 2001), p. 77.
[3] *WOM* 93 (footnote deleted).

These categories of speech acts are also significant in relation to rules, which are statements telling us how to carry on (*WOM* 51). All rules are normative (CM 10). According to Onuf, a distinction between regulative and constitutive rules, frequently used for classification, is impossible. They are always both (*WOM* 51–2 and 86; CIS 7). Regulation and constitution cannot be separated in a socially constructed world because 'what people take to be possible and what society makes permissible depend on vantage point, one's relation to practice' (*WOM* 51). As rules are always statements, Onuf's own categorisation of rules rather derives from his consideration of language as enabling people to perform social acts and achieve ends through statements of assertion, direction and commitment, that is, through speech acts (*WOM* 23; see also 79). Assertives are statements of belief which, by implication, the speaker wishes the hearer to accept. Directives contain an action the speaker wishes the hearer to perform. Thus there is an immediate regulative intent in a directive which the assertive usually lacks. Commissives consist in the declaration of the speaker's commitment to some future action. Therefore they produce rules for the speaker, whereas assertives and directives try to impose rules on the hearer (*WOM* 87–8). Onuf claims that the categorisation of rules in assertives, directives and commissives provides 'an inclusive classificatory scheme for *all* social rules' (*WOM* 91). In other words, 'all rules are either assertives of the form, I state that X counts as Y, or directives of the form, I state that X person (should, must, may) do Y, or commissives of the form, I state that I (can, will, should) do Y. While each is a distinctive category, all three play on each other in the production of rules' (*WOM* 90). Language is crucial to such a consideration of rules. It 'gives rules an autonomous character suited to their function; through language, rules exist in their own right'.[4]

In this conceptualisation all rules are based on speech acts. However, although speech acts may produce rules, not all of them do. Onuf claims that

> when assertive speech acts are successful (their reception confirmed, with normativity attaching), they produce rules however fragile their constitution and tenuous their normativity. When any such rule becomes a convention, constitution of the rule by speech acts accepting its status as a rule begins to supplant its constitution by the repetition of speech acts with complementary propositional content. Then the rule is normatively stronger, its regulative character supporting

---

[4] Onuf, 'Intervention for the Common Good', p. 46.

> its independent constitution, and conversely. The change in condition is signified by a change in nomenclature: constitution becomes institution.
>
> (*WOM* 86)

This process is fundamentally significant as the context of rules makes meaning possible (*WOM* 21–2). The texture of the social world is made up of rules. Rules are the basic ingredient of any social structure. 'General, prescriptive statements, hereafter called *rules*, are always implicated in' (CM 7) the continuous co-constitution of people and society. Rules give people orientation. They 'tell us how to carry on' but they 'cannot provide closure for the purposes of carrying on because rules are not the sufficient agency whereby intentions become equivalent to causes' (*WOM* 51). Although rules provide guidance, they do not determine human behaviour. Accordingly, based on the analysis of rules only general statements about social action are possible. The concept of judgement is significant here. Judgement arises from knowledge about the context of rules involved in a situation and about the consequences of following or violating them (*WOM* 110). It is closely linked to the process of reasoning. Speech acts can be seen as 'instances of applied reasoning' (*WOM* 99). All human beings reason (*WOM* 100). According to Onuf, a 'constructivist interpretation of reasoning extends to learning and knowing, not just in the sense of acquiring propositional knowledge, but learning and knowing how to use that knowledge, including knowledge of rules' (*WOM* 96–7). When people learn how to use rules, rather than just to know their content, they learn how to exercise judgement (*WOM* 110–11). Thus it is the combination of practice and consciousness which creates judgement (*WOM* 119). Judgement leads to the choice of the actual course of action. Onuf perceives individuals as being active participants in the ongoing social construction of the world (*WOM* 114). This, however, cannot be taken to mean that individuals construct reality according to their liking. Deeds have unintended as well as intended consequences.[5] The autonomous individual is an illusion. In fact, this is part of what constructivism means to Onuf: 'To be fully conscious of the implications of making society by making commitments, not rules as such, is to be constructivist. Gone is the autonomous individual – she is an artifact of lower levels of rule experience' (*WOM* 119). The scope for agency is circumscribed by rules which, in addition to material givens, define how individuals may affect reality.[6]

---

[5] See also Kubálková, Onuf and Kowert, 'Constructing Constructivism', p. 21.
[6] Onuf, 'Intervention for the Common Good', p. 47.

Hence, materiality plays a role in Onuf's constructivism. Although we can never leave our constructions, Onuf firmly argues that there is a material world 'out there' (*WOM* 29–30 and 46), presumably *beyond* our constructions, and that this is significant. Material reality circumscribes the boundaries of possibility: 'Some limits are substantially material, and any rule on the subject is beside the point' (CM 9). In his rendering of how the world is constructed, Onuf relates the realm of the social and the material. Therefore, Onuf's constructivism

> does not draw a sharp distinction between material and social realities – the material and the social contaminate each other, but variably – and it does not grant sovereignty to either the material or the social by defining the other out of existence. It does find socially made content dominant in and for the individual without denying the independent, 'natural' reality of individuals as materially situated biological beings. (*WOM* 40)

The concept of deed seen as both social construction and natural event allows him, Onuf argues, to privilege neither world nor word, that is, neither the material nor the social (*WOM* 43).

Thus Onuf perceives the world as consisting of a material and a social realm which are distinct but nevertheless closely related. If one grants the possibility of separating social and material reality, at least for analytic purposes, the concept of deed is a powerful basis for Onuf's constructivism precisely because he sees it as situated at the border between social and material reality. A deed 'is intelligible only as jointly a social construction and natural event, produced by mind and yet phenomenal in its own right' (*WOM* 43). Deeds provide the link between the natural and the social world. As social phenomena they are based on intentions and meanings. Yet they have to be addressed to the natural world in order to function properly. In other words, deeds transport meaning but they have to be related to both the social and the natural world correctly to produce the desired outcomes.[7] Deeds therefore make possible the linkage of the social to the material, the two realms construed as separate by Onuf. This connection is also established through the notion of language and thus, in Onuf's case, speech. This is, of course, only another way of looking at his notion of deed, since the 'point of a speech act is to have an effect on some state of affairs' (*WOM* 98). A speech act is therefore a form of deed. Indeed, as Onuf argues, 'saying is doing:

---

[7] See also Austin, *How to Do Things with Words*.

talking is undoubtedly the most important way that we go about making the world what it is' (C 59). Thus Onuf argues that a 'constructivist view denies that world and words are independent; it sees them as mutually constitutive. If categories of being are linguistically constituted, then they may be said to have social origins' (*WOM* 94). The significance of speech acts also supports the centrality of rules, for rules are based on speech acts. A rule is always a statement and the normativity of a speech act develops through repetition (*WOM* 86). Therefore, rules originate in speech acts and retain this form, but generalise the relation between speaker and hearer (CM 10).

If we use these conceptualisations to analyse the issue of German military involvement abroad after the end of the Cold War, statements and rules become significant. As both are ubiquitous, it is, however, difficult to know where to start. Onuf claims that, given his formulation of constructivism, the 'most obvious implication is that scholars (people, relations) always begin in the middle. Context is unavoidable. So are beginnings' (CM 7). Following this reasoning, my representations in this chapter *make* a world rather than describe one, since 'we (as people, scholars) make the world and the world makes us' (CM 7). This is inevitable, not a problem to be overcome. Moreover, since the world is, according to Onuf's argument, at the same time making me, there is an interactive relationship between my rendering and the practice at issue, between my words and the world they address. As Onuf points out, we 'are always within our constructions, even as we choose to stand apart from them, condemn them, reconstruct them' (*WOM* 43). The implications of this for the status of academic work are taken up in the conclusion of this chapter. For now, I will take the inevitability of asserting a context as a licence to postulate my own beginning.

In Onuf's framework it is impossible to conceive of politics and therefore of the shift towards German military involvement abroad other than in relation to speech acts. Speech acts provide the link between words and world, the two spheres Onuf construes as distinct. As has been argued in relation to Wendt's approach, language is an integral part of human interaction. It is difficult to conceive of any move at all which would not involve a speech act. The very act of deploying the military, sending the navy to the Adriatic Sea, for instance, required a cabinet decision to this effect[8] and multiple other directive speech acts leading to the actual movement of vessels. When one person instructs another to

---

[8] 'SPD-Fraktionsvorstand beschließt Verfassungsklage', *SZ*, 17 Jul. 1992, 1.

do something, speaking is part of the process. As the decision-makers in the FRG were not identical with those who did the soldiering, successful speech acts were crucial. The possibility of sending the Bundeswehr anywhere at all depended on an acceptance of the validity of the speech acts by those who would, as a consequence, move the equipment. Onuf does not discuss the precise conditions of success or failure of speech acts at length. The point of his work is not primarily to elucidate when specific speech acts function according to plan but to make a case for the relevance of speech acts as such and to show how we construct our world through them.

Clearly, directives, and therefore speech acts, are part of the political process, but the significance of this insight is not quite as obvious. After all, if directives translate decision-makers' wishes into material actions, as in bringing about a situation in which surveillance aircraft actually monitor the embargo[9] – that is, if directives set in train actions which change the world (*WOM* 93) – they would seem to function as a neutral tool. Thus, the value added of acknowledging that *words* are used to bring about actions which change the world is difficult to discern in this case. What is important in this conceptualisation, a sceptic might argue, is the action which is brought about, not the speaking which set it off. However, Onuf's crucial point is that speech acts may *themselves* change the world.

The recognition amongst policy-makers that speech acts could be used to change the situation was reflected in the significance attributed to changing the constitution. As has been discussed in chapter 3, the situation surrounding the issue of involvement in international military operations was at least partially defined by the constitution. The directive in Art. 87a of the Basic Law to use the Bundeswehr only for defensive purposes was considered significant, although some argued that it was overruled by the licence, in Art. 24 (2), to become a member of a 'system of mutual collective security'. Two approaches to this situation became relevant. Either the existing rules were understood as in some way faulty, and accordingly changes were proposed. Alternatively, the rules were read as establishing the desired reality and consequently no formal change was attempted. In both cases, speech acts were used in attempts to reinforce or change the existing reality. Such speech acts are amongst the practices which work to strengthen or weaken rules (CIS 18).

[9] Ibid.

The first approach was prominent across the political spectrum in the years immediately after the Gulf War. The parliamentary groups of all parties put forward proposals to change the Basic Law at different times. In July 1992 both smaller opposition groups presented their suggestions for new Art. 24 and 87a. The proposal of PDS/Linke Liste was most restrictive in terms of the conditions under which the use of force would have been permitted. They proposed to rule out even peace-keeping operations. Only self-defence in the event of an attack on the territory of the FRG was to be constitutional.[10] The parliamentary group of Bündnis90/Die Grünen put forward a proposal addressing the issue of 'civilising' international relations more broadly. This included limiting usage of the Bundeswehr to defence and peace-keeping operations, the latter under specific restrictive conditions.[11] The SPD had already, in June 1992, introduced a proposal to change Art. 24 and Art. 87a in order to clarify that, beyond defence, only participation in peace-keeping missions without a combat dimension was constitutional.[12] Finally, in January 1993 the CDU/CSU and FDP parliamentary groups submitted a joint proposal to clarify the Basic Law by supplementing Art. 24 with a section 2a. This envisaged three cases of military involvement: peace-keeping missions on the basis of a UN Security Council decision or of regional agreements as mentioned in the UN Charter of which the FRG is a member; peace-making operations according to Chapters VII and VIII of the UN Charter on the basis of a Security Council decision; and operations according to the right to collective self-defence, as provided for by Art. 51 of the UN Charter, together with other states in alliances and regional agreements of which the FRG is a member.[13] Whilst these various proposals aimed to secure substantially different outcomes, which ranged from ruling out uses of the Bundeswehr other than for territorial defence to enabling it to participate in almost any use of force permitted under international law,[14] they all reflected a strategically similar approach to the issue. All implied that the current state of reality was in need of change, that this reality was defined around

[10] Deutscher Bundestag, *Drucksache*, 12/3055, 21 Jul. 1992. See also their motion: Deutscher Bundestag, *Drucksache*, 12/4755, 20 Apr. 1993.
[11] Deutscher Bundestag, *Drucksache*, 12/3014, 2 Jul. 1992.
[12] Deutscher Bundestag, *Drucksache*, 12/2896, 23 Jun. 1992. See also the reasons given for the proposal in Deutscher Bundestag, *Drucksache*, 12/4535, 10 Mar. 1993.
[13] Deutscher Bundestag, *Drucksache*, 12/4107, 13 Jan. 1993. See also the justification for the proposal: Deutscher Bundestag, *Drucksache*, 12/4135, 15 Jan. 1993.
[14] No grouping aimed to legitimise unilateral military action other than for territorial defence even in the cases permitted by international law.

the existing rules and that therefore a speech act and a speech act alone could change the situation. As Onuf points out, the most important way in which we make the world is through saying things (C 59). The point is, therefore, that all of the proposals show the belief that a reformulation of words, i.e. a change of the law through parliament, would lead to a situation in which it was *possible* for the FRG to take up practices it had never engaged in before. Moreover, they imply that a change of words was *necessary* in order to do so.

In contrast to the at first widely shared belief that the constitution had to be changed, some Conservatives argued that this was not necessary. Chancellor Helmut Kohl's security advisor Horst Teltschik had made this point in the late 1980s.[15] Rupert Scholz, a constitutional lawyer who was defence minister from May 1988 until April 1989, supported this argument.[16] The CSU had long made it its official position.[17] Those supporting this view claimed not to pursue any change but merely to point out an aspect of reality, namely that the Basic Law already permitted military involvement abroad. Nevertheless, in terms of Onuf's analysis of the social world, they used the same strategy as did those who proposed constitutional change: they used speech acts to bolster their position. Those who wanted to amend the Basic Law aimed to change the situation through speech acts. Those who thought the law already provided for the possibility of military involvement abroad stated the existence of a particular state of affairs. Thus, they asserted a particular fit between words and world (*WOM* 93). Wolfgang Schäuble, the chairman of the CDU/CSU parliamentary group, became one of the most vocal supporters of the claim that constitutional change was unnecessary. He repeatedly asserted that the Basic Law already sufficiently regulated the possibilities for using the Bundeswehr outside NATO territory.[18] In order to be able to act upon this conviction, it was necessary to bring about a situation in which a substantial number of people would recognise that Bundeswehr deployments abroad were legal. This, just like

[15] 'Bundesmarine: Germans to the front?', *Der Spiegel*, 49/41, 30 Nov. 1987, 19–21, here 19, and 'Wir müssen erwachsen werden', *Der Spiegel*, 34/44, 20 Jul. 1990, 121–3, here 122.
[16] Philippi, *Bundeswehr-Auslandseinsätze*, p. 36.
[17] Gutjahr, *German Foreign and Defence Policy*, pp. 72–3.
[18] See, for instance, 'Nato-Mitglied, das reicht nicht', interview with the chairman of the CDU/CSU parliamentary group Wolfgang Schäuble, *Der Spiegel*, 4/47, 25 Jan. 1993, 20–3, here 20–1; Wolfgang Schäuble (CDU/CSU) in Deutscher Bundestag, *Plenarprotokoll*, 12/132, 15 Jan. 1993, 11464; 'Die SPD macht uns mehr Kummer als Freude', interview with the chairman of the CDU/CSU parliamentary group Wolfgang Schäuble, *SZ*, 15–16 May 1993, 9.

constitutional change, could be brought about through the use of speech acts, in this case assertives.

Over time the supporters of the position that no constitutional change was required repeatedly asserted their understanding of the supposedly existing reality and the statements of CDU/CSU politicians shifted towards a new framing of the issue. In 1990, the CDU had officially declared that clear constitutional authorisation for deployments abroad had to be 'created'.[19] This implied that such authorisation did not exist and accordingly that participation in international operations would have been illegal unless the constitution was changed. In line with this interpretation, Defence Minister Volker Rühe spoke of a 'necessary' change in the Basic Law in May 1992.[20] However, Rühe was out of tune with the views voiced by his party at this time. By January 1991, Kohl had already said that the constitutional basis for deployments abroad had to be 'clarified'.[21] This change in the wording indicates a significant shift. The assertion that the constitutional basis needed to be 'clarified' rather than 'created' implied that deployments abroad at least *might* already be legal, and the supporters of clarification certainly argued it was, whilst the earlier formulation was based on the belief that they were not.

The conceptualisation of the existing situation shifted gradually. In a speech about Germany's role in Europe in March 1991, Chancellor Kohl argued both that so far the constitution had *restricted* the ability of the FRG to fulfil its obligations as a member of collective security systems and that the Basic Law *required* participation in military operations for the preservation of international security. He claimed that the new position of the unified Germany made it necessary to participate in peace missions and therefore to 'draw the consequences' in terms of the constitution.[22] Kohl did not explain what this 'drawing consequences' meant, whether he was talking about formal changes of the regulations or not, but the context suggests that he was. Thus he implied the necessity of constitutional change, even if this change was merely going to clarify that military involvement abroad had always been legal because of the requirements of UN membership.

---

[19] CDU party platform for the 1990 *Bundestag* election quoted in Philippi, *Bundeswehr-Auslandseinsätze*, p. 85.
[20] 'Langfristig auch Kampfeinsätze', *SZ*, 15 May 1992, 1.
[21] Helmut Kohl (chancellor) in Deutscher Bundestag, *Plenarprotokoll*, 12/5, 30 Jan. 1991, 90.
[22] Helmut Kohl, 'Die Rolle Deutschlands in Europa', in Presse- und Informationsamt der Bundesregierung, *Bulletin*, 33, 22 Mar. 1991, 243.

By November 1992, however, when the extension of the mandate in relation to the embargo against Serbia-Montenegro was at issue, an increasing number of CDU/CSU politicians had apparently begun subscribing to the view, long championed by Schäuble, that changing the constitution was not necessary because the 'participation in collective measures for the restoration of peace' was permitted anyhow.[23] Thus, constitutional change was increasingly seen as 'superfluous'.[24] When the governing parties' proposal to amend the Basic Law was finally under discussion in the Bundestag, Schäuble reiterated the view, now on behalf of the CDU/CSU, that Art. 24 (2) already provided the legal basis for such operations and that the proposed change of the constitution was not necessary but merely desirable to clarify.[25] One of two reasons was given in support of this view. Some argued that Art. 24 (2) Basic Law was a sufficient basis for Bundeswehr operations abroad. It constituted an explicit permission as required by Art. 87a (2). Others, like Scholz, continued to claim that the restrictive Art. 87a was applicable only to internal uses of the armed forces. Both interpretations led to the same conclusion that combat missions abroad were already legal.[26] Accordingly, the aim was to clarify what had always been legal, rather than to create new legal possibilities. An already existing state of affairs had to be asserted rather than brought about through a directive.

The clarification which was sought was, however, difficult to obtain in practice. Members of the governing parties did not agree on what exactly was to be clarified, in other words, on how far the supposedly already existing licence to use force went or should go.[27] Moreover, for those who thought that the external use of force was already permitted, any constitutional change could only lead to reducing the range of options.[28] Besides, even if what was at issue was clarification rather than substantial alteration, it was nevertheless going to be an interference

[23] 'Verstimmung im Kabinett über Adria-Einsatz der "Hamburg"', *FAZ*, 20 Nov. 1992, 1–2, here 2.
[24] 'Rühe ändert seine Ansicht zur Möglichkeit von Kampfeinsätzen', *FAZ*, 23 Nov. 1992, 1–2, here 2; 'Weder Grundgesetzänderung noch Entsendungsgesetz', *FAZ*, 25 Nov. 1992, 1–2, here 2.
[25] Deutscher Bundestag, *Plenarprotokoll*, 12/132, 15 Jan. 1993, 11464.
[26] Philippi, *Bundeswehr-Auslandseinsätze*, p. 86; 'Regierung über Bundeswehr-Einsätze tief zerstritten', *SZ*, 8 Jan. 1993, 2.
[27] See, for instance, 'Bosnier: Waffenembargo aufheben', *SZ*, 7 Jan. 1993, 2; 'Regierung über Bundeswehr-Einsätze tief zerstritten', *SZ*, 8 Jan. 1993, 2.
[28] See 'Verstimmung im Kabinett über Adria-Einsatz der "Hamburg"', *FAZ*, 20 Nov. 1992, 1–2, here 2; 'Ghali für volle Teilnahme Bonns an UNO-Einsätzen', *SZ*, 12 Jan. 1993, 1.

with the text of the constitution. Technically, it was constitutional change. Therefore agreement between CDU, CSU and FDP was not enough. The SPD's consent was needed to be able to amend the constitution which, according to Art. 79 (2) of the Basic Law, requires a majority of two-thirds of members of the Bundestag and the same majority of votes in the Bundesrat.[29]

When it became clear that no agreement with the opposition would be reached, the governing parties shifted their strategy. They abandoned the possibility of formally changing the rules of the Basic Law through a speech act endorsed by the appropriate majority in parliament, and turned to exploiting the claim that deployments abroad were in fact legal. Assuming the legality of deployments abroad created space for a new strategy to achieve the desired constitutional clarification. The aim was to create a situation where the Federal Constitutional Court would state the legality of the envisaged actions. As the option of judicial review does not exist in the constitutional system of the FRG,[30] it was necessary to violate the Basic Law in the eyes of the opposition, who would then find a way to appeal to the court.[31] This meant that the government had to engage in an activity the legality of which was under dispute. The most obvious step, with this aim in mind, would have been simply to deploy soldiers to an international mission. This, however, involved an element of risk. It would have meant dispatching troops to potentially dangerous missions despite the possibility that this could later turn out to have been illegal. The defence minister repeatedly expressed his worry about sending soldiers abroad without a clear legal basis.[32] Alternatively, the governing majority in parliament could pass a law spelling out the conditions under which the Bundeswehr could be deployed abroad. If deployments abroad were illegal as such, then so would be such a law. Either way, this process of testing the limits of permissibility would leave the opponents of such a development with a choice of either appealing to the constitutional court or accepting a

---

[29] The Bundesrat represents the governments of the *Länder*, the constituent parts of the Federal Republic.
[30] See, for example, Heribert Prantl, 'Verfassungsstreit um die Operation in der Adria', *SZ*, 20 Jul. 1992, 6; Helmut Kerscher, 'Ein Gericht als Oberbefehlshaber', *SZ*, 26 Mar. 1993, 4; 'Herzog: Karlsruhe macht keine Gutachten', *SZ*, 27–8 Mar. 1993, 2.
[31] For the exact regulations, see Art. 93 of the Basic Law.
[32] See, for example, 'Rühe ändert seine Ansicht zur Möglichkeit von Kampfeinsätzen', *FAZ*, 23 Nov. 1992, 1–2, here 1; 'Rühe findet Unterstützung in der CDU', *FAZ*, 24 Nov. 1992, 4; 'Weder Grundgesetzänderung noch Entsendegesetz', *FAZ*, 25 Nov. 1992, 1–2, here 2.

new interpretation of the rules:[33] for any new practice would invariably have an influence on the existing rules (*WOM* 101).

When the 1992 SPD party congress failed to authorise its leadership to discuss constitutional regulations which would permit more than peacekeeping operations, Chancellor Kohl, who earlier had been in favour of clarifying the constitution through the democratic process, began to support this new strategy of provoking a decision of the constitutional court.[34] To avoid an actual and potentially illegal deployment, Defence Minister Rühe suggested passing an *Entsendegesetz*, a 'law on dispatching', to form the legal basis for Bundeswehr participation in all UN operations. This law was meant to regulate the external use of the military without constitutional change.[35] The point of this law would not merely have been to regulate an area of policy which had not previously existed, but also to establish the meaning of the constitutional rules. Passing such a law would have forced the SPD opposition to appeal to the constitutional court if it wanted to prevent it.[36] Effectively, this was a move away from the position that the Basic Law itself needed clarification. It was rather based on the assumption that the constitution already established the legality of military involvement abroad. Although only a few months earlier Kohl had argued that court proceedings were not a basis for a serious foreign and security policy, he was now in favour of the plan.[37] It failed, however, because the junior coalition partner, whose support was needed to pass the law, refused to cooperate.[38]

Proposing a law on deployments meant acting on the assumption that military involvement abroad was constitutional. Otherwise passing such a law would have constituted an illegal manoeuvre. The claim that military deployments abroad were not technically illegal but merely construed as such by a misguided reading of the rules therefore created

---

[33] The aim to get the opposition to appeal was repeatedly mentioned in the press. See, for example, 'Eine regelrechte Psychose', *Der Spiegel*, 52/46, 21 Dec. 1992, 18–20, here 20; 'Nato-Mitglied das reicht nicht', interview with the chairman of the CDU/CSU parliamentary group Wolfgang Schäuble, *Der Spiegel*, 4/47, 25 Jan. 1993, 20–3, here 21. See also Philippi, *Bundeswehr-Auslandseinsätze*, pp. 89–90.

[34] 'Rühe findet Unterstützung in der CDU', *FAZ*, 24 Nov. 1992, 4; 'Rühe ändert seine Ansicht zur Möglichkeit von Kampfeinsätzen', *FAZ*, 23 Nov. 1992, 1–2, here 1.

[35] 'Rühe: Militäreinsatz auch ohne Verfassungsänderung', *SZ*, 23 Nov. 1992, 2; 'Rühe ändert seine Ansicht zur Möglichkeit von Kampfeinsätzen', *FAZ*, 23 Nov. 1992, 1–2, here 1.

[36] 'Rühe findet Unterstützung in der CDU', *FAZ*, 24 Nov. 1992, 4; 'Weder Grundgesetzänderung noch Entsendegesetz', *FAZ*, 25 Nov. 1992, 1–2.

[37] Philippi, *Bundeswehr-Auslandseinsätze*, pp. 90–1.

[38] 'Weder Grundgesetzänderung noch Entsendegesetz', *FAZ*, 25 Nov. 1992, 1–2, here 1; Philippi, *Bundeswehr-Auslandseinsätze*, pp. 90–1.

new space for practice. This space turned out to be wider than this first manoeuvre suggested, for on the same basis it was also possible to simply go ahead with participation in international operations, that is, to engage in the new but as yet contested practice. Engaging in the practice is significant because rules are made by and become significant through what people say and thereby do. It is even difficult to distinguish rules from related practices. Onuf calls '[a]ll the ways in which people deal with rules' (C 59) practices. By looking at practices, we may infer what the rules are. However, practices are not merely a realisation or operationalisation of rules. 'Practices are the content of carrying on'[39] in relation to rules and this involves being aware of them in a practical or even reflective way. Through practices people change rules and alter outcomes (*WOM* 101). Every response to rules has an effect on them and their position (C 70). In other words, 'conduct affects the status and content of particular rules, which is to say, it (re)constitutes them'.[40] Thus the government's shift in practice with respect to the constitutional rules would have an effect on the rules themselves. In May 1992 the government sent 150 soldiers acting as paramedics to Cambodia as part of UNTAC.[41] Although the SPD at first considered this operation unconstitutional,[42] the government made sure to acquire their consent.[43] However, after it had become clear that the SPD would not agree to the plans for constitutional change, the government increasingly began to undertake deployments which the opposition was bound to object to. This became particularly clear in relation to the monitoring of the embargo against Bosnia-Herzegovina and the UN mission in Somalia. These operations provided the opportunity not only to discuss the meaning of the rules but to engage in behaviour which would (re)interpret the rules.

Whilst the defence minister had sought the consent of the SPD before soldiers were sent to Cambodia, the Bundeswehr participated in monitoring the UN embargo against Serbia and Montenegro despite explicit SPD opposition.[44] The Bundesmarine had been a part of the WEU operation monitoring the embargo for several months when the mandate was extended to include coercive measures. This posed a problem for

[39] *WOM* 52.
[40] Onuf, 'Intervention for the Common Good', p. 45.   [41] BMV, Official website.
[42] 'SPD: Für Blauhelmeinsatz Grundgesetz ändern', *SZ*, 20 May 1992, 2.
[43] 'Das ist keine Drohgebärde', interview with Defence Minister Volker Rühe, *Der Spiegel*, 30/46, 20 Jul. 1992, 32–5, here 33.
[44] Ibid.

the participating German troops because there was no consensus as to whether the usage of military force abroad for other than strictly defensive purposes was permitted under the Basic Law. Enforcing the embargo rather than just monitoring it would have meant clearly to engage in an activity the legality of which was contested. The FDP opposed the participation of German soldiers in these new measures, as they considered them beyond the scope of what the Basic Law permitted. Defence Minister Rühe and Foreign Minister Klaus Kinkel therefore proposed to let the German destroyer remain part of the operation, but not to authorise its participation in coercive measures. This decision was approved by the cabinet.[45]

However, Chancellor Kohl and several other ministers were unhappy about this construction. They agreed only on the condition that the fundamental question of participation in UN operations would be clarified by 'the coalition and the Bundestag' as soon as possible.[46] Kohl and the CDU/CSU parliamentary group later claimed that it would have been better to let the Bundesmarine participate in the stop-and-search operation. Politicians especially from within the parliamentary group emphasised that Rühe's 'solution' had meant forgoing an opportunity to test the limits of constitutional permissibility. According to this argument, engaging in the new practice despite the possibility that it might be in breach of the constitution would have forced a decision on the matter. The SPD would have appealed to the constitutional court which would have been obliged to decide the matter quickly.[47] On the basis of his expectation that the SPD would have appealed, Schäuble in particular argued that an opportunity to test the limits of the constitution further had been missed.[48] After all, the SPD had already gone to court in July 1992 over the original deployment to the Adriatic. Schäuble and the chairman of the CSU Theo Waigel had explicitly encouraged them to do so.[49]

In this case, the government shied back from what might have turned out to be a blatant violation of the constitution. Yet it continued to send the Bundeswehr on missions considered to be at the border of

---

[45] 'Verstimmung im Kabinett über Adria-Einsatz der "Hamburg"', *FAZ*, 20 Nov. 1992, 1–2, here 1.
[46] Ibid.
[47] 'Kohl verärgert über Rühe', *SZ*, 21–2 Nov. 1992, 2; 'Rühe: Militäreinsatz auch ohne Verfassungsänderung', *SZ*, 23 Nov. 1992, 2.
[48] Philippi, *Bundeswehr-Auslandseinsätze*, pp. 89–90.
[49] 'SPD-Fraktionsvorstand beschließt Verfassungsklage', *SZ*, 17 Jul. 1992, 1; 'CSU ermuntert SPD zur Verfassungsklage', *SZ*, 21 Jul. 1992, 2; 'SPD klagt gegen Bundeswehr-Einsatz in der Adria', *SZ*, 22 Jul. 1992, 1.

permissibility. It gradually involved the military in the UN operation in Somalia. From August 1992 onwards two Transall aircraft of the Bundesluftwaffe were flying food and medical supplies to Somalia.[50] In December this effort was to be quadrupled[51] and the government additionally planned to send paramedics and technical help to rebuild the local infrastructure.[52] Later, plans to deploy infantry to protect the humanitarian mission were reported.[53] Finally, on 17 December the cabinet officially decided to send 1,500 troops to Somalia in January 1993. The soldiers would carry light arms to protect themselves. The government claimed this deployment was in accordance with the constitution, whilst the SPD announced that it would appeal to the constitutional court despite its support for the mission as such.[54]

The position the SPD put forward was twofold. It approved of the provision of medical and logistic support to the Somalia operation but continued to consider changing the constitution necessary. Hence it threatened to appeal to the constitutional court.[55] Some argued that sending German soldiers to Somalia as part of UNOSOM II clearly meant breaking the constitution.[56] Kohl, however, claimed that 'the people starving in Somalia c[ould] not wait until the German parties ha[d] finished their argument about the constitution'.[57] Rühe also said that those who were starving could not wait for a ruling of the German constitutional court.[58] Christian Schwarz-Schilling made a similar argument in relation to Yugoslavia. He even stepped down from his cabinet post because he was 'ashamed' to be part of it as long as nothing was done about the situation in Yugoslavia. He specifically pointed out that a change of policy in relation to international operations after 'the months of exchanging legal reports and then maybe new decisions of party conferences' would be too late to help the Yugoslavs.[59] These politicians therefore appealed

---

[50] 'Bonn will sofort helfen', *SZ*, 12–13 Dec. 1992, 9.
[51] 'Generalinspekteur rät von Militäreinsatz ab', *SZ*, 14 Dec. 1992, 5.
[52] 'Bonn will sofort helfen', *SZ*, 12–13 Dec. 1992, 9; 'Generalinspekteur rät von Militäreinsatz ab', *SZ*, 14 Dec. 1992, 5.
[53] 'Bundeswehr-Infanteristen angeblich nach Somalia', *SZ*, 17 Dec. 1992, 1.
[54] 'Bonn entsendet bewaffnete Soldaten nach Somalia', *SZ*, 18 Dec. 1992, 1; 'SPD droht erneut mit Karlsruhe', *SZ*, 19–20 Dec. 1992, 2.
[55] 'Kinkel strebt breites Bündnis an', *SZ*, 10 Dec. 1992, 1; 'Rechtsprüfung vor Somalia-Einsatz', *SZ*, 11 Dec. 1992, 2.
[56] 'Eine regelrechte Psychose', *Der Spiegel*, 52/46, 21 Dec. 1992, 18–20, here 18.
[57] Quoted ibid.
[58] 'Bonn will sofort helfen', *SZ*, 12–13 Dec. 1992, 9; 'Bonn zu Somalia-Einsatz fest entschlossen', *SZ*, 21 Dec. 1992, 1.
[59] 'Scham über das Kabinett', Schwarz-Schilling's statement about his resignation, *SZ*, 15 Dec. 1992, 6.

to other rules, in Kohl's and Rühe's case to justify the way the government was dealing with the constitutional rules. The moral imperative not to let the Somalis starve was to overrule any potential constitutional restriction. Onuf points out that there is usually more than one rule involved in any situation and that actors may choose which to follow and to what extent (*WOM* 261). An appreciation of the constitutional situation therefore concerns some of the rules which bounded the situation, but not of all of them. In any case, the understanding amongst the governing parties that German soldiers could participate in UN missions involving the use of armed force only after the constitution had been changed was overturned with the decision to participate in UNOSOM II.[60] However, an effort was still made to portray the mission as constitutional. The reasoning was that, as the German army was only going to operate in a 'secure environment', there would not be any encounters with the 'enemy' and, accordingly, the use of force was not the *aim*. As a consequence, this was not a 'deployment', and therefore the operation could not be ruled out by Art. 87a.[61]

Apparently, there was some confusion as to which rules were relevant and what they meant. In an interview with *Der Spiegel*, Defence Minister Rühe seemed to contradict himself with respect to the question of whether the operation was constitutional or not. First he said he was unsure about the legal situation; later he claimed the operation was clearly constitutional. Made aware of the tension between the two statements, he explained that there was no contradiction as the first merely reflected his personal opinion; however, he also claimed that his 'conception of legality [wa]s identical with that of the CDU/CSU'.[62] It was left to the reader to figure out why his personal uncertainty and the party's clear line were in his view not in tension. Neither did Rühe have much of a response to the interviewer's question about his flexibility in legal matters. In October 1992 Rühe had claimed that combat missions would be the exception and that they would require a change in the constitution and the consent of a majority of two-thirds in parliament. Then he wanted a law on deployments. And now he seemed to be able to do without either. Rühe did not attempt to explain his change of mind.[63]

[60] 'Eine regelrechte Psychose', *Der Spiegel*, 52/46, 21 Dec. 1992, 18–20, here 18.
[61] Ibid., 19, and Rühe in 'Raus aus dem Dilemma', interview with Defence Minister Volker Rühe, *Der Spiegel*, 52/46, 21 Dec. 1992, 21–3, here 21–2. See also ch. 3.
[62] 'Raus aus dem Dilemma', interview with Defence Minister Volker Rühe, *Der Spiegel*, 52/46, 21 Dec. 1992, 21–3, here 21–2.
[63] Ibid.

However, this 'flexibility' is surprising and objectionable only if nothing had changed. If rules are not given and unchangeable but are reinforced or altered by practice, as Onuf argues (CIS 18), Rühe's change of mind is less remarkable. The continued involvement of the Bundeswehr in a number of operations apparently worked to reinforce the possibility and, also, legitimacy of such actions. The SPD leadership had early on warned the government not to attempt to evade amending the Basic Law by creating facts.[64] That was, however, precisely what was happening.[65] The government had let the armed forces participate in international military operations, with each deployment more 'military' in nature than the previous one. This can be represented not only as a process of perhaps getting used to the new demands of international military operations, but also as employing rules at a 'level of self-conscious reflection' (*WOM* 52). In other words, this process had a purpose. The expectation was that a persistent new practice would lead to a reinterpretation of the rules. Foreign Minister Kinkel made a related point when he referred to his expectation that the opposition would be forced to acknowledge the 'real' situation: 'But I rely on the power of the facts here. A change in the Basic Law which covers the whole range of potential UN actions is becoming more urgent from month to month. The conflicts do not wait until we are ready and they do not proceed as harmlessly and predictably as some would like to imagine.'[66] Of course, public contemplation about deployments and participation in international missions were part of these powerful 'facts'. Graf Lambsdorff's warning that the CDU/CSU should stop pushing the limit of the constitution,[67] like the SPD's objection to the government's efforts to 'create facts', reflects the fear that this practice had the potential to change the restrictions on action imposed by the rules. As Onuf points out, if 'norms, as rules, guide conduct, then they can, and often do, guide conduct causing the formation of new norms. Every norm has a "source" defined as such by other norms. New norms stem from old norms by way of intervening practice.'[68] In the absence of the power of practice to create reality, those who believed that deployments abroad were unconstitutional should have been able to look forward with confidence to a ruling of the constitutional court.

[64] 'SPD: Für Blauhelmeinsatz Grundgesetz ändern', *SZ*, 20 May 1992, 2.
[65] See also Clemens, 'Opportunity or Obligation?', 245.
[66] Kinkel, 'Verantwortung', 8.
[67] 'Kinkel strebt breites Bündnis an', *SZ*, 10 Dec. 1992, 1.
[68] Nicholas Greenwood Onuf, 'Everyday Ethics in International Relations', *Millennium: Journal of International Studies* 27 (1998), 682.

After all, the legal situation was sufficiently unclear to give them at least an equal chance of victory in the court case the government had arguably provoked.[69]

The government's strategy of increasingly involving the Bundeswehr in international operations had achieved what it was designed to do: the opposition appealed to the constitutional court[70] and as a consequence the court had to establish the legality of the deployments under dispute. In the end, the court indeed had, in some sense, the last word.[71] On 12 July 1994 it ruled that there was no constitutional prohibition against the operations which the opposition claimed to be illegal.[72] This assertive speech act by the court fundamentally changed the situation. It was now possible to deploy the Bundeswehr abroad without significant restrictions. Onuf reminds us that words and words alone may change reality (*WOM* 82). The situation at hand provides a good illustration of this power of speech. The court did nothing other than speak. And yet this speaking had tangible consequences. This speech act made possible the participation in stop-and-search operations in relation to the UN embargo against Serbia and Montenegro,[73] the deployment of ground troops to Bosnia[74] and later the participation in NATO's bombing campaign against Serbia and Serbian troops in Kosovo.[75] Heribert Prantl captured this effect of the court's ruling when he wrote that it changed 'the entire German foreign and military policy'.[76]

This view of the situation relies on an inextricable interconnectedness of speech acts, rules and practices. Rules delimited the issues in some ways but were also susceptible to change through related practices and, significantly, the use of words. As in Kratochwil's approach, norms are fundamentally significant in Onuf's formulation of constructivism. Without reiterating the argument developed in chapter 3, it nevertheless must be pointed out that the indeterminacy of rules and their

---

[69] For more on the constitutional situation, see ch. 3.

[70] The junior coalition partner also appealed. See ch. 3.

[71] See also the comment to this effect in 'Karlsruhe erlaubt UNO-Kampfeinsätze der Bundeswehr', *SZ*, 13 Jul. 1994, 1.

[72] Bundesverfassungsgericht, 'Urteil des Zweiten Senats', 12 Jul. 1994, E90.

[73] 'Bundestag billigt mit großer Mehrheit Einsätze der Bundeswehr in der Adria und in AWACS-Flugzeugen', *SZ*, 23–4 Jul. 1994, 1; 'Bundeswehr in der Adria und in AWACS-Teams', *SZ*, 23–4 Jul. 1994, 2.

[74] 'Die Bundeswehr beginnt ihren gefährlichsten Einsatz', *SZ*, 22 Dec. 1995, 1.

[75] 'Fischer nennt Mission richtig', *SZ*, 20 Nov. 1998, 6; 'Bundeswehr beteiligt sich an Kosovo-Einsatz', *SZ*, 5 Nov. 1998, 5; Renate Flottau et al., 'Alle Serben im Krieg', *Der Spiegel*, 13/53, 29 Mar. 1999, 194–213, here 196.

[76] Heribert Prantl, 'Wir können – aber: sollen wir auch?', *SZ*, 13 Jul. 1994, 4.

interpretations again poses a problem. The lack of clarity as to the rule structure became apparent in the confusion over what the rules meant and whether they needed changing, but also in the potential to appeal to moral norms in order to overrule the disputed requirements of the constitutional regulations. Onuf summarises the role of norms in social life as follows, insisting that rules do not 'govern' everything social:

> People always have a choice, which is to follow rules or not. Instead rules govern the construction of the situation within which choices are made intelligible. The simplest situation is one in which a single rule constitutes the boundaries of choice. Either one follows that rule or not. Most situations are bounded by a number of rules. At choice then is not just whether to follow a rule, but which one, to what extent and so on. (*WOM* 261)

It seems obvious that in this setting the analysis of specific rules will not suffice. Actors may decide to follow different ones. Again, it is therefore problematic to claim that '[w]hat bounds situations are rules' (*WOM* 261). Quite apart from the problem of interpretation, it is not possible to single out certain rules as delimiting situations. Moreover, as we have just seen, practices may influence the rule structure. However, there is less of a clear demarcation between the rule structure, which was largely treated as given by Kratochwil, on the one hand, and actors' practices in relation to it on the other. Onuf's approach emphasises the normative effects of speech acts, even if they are not rules, and they may thus be investigated.

The normative effects of speech acts

Speech acts, because they have normative consequences, are important not only in changing situations but also in defining them. They bestow normativity on practices (*WOM* 183). Speech acts which are repeatedly accepted by the addressees may be institutionalised as rules (*WOM* 86). However, all speaking has normative effects. Assertives imply that the hearer should accept the underlying belief. Directives demand the performance of some action. Commissives, finally, impose duties on the speaker (*WOM* 87–8). The normative effect of speaking can be illustrated by returning to the constitutional problematic discussed above. Early on, there had been a common perception that the constitution had to be changed. Yet the reasons for this belief diverged considerably. This was partially due to opposing views as to the direction in which it should be changed. Whilst some wanted to ensure that the Bundeswehr would not be used for other than defensive purposes, others aimed to enable it to participate in a wide range of international operations.

The position of the FDP on the matter is interesting because it seems at first counterintuitive. Prominent FDP politicians argued that they supported future Bundeswehr involvement in international operations, that the text of the Basic Law as such did not rule it out but that the constitution nevertheless had to be changed before such operations could be considered legal and therefore could be undertaken at all. Genscher categorically claimed that 'under the current constitutional situation no German soldier w[ould] be deployed outside alliance territory'.[77] Kinkel repeatedly argued that changing the constitution might not be necessary legally but that it was politically. He thought that the CDU's shift from considering constitutional change as necessary to doing without it created the impression that the Basic Law was something with which one could do what one liked.[78] Interpretations of the constitution, he argued, could not be changed like a shirt.[79] This refusal to consider deployments abroad without prior constitutional change was based on the belief that one could not change a long-standing constitutional practice just like that, as if the constitution was a meaningless piece of paper. Ulrich Irmer drew attention to the implications of doing that in terms of the FRG's relations to other countries: 'And what should we tell our partners, some of whom have been pushing for German participation for years and who always heard (and believed!) that our constitution does not permit this? That we have only learnt reading now, or, even worse, that we have been shirking successfully so far with the help of a legal trick?'[80] The FDP thereby acknowledged the normative effects of past talking.[81] The implications of past assertions about constitutional restrictions could not be ignored. Speaking, as Onuf points out, has

---

[77] 'Ich habe Kurs gehalten', interview with Foreign Minister Hans-Dietrich Genscher, *Der Spiegel*, 6/45, 4 Feb. 1991, 22–5, here 24.

[78] 'Rühe ändert seine Ansicht zur Möglichkeit von Kampfeinsätzen', *FAZ*, 23 Nov. 1992, 1–2, here 2; 'Regierung über Bundeswehr-Einsätze tief zerstritten', *SZ*, 8 Jan. 1993, 2; Stefan Kornelius and Udo Bergdoll, 'Selbstüberlistung – ein Fall fürs höchste Gericht', *SZ*, 26 Mar. 1993, 3.

[79] Stefan Kornelius and Udo Bergdoll, 'Selbstüberlistung – ein Fall fürs höchste Gericht', *SZ*, 26 Mar. 1993, 3; 'FDP will gegen CDU/CSU in Karlsruhe klagen', *SZ*, 25 Mar. 1993, 1.

[80] Ulrich Irmer, 'SPD darf sich nicht länger verweigern', *Pressedienst der FDP Bundestagsfraktion*, 11 Jan. 1992 quoted in Philippi, *Bundeswehr-Auslandseinsätze*, p. 102.

[81] See also 'FDP beharrt auf Grundgesetzänderung', *FAZ*, 24 Nov. 1992, 4; Hoyer (FDP) in Deutscher Bundestag, *Plenarprotokoll*, 12/132, 15 Jan. 1993, 11468.

normative effects.[82] A related point was made by Robert Leicht in *Die Zeit*. He emphasised that the past assertions about the content and meaning of the Basic Law, that is, the repeated claim that military involvement outside NATO territory was unconstitutional, had legal implications. Therefore it was impossible to overturn them unilaterally. He argued that a continuous practice in combination with *opinio juris* had led to customary law with respect to the constitution. This had created more restrictive conditions for the use of force than the text of the Basic Law suggested, but they were nevertheless binding.[83] It is important to note that these points appeal to the normative consequences not of legal rules but of speaking. Normativity is attached to speech acts which had been repeatedly performed, but which were not acknowledged as 'rules' by the actors. Onuf's approach recognises the normative effects of speaking, and it may therefore be less important to identify specific rules which, as has been shown in chapter 3, is all but impossible.

Normativity also develops from past speech acts. In the case of the FDP's unwillingness to consider military action without constitutional change, reference is made to the normative consequences of an assertion. In the past the representatives of the FRG had asserted that their constitution ruled out such operations and therefore they could not now simply change their mind. A certain reality had been established and, following the argument from within the FDP, one could not ignore this reality. Normative constraints are even more obvious in the case of commissive speech acts, that is, promises. It is the point of a promise to create normative consequences for the speaker. In other words, it 'constitutes a commitment on the speaker's part' (*WOM* 87). Arguably, the normative force of the principles of 'never again war' and 'never again dictatorship' discussed in chapter 3 rested primarily on the prior commitment to them. Andrea Lederer, for instance, pointed out that a commitment had been made and that she could see no reason why it would not be valid any more: 'All parties, especially the SPD, have stated: Never again German soldiers in other countries! War must never again emanate from German soil! – I really ask myself seriously why this should have become different today.'[84] The normative force of the 'never again war' principle has been discussed at length in chapter 3 and will not be taken up again here. In this chapter, I want to draw attention to

---

[82] Onuf, 'Speaking of Policy', p. 77.   [83] Leicht, 'Mit Volldampf', 3.
[84] Andrea Lederer (PDS/Linke Liste) in Deutscher Bundestag, *Plenarprotokoll*, 12/132, 15 Jan. 1993, 11472.

some commitments claimed by those in favour of military involvement abroad. Firstly, they argued that, in becoming a member of the UN, the FRG had promised to participate in military action in the pursuit of international security. Secondly, the government increasingly committed itself to changing the constitution by making implicit and explicit promises in the international realm.

In the discussion about German military involvement abroad, the FRG's accession to the UN in 1973 was represented as a commitment to honouring duties under the UN Charter. Repeatedly, it was emphasised that the FRG had become a member without claiming any exceptions and that therefore it had to contribute troops to UN operations.[85] Chancellor Kohl's then security adviser Teltschik had already argued in 1987 that the Basic Law left more options open than commonly recognised. The supporting argument for claiming this legal room for manoeuvre had been precisely that the FRG had become a member of the UN without any reservation. Therefore, and because of Art. 24 (2) of the Basic Law permitting integration into a 'system of mutual collective security', a deployment would be legal if the UN asked for German soldiers.[86] The argument implied that there was a duty for the member states, under the UN Charter, to contribute troops to UN operations. This was obvious in the 1994 White Paper:

> As a member of the United Nations the Federal Republic of Germany has accepted all rights and duties of the UN Charter. From this derives the active participation in tasks and missions of the community of peoples. The military provisions for the security of our state must therefore not be limited any more to the defence of the country and the alliance.[87]

It remained unclear, however, on which specific regulations the asserted duty was thought to be based. Peace-keeping operations have, considering the long-standing practice, become accepted as customary international law, but they are not mentioned in the UN Charter.[88] Peace-enforcing operations are based on Chapter VII of the Charter. Yet, a duty to commit troops to such operations could derive only from Art. 43 of the UN Charter. Art. 43 envisions each member state contributing armed forces and logistical support which would be available to the

---

[85] See, for example, BMV, *Weißbuch 1994*, p. 47, section 403; Lamers, 'Was die Friedens-missionen lehren', 55.

[86] 'Wir müssen erwachsen werden', *Der Spiegel*, 34/44, 20 Aug. 1990, 121–3, here 122.

[87] BMV, *Weißbuch 1994*, p. 47, section 403.

[88] Philippi, *Bundeswehr-Auslandseinsätze*, p. 29.

UN on its demand. This obligation to commit troops was to be based on a special agreement to be ratified by the member states. Such an agreement has never been concluded.[89] Therefore, there is little evidence that the FRG is under a legal duty to commit troops to UN operations.[90]

Nevertheless, politicians time and again referred to the FRG's commitment to preserving international peace as expressed by its accession to the UN. Genscher claimed that Germany wanted to 'fully observe' its rights and duties in the UN now.[91] Kinkel reiterated that the FRG's international political responsibility had increased. This, he argued, applied especially to the 'obligation, which we took on in subscribing to the statutes of the United Nations, to support the instruments of collective preservation of peace which the UN Charter provides for'.[92] Kohl stressed the necessity of observing the rights and duties which the FRG had accepted by becoming a member of the UN, if it wanted to remain able to act and to shape international politics.[93] Hermann-Otto Solms of the FDP spoke of the 'duties in the United Nations and in other alliances'.[94] He claimed that Germany (*sic!*), by becoming a member of the UN, had committed itself to providing the necessary contribution to the peace policy of the community of peoples.[95] Defending the governing parties' proposal to change the constitution, Schäuble also argued that the FRG had duties under the UN Charter, including participation in military operations.[96] In a commentary in the *Süddeutsche Zeitung*, Dieter Schröder claimed that the logical consequence of not

---

[89] Philippi, *Bundeswehr-Auslandseinsätze*, p. 33; Khan and Zöckler, 'Germans to the Front?', 166; Bundesverfassungsgericht, 'Urteil des Zweiten Senats', 12 Jul. 1994, E90, 352.

[90] Ulrich Fastenrath, 'Müssen die Deutschen Truppen nach Somalia schicken?', *FAZ*, 16 Jan. 1993, 6. Nevertheless, the constitutional court followed the argument that there was a practical even if not legal duty to participate in UN operations. See Bundesverfassungsgericht, 'Urteil des Zweiten Senats', 12 Jul. 1994, E90, 291–2 and 345–55, esp. 352–3.

[91] 'Genscher: UNO-Sicherheitsrat stärken', *SZ*, 16–17 May 1992, 6; also 'Die Welt ist von Grund auf verändert', interview with Foreign Minister Hans-Dietrich Genscher, *Die Zeit*, 30 Aug. 1991, 5–6, here 6.

[92] Deutscher Bundestag, *Plenarprotokoll*, 12/101, 22 Jul. 1992, 8610; see also 'Rühe ändert seine Ansicht zur Möglichkeit von Kampfeinsätzen', *FAZ*, 23 Nov. 1992, 1–2, here 2; 'Rühe verabschiedet deutsche Blauhelme', *SZ*, 12 May 1992, 15.

[93] 'Naumann: Bundeswehr ist bequem und überheblich geworden', *SZ*, 13 May 1992, 1; 'Deutschland soll stärkere Führungsrolle ausüben', *SZ*, 12 Jul. 1994, 1. Kohl's security advisor Joachim Bitterlich also referred to duties in the international community. See Bitterlich, 'La politique communautaire et occidentale', 834.

[94] Deutscher Bundestag, *Plenarprotokoll*, 12/151, 21 Apr. 1993, 12941.

[95] Ibid., 12939; Rühe, 'Es geht nicht um Eroberungskriege', 12.

[96] Wolfgang Schäuble (CDU/CSU) in Deutscher Bundestag, *Plenarprotokoll*, 12/132, 15 Jan. 1993, 11464. See also 'Nahe dran am echten Krieg', *Der Spiegel*, 30/46, 20 Jul. 1992, 22–9, here 28.

contributing troops to UN operations would be to withdraw from the UN altogether.[97] Hence, the past commitment was seen to create consequences for present practice.

This supposed need to contribute to UN and other international operations was reinforced by statements and actions which could be read as commitments. During the Gulf War Chancellor Kohl argued that, in the future, Germany had to be prepared to participate in 'concrete measures for the preservation of peace and stability in the world'.[98] More precisely, it was necessary to make it constitutionally possible for the FRG to contribute to the activities of the UN in the realm of the preservation of peace. According to Kohl there was no 'niche' for Germany in world politics, no possibility of escaping its responsibility.[99] Especially during the Gulf War, members of the government had repeatedly hinted that the FRG would rapidly change its constitution to make participation in military operations possible. Foreign Minister Genscher had even declared in front of the UN Assembly that German forces would participate in UN operations before there was a majority supporting this move in the Bundestag.[100] In a speech in London in March 1993, Defence Minister Rühe assured the audience that he understood that the FRG had to change its constitution. He explained that the government had introduced a bill in parliament to do so but was unlikely to get the required two-thirds majority. Nevertheless, he promised to continue to work hard for a consensus. According to Rühe, a majority of the German population considered 'an appropriate German participation in international crisis management an expression of the normality of a sovereign state'.[101] Concluding his speech, he acknowledged that the FRG would have to change more than others in order to cope with the new challenges of the international world. Yet he had no doubts that Germany would 'catch up with its allies'.[102]

Statements promising constitutional change were combined with behaviour which had the same effect. For instance, the FRG took part in creating a NATO rapid reaction force. This was problematic in itself because the NATO treaty provided no basis for using it outside the treaty area.[103] Arguably, it ignored that intervention without a UN mandate

---

[97] Dieter Schröder, 'Am Ende des Sonderweges', *SZ*, 13 Apr. 1993, 4.
[98] Deutscher Bundestag, *Plenarprotokoll*, 12/5, 30 Jan. 1991, 90.   [99] Ibid.
[100] 'Bundeswehr wird an UNO-Einsätzen teilnehmen', *SZ*, 26 Sep. 1991, 1; 'Grundlage entzogen', *Der Spiegel*, 41/45, 7 Oct. 1991, 45.
[101] Rühe, 'Gestaltung euro-atlantischer Politik', 230.   [102] Ibid., 233.
[103] 'Lieber exklusiv', *Der Spiegel*, 45/45, 4 Nov. 1991, 24–5, here 25.

would be a violation of international law.[104] However, the FRG supported this project, which ultimately necessitated participation in international military operations. This could be seen when NATO decided to support the European intervention forces in the Balkans with its rapid reaction force,[105] which could not function without German helicopters, engineers and transport forces.[106] Moreover, as *Der Spiegel* commented, the government had increasingly from week to week 'committed itself to military participation through its promises in the NATO Council'.[107] Additionally, the FRG joined the Eurokorps, which was also set up to intervene outside NATO territory. The German government stressed that its constitution had to be changed before the Bundeswehr would be able to participate in such operations. This reservation, however, implied a commitment to future participation. Kohl made clear in this context that he considered the constitutional restriction a relic of the times of occupation.[108] Heidemarie Wieczorek-Zeul of the SPD complained that the proposals for the Eurokorps had again created 'false expectations amongst [our] European neighbours'.[109] The actions taken implied a promise to go further, to deploy the military abroad.

Hence, it was not so much that independently existing rules prescribed a specific course of action for the FRG. Rather, looking at the situation with Onuf's reasoning in mind, actors created normative constraints for themselves through the use of speech acts. Onuf points out that, once 'webs of promises become sufficiently generalized and normative in their own terms, they become *commitment-rules*. Agents are most likely to recognize these rules in their effects. These effects are the *rights* and *duties* that agents know they possess with respect to other agents' (C 68). Thus, promises may create new rules which then impose rights and duties. Onuf also points out that liberal society is saturated with commitment rules which lead to a sense of responsibility (*WOM* 121). Liberal society depends on this sense of responsibility to function. Accordingly, disregarding the requirements of acting responsibly is not an option. Unsurprisingly, the need to take responsibility was a

[104] Elmar Schmähling, 'Ein Lagerhaus der Rüstung', *Der Spiegel*, 1/46, 30 Dec. 1991, 32–3, here 33.
[105] 'Deutsche "Tornados" sollen in Bosnien zum Schutz der europäischen Eingreiftruppe eingesetzt werden', *SZ*, 27 Jun. 1995, 1.
[106] 'Wie in Somalia', *Der Spiegel*, 49/48, 5 Dec. 1994, 18–21, here 18.
[107] 'Nur noch Gewalt', *Der Spiegel*, 23/49, 5 Jun. 1995, 30–1, here 31.
[108] 'Im Kriegsfall unter NATO-Befehl', *SZ*, 22 May 1992, 1; Rudolph Chimelli, 'Euro-Korps steht allen Staaten der EG offen', *SZ*, 23–4 May 1992, 2.
[109] 'SPD warnt vor Geheimdiplomatie', *SZ*, 15 May 1992, 2.

significant argument in the debates about German military involvement abroad. In taking up this theme, I will take a closer look at speech acts and their success or failure.

Speech acts: success and failure

Onuf stresses that the 'very act of saying something (a speech act), of giving voice, does what that act says it does' (*WOM* 236). This is what he means by speech being performative. All speech acts in some way perform, rather than describe, an action. Assertives, which seem to merely represent an action, imply 'the speaker's wish or intention that the hearer accept this belief' (*WOM* 87). Therefore, if successful, they do not merely describe a state of affairs but make the addressee accept that it exists. I want to explore the claim that the act of saying something does what it says it does with respect to such an assertive speech act, i.e. a statement of the form X counts as Y, which was repeated frequently in the debates. Time and again it was claimed that the issue of participation in international military operations constituted a test of German reliability, that solidarity was at stake. Schäuble, for instance, forcefully argued that the decision about whether or not to get militarily involved abroad was deeply significant: 'What is at stake is the ability to act, the ability to be part of an alliance, what is at stake is the ability of the Federal Republic of Germany to contribute to peace.'[110] To him, the question of participation in international military operations was about the FRG's reliability and predictability in relation to the task of securing peace and freedom.[111] He urged that the FRG needed to remain able to be an alliance partner within NATO.[112]

This theme became prominent when it seemed possible that the FRG would have to pull out of the international operations to which it had already deployed troops if the constitutional court ruled that these were illegal. Kohl talked about the damage this would do to the FRG's international reputation and about the danger of isolation.[113] In a statement in front of the constitutional court when a temporary injunction was at issue, the government argued that the functioning of AWACS would be seriously hampered without German participation. A temporary

---

[110] Wolfgang Schäuble (CDU/CSU) in Deutscher Bundestag, *Plenarprotokoll*, 12/132, 15 Jan. 1993, 11465.
[111] Ibid.
[112] 'Die Deutschen an die Front', *Der Spiegel*, 6/45, 4 Feb. 1991, 18–22, here 20.
[113] 'Harmlos humanitär', *Der Spiegel*, 25/47, 21 Jun. 1993, 28–9, here 29.

injunction forcing the Germans to pull out would reduce the trust of NATO partners and therefore Germany's defensive capacity. Pulling German forces out of an integrated unit would amount to revoking solidarity in the alliance.[114]

In the Bundestag debate about the participation in the AWACS operation and the UN mission in Somalia, Foreign Minister Kinkel defined the key question as follows: 'Do we, as a unified and sovereign Germany after the end of the bipolar world of the East–West conflict, arrive at a new consensus about foreign and security policy, which makes us a partner of the world community who, in a changed situation in the world, is able to act and is aware of its responsibility?'[115] The question, he said, was whether the Germans were ready to take up the 'tasks for peace' which the world community expected them to fulfil.[116] If the constitutional situation was not resolved, the Germans would find themselves on the political margins in the alliance, the EC and the UN. Their partners had provided security for over forty years. If they left those partners on their own with the new tasks, the Germans would become incapable of being part of an alliance.[117] Kinkel justified the unconventional procedure of referring the decision to the constitutional court with the significance of the issue: 'What was at stake at the end of the day was our calculability as an alliance partner.'[118] Participation in international military operations beyond the traditional peace-keeping that the SPD was prepared to accept was necessary because an 'isolation of Germany in the community of states' had to be prevented.[119] Later, Kohl argued that after forty years of security under the nuclear umbrella the Germans had to show 'support and comradeship' on the Balkans: it was their 'turn now'.[120] These comments implied that they were merely stating an independent reality, namely that German reliability and solidarity was at issue. However, in some sense, they make what they state. Reliability and solidarity cannot be at issue unless this context is invoked through speech acts. They are concepts which depend on linguistic contextualisation. In other words, the effect of these speech acts was that German reliability and solidarity were at issue precisely because this is the state of affairs created through the speech acts. This problem was recognised by Josef Joffe who complained in a commentary in the *Süddeutsche Zeitung* that the AWACS issue had needlessly been turned into a 'fateful

---

[114] Bundesverfassungsgericht, 'Urteil des Zweiten Senats', 8 Apr. 1993, E88, 178–9.
[115] Deutscher Bundestag, *Plenarprotokoll*, 12/151, 21 Apr. 1993, 12925.
[116] Ibid.   [117] Ibid., 12928.   [118] Ibid.   [119] Ibid., 12929.
[120] Quoted in 'Wir sind jetzt dran', *Der Spiegel*, 44/49, 30 Oct. 1995, 34.

question' and that one now had to deal with the consequences of this move.[121]

However, although speech acts may automatically do what they say, although they may change reality, this is not always the case. The speech acts so far considered are only a very small proportion of the statements uttered in relation to the issue of German military involvement abroad. A whole host of things were said with similar intentions of changing or reinforcing the situation, in similar settings, but many of them did not have the same effect. There was a long list of suggestions from those who wanted to avoid military action altogether. The independent member of parliament Wüppesahl, for instance, was prepared to take the idea of responsibility very personally. He wanted to submit a motion asking members of parliament to travel to Iraq and Kuwait and stay there to stop the Americans from attacking. This was rejected by a large majority in the Bundestag, however.[122] Vera Wollenberger of Bündnis90/Die Grünen suggested, in a similar vein, that parliamentarians should travel to the Gulf region to express their opposition to withdrawing all politicians and diplomats from the crisis region in order to make war possible.[123] Wüppesahl's and Wollenberger's speech acts seemed to have no effect on the reality as conceived by their fellow parliamentarians.

Others suggested ways of taking responsibility other than militarily. Peter Glotz of the SPD ridiculed the notion of the pressure which, it was claimed, the world was exerting on the FRG to participate in combat missions. He argued that the FRG's reputation did not depend on whether there were German pilots in AWACS planes. According to Glotz, raising foreign aid to the promised 0.7 per cent would be a stronger expression of responsibility.[124] His party colleague Gerhard Schröder similarly considered increasing aid to this level a better expression of sovereignty than participation in military operations.[125] Moreover, the FRG should contribute towards making international organisations work better. Günter Verheugen therefore thought that responsibility would consist in contributing towards a world domestic policy through politically, financially and materially enabling the UN to do what it was continuously

[121] Josef Joffe, 'Die "peinlichste Kabinettssitzung des Jahres" ', *SZ*, 2 Apr. 1993, 4.

[122] Deutscher Bundestag, *Plenarprotokoll*, 11/235, 15 Nov. 1990, 18852–3.

[123] 'SPD-Chef Vogel warnt vor den Folgen eines Krieges', *SZ*, 12–13 Jan. 1991, 2.

[124] Deutscher Bundestag, *Plenarprotokoll*, 12/151, 21 Apr. 1993, 12969.

[125] 'Schröder: Bruch des Völkerrechts', *SZ*, 17 Jul. 1992, 6.

being asked to do.[126] According to Wollenberger, German money was more important than German troops in order to live up to the growing responsibility. She compared the FRG to Norway in this context.[127] The FRG was especially to provide the financial support necessary for overcoming the division of Europe. Germany's international responsibility lay, as Wieczorek-Zeul of the SPD argued, in financing German unity and the stabilisation of countries in Eastern and Central Europe. There was no need to compete with great powers.[128] Rudolf Scharping later asked what he was to think of a foreign policy which could not spare DM10 million for a project of the THW in Africa or elsewhere but was willing to make available billions for the Gulf War.[129] Scharping also pointed to the parliamentary refusal to found a relief organisation to deal with environmental disasters and catastrophes which would have been a peaceful way to take responsibility.[130] These alternative suggestions as to how to accept responsibility were not taken up by the government. Similarly, the idea of transforming the military into a 'civilary', which would help with natural and industrial disasters or work to repair ecological damage,[131] did not make much impact, although it was proposed more than once. Oskar Lafontaine of the SPD demanded that future plans for the Bundeswehr should consider new tasks, such as fighting epidemics, natural disasters and environmental damage.[132] A similar goal was pursued by Bündnis90/Die Grünen with their proposal to 'civilise' international relations.[133] The Greens would have preferred to replace NATO altogether, with a new security system not based on violence and military force.[134] None of these speech acts, however, had the desired effect of bringing about the state of affairs apparently intended by the speakers.

Now, if Onuf claims that the 'very act of saying something... does what that act says it does' (*WOM* 236), it is not clear why *these* speech acts should have had less effect than others. More broadly, the question is why the government's interpretation that there were no constitutional restrictions won over the traditional interpretation, as supported by the

---

[126] Günter Verheugen (SPD) in Deutscher Bundestag, *Plenarprotokoll*, 12/132, 15 Jan. 1993, 11479.
[127] Ibid., 11472.   [128] Ibid., 11491.
[129] Deutscher Bundestag, *Plenarprotokoll*, 12/240, 22 Jul. 1994, 21170.   [130] Ibid., 21171.
[131] 'Viele bunte Smarties', *Der Spiegel*, 32/46, 3 Aug. 1992, 34–7, here 37.
[132] 'Humanitäre Hilfe verstärken', *SZ*, 4 Jan. 1993, 5.
[133] Deutscher Bundestag, *Drucksache*, 12/3014, 2 Jul. 1992.
[134] 'Draußen wie drinnen', *Der Spiegel*, 32/48, 8 Aug. 1994, 20–1, here 20.

SPD, the FDP and Bündnis90/Die Grünen. J. L. Austin discusses at length why speech acts fail. He calls these 'infelicities' of performatives and refers to such aspects as completeness, correctness and appropriate context.[135] Onuf does not take up this discussion, presumably because his argument is about the general significance of speech acts and not about success or failure of specific occurrences of speech acts. Nevertheless, he implicitly provides us with one criterion a speech act must satisfy: it must be properly addressed to the material circumstances. We cannot construct just anything we like. Materiality constitutes a limit. People are free as agents, Onuf argues, in as far as they are able 'to recognize material and social limits and to evaluate the consequences of ignoring or defying those limits' (CM 9).

However, the exploration of unsuccessful alternatives to government policy shows that the limit of materiality is not a convincing explanation of why the above speech acts failed. For a start, none of them seem to be running up against some physical limit: members of parliament could have travelled to Iraq had they so wished; the FRG could arguably have diverted funding to countries in need and civilian projects; and the military could have been retrained to fulfil disaster relief rather than combat functions. The realisation of these suggestions does not seem impossible as such. Moreover, apparent 'material' limitations did not lead to an abandonment of the practice of participation in international operations. In early 1992 Hans Rühle, a former chief of planning for the Bundeswehr, suggested that the Bundeswehr was not prepared for missions 'out of area'. No complete unit was available for such operations and the soldiers were insufficiently trained for such tasks. There was also the problem of whether draftees could be ordered to do anything beyond fighting an imminent and existential threat to their country.[136] Inspector General Klaus Naumann also claimed in May 1992 that, as things stood, the German armed forces were unable to participate in a large peace-keeping mission.[137] In March 1993, the Bundestag's commissioner of the armed forces, Alfred Biehle, contended that, because of the consequences of restructuring and a lack of material and equipment, the Bundeswehr was not fully fit for action.[138] German troops did not have the right equipment for the operation in Cambodia. Their uniforms

135 Austin, *How to Do Things with Words*, esp. Lecture II.
136 Hans Rühle, 'Und jetzt der Krieg?', *Der Spiegel*, 9/46, 24 Feb. 1992, 108; Stephan-Andreas Casdorff, 'Nur bedingt einsatzbereit', *SZ*, 17 Jul. 1992, 4.
137 'Naumann: Bundeswehr ist bequem und überheblich geworden', *SZ*, 13 May 1992, 1.
138 'Wehrbeauftragter: Bundeswehr nicht voll einsatzfähig', *SZ*, 24 Mar. 1993, 1.

and boots were too heavy for the climate, they had no mosquito nets and their insect repellent proved ineffective.[139]

Scenarios discussed in the Defence Ministry also suggested some limitations. They showed that, even if German troops were allowed to go abroad, they would, for the time being, be unable to do so. There were not enough pilots to fly the Transall transport planes. Engineers could transport their equipment to Somalia within three weeks, but that would have left insufficient time to prepare troops for the operation. The radio equipment of the signals corps was incompatible with that of US troops. A field hospital was available from the supplies of the former East German army, but because of the operation in Cambodia, no doctors or auxiliary staff could be provided.[140] Moreover, the helicopters of the Bundeswehr were unlikely to function in the Somali climate. The helicopters had to be re-equipped for combat conditions, adding machine guns and protection against enemy fire, making them much heavier, whilst the heat of the desert reduced the power of their engines. This meant that on hot days they could not carry the weight of the gunners as well as that of the pilots, let alone transport any equipment as they were meant to. The helicopters were also insufficiently protected against the effects of sand and dust on their engines.[141]

In early 1993 politicians from different parties came out in favour of military involvement in Yugoslavia. However, the Luftwaffe would at this point in time have been unable to participate in air drops of supplies to fight starvation in East Bosnia because the pilots of the German Transall aircraft were lacking both equipment and training.[142] With the Somalia operation the limit of the Bundeswehr's capacity had, according to the defence minister, been reached.[143] The lack or inadequacy of equipment and personnel could certainly be interpreted as a material limitation to performing the practice of military involvement abroad. Yet in the political debates it was never suggested that these problems should lead to reconsidering the practice. They were problems to be overcome, not boundaries to which kinds of deeds or speech acts were possible. Some limits may be 'substantially material', as Onuf claims (CM 9), but material conditions, even if constraining, are, as this case shows, not always a limit.

[139] 'Möglichst unauffällig', *Der Spiegel*, 23/46, 1 Jun. 1992, 125.
[140] 'Feldjäger in die Wüste', *Der Spiegel*, 51/46, 14 Dec. 1992, 24–5.
[141] 'Bleierne Libellen', *Der Spiegel*, 28/47, 12 Jul. 1993, 47.
[142] 'Hohe Höhe', *Der Spiegel*, 9/47, 1 Mar. 1993, 30–2, here 30.
[143] 'Helden in der Wüste', *Der Spiegel*, 26/47, 28 Jun. 1993, 26.

Therefore, another explanation seems necessary for the success and failure of certain speech acts. Onuf argues that the 'nexus of directing and direction, giving and taking, suggests that politics has to do with contests of wills or . . . struggle' (*WOM* 5). Clearly, there was such a contest over whether the Bundeswehr would be sent abroad. Onuf has this to say about what happens in a political struggle:

> If directing is at the core of politics, it is because some or all members of a social unit treat some matter as important enough to expend resources to affect the disposition of that matter. What they say serves as a direction to others, with consequences that we think of as mapping the direction in which the matter goes. (*WOM* 5)

Some are, of course, more able to influence 'the direction in which the matter goes' than others. Onuf's discussion of resources goes some way towards elucidating this issue. He notes the uneven access to resources and the ensuing differential control over social relations (*WOM* 60), which ultimately leads him to consider the problem of exploitation. He starts with rules to 'show how rules make agents and institutions what they are in relation to each other. Then we can show how rules make rule, and being ruled, a universal social experience' (*C* 63). Onuf views rule as always exploitative, a fact we cannot change. This should not, however, stop us from calling exploitation what it is (*WOM* 288–9). Exploitation is ingrained in what we call order. Rules establish stability in social institutions by privileging certain people (*WOM* 122). Stability ensues precisely because those who made the order benefit from it (*WOM* 158). We usually call this phenomenon order. However, '[w]hen we speak of order, we choose a fiction to believe in. "Order" is a metaphor, a figure of speech, a disguise. It is constituted by performative speech and constitutes propositional content for such speech' (*WOM* 155). The problem of order, in which Onuf has been interested for a long time,[144] is therefore the other side of the problem of privilege. Privilege, as Onuf conceptualises it, is related to the asymmetrical distribution of benefits based on rules, that is, what he calls rule (*WOM* 21–2 and 122).

Questions of 'rule' seemed to play a role in the debates about German military involvement abroad not only in terms of why it was one side rather than the other who managed to dominate the debate and bring about the state of affairs they had hoped for. The consideration of rule also mattered in terms of the reasons why politicians either supported

---

[144] Onuf, 'International Legal Order'.

or opposed participation in international operations. Those who were against taking up such a practice worried about an inappropriate use of rule by the Germans. The spokesman on defence of the FDP parliamentary group, Werner Hoyer, for instance, criticised the Stoltenberg paper, which laid out the new planning for the Bundeswehr, on the grounds that it constituted a 'postcolonial trip'.[145] Similar worries were reflected in the fear that such practices might lead to a fundamental remilitarisation of German policy.[146] On the other side, those who supported military involvement abroad feared that failure to do so would mean ending up on the wrong side of rule. Rühe claimed that the ability to participate in international military operations was necessary because a passive role would not be in the FRG's interest. As he put it: 'Only those who act have international influence; those who watch don't.'[147] This assessment of the situation was supported by the observation of a British NATO diplomat that foreign policy in Europe was made by those who were willing and able to act and that the Germans were 'so far not part of this game'.[148] Moreover, the British demanded that only officers of countries providing troops for international operations should be represented at the new joint headquarters of NATO and the WEU.[149] The German military leadership claimed that those who did not provide troops would get no say in new UN structures.[150] This relationship between the provision of armed forces to UN operations and the ability, or even right, to shape organisational structures within the organisation was also asserted by the German government. Bonn, Foreign Minister Kinkel said, would participate in discussions about the reform and expansion of the UN Security Council only once the constitutional situation was clarified.[151] These points suggest that the FRG's shift towards participation in international military operations was not (only) related to constraints created by past commissive speech acts or indeed to an imposition of materiality, but that the relationship between rules and rule was significant.

Yet, despite Onuf's concern with the problem of privilege, we do not gain extensive insight about this phenomenon through his approach.

---

[145] 'Kontroverse um Militärstrategie', *FR*, 20 Feb. 1992, 1.
[146] See, for example, Andrea Lederer (PDS/Linke Liste) in Deutscher Bundestag, *Plenarprotokoll*, 12/151, 21 Apr. 1993, 12942.
[147] Rühe, 'Gestaltung euro-atlantischer Politik', 230.
[148] Quoted in 'Dabeisein ist alles', *Der Spiegel*, 26/49, 26 Jun. 1995, 22–5, here 23.
[149] 'Rote Ohren', *Der Spiegel*, 6/48, 7 Feb. 1994, 23–4, here 23.
[150] 'Lego für die Uno', *Der Spiegel*, 11/48, 14 Mar. 1994, 23–4.
[151] 'Ghali für volle Teilnahme Bonns an UNO-Einsätzen', *SZ*, 12 Jan. 1993, 1.

Given Onuf's preoccupation also with rule, it is surprising that he categorically refuses to discuss the dimension of power. He explicitly avoids 'using the term "power" except in an obviously metaphorical way' because of conceptual ambiguities (*WOM* 237). Although he has a point – power is certainly not an unambiguous notion – this refusal to address the problematic character of the concept seems to leave him in a difficult position not only in terms of explaining why practice takes one direction rather than another, but also of providing a way to deal with or think about the problem of rule which is so important to him; for rules and rule are two sides of the same coin to him. Onuf prefers the terms 'resources' or 'capabilities' over the ambiguous 'power' (*WOM* 237). His discussion of resources goes some way towards addressing the issue I am concerned with here. Clearly, the uneven access to resources and the ensuing differential control over social relations noted by Onuf is related to the issue of what I would call power relations (*WOM* 60).[152] According to Onuf, resources are 'the material component in all human endeavor' and they become important through rule (*WOM* 64; see also 285). Rules, he argues, 'constitute a resource themselves' (*WOM* 64). The problem is that deploying power through rules is more than 'socially defined use' of 'raw materials of nature' (*WOM* 285). Resources, in Onuf's approach, fashion a link between the social and the material. This is, in my view, not the only realm in which power might matter. Rather the representation of reality in particular ways in the first place is a question of power. What is more, the replacement of power with resources is premised on the idea that the social and the material are somehow separate but nevertheless inextricably linked. The next section will discuss why this is fundamentally problematic. Here, it remains to note that, in analysing our social world, Onuf points out 'a pattern of unequal consequences, which does engage [his] moral sense' (*WOM* 283). Surely, he is in good company with this sense of unease. Disappointingly, this is not the starting point for a fruitful argument about rule and privilege but rather where Onuf ends.

The politics of words and worlds

The investigation of privilege is not the only aspect in which Onuf's approach leaves off before getting to the practicalities. He prefers to think about grand shifts, such as in the meaning of modernity, rather than

---

[152] See also Onuf's critique of Giddens' structuration theory (*WOM* 63–4).

to search for the meaning of events which, he claims, can be properly understood only in relation to the meaning of modernity.[153] This entails an engagement with such large issues as the centrality of humans and their individuality in modern thinking, what Onuf refers to as 'ideas', rather than specific manifestations of the problem he addresses, what he calls 'events'.[154] Whilst an exploration of ideas is worthwhile, it is unfortunate that it is opposed to and wins out over the analysis of concrete occurrences.

Onuf's conceptualisation of the relationship between words and world provides little to work with for those wishing to analyse what is construed as the empirical reality of international politics. His approach is abstract. He works through in detail where the different logics of the three basic categories of speech acts can be traced in social reality. These discussions provide a novel way of conceptualising this reality but it never becomes quite clear why this should matter beyond the important point that social life is always conducted in more than one mode. Onuf's categories may be pure and comprehensive, as he claims (*WOM* 24 and 91), but, other than satisfying his personal preference for neat ordering (*WOM* 94), what is their purpose? What are the questions his approach aims to answer or the problems it aims to address? Onuf's goal seems to be at least twofold. On the one hand, he informs us that he wants to reconstruct the discipline of IR; on the other hand, the presentation of his approach as a matter of rules and rule suggests that he is concerned with the problem of privilege. These seem disparate projects. In Onuf's argument they are related because they are both, as everything in his world, related to speech acts.

Speech acts are a difficult operation for at least two reasons. Firstly, they are inextricably related to the idea of intentionality and appropriate context. A promise, for instance, will usually be recognised as one only if it was intended as such and if minimum conditions are met, for instance the ability in principle to deliver the promise. These assumptions are more problematic than it may at first seem. The question of the possibility of speech acts has been analysed by Jacques Derrida (*LI*) and I will come back to his critique of context in chapter 5. At

---

[153] Onuf, 'Sovereignty', 429.

[154] Onuf, 'Sovereignty', 426. See also Nicholas Greenwood Onuf, 'Imagined Republics', *Alternatives* 19 (1994), 315–37; Nicholas G. Onuf and Thomas J. Johnson, 'Peace in the Liberal World: Does Democracy Matter?', in Charles W. Kegley Jr (ed.), *Controversies in International Relations Theory: Realism and the Neorealist Challenge* (New York: St. Martin's Press, 1995), pp. 179–99; and Nicholas Greenwood Onuf, *The Republican Legacy in International Thought* (Cambridge University Press, 1998).

this point, I want to raise the second difficult aspect of speech acts. As the 'point of a speech act is to have an effect on some state of affairs' (*WOM* 98), speech acts are conceptualised as located at the boundary between the linguistic realm and what we call the world, whilst they are at the same time supposed to transcend it. In other words, I want to raise the problem of Onuf's simultaneous efforts at dissolving the clear demarcation between actors and observers and the necessity, for his approach, of confirming the existence of separate social and material worlds. Onuf claims that 'tendencies in practice and observers' portrayals are separately constituted but mutually reinforcing' (*WOM* 23–4) and that 'the distance between the observer and most pictures of social and political space is imagined'.[155] In the context of traditional IR theory, which relies on the transhistorical continuity of practice unrelated to its study, these are radical claims, especially when Onuf goes on to say that it does not matter '[w]hether professors profess an interest in shaping social reality with their conjectures, shape it they do' (*WOM* 106).

In the context of the debates on German military involvement, there were a number of professors and other 'experts' who showed an interest in shaping reality. One example may suffice here. Hanns Maull strongly argued the case for ensuring that the FRG remained what he called a 'civilian power'. Maull claimed that international politics should and could be civilised. This is possible through the mobilisation of 'civilian power', that is, 'a specific form of exercising influence on the course of international relations with the aims of taming the use of organised social violence, of the legal regulation of social relations, of the development of participatory forms of decision-making, of the channelling of conflict resolution and finally of social justice'.[156] This rules out the use of force other than for individual and collective self-defence both between and within states, and means, on the other hand, that the principle of non-intervention has to be overturned; for, as a last resort, military action as police action to restore peace would be necessary. This would require the willingness to put national forces under collective command.[157] Maull went on to argue that, in this process of the civilisation of international relations through the use of civilian power, 'civilian powers', that is, actors whose foreign policy behaviour is particularly conducive to these

---

[155] Nicholas Onuf, 'Levels', *European Journal of International Relations* 1 (1995), 43.

[156] Hanns W. Maull, 'Zivilmacht Bundesrepublik Deutschland. Vierzehn Thesen für eine neue deutsche Außenpolitik', *Europa-Archiv* 47 (1992), 271.

[157] Maull, 'Zivilmacht', 271–2.

processes, play a significant role.[158] The FRG should aim to take on the role of civilian power to its full extent, as its vital interests could be guaranteed only through a civilisation of the international order.[159] Maull stressed that a civilian power could not do without the military instrument. However, its function was to channel the resolution of conflicts into non-military forms.[160] The upshot of Maull's argument was that Germany would prefer to play the role of civilian power.[161] This argument was relevant to policy problems the German government saw itself confronted with at the time. Indeed, the SPD arguably was influenced by these ideas. William Paterson, in describing the foreign policy of the FRG, speaks of a 'civilian power reflex'.[162] However, even if Maull's arguments are related in substance to ideas presented by politicians in debates about military involvement abroad, this does not tell us what their relationship is. Neither does Onuf's argument, which is not merely about those who, like Maull, want to shape reality but also about unintended constitutive effects.

Maybe it is more helpful then, in terms of appreciating the implications of Onuf's argument, not to look at academic work 'out there' but, more fundamentally, to question our own activity of producing such work. Onuf contests not only disciplinary boundaries but also the epistemological assumptions on which IR has been operating. He disagrees with positivist and empiricist but also realist[163] leanings in the discipline. According to Onuf, there is no single truth. Rather '[t]ruths as we take them to be are inextricable from the arguments offered for them' (*WOM* 35). This is related to the notion that observers cannot detach themselves from the matter investigated. It is crucial for Onuf's conception of knowledge to understand that we can never leave the world of constructions: 'We are always within our constructions, even as we choose to stand apart from them, condemn them, reconstruct them' (*WOM* 43). Ideas and events necessarily interact.[164] Onuf quotes Giddens to the effect that the 'point is that reflection on social processes

---

[158] Confusingly, Maull uses the term 'Zivilmacht', civilian power, to signify both a capacity and a country which aims to act in accordance with this capacity. He uses an article only with the latter.
[159] Maull, 'Zivilmacht', 276.   [160] Maull, 'Zivilmacht', 278.
[161] Maull, 'Allemagne et Japon', 487.
[162] Paterson, 'Beyond Semi-Sovereignty', 180. See also Thomas U. Berger, 'Past in Present', 40; Carl Cavanagh Hodge, 'Germany and the Limits of Soft Security', *European Security* 7 (1998), 111; Kelleher and Fisher, 'Germany', p. 171; Livingston, 'United Germany', 166; Michael Hennes, 'Der Krieg und die deutsche Politik', *Gewerkschaftliche Monatshefte* 44 (1993), 193–5; Michael E. Smith, 'Sending the Bundeswehr', 51.
[163] This refers to realism in philosophy.   [164] Onuf, 'Sovereignty', 426 and 429.

(theories, and observations about them) continually enter into... the universe of events that they describe'.[165] Thus we always know from within. We can never get some eternal, unchanging truth. Rather, we 'construct worlds we know in a world we do not' (*WOM* 38). By giving certain concepts meaning we create a starting point in relation to which other aspects of social reality gain meaning. We can know only by creating 'an appropriate vocabulary' which assigns occurrences to 'conceptual homes'.[166]

This suggests the necessity of a new attitude towards our *own* work: for, if academic work does not merely describe or analyse the reality of international politics but helps to constitute it, then it is implicated in that process of making rules and rule which Onuf considers ubiquitous in political society. Clearly, this book seems to bear out the point that we cannot leave our constructions, that reality gains meaning only in relation to a vocabulary we create. Although we are able to conceive of chapters 2, 3 and 4 as analysing, in some sense, the same situation, what this situation *was* depended on how it was constructed in relation to different constructivist approaches. In my explaining what the issue was, it was constituted. In Onuf's terms, it therefore makes no sense to ask, having gone through different analyses, whether the matter discussed in this book was 'really' about identity change in the international realm, about a competition between contradictory norms, about establishing a new relationship between the social and the material or about something different altogether. The best we can do is examine the elements of the picture in relation to each other rather than from the unattainable position of a detached observer.[167] No matter what we do, we always 'end up ordering sets of relations, not as such, but as represented in our theories'.[168]

This suggests not only that we would help make the world with our 'pictures' of it, even if we had no intention of doing so, even if we aimed merely to describe it. It also reads like an invitation to investigate meanings only in relation to each other. Yet Onuf frequently argues at other points that something else matters: materiality. Rules make agents who are able to act upon the world and their 'acts have material and social effects; they make the world what it is materially *and* socially' (CM 8). Deeds therefore link the material and the social. Social reality is linguistically constituted (*WOM* 94); material reality is 'out there'. The latter

[165] Giddens, *Constitution of Society*, p. xxxiii, quoted in Onuf, 'Sovereignty', 426.
[166] Onuf, 'Sovereignty', 439.   [167] Onuf, 'Levels', 43.   [168] Onuf, 'Levels', 52.

provides the materials for construction and marks the limit of the possibilities for the former. As Onuf puts it: 'Human beings, with whatever
equipment nature and/or society provides [*sic*], construct society, and
society is indispensable to the actualization of whatever human beings
may "naturally" be; society constructs human beings out of the raw materials of nature, whether inner nature or, less problematically, the outer
nature of their material circumstances' (*WOM* 46; see also 292). If construction is based on material preconditions, then it is only logical that
these conditions also circumscribe the possible. The freedom of agents,
Onuf argues, 'depends on the ability to recognize material and social
limits and to evaluate the consequences of ignoring or defying those
limits' (CM 9). Apparently, Onuf's constructivism starts from a duality
of the material and the social. Although Onuf claims that there are no
essentialist tendencies in his theory (*WOM* 293), he makes a universal-
ist claim on the basis of *a priori* existing material conditions: 'I suggest
that our sensory experience of the world and of our bodily selves in
that world, reinforced by our appreciation of possible relations of in
and out, wholes and parts, yields a universal set of three categories
of reasoning, not to mention many other social practices' (*WOM* 292).
Thus, because all humans share the same experiences of themselves and
their environments, their social practices turn out to be similar as well.
Whilst this seems to be a contentious claim from a whole range of perspectives, what is problematic is that it is not clear how Onuf's different
pronouncements on the existence and relationship of social and material
reality are to be reconciled with each other and with his constructivist
argument.

   It is difficult to see, especially in relation to a particular issue such as
German military involvement abroad, how Onuf can, on the one hand,
conceptualise words and world as inseparable and mutually constituted
and, on the other hand, propose to examine the 'direction of fit' between
words and world. Onuf offers an extended discussion of the 'words-to-
world' fit of assertives, directives and commissives. Directives fit world
to words, that is, they change the world through words (*WOM* 93).
This seems to make immediate sense. We are all familiar, for instance,
with the tangible consequences of the order by NATO governments,
including that of the FRG, to bomb Serbia and the Serbian military in
Kosovo. Onuf's split between words and world is, however, in danger
of inviting the cheap objection that the damage on the ground was not
caused by the speech act but by the bomb. To be sure, this discussion
which must refer to separate consequences of the order *versus* the bomb

seems nonsensical in terms of the overall drift of Onuf's approach: for
the whole point of introducing speech act theory is to draw attention to
the interconnectedness of both, to dispel the myth of the possibility of
analysing each in separation from the other.

If directives supposedly fit world to words, commissives, Onuf argues, work the other way around. They fit words to the world because
to 'commit oneself is to project a desired state of affairs and bring it
to bear on oneself' (*WOM* 93). I take this to mean that, for instance, if
we understand the FRG's membership in the UN as a commissive, it
had to provide the troops for UN missions in the pursuit of preserving
international security. The promise to secure international peace militarily must lead to an actual deployment. Why this should mean fitting
words to the world is not clear. It seems to me that following through
with promises leads to something which has an effect on the world
and therefore potentially changes it. It is difficult to see how words and
world, in the case of a promise which necessarily addresses future states
of affairs, should be separable in this way. Things become even more
puzzling when Onuf informs us that assertives 'either reflect an existing words-to-world fit or propose a new one. They do not endeavor
to change an existing arrangement.'[169] It seems strange to suggest that
proposing a new words-to-world fit would *not* change an existing arrangement. The assertion that the Basic Law did not rule out military
deployments abroad, for example, in my view, led to significant changes
in the 'existing arrangement'. The ruling of the Federal Constitutional
Court, which asserted that Art. 24 provided a basis for the deployments in question, clearly led to immediate material consequences as the
Bundestag lifted restrictions on Bundeswehr operations.[170] It made
German participation, for instance in the bombing of Serbia, possible.

It is strange how Onuf stresses, on the one hand, the performativ-
ity of language, that is, a concept which undermines the possibility of
distinguishing between words and world, and, on the other hand, puts
so much emphasis on this very distinction. He ends his discussion of
performative language with the claim that if he is right 'in this reconstruction of the ways in which words and world fit, ontological categories match functional categories of speech acts and rules' (*WOM* 94).
It is hard to see, however, how 'ontological categories' and 'functional

[169] *WOM* 93 (footnote deleted).
[170] 'Bundestag billigt mit großer Mehrheit Einsätze der Bundeswehr in der Adria und in
AWACS-Flugzeugen', *SZ*, 23–4 Jul. 1994, 1; 'Bundeswehr in der Adria und in AWACS-
Teams', *SZ*, 23–4 Jul. 1994, 2.

categories of speech acts and rules' can be separate concepts within his approach in the first place. The words–world distinction is, of course, one that is frequently alluded to by policy-makers. Kinkel, for instance, argued at one point that those who, despite their opposition to war, were 'not willing to militarily resist the war-monger if necessary, [we]re not able to create peace or protect human rights. They pursue[d] only a policy of words.'[171] Yet, a speech act approach suggests that there cannot possibly be such a thing as resistance without a 'policy of words'.

Onuf's conceptualisation of words and world as inextricably related but nevertheless distinct, with the latter circumscribing the conditions of possibility for the former, suggests that there is something behind our constructions which is in some way more real. This certainly seems to be conveyed in Onuf's claim that 'the ongoing (re)construction of reality is rarely distinguishable from the known, felt, lived in world we "really" inhabit' (*WOM* 157). If they are to be distinguished at all, they must be in some sense separate. 'Reality' was also frequently invoked as a background and limit in the debates on German military involvement abroad. *Der Spiegel* argued that reality had been 'catching up with the Germans at the Gulf'.[172] Hans-Ulrich Klose complained, also in relation to the Gulf War, that it was unacceptable that politics tried to hide from reality.[173] What exactly this 'reality' was meant to be was never clear except that it was something which supported the position of the speaker, as you cannot argue with reality.

One theme in particular invoked a 'natural' limit: death. There was no good reason why soldiers of other countries should be risking their lives whilst the Germans safely sat at home. No amount of financial aid or other forms of helping out in crisis situations could justify that German soldiers should not die if others did. Defence Minister Rühe rhetorically asked why a nineteen-year-old Polish soldier should carry more responsibility than a nineteen-year-old German soldier.[174] He said that the Germans were 'confronted with the task that Germany take on the same responsibility as its neighbours in a new and changed international system'.[175] If Germany, and so by implication the Germans, were to be equal, they had to be prepared to do this. Foreign Minister Kinkel talked about the questioning looks of alliance partners when, together with his European colleagues, he had been commemorating a British

[171] Deutscher Bundestag, *Plenarprotokoll*, 12/240, 22 Jul. 1994, 21167.
[172] 'Den Ernstfall nicht gewagt', *Der Spiegel*, 7/45, 11 Feb. 1991, 18–26, here 22.
[173] Klose, 'Die Deutschen und der Krieg am Golf', 6.
[174] Deutscher Bundestag, *Plenarprotokoll*, 12/132, 15 Jan. 1993, 11483.   [175] Ibid.

soldier killed on a UN operation. He explained that such a minute's silence had then been necessary at practically every meeting of the foreign ministers and went on to say: 'I at least am unable to forget the fair but questioning looks of my colleagues and also to suppress them just like that: for how long can and does Germany want to permit itself only to see to it that other peoples deploy their soldiers for the protection of peace and accept all the consequences?'[176] Irmer of the FDP asked the SPD: 'Do you believe that the tears flow less hotly when zinc coffins with dead soldiers are delivered in Ireland, Italy or India? What kind of an attitude is it after all to say: we pay, and the others should just put their heads on the chopping block!?'[177]

However, despite the pretence that one could not argue any more once death was involved, matters were more complicated than that. What was important was not any actual death but how it was and could be represented. As will be demonstrated in more detail in chapter 5, in relation to the Somalia mission it was arguably more important to the German government whether the deployment was *seen* to endanger the lives of German soldiers than whether it actually did.[178] Indeed, the danger to soldiers' lives was declared not to be decisive to decision-making in relation to international military operations.[179] Furthermore, it greatly mattered *whose* death was at issue. The life of a Kosovar refugee was not necessarily as important to the decision-makers in the FRG as was the life of one of their nationals.[180] Hence, even when something as suggestively 'real' as death is concerned, interpretation is needed to assess how it matters and indeed, I would argue, what it is. Therefore, it is unconvincing to portray a background reality or materiality as an indisputable limit to our constructions.

Onuf's appeal to material conditions as *a priori* existent and providing the context of constructions seems to reflect common-sense conceptions of reality. It is interesting to note that in the title of the book containing the detailed formulation of his constructivist position Onuf speaks of only one 'world of our making'. This is not surprising because, if we all share certain material conditions, there is a 'natural' limit to the way we may construct our world(s). Political events are, however, never just material. 'Unlike earthquakes, political events never just happen; events and

[176] Ibid., 11476.
[177] Deutscher Bundestag, *Plenarprotokoll*, 12/151, 21 Apr. 1993, 12966.
[178] See Stefan Kornelius, 'Ein mehrfach ungewisses Abenteuer', *SZ*, 18 May 1993, 4.
[179] Martin E. Süskind, 'Ein Militär-Kompromiß ist möglich', *SZ*, 10 Aug. 1993, 4.
[180] 'Möglichst gut rauskommen', *Der Spiegel*, 36/53, 6 Sep. 1999, 190–2, here 192.

concepts depend on each other. Together they are deeds, and through our deeds we make the world we know.'[181] Clearly, there are tensions within this conceptualisation. The argument is problematic because it seems to be dangerous in its own terms. Following Onuf's argument, the problem is not our inability to find truth but our implication, through the use of language, which is rule-governed, in the distribution of privilege.

It seems awkward then to present material reality as the explanation for the limitations of our constructions. By Onuf's own admission, we cannot leave our constructions. This sits uneasily with the notion that there is something *behind* them, so to speak. Even if there was, it could never matter to us other than within our constructions. Even if material reality imposed a limit, what is significant is how we conceptualise this limit. Supporters of military involvement abroad managed to present it as demanded by reality and all alternatives as out of touch with reality. In contrast, the 'limit of reality' did not seem to matter in terms of the obstacles which Bundeswehr deployments faced. Here, obstacles which might be construed as material were simply seen as problems to be overcome, not as fundamental hindrances.

The question of when the material is recognised as a limit therefore seems to be more political than can be acknowledged within Onuf's approach. In remaining abstract and aloof from particular constructions of reality, Onuf seems to exclude the problematic of the political character of constructions. This is significant because the whole point of his enterprise, he argues, is to reconstruct International Relations in a way that takes into account their political character. In Onuf's conceptualisation, politics is inextricably linked to the problem of privilege, to the asymmetry of contests and consequences (*WOM* 5). In presenting materiality as a limit, Onuf tends to privilege the world as it is presented to us, that is, the status quo. His view of how we make our world seems to pay insufficient attention to how this asymmetry is already invested into what he calls the raw materials of our constructions. He therefore seems to favour those who are privileged already, who have the means to present the way things are as 'reality'.

[181] Onuf, 'Sovereignty', 429.

5 The politics of 'reality': Derrida's subversions, constructivism and German military involvement abroad

So far this book has highlighted tensions within each of the different constructivisms under consideration. Each chapter focused on a problematic key move: Alexander Wendt's approach is based on a conception of identity which is contradictory, Friedrich Kratochwil's on a notion of norms which does precisely what he wants to avoid and Nicholas Onuf's on a conceptualisation of the relationship between words and world which unravels in relation to his other claims. In the preceding chapters, these shortcomings were illustrated chiefly in relation to the FRG's shift towards participating in international military operations. My analysis was informed by Jacques Derrida's thought without, however, explicitly detailing how the specific claims used relate to his fundamental challenge to Western thought. Here I want to provide a brief introduction to my reading of Derrida's work, focusing specifically on what I call the 'politics of reality'.

Derrida's plot is as simple as it is subversive: he sets out to demonstrate that our thought, which he terms 'logocentric', cannot function on the basis of its presuppositions. The result of this subversion is a fundamentally different conception of the 'real' which undermines the value-laden hierarchy reality/representation. Following Derrida, even if there were a real, we could never have access to it other than through our representations. As a consequence, what we conceptualise as real is itself an effect of representations. This means that appeals to reality, which were frequent in relation to German military involvement abroad, are not neutral factual statements. The discourse on reality establishes what is represented as possible and what is not. By arguing that the reality which is portrayed as the limit for our constructions and for the scope of our responsibility is itself the effect of representations, Derrida's thought questions the inherent closures. Therefore it can be employed to draw attention to the depoliticising moment of the politics of 'reality'.

All constructivisms critiqued in this book posit 'reality' as a significant point of reference. In engaging further the problems with these constructivisms, I will focus on different but ultimately related uses of 'reality' in each approach: the 'reality' of international politics for Wendt, everyday 'reality' for Kratochwil and 'reality' as raw material for Onuf. This will allow me to make two significant points. Firstly, each use of reality constitutes a closure, an unfounded violence. That is, as will be explained in this chapter, it closes off avenues of thought on grounds which, upon investigation, turn out to be based on nothing but a prior decision. Secondly, despite fundamental differences between the three approaches, they are vulnerable to similar criticisms as the appeals to reality create similar closures. In other words, the conceptual problems with identity, norms and materiality respectively are different expressions of representing 'reality' as a limit to the possible and therefore to our responsibility.

The impossibility of pure presence and the politics of the 'real'

Western thought has, according to Derrida, always been structured by dichotomies or polarities, such as good/evil, presence/absence, truth/error, identity/difference, nature/culture, speech/writing. These opposites are neither equal in value nor independent of each other. Rather, as Barbara Johnson explains, the 'second term in each pair is considered the negative, corrupt, undesirable version of the first, a fall away from it'.[1] Thus the opposition implies a hierarchical order. The first term is temporally and qualitatively prior. 'In general, what these hierarchical oppositions do is to privilege unity, identity, immediacy, and temporal and spatial *presentness* over distance, difference, dissimulation, and deferment.'[2] Western philosophy has, in other words, conceptualised being or the 'real' as presence (*OG* 12 [23]).[3] That which is seen to be immediately present, temporally and spatially, is thus valued

[1] Barbara Johnson, 'Translator's Introduction', in Jacques Derrida, *Dissemination*, translated, with introduction and additional notes, by Barbara Johnson (University of Chicago Press, 1981), p. viii.
[2] Johnson, 'Translator's Introduction', p. viii.
[3] As noted earlier, in references to Derrida's work, numbers in brackets refer to the location in the French originals listed in the bibliography.

over the removed. This, Derrida argues, can be seen in how speech is valued over writing in the history of Western philosophy. The immediacy of speech, which requires speaker and listener to be in the same place at the same time, seems to ensure that they are able to grasp the meaning of their communication. Meaning is thought to be self-present to both sides. As Barbara Johnson explains: 'Whether or not perfect understanding always occurs *in fact*, this image of self-present meaning is, according to Derrida, the underlying ideal of Western culture. Derrida has termed this belief in the self-presentation of meaning "Logocentrism", from the Greek word *Logos* (meaning speech, logic, reason, the Word of God).'[4] Logocentrism, Derrida argues, supports 'the determination of the being of the entity as presence' (*OG* 12 [23]). This has far-reaching implications for all our thinking, basing it on the value of presence.[5] In order to prove the worth of our ideas, for example, we 'show', 'reveal', 'make clear'. In other words, we aim to demonstrate how they are in accordance with a presence. From this point of view, of what Derrida terms the 'metaphysics of presence',[6] representation is always already inferior to the 'real' and present. However, Derrida argues that this conceptualisation of being cannot work. It is built on clear distinctions between presence and absence, identity and difference, and entity and supplement. Yet on investigation we find that each of the terms cannot work without elements of its presumed opposite.

Presence can serve as a secure foundation for our thought only if it is given, pure and absolute. Derrida argues, however, that there can be no pure presence. On the contrary, the 'notion of presence is derived: an effect of differences'.[7] If one considers, for instance, the flight of an arrow, a paradox is produced by thinking of reality as presence: the movement of the arrow cannot be thought as presence. At any instant the arrow is at a particular spot and thus not in motion. The motion of the arrow becomes conceivable only if we accept that every instant is already marked by its past and future. Hence 'something can be happening at a given instant only if the instant is already divided within itself, inhabited by the nonpresent'.[8] Thus, although our thinking is based on the notion of presence as absolute presence, thinking about an everyday occurrence

---

[4] Johnson, 'Translator's Introduction', pp. viii–ix. See also *OG* 3 [11–12].

[5] Jonathan Culler, *On Deconstruction: Theory and Criticism After Structuralism* (London: Routledge, 1983), p. 94. See Jacques Derrida, *Writing and Difference*, translated, with introduction and additional notes, by Alan Bass (London: Routledge, 1978), p. 279 [p. 411].

[6] See, for example, *OG* 49 [71].

[7] Culler, *On Deconstruction*, p. 95. See *OG* 157 [226] and *P* 26 [37–8].

[8] Culler, *On Deconstruction*, p. 94.

such as motion is at the same time possible only because we abandon the purity of the notion of presence. The idea of presence is therefore contaminated by its opposite.

Derrida introduces the notion of *différance* in order to overcome the mutual exclusiveness of presence and absence which he has identified as impossible. *Différance* plays on the two meanings of the French word *différer*: to differ and to defer. Introducing the letter *a* into the word *différence* signals the active character of *différance* whilst remaining hidden when the word is pronounced. *Différance* therefore in one sense refers to something not being identical, or being other, discernible. In the other sense, it means a 'temporal or temporizing mediation or a detour that suspends the accomplishment or fulfillment of "desire" or "will", and equally effects this suspension in a mode that annuls or tempers its own effect'.[9] *Différance* always has several meanings which cannot be reduced to one another. *Différance*

> is a structure and a movement no longer conceivable on the basis of the opposition presence/absence. *Différance* is the systematic play of differences, of the traces of differences, of the *spacing* by means of which elements are related to each other. This spacing is the simultaneously active and passive . . . production of the intervals without which the 'full' terms would not signify, would not function.[10]

Différance not only marks the movement of delay, detour or post-ponement inherent in signification; it is also that which produces differences and as such makes possible the oppositional concepts in our language, for instance, sensible/intelligible, intuition/signification, nature/culture (*P* 8–9 [17]).

All signification is based on *différance*. 'Essentially and lawfully, every concept is inscribed in a chain or a system within which it refers to the other, to other concepts, by means of the systematic play of differences.'[11] To grasp this idea it is helpful to analyse a more common conception of meaning. It is plausible to claim – and this is what speech act theorists do – that the meaning of a word is based on how it is used, on what speakers mean by it. Thus, the meaning of a word at any given point in time depends on prior communication, and, analogously, the structure of the language, its rules and norms, are based on prior events or speech acts. This implies, however, that each event which is said to determine

---

[9] Jacques Derrida, *Margins of Philosophy*, translated, with additional notes, by Alan Bass (University of Chicago Press, 1982), p. 8 [p. 8].
[10] *P* 27 (footnote deleted) [38–9].   [11] Derrida, *Margins*, p. 11 [p. 11].

structures or meaning must itself already be determined by yet prior events. Thus the structures are always already products no matter how far back one goes. As a result, it is impossible to imagine an origin of language without assuming prior organisation and differentiation.[12] Hence, *différance* puts into question the search for origins or essences.[13] All we can ever find are 'nonoriginary origins'.[14]

The implications of Derrida's claim that all signification rests on the simultaneous movements of difference and deferral are profound. Usually, the sign is said to stand for a thing, where the 'thing' may be a meaning or a referent. In other words, it represents a presence in its absence. When we cannot show the thing itself, 'we go through the detour of the sign'.[15] The sign is deferred presence. Thus, Derrida argues, the possibility of the sign, although predicated on the representation of a presence, already introduces the element of difference and deferral, that is, *différance*. 'Nothing, neither among the elements nor within the system, is anywhere ever simply present or absent. There are only, everywhere, differences and traces of traces' (*P* 26 [38]). *Différance* therefore questions the 'authority of presence'.[16] This is crucial because, as we have seen, Western thought, according to Derrida, is based precisely on that authority.

The iterability of signs underscores Derrida's point that signification is based on *différance*. Signification is possible only on the basis of iterability. In other words, '[s]omething can be a signifying sequence only if it is iterable, only if it can be repeated in various serious and non-serious contexts, cited and parodied. Imitation is not an accident that befalls an original but its condition of possibility.'[17] This means that a sign can function only if it can retain aspects of the same whilst changing. Iterability therefore 'supposes a minimal remainder . . . in order that the identity of the selfsame be repeatable and identifiable *in*, *through* and even *in view* of its alteration. For the structure of iteration . . . implies *both* identity *and* difference' (*LI* 53 [105]). It must be possible to recognise a sign whilst giving it a different signification according to the situation. Meaning depends on the context. This, however, means that meaning can never be wholly clear as the context cannot be circumscribed.[18] In other words, 'no context is absolutely saturable or saturating. No context

[12] Culler, *On Deconstruction*, pp. 95–6.   [13] Derrida, *Margins*, p. 6 [p. 6].
[14] Culler, *On Deconstruction*, p. 96.   [15] Derrida, *Margins*, p. 9 [p. 9].
[16] Derrida, *Margins*, p. 10 [p. 10].   [17] Culler, *On Deconstruction*, p. 120.
[18] Culler, *On Deconstruction*, p. 123.

can determine meaning to the point of exhaustiveness.'[19] Because of the potential multiplicity of contexts, meaning is also the product of a process of 'grafting', of different texts and contexts being superimposed on each other and working together in a signifying chain.[20] Meaning cannot be determined other than in relation to a context but, because context can never be specified unambiguously, meaning itself remains inherently indeterminable.

If signification cannot be the representation of an absent presence because there never is an absolute presence which could be thus represented, prior to signification itself, then 'signified presence is always reconstituted by deferral, *nachträglich*, belatedly, *supplementarily*'.[21] Thus supplements are an integral part of signification. The supplement is what Derrida calls an 'undecidable'. Undecidables do not function within logocentrism but have their own logic. They are '"false" verbal properties (nominal or semantic) that can no longer be included within philosophical (binary) opposition, but which, however, inhabit philosophical opposition, resisting and disorganizing it, *without ever* constituting a third term, without ever leaving room for a solution in the form of speculative dialectics' (*P* 43 [58]). The undecidable is not a contradiction in the Hegelian sense which needs to be or could be resolved. It simultaneously points to and ignores contradiction as contradiction is part of the logic of speech, discourse, presence, truth, etc. (*P* 101, n. 13 [60, n. 6]). Undecidables, in other words, 'contain *within themselves* an ambiguity, a duplicity of meaning. They are *neither* one thing *nor* the other, and at the same time they are simultaneously *both*.' They 'embody *différance* within themselves'.[22]

The supplement itself acquires the character of an undecidable through embodying the two contradictory but mutually complementary meanings of *suppléer*, to complement and to replace. Derrida discusses the supplement in relation to the traditional idea in philosophy, as exemplified in Jean-Jacques Rousseau's thought, that writing is merely a representation of speech and thus secondary to speech. Writing, in this view, is less immediate, less present, less natural than speech. Writing is added only when speech is unable to protect the presence of thought.

[19] Jacques Derrida, *Aporias*, translated by Thomas Dutoit (Stanford University Press, 1993), 9 [312].
[20] Culler, *On Deconstruction*, pp. 134–5.
[21] Derrida, *Writing and Difference*, pp. 211–12 [p. 314].
[22] Jenny Edkins, *Poststructuralism and International Relations: Bringing the Political Back In* (Boulder and London: Lynne Rienner Publishers, 1999), p. 70.

In contrast to the immediate presence of thought to speech, writing provides only representation and imagination. Writing is not only inferior to speech but becomes dangerous when it claims its own presence, when it makes us, through its very functioning, forget its derived and artificial character. The supplement, Derrida points out, is always dangerous because it necessarily contains two contradictory dimensions. On the one hand, the supplement adds itself, enriches another plenitude and thus functions as a surplus (*OG* 144 [208]). On the other hand, however, 'the supplement supplements. It adds only to replace. It intervenes or insinuates itself *in-the-place-of*; if it fills, it is as if one fills a void' (*OG* 145 [208]). Thus, whilst the supplement enriches the presence, it at the same time endangers it by replacing it.

This can be seen with respect to the relation of the sign to what it is thought to stand for. As the 'sign is always the supplement of the thing itself' (*OG* 145 [208]), it 'takes its place' in both meanings of the term: it stands for it in its absence but at the same time already replaces it. The supplement is not an essentially superfluous addition. Rather the 'presence' which it is thought to be added on to is derived from the supplement. Therefore, the supplement endangers the possibility of pure presence. As the sign is a supplement, the logic of the supplement is fundamental to Derrida's claim that there is *'nothing outside of the text'* (*OG* 158 [227]), that the real is an effect of representation, that it is 'constituted by the logic of supplementarity'.[23] I will return to this claim in more detail in relation to Onuf's portrayal of material reality as behind our constructions. At this point, it is important to recognise that the logic of the supplement requires us to abandon forms of analysis which rely on the possibility of pure presence. Therefore Derrida resorts to a strategy which takes into account this logic: deconstruction.

Deconstruction is practised in two styles which complement one another: 'One takes on the demonstrative and apparently ahistorical allure of logico-formal paradoxes. The other, more historical or more anamnesic, seems to proceed through readings of texts, meticulous interpretations and genealogies' (FoL 959/958). Both strategies aim to subvert the logic of a text by taking this logic seriously. As Jonathan Culler explains, to 'deconstruct a discourse is to show how it undermines the philosophy it asserts, or the hierarchical oppositions on which it relies, by identifying in the text the rhetorical operations that produce the

---

[23] Culler, *On Deconstruction*, p. 105.

supposed ground of argument, the key concept or premise'.[24] Derrida employs a *'general strategy of deconstruction'* (*P* 41 [56]) to deal with the oppositions and contradictions necessarily involved in all language without making them disappear in a Hegelian *Aufhebung*.[25] Deconstruction involves a double movement of inversion and displacement. This is meant to address the oppositions without either neutralising them or staying within them and reaffirming them:

> On the one hand, we must traverse a phase of *overturning* . . . To do justice to this necessity is to recognize that in a classical philosophical opposition we are not dealing with a peaceful coexistence of a *vis-à-vis*, but rather with a violent hierarchy. One of the terms governs the other (axiologically, logically, etc.), or has the upper hand. To deconstruct the opposition, first of all, is to overturn the hierarchy at a given moment. To overlook this phase of overturning is to forget the conflictual and subordinating structure of the opposition.[26]   (*P* 41 [56–7])

This move is necessary to avoid a neutralisation of the opposition, which in practice would leave the hierarchy in place. Without going through this phase one cannot intervene in the field of signification. One has to go through this phase continuously; it is an interminable analysis because the hierarchy of binary oppositions always re-establishes itself (*P* 42 [57]). However, overturning the hierarchy is not enough, as this move remains within the deconstructed system. Thus, in a second phase, one has to move towards the emergence of a new term which is not part of the previous regime any more (*P* 42–3 [57–9]). This is the displacement. In other words, two steps are involved. Firstly, one reveals the opposition as a metaphysical and ideological imposition by making clear its presuppositions and role in the value system and by showing how it is undone in the texts that are based on it. Secondly, one at the same time maintains the opposition by employing it in one's own argument and by displacing it through a reversal.[27] Deconstruction therefore works through a 'double gesture' (*LI* 21 [50]): a reversal and a displacement. 'To deconstruct an opposition is to undo and displace it, to situate it differently.'[28]

It is crucial to realise that deconstruction wants neither to uncover meaning nor to establish the relationship between the text and 'reality'.

---

[24] Culler, *On Deconstruction*, p. 86.
[25] Rodolphe Gasché, *The Tain of the Mirror: Derrida and the Philosophy of Reflection* (Cambridge, MA, and London: Harvard University Press, 1986), p. 142.
[26] The sentence omitted does not appear in the English translation. See also *LI* 21 [50].
[27] Culler, *On Deconstruction*, p. 150.   [28] Culler, *On Deconstruction*, p. 150.

Derrida conceptualises the whole of our experiences as text, so that the problem of the connection between text and reality does not arise within his thinking. Johnson draws attention to the close relationship between 'deconstruction' and 'analysis', as the latter means 'to undo', in other words, 'to de-construct'. Thus, deconstruction aims to draw out the different forces of signification already within a text and the contradictions which lie within them. Thereby 'the deconstructive reading does not point out the flaws or stupidities or weaknesses of an author, but the *necessity* with which what he *does* see is systematically related to what he does *not* see'.[29] Thus, a deconstructive critique teases out the heterogeneity of signification. In order to do so it starts from value-laden hierarchies and points of condensation, in which one term serves to integrate several lines of argument.[30] In the sense that critique is an analysis of the premises of a system's possibility, deconstruction is a form of critique. Deconstruction therefore aims not at making meaning transparent but at making visible the presuppositions of statements.[31]

Deconstruction is not the solution to the problem of the metaphysics of presence. It does not offer a way out. It merely makes possible an analysis of the problem, if only in its own terms:

> Theories grounded on presence . . . undo themselves, as the supposed formation or ground proves to be the ground of a purely differential system, or rather, of difference, differentiation, and deferral. But the operation of deconstruction or the self-deconstruction of logocentric theories does not lead to a new theory that sets everything straight . . . there is no reason to believe that a theoretical enterprise could ever free itself from logocentric premises.[32]

Deconstruction then remains, and must remain, within the system it aims to breach.[33] It 'appeals to no higher logical principle or superior reason but uses the very principle it deconstructs'.[34] Deconstruction works to subvert the text, it creates a profound recontextualisation (*LI* 136 [252]), but at the same time it cannot escape the text because there is nothing outside of it. Deconstruction uses the very concepts and assumptions it subverts. Concepts can be deconstructed only by operating within them.

Obviously, deconstruction faces a problem if it has to operate within the confines of what it aims to subvert, if it has to be based on the logic

[29] Johnson, 'Translator's Introduction', p. xv.   [30] Culler, *On Deconstruction*, p. 213.
[31] Johnson, 'Translator's Introduction', pp. xiv–xvi.
[32] Culler, *On Deconstruction*, p. 109.   [33] Culler, *On Deconstruction*, p. 86.
[34] Culler, *On Deconstruction*, p. 87.

which disintegrates under the deconstructive gaze. The criticism that deconstruction defeats its own purpose because it has to fall back on the terminology and logic it critiques seems obvious. Derrida is aware that the deconstructive approach threatens to be circular. *'There is no sense* in doing without metaphysics in order to shake metaphysics. We have no language – no syntax and no lexicon – which is foreign to this history; we can pronounce not a single destructive proposition which has not already had to slip into the form, logic, and the implicit postulations of precisely what it seeks to contest.'[35] Therefore the necessity of remaining within the language which is being critiqued is not merely a problem, an inconvenience which one must accept. On the contrary, it is this borrowing of concepts which makes an intervention in the discourse possible in the first place.[36] Deconstruction 'must, through a double gesture, a double science, a double writing – put into place a *reversal* of the classical opposition *and* a general *displacement* of the system. It is on that condition alone that deconstruction will provide the means of *intervening* in the field of oppositions it criticizes and that is also a field of nondiscursive forces' (*LI* 21 [50]). Thus, the impossibility of escaping the discourse of metaphysics is both an ever-present danger and obstacle for deconstruction, and the very condition of its success and even possibility. Derrida insists that 'we cannot give up this metaphysical complicity without also giving up the critique we are directing against this complicity'.[37] He speaks of the necessity of accepting logocentric logic but at the same time looking elsewhere: 'It is a logic, logic itself, that I do not wish to criticize here. I would even be ready to subscribe to it, but with one hand only, for I keep another to write or look for something else' (*OH* 69 [68]). This move remains unsatisfactory as long as we expect deconstruction to be something it is not: a solution to the metaphysical problems it points out. What Derrida is driving at is precisely that we cannot escape the logic of logocentrism, which should, however, not stop us from questioning it.

Derrida sees deconstruction as 'a way of taking a position'.[38] As such it is inherently and unavoidably political. Nevertheless, critics argue that Derrida's work is apolitical and must end up reinforcing existing power structures. Derrida himself certainly does not consider deconstruction

---

[35] Derrida, *Writing and Difference*, pp. 280–1 [p. 412] (italics in French original).
[36] Gasché, *Tain of the Mirror*, p. 168.   [37] Derrida, *Writing and Difference*, p. 281 [p. 413].
[38] Jacques Derrida, 'The Conflict of Faculties', in Michael Riffaterre (ed.), *Languages of Knowledge and of Inquiry* (New York: Columbia University Press, 1982), quoted in Culler, *On Deconstruction*, p. 156. See also *P* 93 [129].

to be apolitical or not concerned with 'reality'. On the contrary, although here addressing the work of others, he speaks of

> the most radical programs of a deconstruction that would like, in order to be consistent with itself, not to remain enclosed in purely speculative, theoretical, academic discourses but rather... to aspire to something more consequential, to *change*... things and to intervene in an efficient and responsible, though always, of course, very mediated way... in what one calls the *cité*, the *polis* and more generally the world.
>
> (FoL 931–2/930–1)

Derrida rejects the notion that a deconstructionist is a 'skeptic–relativist–nihilist' and argues that 'of course there is a "right track" [*une "bonne voie"*], a better way' (LI 146 [269]). He speaks of 'deconstructive (i.e. affirmative) interpretation'.[39] It is then important to consider how Derrida's thought can be considered political, an intervention in the world.

The political character of Derrida's work lies in drawing attention to how discourses depoliticise. His arguments reveal, according to Jenny Edkins, how 'logocentric approaches depoliticise through their claims to knowledge', through what she calls 'technologization'.[40] Derrida makes this depoliticising move impossible or at least suspect in two ways. Firstly, he questions the metaphysics of presence and, as a consequence, the idea of a determinable and exterior origin or an absolute context. The determination of context inherent in communication then involves the creation of 'non-natural' relationships to others, that is, politics (LI 136 [251]). Secondly, he introduces concepts, such as the undecidable, which are based on the irreducible ambiguity of situations, thereby countering any attempt to provide a technical 'solution' to dealing with them. Far from being an apolitical, disengaged and conservative method, deconstruction actually asks us to get involved, and incessantly to remain so, for there is always a movement towards depoliticisation which is to be countered. 'Politicization... is interminable even if it cannot and should not ever be total' (FoL 971/970).

The political impact of Derrida's thought is particularly apparent in his arguments about identity as always already encompassing difference within itself, about the impossibility of communication as traditionally conceived, about the inevitability of an unfounded violence implicated

[39] Jacques Derrida, *Spurs: Nietzsche's styles/Eperons: les styles de Nietzsche*, English translation by Barbara Harlow (Chicago and London: University of Chicago Press, 1979), p. 37/36.
[40] Edkins, *Poststructuralism and International Relations*, p. 80; see also pp. 9–14.

in the founding of the law and the necessity of escaping the certainty of rules in order to make responsible action possible and about the impossibility of a meeting with the purity of the real. These aspects will be explored in some detail in this chapter. Fundamentally, Derrida's thought subverts the possibility of appealing to a given, although possibly changeable, value-neutral reality. Identifying some things as present, as real and therefore more important is not a simple acknowledgement of given constraints for practice. Rather these constraints, as will be illustrated in the following sections of this chapter, become established through their representation as such. The implicit valorisation of the real over the represented is crucial in making the limit appear as one which is imposed by the world rather than a limit of our thinking.

The 'reality' of international politics

Alexander Wendt claims that the reality of international politics is one of anarchy, of self-help (A 394–5). Moreover, states are 'the principal units of analysis' and what matters is the international realm rather than the domestic.[41] These claims reflect widespread beliefs about international reality in International Politics[42] at the time of his writing. Equally, they are in accordance with common ways of talking about international politics and specifically with how the reality of international politics was portrayed in the debates about German military involvement abroad. The international realm was seen as one in which wars were possible (again), and in which violence had to be countered with violence.[43] The international was recognised as of overriding significance in claims that, no matter what the Germans themselves thought about the use of force, pressure from abroad made it imperative.[44] The idea, finally, that the

---

[41] Wendt, 'Collective Identity Formation', 385. See also *STIP* 8–10.

[42] In this book, International Politics refers to the discipline, and international politics to what is construed as its empirical subject matter.

[43] See, for example, Volker Rühe (defence minister) in Deutscher Bundestag, *Plenarprotokoll*, 12/132, 15 Jan. 1993, 11484; Joschka Fischer, 'Die Katastrophe in Bosnien und die Konsequenzen für unsere Partei', reprinted in *Blätter für deutsche und internationale Politik* 40 (1995), 1147; Helmut Kohl, 'Ziele und Prioritäten der Innen- und Außenpolitik', in Presse- und Informationsamt der Bundesregierung, *Bulletin*, 84, 25 Jul. 1992, 811; Klaus Kinkel (foreign minister) in Deutscher Bundestag, *Plenarprotokoll*, 12/240, 22 Jul. 1994, 21166; Naumann, *Bundeswehr*, p. 129.

[44] See, for example, Christian Schmidt (CDU/CSU) in Deutscher Bundestag, *Plenarprotokoll*, 12/150, 26 Mar. 1993, 12880; 'Feldjäger in die Wüste', *Der Spiegel*, 51/46, 14 Dec. 1992, 24–5, here 24; Klaus Kinkel quoted in 'Eine regelrechte Psychose', *Der Spiegel*, 52/46, 21 Dec. 1992, 18–20, here 19.

conflicts in the Balkans or the plight of the Somalis were problems the FRG had to confront *qua* German state relied on the centrality of states. Thus, the world Wendt pictures resonates not only with claims in International Politics but also with common-sense notions of international politics.

Wendt's departure lies in the claim that this situation is not an expression of natural necessity but a construction. This is based, I argued in chapter 2, on conceiving of state identity as at the same time changeable and relatively stable. I discussed identity as a crucial concept both in Wendt's constructivism and in the debates about German military involvement abroad. Bringing the two together in my analysis, I found Wendt's approach wanting in a number of ways. Firstly, I argued that his notion of identity excluded much of what seemed significant to *how* identity was constructed in relation to military involvement abroad. The failure to explore linguistic processes as well as the strict separation between the domestic and international realms and indeed the exclusion of the former were raised as problems. Moreover, I claimed that Wendt's approach implied that it was possible to determine an actor's identity at any point in time and that this failed to take account of the complexity of the phenomenon of identity. What is important about these shortcomings and misconceptualisations is that they lead us to reach particular conclusions whilst barring us from considering alternative possibilities. Thus, the starting point of Wendt's constructivism already encompasses within it the scope of possible outcomes of the analysis.

An understanding of this closure was then developed further through an exploration of the necessarily ambiguous character of German identity as presented in the debates. I showed that the arguments against military involvement abroad were based on treating 'the FRG', 'Germany' and 'the Germans' as coterminous. These equations reflect the idea that the relevant agent in the political situation at issue is in some significant way the successor of the Third Reich. In other words, insofar as the FRG is Germany, it is in some way identical with the Third Reich. However, this alleged identity is only part of the story. The FRG is not only attributed with characteristics which are different from, indeed diametrically opposed to, those of the Nazi state, such as its non-military role in the international realm, the FRG was also *classified* differently in that it was considered part of 'the West' and 'the community of peoples'. Thus, the representation of German identity involved a tension, an inescapable 'difference *with itself*' (*OH* 9–10 [16]). Similarly, the solutions to the dilemma of military involvement abroad which were considered possible revolved around both identity and difference with the Nazi past. The FRG could take part in international military operations and thereby, on the one hand, confirm its integration with the West and therefore its overcoming of the Nazi past, whilst, on the other hand, making use of its military beyond defence and therefore recalling the militarist practices of the Nazi state. Alternatively, it could withdraw at least from further international integration to avoid participation in military operations. This would have made it possible to reconfirm the non-military character of the FRG as an international actor, thereby setting it apart from the Nazi state, whilst, however, taking the FRG out of the partnership with the Western countries and therefore establishing another identity with the Third Reich. Neither option provided an escape from difference within identity.

My analysis destabilised the possibility of conceiving identity as proposed by Wendt. A closer engagement with Derrida's thought makes it possible to explore further the serious consequences of nevertheless operating on the basis of the possibility of identity. Representations of identity were at the base of both what was construed as the 'problem' of participation in international military operations and of what were proposed as solutions. Crucially, the situation was conceived as one for 'Germany'. Although the Gulf War and the operations in Somalia or Kosovo can be understood as situations in which the UN and/or NATO and its member states engaged in practices equally as new to them as to the FRG,[45] the debates in Germany focused on the problem as one for the *German* state. Christian Schmidt of the CDU/CSU detected a wrestling with the question 'Whither Germany?'[46] Whether the FRG should, and how far it could, send its military abroad was discussed in relation to a representation of identity which referred to history. The FRG's inability and unwillingness to use force, even in the context of the UN and for purposes justified by international law, were based on the idea that there were constraints on the country due to its past. The perceived constitutional restrictions were also considered a consequence of the past.

History was construed as an important source of identity. Catherine Kelleher and Cathleen Fisher point out that the domestic debates about participation in international military operations revolved around basic definitions of identity and security, that is, around questions about the Germans' understanding of history and their definition of the future.[47]

[45] See, for example, 'NATO schießt vier serbische Militärflugzeuge ab', *SZ*, 1 Mar. 1994, 1.
[46] Deutscher Bundestag, *Plenarprotokoll*, 12/151, 21 Apr. 1993, 12971.
[47] Kelleher and Fisher, 'Germany', p. 161.

Who the Germans had been in the past and how they had used force was to establish who they were now and ultimately how they could and should use force today. This attitude towards history was displayed by Chancellor Kohl when he outlined the policy of the first government of the unified Germany. He stated that an '[a]wareness of German history in all its parts and of the responsibility which follows from it [would] have a formative influence on the policy of the Federal Government. Only those who know and accept their origin have a compass for the future.'[48]

In relation to the issue of using force, the history of the Third Reich and the Second World War were portrayed as salient. Foreign Minister Genscher's opposition to military deployments abroad was based on his conviction, influenced by his experience of the Second World War, that war could never be a means of politics.[49] He made this an important part of the narrative in his memoirs.[50] A similar point was made by Heidemarie Wieczorek-Zeul on behalf of the SPD. She pointed out that people, because of the history of the Second World War, rejected war.[51] Also based on the historical experience, as Willi Hoss of Bündnis90/Die Grünen argued, the Greens conducted a flyer campaign in relation to the Gulf War in which they asked German soldiers not to let themselves be used as cannon fodder, to refuse to serve in war and, if deployed to the Gulf, to desert.[52] Gregor Gysi, the chairman of the PDS, moreover, claimed that because of German history the FRG should exercise self-restraint and engage in war only if it was itself attacked.[53] Gysi complained that forty-five years after the Second World War but only three months after unification Germany was getting involved in war again.[54] These statements of politicians from different parties illustrate that the history of the Third Reich – sometimes referred to simply as 'the history'[55] – was asserted as an obvious starting point in discussing the external use of force. As Detlef Kleinert put it, the 'root was after

[48] Deutscher Bundestag, *Plenarprotokoll*, 11/228, 4 Oct. 1990, 18019. On Kohl's use of history, see Banchoff, 'German Policy Towards the EU', 61–6.
[49] 'Die Deutschen an die Front', *Der Spiegel*, 6/45, 4 Feb. 1991, 18–22, here 19.
[50] Genscher, *Erinnerungen*.
[51] Deutscher Bundestag, *Plenarprotokoll*, 12/2, 14 Jan. 1991, 41.
[52] Deutscher Bundestag, *Plenarprotokoll*, 11/235, 15 Nov. 1990, 18850.
[53] Deutscher Bundestag, *Plenarprotokoll*, 12/2, 14 Jan. 1991, 35. See also the motion of PDS members of parliament in Deutscher Bundestag, *Drucksache*, 12/28, 11 Jan. 1991.
[54] Deutscher Bundestag, *Plenarprotokoll*, 12/3, 17 Jan. 1991, 53.
[55] Christian Schwarz-Schilling (CDU/CSU) in Deutscher Bundestag, *Plenarprotokoll*, 12/219, 14 Apr. 1994, 18923.

all 1945'.[56] According to this position, German identity *had* to be understood in reference to the Nazi past. This past was thus represented as the origin of German identity.

References to history endow actions with meaning. History is often used as a source of truth. As Culler explains, 'history invoked as ultimate reality and source of truth manifests itself in narrative constructs, stories designed to yield meaning through narrative ordering'.[57] The authority of history is particularly significant in relation to questions of identity. Who we are depends, in this thinking, on who our predecessors were, on where we come from. Derrida's thought, however, leads to questioning first origins and thus to a subversion of the mystification of the origin, for there are only 'nonoriginary origins'.[58] Every event which may be construed as originary presupposes something yet prior to it. Hence, it is impossible to return to 'the source' to find meaning. Moreover, Derrida argues that the attempt to tell a singular story about oneself must always lead to a myth:

> This can be said, inversely or reciprocally, of all identity or all identification: there is no self-relation, no relation to oneself, without culture, but a culture of oneself *as* a culture *of* the other, a culture of the double genitive and of the *difference to oneself*. The grammar of the double genitive also signals that a culture never has a single origin. Monogenealogy would always be a mystification in the history of culture.
>
> (*OH* 10–11 [16–17])

Identity must cope with difference within itself. Derrida argues that there is never such a thing as a unified, self-present identity. It is not that culture does not have an identity or is not able to identify itself, but that we are able to 'take the form of the subject only in the non-identity to itself, or, if you prefer, only in the difference with itself [*avec soi*]. There is no culture or cultural identity without this difference *with itself*' (*OH* 9–10 [16]).

The identification of the Third Reich as 'the root' or origin made possible a representation of identity as a linear development from the Nazi state via the old FRG through to the new FRG. What held this ancestral line together was that all three were seen as expressions of 'Germany'. This not only lent some logical necessity to the link but also significantly excluded the history of the other Germany, the GDR. Although

---

[56] Detlef Kleinert (FDP) in Deutscher Bundestag, *Plenarprotokoll*, 12/151, 21 Apr. 1993, 12952.
[57] Culler, *On Deconstruction*, p. 129. See also *OG* 85 [127].
[58] Culler, *On Deconstruction*, p. 96.

this history was sometimes referred to, it only ever made an appearance as merely another manifestation of what the Third Reich stood for. According to Foreign Minister Kinkel, the historical experience, 'namely the period of the National-Socialist dictatorship with an inhuman and destructive regime and the regime of injustice of a different kind in the former GDR, really establishe[d] a special responsibility for German foreign policy to actively promote peace and human rights in the international realm'.[59] Thus the history of the GDR was considered relevant only insofar as it reaffirmed the Third Reich as the origin. The history of the GDR as an origin in itself, in contrast, was erased; for the mono-genealogy made possible the crucial claim that military involvement abroad was in the tradition of Germany's cooperation with its partners. According to Defence Minister Rühe, the European partners considered it a break with past practice that the Germans were not at their side in relation to new military tasks.[60] Foreign Minister Kinkel argued that it was necessary to show solidarity because 'Germany' had received protection and solidarity with respect to security issues from its Western allies during the Cold War.[61]

This claim that solidarity had to be returned and that participation in international military missions was in line with a long-standing practice of cooperation was possible only on the basis of the deliberate exclusion of the GDR and its citizens, who neither were protected by the Western allies during the Cold War nor had a habit of cooperating with and integrating into Western institutions. Derrida's discussion of J. L. Austin's speech act theory, which will be explored in detail later, shows that exclusions can be crucial for the argument and that they support hierarchies of values. As Edkins points out, for 'Derrida, the drawing of boundaries by a process of exclusion, which places something "outside" and thus defines an "essence", or an inside, is a process that is typical of logocentric analysis, the form of analysis that is familiar in metaphysics, and Western thought more generally'.[62] In this case, the old FRG and its history, perceived as a linear development originating from the catastrophe of the Third Reich, became 'the essence' through excluding from consideration the experience of the other Germany as

---

[59] Klaus Kinkel (foreign minister) in Deutscher Bundestag, *Plenarprotokoll*, 12/101, 22 Jul. 1992, 8609.
[60] Deutscher Bundestag, *Plenarprotokoll*, 12/240, 22 Jul. 1994, 21187.
[61] Deutscher Bundestag, *Plenarprotokoll*, 13/48, 30 Jun. 1995, 3956.
[62] Jenny Edkins, 'Legality with a Vengeance: Famines and Humanitarian Relief in "Complex Emergencies"', *Millennium: Journal of International Studies* 25 (1996), 555.

accidental and marginal. The argument for military involvement abroad relied on this exclusion.

The selective telling of history privileged a partial experience and derived guidance for the future therefrom. The historical 'compass' was not a neutral instrument to ascertain where different paths might lead. It firmly pointed where the decision-makers believed 'the West' to be. The significance of the West was reflected in the wish to be 'normal'. Kinkel claimed that the 'return to normality... reflect[ed] a deep desire of [the] population since the end of the war'.[63] The concept of 'normality' was thus invoked as self-evident and self-evidently valuable. It referred to the notion that the FRG, Germany and the Germans were in some way tarnished by the past and that the appropriate response to this lay in cooperation with the West. This idea provided the link between the experiences of the past and the requirements of the future. The implication was that the Germans had to be enabled 'to participate normally with [the] Bundeswehr in the tasks which are now central to world foreign and security policy'.[64] Inspector General Admiral Dieter Wellershoff supported participation in Gulf War-style international operations with the words: 'At some point this state has to become normal again.'[65] Uwe-Jens Heuer of PDS/Linke Liste, on the other hand, argued that for him 'German normality firstly mean[t] retaining... military restraint.'[66] As Gysi pointed out, most states did not participate in military conflicts abroad. It was only the leading Western states who engaged in such military operations. Therefore, according to Gysi, a 'normal' role would not be a military one.[67]

It comes as little surprise that the substance of what was considered 'normal' was contentious. Definitions of normal behaviour for Germany ranged from carrying on with the FRG's non-military role to dominating Europe.[68] As Derrida points out, 'the criterion between normal and not-normal is essentially elusive' (LI 82 [154]). The impossibility of distinguishing normality from its opposite is a specific occurrence of the impossibility of defining presence and absence as mutually exclusive.[69]

---

[63] Kinkel, 'Verantwortung', 8.
[64] 'Abschied von der Ära Genscher', interview with Foreign Minister Klaus Kinkel, SZ, 13 May 1993, 11.
[65] Quoted in 'Auch SPD jetzt für Beteiligung an Militäreinsätzen', SZ, 4 Mar. 1991, 2.
[66] Deutscher Bundestag, Plenarprotokoll, 12/151, 21 Apr. 1993, 12956.
[67] Deutscher Bundestag, Plenarprotokoll, 12/240, 22 Jul. 1994, 21181.
[68] For the various conceptions of normality used in the debates, see McKenzie, 'Competing Conceptions', esp. 2–4.
[69] Culler, On Deconstruction, p. 94.

In other words, the opposition normal/abnormal is possible only on the basis of *différance* (*P* 8–9 [17]). The significant point here is not only that normality as a concept cannot function without elements of what is construed as its opposite, but that the dichotomy is dominated by normality. Thus, as a result of the metaphysics of Western thought, normality is valued over abnormality. Normality was important not because any substantial form of behaviour was seen as necessary. All the government wanted to achieve, according to Defence Minister Rühe, was the vague aim of being able to react just like the FRG's 'democratic European neighbours'.[70] What was significant was not to achieve a positive goal but to avoid abnormality.

The emphasis was on avoiding a *Sonderweg* (special path) or *Sonderrolle* (special role). As Foreign Minister Kinkel put it: 'I think that a lesson from this history really can only be: never again to step out of line of the community of Western peoples, never again special paths, also not the one of a moral know-all manner and the ethics of absolute ends!'[71] This reasoning relied on the notion that every time Germany had asserted itself as different in the past, this had led to disaster, to a world war. Rühe set up this argument as a series of rhetorical questions:

> Why does Germany always have to be different from others then? . . . And why then do you now believe that you are more moral than others? Why can we not find the way by asking ourselves how our two important neighbours in the East and the West, France and Poland, see the situation in Europe, what is moral and immoral for them? Is this not a good guideline for German policy at the end of the century? Why do we always have to be something special?[72]

The implication of this line of reasoning was clear: NATO and the UN approved of military operations. Therefore, the Germans had to. Despite the emphasis on normality as the key term, as what was desired, it was defined by its opposite. This reflects what Henry Staten refers to as the constitutive function of the outside.[73] Phenomena are not constituted by their essence; rather the essence is derived from exclusion, from what is declared to be outside.

Moreover, the strategy of justifying participation in international military operations with the need to avoid a special role betrays that the

---

[70] 'Das ist keine Drohgebärde', interview with Defence Minister Volker Rühe, *Der Spiegel*, 30/46, 20 Jul. 1992, 32–5, here 34.
[71] Deutscher Bundestag, *Plenarprotokoll*, 12/151, 21 Apr. 1993, 12928.
[72] Deutscher Bundestag, *Plenarprotokoll*, 12/132, 15 Jan. 1993, 11484.
[73] Henry Staten, *Wittgenstein and Derrida* (Oxford: Basil Blackwell, 1985), p. 16.

concept of 'normality' is already contaminated by traces of the abnormal; for 'the opposition of "normal" and "abnormal" will always be lacking in rigor and purity' (*LI* 82 [154]). Neither term can work without elements of its supposed opposite. Two interrelated strategies of reasoning for the need to be normal were presented, and both relied on the idea that Germany was in some way special. The first was based on Germany's past, especially the history of the Third Reich. The second concerned Germany's future, especially its role in the UN. The arguments quoted above make reference to the history of difference. Germany was not to assert policies different from those of its neighbours, it was not to express opinions diverging from others, because of its singular, special, abnormal past. The term 'special path', used by Kinkel and others, had been coined in historical scholarship to refer to and explain Germany's development in the past which was conceived of as an aberration from the norm. In 1973, historian Hans-Ulrich Wehler had put forward the so-called *Sonderweg* (special path) thesis.[74] Germany had diverged from the West European norm in a number of ways, such as 'late unification and nation-building, the failure of the German revolutions and the weakness of liberalism'.[75] As a result, '[s]ocial hierarchies and values stayed premodern.'[76] In the popular usage of the term, the *Sonderweg* thesis usually referred to the more general notion that Germany had historically developed differently from the West, and that this had made Nazism possible.[77] This portrayal of Germany having historically constituted an aberration from the norm made the idea of being anything other than 'normal' unappealing. Crucially, however, normality was defined on the basis of already conceiving of Germany as non-normal.

This abnormality continued to threaten the attainment of normality throughout. Even as politicians were arguing for normality, they retained a belief in the special character of the German state because of its history. Traces of abnormality were apparent in each supposed move towards normality. In relation to the potential deployment of ECR-Tornados NATO had requested, one commentator asked whether the Germans were 'prepared to give up their special role in order to protect NATO allies from the Serbian air defence with their superior

[74] Evans, *Rereading German History*, pp. 12–13.
[75] Ian Varcoe, 'Identity and the Limits of Comparison: Bauman's Reception in Germany', *Theory, Culture and Society* 15 (1998), 58. See also Evans, *Rereading German History*, pp. 12–13, and Geoff Eley, 'Nazism, Politics and the Image of the Past: Thoughts on the West German *Historikerstreit* 1986–1987', *Past and Present* 121 (1988), 203.
[76] Evans, *Rereading German History*, p. 13.
[77] Eley, 'Nazism, Politics and the Image of the Past', 182.

weapons technology'.[78] The government insisted that they were. Yet at the same time they upheld the so-called Kohl doctrine which ruled out deployments to the Balkans. In supposedly giving up the special role, a new one was created as the mandate for German Tornados was limited. They could protect only NATO's rapid reaction force.[79] Joschka Fischer also drew attention to this. He stressed the tension between the government's argument that the deployment was necessary to show solidarity in the alliance and the continued limitation of the FRG's involvement. No ground troops were sent. He pointed out that the government had always rejected the possibility of deploying troops to the former Yugoslavia on the grounds of the historical argument.[80] Thus, whilst a new normality was asserted, another abnormality was upheld.

'Germany' was construed as non-normal not only because of its past but also because of its position and capabilities. One commentator warned that '[t]hose who now talk of "normality" must not deny that the German situation since the founding of the first unitary German state just was and remains the normality of an extremely difficult situation.'[81] Kinkel was concerned that the FRG had to become equal in its ability to shape politics. He went on to say: 'I do not claim that German ships, German soldiers and German UN soldiers can deal with things better. But it cannot be right that the economically most significant power and also the biggest country in Europe in terms of population has to pursue a foreign policy which is in many ways restricted.'[82] This amounts to claiming that the FRG must be enabled to do what every other state supposedly does, that is, to act 'normally', because it is not normal, because it is bigger and more powerful than other states. This was again reflected in the justification for the Somalia mission. Whilst Kohl justified the decision to participate by arguing that there was a growing danger that Germany would become isolated internationally,[83] he also argued that it was 'appropriate to the size and significance of Germany'.[84]

The Germans also became abnormal in the sense that their behaviour became an issue. No one was interested in the abnormality of Costa Rica being a UN member without a military and hence without the

[78] Udo Bergdoll, 'Aus Bonn ein vernebeltes Nein', *SZ*, 8 Dec. 1994, 4.
[79] Stefan Kornelius, 'Einsatzplan im politischen Fadenkreuz', *SZ*, 28 Jun. 1995, 1.
[80] Deutscher Bundestag, *Plenarprotokoll*, 13/48, 30 Jun. 1995, 3972.
[81] Leicht, 'Mit Volldampf', 3.
[82] 'Mit allen zwölfen durchs Ziel', interview with Foreign Minister Klaus Kinkel, *Der Spiegel*, 40/46, 28 Sep. 1992, 32–5, here 33.
[83] 'Eine regelrechte Psychose', *Der Spiegel*, 52/46, 21 Dec. 1992, 18–20, here 18.
[84] Quoted ibid., 19.

potential to contribute to UN operations. In contrast, UN strategists saw the Germans as ideal for jobs in the Third World because of their supposedly minimal colonial past. Moreover, German equipment could be used to solve technical problems and the Germans would be able to pay for their forces themselves.[85] The German government also envisaged a 'beyond normal' role within the UN for themselves. As Kinkel put it: 'We now have to prove our ability to be normal inside and outside if we do not want to be seriously damaged politically. Part of this normalisation is also a German permanent seat in the UN Security Council if new members are admitted to this body.'[86] Even if the Security Council was to be enlarged, being part of this body would not, by any stretch of the imagination, be 'normal'; but this representation provided a crucial link. The wish to become part of the Security Council was in turn used to support the argument that changing the constitution or, more precisely, taking part in UN military operations was necessary.[87] Björn Engholm, Oskar Lafontaine and Hans-Ulrich Klose, who represented most of the SPD leadership at the time, therefore agreed that the FRG would be unable to stay out of military operations.[88] Thus the abnormal desire to be part of the Security Council became the reason for the necessity of what was represented as normalisation.

It is impossible to draw a clear distinction between the normal and the abnormal. As mentioned before, the dichotomy of normal versus abnormal is never rigorous or pure (*LI* 82 [154]). It is not merely that different opinions can be held as to what is normal and what is not. Rather, the distinction 'between normal and not-normal is essentially elusive' (*LI* 82 [154]). Only *différance* makes possible their functioning as a dichotomy whilst at the same time making impossible their opposition as mutually exclusive. The systematic play of differences is necessary to produce the dichotomy but it also means that the opposite is always already inscribed within each term, thus making a clear demarcation between both terms impossible. We cannot, therefore, rigorously distinguish between normal and special, not-normal, abnormal at all. Each 'normality' proposed already contained within it elements of the not-normal. The

---

[85] 'Uno: "Wir machen das alles ganz zivil" ', *Der Spiegel*, 21/46, 18 May 1992, 184–6, here 185.

[86] Kinkel, 'Verantwortung', 8. The willingness to take 'responsibility also in the context of a permanent membership in the Security Council' is stated in the 1994 White Paper: BMV, *Weißbuch 1994*, p. 69, section 469.

[87] 'Dort spielt die Musik', interview with Foreign Minister Kinkel, *Der Spiegel*, 39/47, 27 Sep. 1993, 23–4, here 23.

[88] 'Ins Allerheiligste der Uno', *Der Spiegel*, 7/46, 10 Feb. 1992, 18–20, here 20.

abnormality of the Germans, both in terms of their history and their current position, made the ideal of normality desirable. Normality had a powerful appeal unrelated to its content. It was used by politicians on both sides of the debate.

Moreover, the failure to live up to what was portrayed as normal tended to arouse strong emotions, such as shame. Not being able to take part in the Gulf War, despite being as capable as soldiers of other countries, had supposedly created an inferiority complex in the military, the so-called Gulf War trauma.[89] Officers found it personally hurtful to be accused of shirking in relation to the Gulf War.[90] The soldiers serving in the Adriatic Sea were unhappy with the restrictions on what they were allowed to do.[91] Orders to go into action for vessels monitoring the UN embargo there singled the Germans out as different, as they often included the addendum '. . . or are you German?'[92] German soldiers also considered it a disgrace to have to rely on military protection of Italian forces during the Somalia operation.[93] Their shame was shared by Foreign Minister Kinkel who said he felt stupid and ashamed when discussing more determined military intervention in Yugoslavia because, in view of the constitutional situation, he would have been unable to contribute to it.[94]

To sum up, the identity asserted to support military involvement abroad relied on the myth of an origin made possible by exclusions. It also appealed to an impossible normality. Arguing in terms of concepts such as normality is problematic because their implied rigour is impossible. Nevertheless, normality was valued because of the underlying logic of our thinking; for, as Derrida points out, our thinking is structured by dichotomies which imply a valorisation.[95] Derrida points out that Western thought relies not only on dichotomies but implicitly values one of the opposed terms over the other. This aspect of his argument has just been employed in relation to the normal/abnormal opposition which contextualised the issue of military involvement abroad. It is also important to consider the identity/difference dichotomy where the former is privileged over the latter.[96] Although identity is an effect of differences, identity is the valued term. The representation of an

[89] 'Wenn es die Führung will', *Der Spiegel*, 13/45, 25 Mar. 1991, 82–93, here 83; 'Größenwahn der Generäle', *Der Spiegel*, 15/46, 6 Apr. 1992, 18–21, here 20.
[90] 'Papa, bitte nicht in Uniform', *Der Spiegel*, 20/46, 11 May 1992, 59–73, here 66.
[91] 'Wir wollen nicht beiseite stehen', *Der Spiegel*, 50/46, 7 Dec. 1992, 114–15.
[92] 'Nun siegt mal schön', *Der Spiegel*, 29/48, 18 Jul. 1994, 23–6, here 23–5.
[93] Ibid., 23.   [94] Dirk Koch, 'Nur nicht drängeln', *Der Spiegel*, 41/46, 5 Oct. 1992, 26.
[95] See, for example, *LI* 93 [174].   [96] Johnson, 'Translator's Introduction', p. viii.

identity as the relevant subject in the first place is significant. Politicians frequently spoke of 'the Germans' or simply used the pronoun 'we'. This is, of course, a common way of speaking in politics. However, accepting this as a given starting point has political consequences. The dominance of the identity problem arguably led to a lack of consideration of the practicalities of military involvement. What was at issue was the confirmation of 'German' identity as 'normal' rather than a consideration of the needs of the other. The circling around the self led to a narrow politics, repeated in the reaction to the situation in Kosovo, which conspicuously failed to take into account the effect reaffirming the West's identity as both unitary and ethical would have on the people who were supposedly being protected.[97] Such an ultimately destructive politics can be avoided only through a recognition of the other. Derrida points out the significance of 'the *heading of the other*, before which we must respond, and which we must *remember, of which* we must *remind ourselves*, the heading of the other being perhaps the first condition of an identity or identification that is not an ego-centrism destructive of oneself and the other' (*OH* 15 [20–1]).

The portrayal of a chosen starting point as an inevitable reality is problematic as identification is never natural (*OH* 26–7 [31]). And yet this is the upshot of representing the succession of Third Reich, old FRG and new FRG as the history which gives meaning to who the Germans are today. The assertion that this is 'the' history, the only relevant reality, involves a depoliticisation. Derrida recognises that the history of a culture presupposes an identifiable heading. Yet, he argues, it also presupposes that this heading not be given, that it is not identifiable in advance (*OH* 17–18 [22–3]). Identity needs telling and retelling, construction and reconstruction. In order to show the difference within identity, in order to make possible its continuous telling and retelling, in order to avoid closure which can only mean

---

[97] The independent evaluation of the UNHCR's response to the refugee crisis claims the interests of key donor states were related to 'the NATO military campaign and not necessarily to universal standards of refugee protection': United Nations High Commissioner for Refugees Evaluation and Policy Analysis Unit, *The Kosovo Refugee Crisis: An Independent Evaluation of UNHCR's Emergency Preparedness and Response*, pre-publication edn (Geneva: February, 2000), chapter 6, section 438. See also, for example, Gerhard Schröder (chancellor), in Deutscher Bundestag, *Plenarprotokoll*, 14/31, 26 Mar. 1999, 2571–2; Manfred Ertel et al., 'Das Gespenst von Vietnam', *Der Spiegel*, 14/53, 5 Apr. 1999, 150–64, here 157–8; Rainer Pörtner and Alexander Szandar, 'Alle hatten Skrupel', interview with Defence Minister Rudolf Scharping, *Der Spiegel*, 13/53, 29 Mar. 1999, 218–19, here 219; 'Nach dem letzten Moment', *SZ*, 25 Mar. 1999, 3; 'Albright deutet Änderung der Nato-Strategie an', *SZ*, 6 Apr. 1999, 1.

depoliticisation, it is necessary to engage continuously in the double gesture of deconstruction.

This resistance to depoliticisation is what Wendt's constructivism lacks and must lack. State agents exist *a priori*. Their identities are merely refined in interaction (A 402–4). These identities then lead to specific interests.[98] Wendt is frequently criticised for exclusions, especially for exogenising the domestic realm. More radically, he is faulted for ignoring the genesis of the subject.[99] Jenny Edkins and Véronique Pin-Fat suggest that it is necessary to go beyond an exploration of 'identity' as such investigations presuppose a pre-existing subject which acquires an identity in interaction.[100] Poststructuralist thought asserts that there 'are no settled identities; the subject never achieves the completion or wholeness toward which it strives. It remains haunted by that which has to be excluded for subjectivity to be constituted in the first place.'[101]

Wendt's starting point establishes a number of exclusions. These are not, as he presents them, innocent methodological choices.[102] On the contrary, such exclusions 'form the often unspoken basis of the argument'.[103] They lead to hierarchies of values. As Derrida argues, 'there is no limit to the effects of a decision that, presenting itself as methodological, organizes and hierarchizes all the delimitations that have here been called problematic closures'.[104] Domestic politics, linguistic processes and normative considerations are not only 'bracketed', they are excluded as unimportant. These exclusions close down the range of possible solutions but they return to haunt the analysis. The problem is that the closures of this approach have significant political consequences. They define not only what is important but what can be thought.

Wendt's starting point makes possible certain solutions whilst excluding others. Viewed in the context of his framework the issue must be construed as a problem *for a state with an identifiable identity*, what is denoted by 'Germany'. The insecurity of the German state's identity can thus at best be considered a curiosity. Other identities or subject positions cannot be addressed. Although Wendt claims that '[h]istory matters' (*STIP* 109), multiple histories do not. 'Germany' makes an appearance

[98] A 398; *STIP* ch. 5.   [99] Campbell, 'Epilogue', pp. 220–1.
[100] Jenny Edkins and Véronique Pin-Fat, 'The Subject of the Political', in Edkins, Persram and Pin-Fat, *Sovereignty and Subjectivity*, p. 1. See the whole volume for explorations of this point.
[101] Edkins and Pin-Fat, 'Subject of the Political', p. 1.
[102] See, for example, *STIP* 6–15; see also 35.
[103] Edkins, 'Legality with a Vengeance', 555.   [104] Derrida, *Aporias*, p. 54 [p. 329].

only as a unified entity. This privileging of unity and identity is, according to Johnson, an expression of logocentrism.[105] Considering identity, in this setting, does not make thinking more problematic. Rather, as David Campbell points out, identity is construed in an essentialist way such that it can be plugged into already existing theoretical frameworks.[106] There is certainly no space for considering the impact of Derrida's claim that 'difference to itself [*différence à soi*], that which differs and diverges from itself, of itself' is always part of cultural identity (*OH* 10 [16]). Consequently, Wendt's constructivism reinforces widespread but ultimately contradictory ways of thinking.

Wendt needs identity to be identifiable but identity is 'never given, received or attained'.[107] Derrida argues that 'identity or identification in general . . . belongs, therefore *must* belong, to this *experience and experiment of the impossible*' (*OH* 45 [46–7]). As we have seen, the participants in the debates about German military involvement abroad appealed to the idea of an origin from which history and political action were to derive meaning. The problem is that this has serious political consequences. It closes down thinking space. Peter Glotz, for instance, was concerned that the space for discussion should be kept open. He complained that the Germans, because of their historically derived commitment to multilateralism, thought they 'obviously' had to participate in the Gulf War.[108] More significantly, perhaps, the closures supported action that had tangible consequences. For instance, the Bundeswehr participated in bombing Serbs in the name of the FRG's identity as a NATO ally.[109] The concern for the self rather than the other became apparent in the failure to consider the likely fate of the Kosovars.[110] The problem thus is not only that Wendt's position is, as I argued in chapter 2, intellectually impossible. It is also that its presentation as possible and even natural has political consequences.

Constructivism in its Wendtian variant is unable to challenge the way things are because it does not take into account the structures of our

[105] Johnson, 'Translator's Introduction', p. viii.   [106] Campbell, 'Epilogue', p. 218.
[107] Derrida, *Monolingualism of the Other*, p. 28 [p. 53].
[108] Glotz, 'Der ungerechte Krieg', 38.
[109] See Gerhard Schröder (chancellor), in Deutscher Bundestag, *Plenarprotokoll*, 14/31, 26 Mar. 1999, 2571–2; 'Annan: Militärschlag im Kosovo möglich', *SZ*, 27 Jan. 1999, 9.
[110] See, for example, 'Nach dem letzten Moment', *SZ*, 25 Mar. 1999, 3; Heribert Prantl, 'Das deutsche Asylrecht – blind für den Kosovo', *SZ*, 1–2 Apr. 1999, 4; Peter Münch, 'In Sicherheit und dennoch in der Falle', *SZ*, 6 Apr. 1999, 2; Heribert Prantl, 'Es gibt nichts Gutes, außer man tut es', *SZ*, 6 Apr. 1999, 4; 'SPD-Linke fordert sofortiges Ende der Kampfhandlungen', *SZ*, 7 Apr. 1999, 6; 'Nato-Bombe trifft offenbar Wohngebiet', *SZ*, 7 Apr. 1999, 5.

thought. Wendt may claim that he wants to explain, not to change. The point is, however, that constructivism, even in its own terms, also 'changes' the world in that it reinforces what 'is'. The 'way things are' is treated as the way things must be. The 'reality' of international politics must be taken into account. This represents as natural what is political and obscures inherent value judgements. This is particularly problematic when the claim is that what is being investigated is how the world is constructed. Derrida's approach is useful to unmask the politics of the conceptualisations we rely on. His insistence on questioning such common-sense notions as normality, identity and unity, on challenging their very possibility, opens up the thinking space which constructivism closes down. As we will see later, Derrida's thought challenges the notion that this 'reality', which Wendt's constructivism makes central, is more real, more authentic or more present than are representations.

Everyday 'reality'

Friedrich Kratochwil starts from the pragmatics of language in order to analyse how we construct our world because appropriateness to the situation is important (*RND* 30). According to Kratochwil, we 'demand, warn, threaten, claim, criticize, assert, consent, suggest, apologize, pressure, persuade, praise, grade, promise, forbid, appoint, authorize, contract, or even bet, in order to further our goals' (*RND* 7). He argues that 'we have to understand how the social world is intrinsically linked to language and how language, because it is a rule-governed activity, can provide us with a point of departure for our inquiry into the function of norms in social life' (*RND* 6). Relying on speech act theory allows us, he claims, to analyse the problem of the conditions of effective communication (*RND* 7). In this context, rules and norms become relevant because they 'constitute a practice within which certain acts or utterances "count" as something' (*RND* 7). Kratochwil's approach to language and its role in social action entails listening in on actors' narratives about themselves, on the reasons they present for their actions and on the metaphors or 'commonplaces' they share, enabling them to understand each other. His world is one of intended, serious and determinable meaning.

Derrida questions the presuppositions of this starting point. He argues that '"everyday language" is not innocent or neutral. It is the language of Western metaphysics, and it carries with it a considerable number of presuppositions of all types, but also presuppositions inseparable from metaphysics, which, although little attended to, are knotted into a system' (*P* 19 [29]). As a consequence, Derrida fundamentally critiques the model of communication on which Kratochwil's approach is based. Kratochwil relies on norms making shared meaning possible. In chapter 3 I discussed norms and normativity as a crucial aspect of his constructivism and of the debates about German military involvement abroad. I argued that there was a twofold problem. Firstly, the reliance of the argument on norms as the basis of intersubjectivity proved elusive. Secondly, the consideration of norms as rules led to an exclusion, rather than inclusion, of the political. My concern was that the upshot of this was that, despite Kratochwil's stated aim of bringing the normative back into the analysis of international relations, his approach was bound to reinforce the separation of the normative from the political. Derrida's challenge to logocentric thinking supports this argument in three ways, which I will explore here. He critiques the model of communication on which Kratochwil relies, he draws attention to the political character of the norms themselves and he offers a different notion of responsibility which aims to escape the depoliticising effect of applying norms as rules.

Derrida's notions of *différance*, iterability and the supplement subvert the metaphysics of presence and thus the presupposition of linguistic philosophy that there is such a thing as self-present and unified meaning. In his 'Signature Event Context' and two related essays,[111] he employs deconstruction to show, amongst other things, that Austin's theory of speech acts is predicated on assumptions that threaten to undo its claims. Derrida starts by questioning the traditional conception of 'communication' as signifying the transmission of unified meaning. 'Communication presupposes subjects (whose identity and presence are constituted before the signifying operation) and objects (signified concepts, a thought meaning that the passage of communication will have neither to constitute, nor, by all rights, to transform). *A* communicates *B* to *C*' (*P* 23 [34–5]). Derrida draws attention to the impossibility of limiting 'communication' to semantics or semiotics as communication always includes the possibility of nonsemantic moves (*LI* 1 [17]). Communication may take place when no language is involved. A shock may, for instance, be communicated, that is, transmitted. One may object that the ambiguity of the meaning of the word 'communication'

---

[111] Collected in *LI*.

is reduced to a large extent by the context within which it is used. Derrida rejects this possibility and aims to show why the determination of context is never 'entirely certain or saturated' (*LI* 3 [20]). The problem is that meaning depends on context but context is boundless. This would then mean that the current concept of context as determining meaning is inadequate and, he claims, that the concept of writing must be displaced, as it is based on the untenable notion of communication as the transmission of meaning.

According to Derrida, in philosophy, writing has been seen as a means of communication which extends its reach, in other words, a transmission of the meaning or content of a semantic message by different means, which involves only an accidental alteration of the meaning of the message, if it involves any alteration at all (*LI* 3 [20–1]). Derrida focuses on how this conceptualisation of writing is predicated on the notion of absence. Writing becomes necessary because of the absence of the addressee. It represents the presence in its absence, supplants it (*LI* 5 [24]). For writing to function as written communication it must be readable, that is repeatable, iterable. 'Such iterability – (*iter*, again, probably comes from *itara, other* in Sanskrit, and everything that follows can be read as the working out of the logic that ties repetition to alterity) structures the mark of writing itself' (*LI* 7 [27]). Writing, therefore, in principle functions without the presence of either the addressee or the writer (*LI* 7–8 [27–9]).

Derrida proceeds to discuss the problematic of iterability and meaning in relation to the performative.[112] The performative seems to destroy the concept of communication as a purely semiotic, linguistic or symbolic concept. Austin conceptualises speech acts as acts of communication and therefore has to conceive of communication as action rather than as the transmission of thought-content, as having no referent outside itself and as following not the logic of a true/false opposition but rather a logic of force (*LI* 13 [36–8]). The performative does not describe something outside language as the constative supposedly does. Rather it creates and changes situations in the 'real' world and therefore is related to notions of force. Nevertheless Austin fails to see, according to Derrida, that the structure of locution is graphematic and that as a result the oppositions Austin aims to set up in rigour and purity are blurred. Austin's analysis is predicated on a notion of context, moreover an exhaustively

---

[112] A performative *is* an action rather than a description of one: Austin, *How to Do Things with Words*, p. 6.

determined context, a 'total context'. One essential element in this context is consciousness. The conscious intention of the speaker must be present in the speech act. Performative communication is the communication of intentional meaning (*LI* 14 [38–9]).

Austin investigates why speech acts fail, what he calls 'infelicities'[113] of performatives. This analysis is based on the idea that the speaker knows what the speech act is meant to do. If the desired effect is not accomplished the performative has failed. Austin identifies six necessary if not sufficient conditions of success. As Derrida points out: 'Through the values of "conventional procedure", "correctness", and "completeness", which occur in the definition, we necessarily find once more those of an exhaustively definable context, of a free consciousness present to the totality of the operation, and of absolutely meaningful speech [*vouloir-dire*] master of itself: the teleological jurisdiction of an entire field whose organizing center remains *intention*' (*LI* 15 [40]).[114] Austin is aware that a speech act is a precarious operation which may fail if, for instance, the procedure for the speech act is not strictly adhered to, if the speaker did not have the appropriate thoughts or feelings or if the speaker was not entitled to perform the speech act. What Derrida points to is that, although Austin recognises the structural possibility of failure, he at the same time wants to exclude that risk as 'accidental, exterior, one which teaches us nothing about the linguistic phenomenon being considered' (*LI* 15 [40]).

Derrida takes this move to be typical for the Western philosophical tradition. In this spirit, Austin excludes any 'non-serious' use of performances, such as in a play or in soliloquy, from consideration as they are '*parasitic*' on the 'normal use' of language.[115] Derrida argues, on the contrary, that precisely this citationality or iterability is the condition of a 'successful' performative. We can identify performatives only because they conform to an iterable model (*LI* 17–18 [43–6]). The exclusion of certain uses of language from the analysis creates hierarchies of values in favour of the serious and literal (*LI* 71 [135–6]). The problem is that these exclusions enter into the discourse as valorisations. 'This discourse thus finds itself an integral part – part and parcel, but also *partial* – of the object it claims to be analyzing. It can no longer be impartial or neutral, having been determined even before the latter could be determined by it' (*LI* 71 [136]). The exhaustiveness of context necessary to Austin's

---

[113] Austin, *How to Do Things with Words*, esp. Lecture II.
[114] See also Austin, *How to Do Things with Words*, pp. 14–15.
[115] Austin, *How to Do Things with Words*, p. 22.

analysis is impossible because of the impossibility of a total presence of meaning. 'In order for a context to be exhaustively determinable, in the sense required by Austin, conscious intention would at the very least have to be totally present and immediately transparent to itself and to others, since it is a determining center [*foyer*] of the context' (*LI* 18 [46]). This is impossible. Therefore, although communication has intended effects, it must at the same time presuppose their opposite as a general possibility (*LI* 19 [47]).

The general possibility of failure in the communication of 'meaning' seems to have been amply demonstrated by the competing significations of the norms in relation to German military involvement abroad. Kratochwil's conceptualisation of norms, which make communication possible (*RND* 11), is indebted to speech act theory. Kratochwil claims that meaning can be shared among actors and also becomes accessible to analysts through norms and norms-based reasoning. In chapter 3, the question of shared meaning was explored with respect to the norms considered significant in relation to the issue of participation in international military operations. A discussion of constitutional regulations as well as extra-legal normative notions, such as the principles against war and oppression, showed that it would be difficult to argue that meaning in relation to them was shared. On the contrary, it seemed that, although actors referred to the same normative notions, they had radically different, even contradictory, interpretations of them. 'Never again war' was interpreted as ruling out the use of force altogether by some and as requiring the use of force to stop war by others. Thus, the result of a detailed analysis of the debates was that the precise impact of norms had become more rather than less unclear. Context certainly did not make meaning self-present. This, I argued, is problematic for Kratochwil as his approach rests on the possibility of intersubjectivity, especially in terms of his epistemology and methodology. The discussion rather suggested that '[m]eaning [*sens*, MZ] and effect are never produced or refused absolutely; they always keep a reserve at the disposition of a potential reader, a reserve that has less to do with a substantial wealth and more with an aleatory margin in the trajectories, an impossibility of saturating a context.'[116]

The indeterminate character of signification is illustrated by the shifts in meaning observed in the debates. It has already been pointed out that

---

[116] Jacques Derrida, *Points . . . Interviews, 1974–1994*, edited by Elisabeth Weber, translated by Peggy Kamuf and others (Stanford University Press, 1995), p. 175 [p. 187].

the 'never again war' principle had been rearticulated. In 1946, Carlo Schmid, a prominent Social Democrat, had argued: 'Never again do we want to send our sons to the barracks. And if again somewhere this insanity of war should break out, and if fate should want it that our land becomes a battlefield, then we shall simply perish and at least take with us the knowledge that we neither encouraged nor committed the crime.'[117] Similarly, in the 1949 election campaign, Franz-Josef Strauß of the CSU said, somewhat drastically, that the hand of any German who touches a gun should fall off.[118] These clear statements against Germans participating in any use of force whatsoever were recalled by Detlef Kleinert in 1993: 'Between 1945 and 1950 at least no one in this country would have come up with the idea that it would be possible ever again that a German would take up a weapon again – no matter for what purpose.'[119] That Kinkel was able to portray his support for deploying armed forces to Bosnia as in the same tradition of the rejection of war – the decision was, he said, not about waging war but about preventing war[120] – highlights the possibility of weaning statements from their contexts, that is, iterability. A sign can function only if it is possible to repeat it in different contexts, if it can retain aspects of the same whilst changing (*LI* 53 [105]). For Kinkel's argument to make an impression, his reference to the rejection of war had to be understood as a citation of important earlier statements to this effect whilst at the same time signifying something new and thereby supporting military involvement abroad.

Making the need to take responsibility a key justification for enabling the FRG to participate in international military operations worked in a similar way. A 'policy of responsibility' had long formed part of the FRG's declared foreign policy. In an interview Foreign Minister Genscher explained the idea: 'One has to know whether one wants to pursue a policy of responsibility or the power politics of yesterday. The politician pursuing power politics will try to gain unilaterally from the problems of his opponent. The politician pursuing a policy of responsibility sees the problems of the partners and is interested in

---

[117] Carlo Schmid, *Erinnerungen* (Bern and Munich, 1979), p. 490, quoted in Abenheim, *Reforging the Iron Cross*, p. 43.
[118] Kaiser and Becher, *Deutschland und der Irak-Konflikt*, p. 8.
[119] Detlef Kleinert (FDP) in Deutscher Bundestag, *Plenarprotokoll*, 12/151, 21 Apr. 1993, 12952.
[120] Deutscher Bundestag, *Plenarprotokoll*, 13/48, 30 Jun. 1995, 3957.

solving them.'[121] He conceptualised responsibility as one towards future generations, which required protecting the environment and preserving peace. It also entailed a policy of development. A new, more just world order was needed.[122] Responsibility had never been related to using the military. Indeed, Genscher did not think that the military realm would provide the best forum in which to act responsibly.[123]

However, in a move which encompassed both citation and alteration, responsibility became displaced to a different context. The assistance to Kurdish refugees from Iraq was portrayed as the first opportunity to show after the Gulf War, that, as Genscher put it, the Germans 'were able to live up to the increased responsibility [they had] gained through unification'.[124] Thus Genscher linked responsibility to the deployment of the Bundeswehr. This move was repeated time and again. Rühe represented the operation in Cambodia as a significant political step towards the willingness to accept more responsibility internationally.[125] Kinkel justified the participation in the surveillance of the UN embargo against Bosnia-Herzegovina in the same way. He argued that 'Germany could not and cannot evade its increased responsibility. This is not about a demonstration of military might but a contribution to strengthening the instruments of collective security.'[126] It did not come as a surprise after all these declarations that the governing parties would justify their intention to make the external use of the military legally possible in view of their claim that the FRG had to take 'more responsibility for international security'.[127] These repeated declarations meant that 'responsibility' came to signify something new. This was recognised by Genscher who, after he had retired from his post as foreign minister, complained that in the government's argument 'new responsibility mean[t]: Bundeswehr deployments abroad'.[128] Such a definition of responsibility seems narrow. It reflects what Derrida would call *'responsibility as irresponsibility'* (*OH* 72 [71]), responsibility reduced to the technical question of troop deployments. The existing

[121] 'Nicht den Buchhaltern überlassen', interview with Foreign Minister Hans-Dietrich Genscher, *Der Spiegel*, 20/44, 14 May 1990, 28–30, here 28.
[122] 'Geheimnis des Genscherismus', interview with Foreign Minister Hans-Dietrich Genscher, *Der Spiegel*, 40/44, 1 Oct. 1990, 30–5, here 33–4.
[123] Ibid., 35.
[124] Quoted in 'Hering in Senfsoße', *Der Spiegel*, 20/45, 13 May 1991, 32–3, here 32.
[125] 'Gewachsene Instinkte', *Der Spiegel*, 21/46, 18 May 1992, 27–30, here 30.
[126] Deutscher Bundestag, *Plenarprotokoll*, 12/101, 22 Jul. 1992, 8612.
[127] Reasoning for the CDU/CSU and FDP proposal to change the Basic Law, Deutscher Bundestag, *Drucksache*, 12/4135, 15 Jan. 1993.
[128] Quoted in 'Einsatz ins Ungewisse', *Der Spiegel*, 5/49, 30 Jan. 1995, 68–79, here 75.

referent of a 'policy of responsibility' gradually altered into a military matter.

Derrida's analysis destabilises the possibility of conceptualising inter-subjectivity as the politically neutral realm of the shared through which communication becomes possible. Consequently, the political character of norms becomes salient. Despite Kratochwil's apparent aim to link the normative and the political, the focus on norms as general statements applicable to all comparable situations works, I claimed in chapter 3, to separate the normative from the political. It obscures the political character of norms themselves. This problematic role of norms was il-lustrated in terms of how the debate about participating in international military operations was represented as a competition between two con-tradictory abstract norms which had to be either accepted or rejected. The choice was portrayed as one between being willing in principle to deploy troops abroad and refusing, again in principle, to use armed force for any purpose other than defence. I used Fischer's arguments to show that deciding for or against one course of action *in principle* was not responsible at all. Rather, it was necessary to recognise the need to make a decision in relation to each specific case, even if it would never be fully responsible. Kratochwil's argument, which does not recognise the political character of the norm structure itself, supports, I claimed, a conceptualisation of responsibility as programme. Thereby the argu-ment in effect defines responsibility in a way which is in tension with the necessity of taking into account the particular situation, which is part of responsibility if it is to be possible at all.

Derrida's argument about responsibility relates to his discussion of law and morality or justice. Both make clear the political implications of his thought rooted in the strategy of deconstruction itself. Any attempt to separate law and morality from politics, Derrida argues, relies on the notion of an origin, a source. A 'deconstructive line of questioning' is through and through a 'problematization of the foundations of law, morality and politics' (FoL 931/930). Such an investigation leads to the disconcerting insight that, '[s]ince the origin of authority, the foundation or ground, the position of the law can't by definition rest on anything but themselves, they are themselves a violence without ground' (FoL 943/942). Thus the foundational moment of law is inextricably linked to force. Derrida points to two aspects of the 'force of law'. Firstly, law is always backed by a force, 'enforced'. The concept of law always struc-turally implies the possibility of it being enforced. Law is 'a force that justifies itself or is justified in applying itself' (FoL 925/924). Secondly, there is the aspect of violence which is always deemed unjust (FoL 927/926). This duplicity of meaning is also inherent in the German term *Gewalt*, which 'is both violence and legitimate power, justified authority' (FoL 927/926). The problem Derrida addresses is the impossibility of clearly distinguishing between these two meanings of the force of law. This becomes apparent with respect to the founding moment of the law. Derrida asks how we are 'to distinguish between the force of law of a legitimate power and the supposedly originary violence that must have established this authority and that could not itself have been authorized by any anterior legitimacy, so that, in this initial moment, it is neither legal nor illegal – or, others would quickly say, neither just nor unjust' (FoL 927/926). The emergence of justice and law necessarily involves a moment of performative and interpretative force. At this stage law cannot yet be an instrument of the dominant power; rather, in this sense, law must 'maintain a more internal, more complex relation with what one calls force, power or violence' (FoL 941/940). The disconcerting thought thus is that 'the operation that consists of founding, inaugurating, justifying law (*droit*), making law, would consist of a *coup de force*, of a performative and therefore interpretative violence that in itself is neither just nor unjust' (FoL 941–2/940). Any recourse to the law or to justice would then be bound up with this original *coup de force*.

Although Derrida discusses justice and law together in many respects, they are profoundly different. When we apply a good rule to a particular case, law (*droit*) is accounted for but not justice. Law represents the element of calculation. Justice, however, requires the experience of aporia, that is, 'moments in which the decision between just and unjust is never insured by a rule' (FoL 947/946). Justice consists in a singular act and not in the mechanical application of a rule (FoL 949/948). Justice therefore takes place only when a decision is made freely. A free decision must go through the aporia of the undecidable:

> The undecidable . . . is not merely the oscillation between two significations or two contradictory and very determinate rules, each equally imperative . . . The undecidable is not merely the oscillation or the tension between two decisions; it is the experience of that which, though heterogeneous, foreign to the order of the calculable and the rule, is still obliged . . . to give itself up to the impossible decision, while taking account of law and rules. A decision that didn't go through the ordeal of the undecidable would not be a free decision, it would only be the programmable application or unfolding of a calculable process.
>
> (FoL 963/962)

The decision does not resolve the problem and go beyond the unde-cidable. The undecidable is not surmounted; it remains caught in every decision and makes it impossible to call any decision fully just.

The question of responsibility concerns a similar problematic. Re-sponsibility, like justice, addresses the relation of the singular act to the abstract rule structure. The problem of ethico-political responsibility lies in 'the disparities between law, ethics, and politics, or between the unconditional idea of law (be it of men or of states) and the concrete conditions of its implementation' (*OH* 57 [57]). Thus responsibility, like justice, is linked to the undecidable. This is hardly surprising as in our thinking both are related to the idea of a free decision. According to Derrida, political and moral responsibility only exists when one has to go through the aporia of the undecidable (*LI* 116 [210]). Otherwise it is not a free decision but a mechanical application of rules:

> I will even venture to say that ethics, politics, and responsibility, *if there are any*, will only ever have begun with the experience and experiment of aporia. When the path is clear and given, when a certain knowledge opens up the way in advance, the decision is already made, it might as well be said that there is none to make: irresponsibly, and in good con-science, one simply applies or implements a program . . . The condition of possibility of this thing called responsibility is a certain *experience and experiment of the possibility of the impossible: the testing of the aporia* from which one may invent the only *possible invention, the impossible invention.*
> (*OH* 41 [43])

The experience of the impossible is crucial, as any attempt to elimi-nate it, Derrida claims, will lead to eliminating responsibility itself. The application of a rule, direction or programme is not responsible, for it 'makes of action the applied consequence, the simple application of a knowledge or know-how. It makes of ethics and politics a technol-ogy' (*OH* 45 [46]). Turning political questions into technical problems leads to the irresponsible. It is, then, not the aporia of the undecid-able which may make responsibility impossible; it is depoliticisation, which turns ethical questions into technical problems awaiting technical solutions:

> To have at one's disposal, already in advance, the generality of a rule [*règle*] as a solution to the antinomy . . . to have it at one's disposal as a given potency or science, as a *knowledge* and a *power* that would pre-cede, in order to settle [*régler*] it, the singularity of each decision, each judgment, each experience of responsibility, to treat each of these as if they were a case – this would be the surest, the most reassuring

definition of *responsibility as irresponsibility*, of ethics confused with
juridical calculation, of a politics organized within techno-science.
(*OH* 71–2 [70–1])

To bypass the aporia, the experience of the undecidable, would amount
to a dangerous mystification: it allows us to be immoral whilst retaining
a good conscience. Good conscience is, however, what it is imperative
to avoid.[129]

Considering these points, the development which involved the shifting signification of 'responsibility' was important not only because responsibility came to refer to something it had not been associated with
in the past. Genscher's remark also drew attention to a closure. How to
act responsibly was treated as a matter which could be decided through
knowledge. One could know responsible behaviour and adhere to it
without regard for the concrete situation in which being responsible was
at issue. One side portrayed the willingness to participate in military operations as such as taking responsibility, the other the principled refusal
to do so. Yet subscribing to such a 'programme', which lays out a given
path for the future, represents an escape from responsibility, according
to Derrida's argument (*OH* 41 [43]). Derrida insists that responsibility is possible only when we go through the aporia of the undecidable
(*LI* 116 [209–10]). The undecidable is the 'condition of the decision as
well as that of responsibility'.[130] In other words,

there is no responsibility that is not the experience and experiment of
the impossible . . . when a responsibility is exercised in the order of the
possible, it simply follows a direction and elaborates a program . . . It
makes of ethics and politics a technology. No longer of the order of
practical reason or decision, it begins to be irresponsible.
(*OH* 44–5 [46])

Situations which require the performance of responsibility are precisely
situations in which knowledge is of little help. If we *know* the best
solution, the matter at issue is not one of responsibility. Settling the
issue by claiming that participation in international military operations
was virtually coterminous with taking responsibility meant pretending
that 'a certain knowledge opens up the way in advance' (*OH* 41 [43]).
The claim was a general one, that, as 'a people of 80 million, as the
economically strongest country in central Europe we carry, whether we

[129] Derrida, *Aporias*, p. 19 [p. 316].
[130] Derrida, *Monolingualism of the Other*, p. 62 [p. 119].

like it or not, a special, partially new responsibility'.[131] Although some claimed that, after committing the FRG to using force abroad in principle, it was still necessary to decide to which specific operations the Bundeswehr would be deployed,[132] that creating the general possibility of using armed force in the international realm would broaden the scope of politics and enhance the FRG's capability to act,[133] this was unlikely to provide space for acting responsibly in the Derridean sense.

The representation of military involvement abroad as responsibility closed down political space. This danger was raised by Glotz of the SPD. He worried that the debate was creating a situation in which the Germans, unlike the citizens of other states, could not differ over whether to engage in war or not. Their military involvement was necessary to live up to their responsibility and to repay their debt to the Western allies.[134] He was concerned that this closed down the space for discussion. Uta Zapf, also of the SPD, called the Bundestag session about participation in NATO and WEU operations implementing the embargo in the Adriatic Sea and the flight ban over Bosnia-Herzegovina in July 1994 after the ruling of the constitutional court a farce. She pointed out that the logic of solidarity in the alliance made any form of autonomous decision impossible: 'When Herr Lamers says that there will of course be a national decision in each case but basically means with this that this national decision is not open any more, because, you see, we must vote the same way as the alliance partners, then we can skip such sittings in which we as parliamentarians decide.'[135] The problem was that what was at issue was not the concrete situation in relation to which an act could never be fully just, but a dichotomous choice between deploying the Bundeswehr represented as taking responsibility, and not doing so represented as shirking. This was apparent in the failure of the parliamentary debates to refer to the situations into which the armed forces were to be sent except in a cursory way. As Derrida reminds us, exclusions are important (*LI* 15–18 [40–7]). This exclusion was significant also because it left important questions unanswered: 'And responsible before whom? Before what memory? For what promise?' (*OH* 13 [19]).

[131] Kinkel, 'Verantwortung', 8.
[132] Karl Lamers (CDU/CSU) in Deutscher Bundestag, *Plenarprotokoll*, 12/240, 22 Jul. 1994, 21192.
[133] Volker Rühe (defence minister) in Deutscher Bundestag, *Plenarprotokoll*, 12/132, 15 Jan. 1993, 11485; Kohl, 'Europäische Sicherheit', 134; 'Die Zukunft steht auf dem Spiel', interview with FDP chairman Klaus Kinkel, *Der Spiegel*, 47/47, 22 Nov. 1993, 41–4, here 44.
[134] Glotz, 'Der ungerechte Krieg', 38.
[135] Deutscher Bundestag, *Plenarprotokoll*, 12/240, 22 Jul. 1994, 21207.

Yet at times the debates opened towards a Derridean view of responsibility. Fischer explicitly spelt out the impossibility of deciding the issue one way or another whilst remaining fully just. He suggested that there was no course of action with respect to Yugoslavia which was responsible as such. Rather one was likely to become guilty both through interference and through a failure to get involved.[136] Both 'never again war' and 'never again Auschwitz' were crucially important to him. However, he recognised that their application in the case of the former Yugoslavia created a problem, as it was possible that only war could prevent Auschwitz in the situation at hand. He thereby acknowledged what Derrida calls a 'double contradictory imperative' (*OH* 79 [77]). What set Fischer's deliberations apart from those of others was that he stressed the impossibility of resolving this contradiction. Rather he wanted his party to stand up for it.[137] This strikes me as a Derridean position because it rejects the possibility of morality or responsibility as a rule. Derrida speaks of 'the responsibility to think, speak, and act in compliance with this double contradictory imperative' (*OH* 79 [77]). This is, of course, a difficult task. The question is, according to Derrida, the following: 'And above all, how does one assume a responsibility that announces itself as contradictory because it inscribes us from the very beginning of the game into a kind of necessarily double obligation, a *double bind*?' (*OH* 29 [32–3]).

Fischer's reasoning was more clearly explicated in an open letter to his party entitled 'The Catastrophe in Bosnia and the Consequences for Our Party', published in summer 1995. In it he acknowledged that a political alternative which would avoid victims and violence was not currently available and argued that this was a challenge to a pacifist party.[138] War, he said, had 'returned with all its cruelty and barbarism'.[139] He rhetorically asked whether 'pacifists, and especially a position of non-violence, [could] just accept the victory of brutal, naked violence'.[140] The question was, he claimed, at what point tolerance towards a policy of violence had to end. He thought that the German left was in danger of losing its soul if it ducked the challenge of this new fascism and policy of violence. He asked whether one could value 'principles more than human lives' and what would become 'of the principle of non-violence

---

[136] Deutscher Bundestag, *Plenarprotokoll*, 13/48, 30 Jun. 1995, 3971.
[137] 'Das wäre blutiger Zynismus', *Der Spiegel*, 34/49, 21 Aug. 1995, 27–9, here 29.
[138] Fischer, 'Die Katastrophe', 1143.   [139] Fischer, 'Die Katastrophe', 1147.
[140] Fischer, 'Die Katastrophe', 1148.

if it submit[ted] to inhuman violence'.[141] He detected a fundamental conflict between three basic values of the Greens: 'Life and liberty stand against the principle of non-violence.'[142] In the end, although he almost hid it between the lines, he backed the use of force in Bosnia.[143] He pointed out, however, that any decision would in some way have to deal with the fundamental contradiction of values he had identified.[144] Crucially, his recognition of the double contradictory imperative did not therefore stop him from making a decision. It merely prevented him from having the good conscience which, according to Derrida, has to be avoided 'at all cost'.[145] His ability to make decisions in view of the moral dilemma, despite the impossibility of these being fully responsible or just, and to acknowledge the impossibility of good conscience was reflected again in his role, having become foreign minister, in relation to the Kosovo crisis.[146] His peace plan, which envisaged a 24-hour interruption of the air campaign if Milošević started withdrawing his armed forces from Kosovo,[147] made little impact and the press frequently commented that he was acting just as any other politician would have in his position.[148] Significantly, however, his recognition of the irresolvable moral dilemma did not lead to paralysis.[149]

Kratochwil is, of course, deeply concerned with our responsibility for the world.[150] He is aware of the significance of considering something as within or outside the realm of responsibility. As he puts it, '[s]ituating the problem in the *discourse of choice and responsibility* instead of that of "natural phenomena" dramatically alters the story' (*RND* 219). Kratochwil's explanation of what it means to do justice, moreover, seems to echo Derrida's insistence that justice, as opposed to law, deals with the singular. Doing justice, Kratochwil argues, 'involves, above all, the exercise of practical judgments in which abstract norms and concrete circumstances are fitted together' (*RND* 241). This seems rather similar

[141] Fischer, 'Die Katastrophe', 1148. [142] Fischer, 'Die Katastrophe', 1149.
[143] Fischer, 'Die Katastrophe', 1150. [144] Fischer, 'Die Katastrophe', 1152.
[145] Derrida, *Aporias*, p. 19 [p. 316].
[146] 'Bundeswehr beteiligt sich an Kosovo-Einsatz', *SZ*, 5 Nov. 1998, 5; Kurt Kister, 'Bundesregierung setzt verstärkt auf Diplomatie', *SZ*, 7 Apr. 1999, 6.
[147] Udo Bergdoll, 'Bonn setzt jetzt auf Annan', *SZ*, 14 Apr. 1999, 1; Jürgen Hogrefe et al., 'Aus freier Überzeugung', *Der Spiegel*, 16/53, 19 Apr. 1999, 22–32, here 24.
[148] Kurt Kister, 'Bundesregierung setzt verstärkt auf Diplomatie', *SZ*, 7 Apr. 1999, 6; 'EU will Annan in Friedenslösung einbinden', *SZ*, 15 Apr. 1999, 6; 'Ich darf nicht wackeln', *Der Spiegel*, 14/53, 5 Apr. 1999, 22–8, here 23; Winfried Didzoleit et al., 'Ernstfall für Schröder', *Der Spiegel*, 13/53, 29 Mar. 1999, 22–30, here 26; Jürgen Hogrefe et al., 'Aus freier Überzeugung', *Der Spiegel*, 16/53, 19 Apr. 1999, 22–32, here 22 and 29.
[149] See, however, ch. 6.   [150] See, for instance, Kratochwil, 'Errors', 319.

to Derrida's description of the problem of ethico-political responsibility as the problem of 'the disparities between law, ethics, and politics, or between the unconditional idea of law . . . and the concrete conditions of its implementation' (*OH* 57 [57]). Derrida also acknowledges the significance of the general. According to him, it 'would be necessary to recognize both the typical or recurring form and the inexhaustible singularization – without which there will never be any event, decision, responsibility, ethics, or politics' (*OH* 80 [78]). However, the problem with Kratochwil's approach is that it takes the underlying rule structure as an unproblematic starting point and therefore in effect as a value-free reality. The consideration of responsibility in terms of Kratochwil's approach is related to the problem of norms. Relying on norms which cannot be based on anything other than a *coup de force* is problematic. It also makes the reduction of responsibility to a technical solution, in this case the use of military force, possible. This in turn means excluding consideration for the other on whose behalf responsibility is nominally taken.

The problem seems to be that Kratochwil starts with everyday language, everyday reality. He appeals to an understanding of the social world 'upon which reasonable persons can agree' (*RND* 229). He acknowledges that this already involves a value judgement. Nevertheless, his conceptualisation of the social world as well as his methodological commitments for academic research are based on shared understandings.[151] This means not only that those who disagree with common-sense understandings of the world are by default unreasonable and therefore insignificant, but also sneaks in the claim that the shared reality Kratochwil starts with is more than merely a representation. The implications of this dichotomy between reality and representation in which the former is valued over the latter can be explored further in relation to Onuf's work.

'Reality' as raw material

Nicholas Onuf repeatedly appeals to reality as the basis for and a limit to our constructions. 'Human beings, with whatever equipment nature and/or society provides, construct society, and society is indispensable to the actualization of whatever human beings may "naturally" be; society constructs human beings out of the raw materials of nature,

---

[151] See ch. 3.

whether inner nature or, less problematically, the outer nature of their material circumstances' (*WOM* 46; see also 292). Accordingly, he conceives of agents' freedom as the ability to deal successfully with these limitations. It 'depends on the ability to recognize material and social limits and to evaluate the consequences of ignoring or defying those limits' (CM 9). He even speaks of 'the known, felt, lived in world we "really" inhabit' as different from 'the ongoing (re)construction of reality' (*WOM* 157). In chapter 4, I discussed the appeal to material reality as a boundary to how, in Onuf's conceptualisation of constructivism, the social world may be constructed and, analogously, as an argument in the debates about military involvement abroad. In Onuf's constructivism the biological givenness of our existence at least partially determines what we are able to do. This way of thinking about the world was echoed in arguments about participation in international military operations, but I argued that the underlying distinction between the material and the social is at the same time rendered impossible by Onuf's arguments. Again, what is significant is that presenting material 'reality' as a 'natural' limit makes it impossible to consider alternatives which are not accepted as within the realm of the real. Thus, the representation of biology as the basis of all construction already delimits the possible outcome of the analysis and the potentialities for practice.

Although material 'reality' was asserted as a limit both by Onuf and as part of the argumentation on behalf of military involvement abroad, I argued that the situation was more complex than this rendering of the issue allowed. An exploration of the debates showed that material constraints were neither the most crucial limit to reality construction – alternative suggestions as to how responsibility could be taken or how wars could be ended failed, although there was no physical hindrance to what was proposed – nor were supposedly adverse material conditions automatically recognised as a limit – serious limitations of the capabilities of the Bundeswehr were construed as problems to be overcome rather than as indisputable hindrances. I was concerned that Onuf's practice of distinguishing between 'words' and 'world' threatened to undo a key move of speech act theory, namely the conceptualisation of language and practice as inextricably linked. Their separation was used by policy-makers to portray their own position as inescapable, such as in the denunciation of objections to military involvement as merely a 'policy of words' and the appeal to death as the ultimate natural limit which could not be discussed away. The argument that there is something *behind* our constructions that is crucial although, following Onuf's reasoning, we are unable to leave our constructions (*WOM* 43) is not only difficult to sustain; it also obscures that nature or material 'reality', even if they exist, are not always accepted as limits. In other words, the limit of reality is itself a construction and Onuf's approach excludes this important point from consideration.

This analysis challenged the possibility and innocence of Onuf's conceptualisation of the constructed world as a result of an interaction between the social and the material. Derrida's notion of the real as text provides the possibility of further exploring this issue. Derrida argues that there can be no signification without supplements. Signification is not the representation of an already existing (but absent) presence. Rather 'signified presence is always reconstituted by deferral, *nachträglich*, belatedly, *supplementarily*'.[152] However, the supplement, at the same time as making signification possible, endangers it. This dual character of the supplement is based on its two contradictory but mutually complementary dimensions. The supplement, on the one hand, functions as an addition and an enrichment. On the other hand, the supplement never merely enriches a presence; it always threatens to replace it (*OG* 144–5 [208]). The ambiguity of the logic and functioning of the supplement may be demonstrated with respect to Rousseau's relationship to Thérèse, which he writes about in his *Confessions*. Although Rousseau sought her intimacy only for amusement at first, she came to be a successor to Mamma, the supplement he needed. Mamma already stands for and replaces an unknown mother. So there is a chain of supplements which fills in for the lack of a presence. 'Through this sequence of supplements a necessity is announced: that of an infinite chain, ineluctably multiplying the supplementary mediations that produce the sense of the very thing they defer: the mirage of the thing itself, of immediate presence, of originary perception. Immediacy is derived' (*OG* 157 [226]). This turns logocentric logic on its head. If immediacy is derived it seems to be possible not to conceive of absence as the negation of presence but of presence as the effect of a general absence. Derrida's conception of constitution then can be schematised in the following way: 'X is constituted by non-X. X here means essence or self-identity as conceived by philosophy, and non-X is that which functions as the "outside", or limit, yet in limiting it remains the positive condition of the possibility of the positive assertion of essence.'[153] Henry Staten therefore speaks of the

---

[152] Derrida, *Writing and Difference*, pp. 211–12 [p. 314].
[153] Staten, *Wittgenstein and Derrida*, p. 17.

'constitutive outside',[154] as the outside is necessary for the constitution of any phenomenon.

According to Derrida there is no such thing as a pure essence of meaning. Thus the reading of a text cannot simply be a reproduction of its content, of what the writer consciously, voluntarily and intentionally meant to convey. However, neither can a reading rely on a referent outside of the text:

> Yet if reading must not be content with doubling the text, it cannot legitimately transgress the text toward something other than it, toward a referent (a reality that is metaphysical, historical, psychobiographical, etc.) or toward a signified outside the text whose content could take place, could have taken place outside of language... *There is nothing outside of the text* [there is no outside-text; *il n'y a pas de hors-texte*].[155]
>
> (*OG* 158 [227–8])

This claim that there is nothing outside of the text has created much indignation. Crucially, it does not imply that the 'real world' with its material effects does not exist. Derrida elsewhere states his point less provocatively: 'there is nothing outside context' (*LI* 136 [252]). Derrida's original formulation is, however, significant. What he calls text 'is also that which "practically" inscribes and overflows the limits of such a discourse' (*P* 59 [82]) which is 'entirely regulated by essence, meaning, truth, consciousness, etc.' (*P* 59 [81]).[156] It is not confined to the semantic, representational or symbolic spheres. Text 'implies all the structures called "real", "economic", "historical", "socio-institutional", in short: all possible referents' (*LI* 148 [273]). Reality is not confined to books (*P* 44 [61]), as the statement, taken out of context, might suggest. That there is nothing outside of the text means that 'all reality has the structure of a differential trace, and that one cannot refer to this "real" except in an interpretive experience' (*LI* 148 [273]). Originally Derrida went on to explain his point using the logic of supplementarity:

> *There is nothing outside of the text* [there is no outside-text; *il n'y a pas de hors-texte*]. And that is neither because Jean-Jacques' life, or the existence of Mamma or Thérèse *themselves*, is not of prime interest to us, nor because we have access to their so-called "real" existence only in the text and we have neither any means of altering this, nor any right

---

[154] Staten, *Wittgenstein and Derrida*, p. 16.

[155] Here, it is particularly useful to refer to the original to avoid the impression of the less than happy translation of *il n'y a pas de hors-texte*.

[156] The translation renders both 'sens' and 'vouloir-dire' as 'meaning' and drops 'idéalité' altogether.

> to neglect this limitation ... What we have tried to show by following
> the guiding line of the 'dangerous supplement', is that what one calls
> the real life of these existences 'of flesh and bone', beyond and behind
> what one believes can be circumscribed as Rousseau's text, there has
> never been anything but writing; there have never been anything but
> supplements, substitutive significations which could only come forth
> in a chain of differential references, the 'real' supervening, and being
> added only while taking on meaning from a trace and from an invoca-
> tion of the supplement, etc.   (*OG* 158–9 [227–8])

Again, presence is always deferred. What seems to lie outside of texts is
more supplements, more chains of supplements and thus what Derrida
calls 'text'. It is in this sense, that there is nothing outside of the text or,
rather, that there is no such thing as an 'outside-text', an *hors-texte*. It
is not that there is no existence beyond empirical texts. Rather, because
there are chains of supplements both within and outside the empirical
texts, because we therefore conceive what we think of as life on the model
of a text, the seemingly clear distinction between inside and outside is
blurred. There is nothing more real than the supplement, no presence
prior to the signification of the supplement. 'One wishes to go back *from
the supplement to the source*: one must recognize that there is *a supplement
at the source*' (*OG* 304 [429]). In other words, as we have already seen,
there are only 'nonoriginary origins'.[157] Hence, what we call 'real life'
turns out to be 'constituted by the logic of supplementarity'.[158]

This argument is important not only in relation to Onuf's insistence
that our constructions must refer to a reality beyond all constructions,
but also in relation to the strategy of representing military involvement
abroad as required by reality. Sometimes this worked merely by stating
what was believed to be the case: 'The war is there.'[159] Therefore, by
implication, any proposals for dealing with the situation which did not
deal with the pregiven reality of the Gulf War were irrelevant. As another
commentator put it, '[w]ar is not abolished or impossible just because
we declare it to be immoral or because we do not regard it as a means
of politics any more.'[160] His conclusion was that '[m]orality and politics
are incompatible in the end. Politics must ask for results. The results
of our politics are not optimal but there was no opportunity to stay
out of this conflict.'[161] Clearly, the assertion that reality 'is' some way

---

[157] Culler, *On Deconstruction*, p. 96.   [158] Culler, *On Deconstruction*, p. 105.
[159] Jürgen Busche, 'Die Entpolitisierung der Golf-Debatte', *SZ*, 3 Jan. 1991, 4.
[160] Dieter Schröder, 'Deutsche an die Front?', *SZ*, 2–3 Feb. 1991, 4.
[161] Ibid.

rather than another limits the range of options which may reasonably be contemplated. Suggestions which do not deal with the asserted reality appropriately can be dismissed as unrealistic, impossible or naive.

Accordingly, the attempt to portray the suggestions and ideas of political opponents as out of touch with reality or, conversely, to present preferred alternatives as in tune with reality was an important strategy. *Der Spiegel* appeared to summarise the point with the following claim: 'In the Gulf reality caught up with the Germans.'[162] However, not all Germans seemed ready for this so-called new reality. As Glotz observed: 'The Germans on the other hand go mad. They avoid reality and use their guilty conscience to produce bad philosophy.'[163] Klose – who disagreed with the rejection of military involvement abroad by most of his party colleagues – spoke, in reference to them, of an 'attempt of politics, often elaborately concealed with words, to hide from realities'.[164] This, he argued, was unacceptable and embarrassing. When the Easter march movement protested against the AWACS mission, the Defence Ministry reproached them with a 'lack of contact with reality'. They should, the Ministry recommended, demonstrate for an enforcement of human rights and the protection of the population in the former Yugoslavia.[165] In an open letter, Fischer, a leading figure of the 'realist' wing of the Green party, accused two of his party colleagues of the 'fundamentalist' wing, Ludger Volmer and Jürgen Trittin, who rejected the use of armed force, of 'escaping reality'.[166] Similarly, sending minesweepers to the Gulf was represented as reflecting the first adaptation of foreign and security policy to the 'new realities'.[167] Karl Lamers talked about adjusting constitutional practice to 'the new realities'.[168] Inspector General Klaus Naumann based the renewed significance of the armed forces on claims about 'the changed situation in the world'[169] and 'the reality of our restless world'.[170]

These claims that reality made military involvement necessary are suspect because the precise character of the asserted reality was rarely specified and because it was used to support diametrically opposed positions. Karsten Voigt, for instance, rejected the use of force with

---

[162] 'Den Ernstfall nicht gewagt', *Der Spiegel*, 7/45, 11 Feb. 1991, 22.
[163] Glotz, 'Der ungerechte Krieg', 38.
[164] Klose, 'Die Deutschen und der Krieg am Golf', 6.
[165] 'Heftiger Protest gegen AWACS-Einsatz', *SZ*, 13 Apr. 1993, 5.
[166] 'Grünen-Vorstand lehnt deutschen Bosnien-Einsatz ab', *SZ*, 29 Nov. 1995, 2.
[167] Anon. (UB), 'Minensucher auf dem Weg zum Golf', *SZ*, 7 Mar. 1991, 4.
[168] Quoted in 'Sozis in der Klemme', *Der Spiegel*, 20/45, 13 May 1991, 31.
[169] Naumann, *Bundeswehr*, pp. 8 and 137.   [170] Naumann, *Bundeswehr*, p. 143.

the same type of argument. He claimed that the 'reinterpretation, the breaking of the constitution [was] real; the hope of people in Bosnia for effective help remain[ed] illusion'.[171] Assertions about what reality requires are not value-neutral. This was apparent in the argument of the Catholic bishop of the military, Johannes Dyba. He said that the Sermon on the Mount was only a guideline. One could not ignore reality. 'If a bomber pilot destroys missile bases, the central bunker of a dictator or of warmongers, then this is a *good* thing.'[172] What is significant is the effect of such claims. The claim that reality demands military involvement abroad – or avoiding it, whichever the case may be – squarely removes the matter from the realm of choice. The issue is then recognising reality and responding to it appropriately, rather than choosing from a variety of alternative possibilities. It becomes a technical rather than political matter.

As a consequence, the government could, for instance, be construed not to be responsible for what it was doing, for reality was forcing them to act in particular ways, or so the argument went. As Kinkel put it: 'The constitutional court or reality will force us to reconsider the situation anyway.'[173] Or, as he had argued elsewhere: 'We have to, whether we want to or not.'[174] According to Kinkel, 'the idea that the economically strongest and most populated state in the middle of Europe may retreat into a kind of snail-shell after the fall of the wall and the iron curtain, whilst [its] partners get the chestnuts out of the fire, does not stand up to reality'.[175] Or again: 'We do not make our life easier by refusing necessary changes.'[176]

The question is, however, whether 'reality' means anything at all. Never did anyone bother to clarify what this reality was actually meant to be, what its salient features were or why it mattered: for reality is there for everyone to see and it is self-evidently important. The political opponent was accused of '[m]alicious denial of reality'[177] whilst one's own position was supported with the simple words: 'Such is reality.'[178]

[171] Karsten Voigt (SPD) in Deutscher Bundestag, *Plenarprotokoll*, 12/151, 21 Apr. 1993, 12931.
[172] Quoted in 'Militärbischof Dyba gegen radikalen Pazifismus', *SZ*, 16 Mar. 1991, 2 (italics added).
[173] Quoted in 'Zweiter Bundeswehrverband in Somalia', *SZ*, 30 Jul. 1993, 2.
[174] Deutscher Bundestag, *Plenarprotokoll*, 12/151, 21 Apr. 1993, 12926.
[175] Ibid., 12928.   [176] Kinkel, 'Verantwortung', 8.
[177] Peter Harald Rauen (CDU/CSU) in Deutscher Bundestag, *Plenarprotokoll*, 12/132, 15 Jan. 1993, 11481.
[178] Heidemarie Wieczorek-Zeul (SPD), ibid., 11490.

The self-evident character of 'reality' was especially important in relation to one limit which was often invoked: death.

As we have already seen in chapter 4, death was sometimes used as the ultimate argument. It was not only that the killing could not, according to this reasoning, be stopped with words alone.[179] Rather the death of soldiers in such international operations as were envisaged seemed to symbolise the limit imposed by the real. Their deaths could neither be avoided nor discussed away. Those opposed to German military involvement abroad were accused of implying that the loss of soldiers of other nationalities was less serious,[180] that they were willing to defend UNPROFOR's position in Bosnia to the last Frenchman or Briton.[181] In this context, the willingness to send their own nationals to die became the ultimate proof of solidarity. When Belgian paratroopers saved Germans in Rwanda, it was asserted that the FRG had to be willing to endanger its soldiers to save citizens of partner countries in the same way.[182] Michael Glos of the CSU even spoke of 'Belgian fellow citizens'.[183] Rühe addressed the SPD candidate for chancellor Scharping directly in relation to this issue, referring to the ceremony in Belgium honouring the widow of the commander who, together with nine others, had died in action in Rwanda: 'Herr Scharping, the concrete question which poses itself is after all this: how should one explain to such a woman that Belgian soldiers are permanently to evacuate German citizens who are in mortal danger? I can't do it. Can you?'[184] It was clear then, that the ruling which had made German military involvement abroad possible was 'in its final consequence also a deadly ruling – for German soldiers who w[ould] be deployed as peace-keepers or even in combat missions in the areas of crisis of the world'.[185] In the face of the possibility of death, alternatives vanished because the reality of death could not be disputed. No other contribution to peace, justice or prosperity in the world could offset the failure to contribute lives. Derrida, however, challenges such talk about death. He disputes the underlying assumption which 'takes the

[179] Klaus Kinkel (foreign minister) in Deutscher Bundestag, *Plenarprotokoll*, 12/151, 21 Apr. 1993, 12928.
[180] Ulrich Irmer (FDP), ibid., 12966.
[181] Klaus Kinkel (foreign minister) in Deutscher Bundestag, *Plenarprotokoll*, 13/48, 30 Jun. 1995, 3957.
[182] 'Kinkel: Deutschland wird auch in Zukunft öfter nein als ja sagen', *FAZ*, 18 Apr. 1994, 2; Karl-Heinz Hornhues (CDU/CSU) in Deutscher Bundestag, *Plenarprotokoll*, 12/219, 14 Apr. 1994, 18913.
[183] Deutscher Bundestag, *Plenarprotokoll*, 12/240, 22 Jul. 1994, 21176.
[184] Volker Rühe (defence minister), ibid., 21186.
[185] Heribert Prantl, 'Wir können – aber: sollen wir?', *SZ*, 13 Jul. 1994, 4.

form of an "it is self-explanatory": everybody knows what one is talking about when one names death'.[186] Although Derrida recognises death as a limit, it is not, as these portrayals suggest a self-evident, natural limit. Derrida insists that '[d]ying is neither entirely natural (biological) nor cultural.'[187] Rather, as Drucilla Cornell points out, it is the 'limit of any system of meaning [which] is, for Derrida, graphically represented to us in death'.[188]

That the potential 'reality' of death was not always the foremost consideration became apparent in the Somalia mission. Contrary to claims that 'words' were somehow less important than what was portrayed as 'the facts' or 'reality', in this case representations were, in a move of inversion, considered more significant. The government insisted that German troops would be deployed only to 'secure environments' or 'safe areas'. Given all the talk about the significance of reality, one might naively have assumed that this meant the Bundeswehr would be sent only to places where the safety of the soldiers could reasonably be expected. This was not, however, the case. Military circles in Bonn explained delays in the deployment by saying that the UN 'had to create a document on the highest level in which the area around Bosaso is officially declared secure'.[189] At issue was apparently not the security of the area but its representation as such. As one commentator observed, this meant that the German soldiers were 'deployed to an area which counts as secure *per definitionem* – that is, only according to the orders'.[190] Definitional matters also took on great significance when it came to discussing different proposals for changing the Basic Law. Despite the frequent claim that the responsibility towards the soldiers was paramount, different missions and therefore different decision-making mechanisms in relation to them were not related to their well-being: 'The criterion whether the life of soldiers is endangered cannot be decisive. Decisive is how the UN defines task and aim.'[191] Thus, that which is considered only linguistic and therefore, following Onuf, social (*WOM* 94) sometimes turns out to be more significant than the so-called real, conceptualised as material and beyond human influence. The overriding importance of the real and its valorisation

---

[186] Derrida, *Aporias*, p. 25 [p. 319].   [187] Derrida, *Aporias*, p. 42 [p. 324].
[188] Drucilla Cornell, *The Philosophy of the Limit* (New York and London: Routledge, 1992), p. 1.
[189] 'Probleme vor Somalia-Einsatz', *SZ*, 10 May 1993, 1.
[190] Stefan Kornelius, 'Ein mehrfach ungewisses Abenteuer', *SZ*, 18 May 1993, 4.
[191] Martin E. Süskind, 'Ein Militär-Kompromiß ist möglich', *SZ*, 10 Aug. 1993, 4.

over linguistic or social context thus seems less obvious than was often implied.

Significantly, if it is impossible to meet a 'real' outside the text, outside our interpretations of it, then the reality which is invoked is itself a construction. In Derrida's conceptualisation what we call 'real life' is, as everything else, 'constituted by the logic of supplementarity'.[192] Signifying chains create the image of presence. Thus, '[i]mmediacy is derived' (*OG* 157 [226]). The real is then merely something which is signified. However, if the real is not more authentic than a sign, it loses the special significance it is accorded by the appeals to reality in the debates and also by Onuf's appeals to a materiality beyond our constructions.

The problem with this conceptualisation lies in positing a 'reality' beyond the social world as outside language, as free of traces of humanness. The claim that something is demanded by reality becomes problematic, particularly as it is based on the notion that the scope of our constructions is limited by the underlying biology. Edkins and Pin-Fat comment that we 'seek to convince ourselves of the existence of "reality" by trying to trace the outline of objects over and over again. As Wittgenstein points out, this is a trick of language.'[193] Derrida similarly argues 'that the truth is precisely limited, *finite*, and confined within its borders'[194] but that we fail to recognise the limit for what it is. If we do not acknowledge that the boundary we believe we experience is a limit of our conceptualisations rather than the interference of an independent materiality, we consider our choices limited by a mysterious outside power that we cannot ever directly experience. As a result, we limit our responsibility. This conceptualisation is therefore deeply political. The assertion of an independently existing reality, which in itself cannot be proved and seems to demand no proof, works to support particular political positions and to exclude others from consideration.

The politics of constructivism

To some extent Wendt's, Kratochwil's and Onuf's projects are profoundly different from each other. Wendt arguably aims to provide a better explanation for a world Realists would easily recognise. Kratochwil's

[192] Culler, *On Deconstruction*, p. 105.
[193] Edkins and Pin-Fat, 'Subject of the Political', p. 4. See Wittgenstein, *Philosophical Investigations*, §§ 114–15.
[194] Derrida, *Aporias*, p. 1 [p. 310].

and Onuf's departure is more fundamental. They challenge the idea that the international world is anarchic in the first place, address the impact of language on constructions and make normative considerations central. Nevertheless, their projects are similar in that they do not address the structures of our thought and therefore end up reinforcing, rather than challenging, 'common-sense' ways of thinking. Constructivism operates on the basis of accepting reality as a limit. Deconstruction, in contrast, concerns the 'limits *declared* to be insurmountable'.[195]

Employing deconstruction, Derrida questions and turns on their head some of our most intuitive beliefs about reality. Several points seem relevant in relation to reality constructions and constructivist portrayals of them. Most fundamentally, perhaps, Derrida makes untenable the notion that we can clearly distinguish between the 'real' and its representation. We experience the world in both its material and immaterial aspects in the context of signification. There can be no meeting with the purity of the 'real' outside this context – or, in Derrida's words, outside of the text – and there is no escape from the 'real' within any of our (con)texts. The positive value attached to the 'real' as opposed to the represented, the signified, the supplement is not natural; treating it as such is political.

If the 'real' is not natural, if we cannot ever go back to a definitive origin, then any claim to an origin will need to be questioned. Narratives of identity start somewhere. They claim possession of an origin. Metaphors or commonplaces used in political discourse claim to be able to identify the relevant context. This is suspect as it closes down fields of signification. If the 'real' is not natural, what is held to be real must be questioned. This, however, means shifting away from the serious and intended content of the justifications actors give for their behaviour. We do not remind ourselves and others of what we think is obvious. Therefore, Derrida's thought leads us not only to question the presuppositions of what is being said and its meaning, conscious and intended or otherwise, but also to investigate what is not being said (*P* 3 [11]). It may precisely be the silence and the exclusions that tell us most about what is accepted as given, 'real'.

What concerns me most, however, is how the politics of the 'real' is played out. Being able to define the 'real' in political discourse is the first step towards getting to define the solution. Being able to dominate

---

[195] Jacques Derrida, *Archive Fever: A Freudian Impression*, translated by Eric Prenowitz (Chicago and London: University of Chicago Press, 1996), p. 4 [p. 15].

a value-laden hierarchy, such as responsible/irresponsible, may help as well as being able to portray a technical solution as a matter of ethics, responsibility. What deconstruction leads us to do then is to demonstrate how each of these steps involves a depoliticisation; for the key move of the politics of reality is to hide the politics, the unfounded violence of the foundational moment of any determination of context, and to portray itself as just the supposed opposite of politics: reality.

This is exemplified in the assertion of given and seemingly neutral starting points in constructivist approaches. My analysis in chapters 2 through 4 showed that this has political implications, an argument which was developed further in this chapter by making use of Derrida's work. Constructivists tell us openly what they take as given. Wendt makes it clear, for instance, that he begins with the assumption that state agents are central (ISC 48; *STIP* 8). Onuf specifically states the problem that there is no given beginning, but concludes that one must be invented. He chooses rules (CM; C 59). Kratochwil claims, *contra* Wendt, that 'there are no simple givens for constructivists',[196] but he nevertheless posits the centrality of rules and certain aspects about their role (*RND* 10–11). Thus my claim that constructivist work always starts with givens, which are not themselves problematised, is not necessarily contentious.

However, my line of reasoning hinges not only on the existence of given starting points but also on their status, on the claim that this constitutes a problem. As we all have to start somewhere, positing a specific starting point might be considered a necessary methodological choice. Wendt stresses that such choices must not 'turn into a tacit ontology' (*STIP* 35).[197] In other words, it is necessary to remember that starting with states is a matter of convenience, possibly even necessity, for a systemic theory of international politics. It is not, and must never be understood as, a claim about the ontology of states. 'Bracketing' certain aspects of the world, such as the domestic construction of states, is necessary for the pursuit of certain analytic goals, to make it possible to focus on an object of analysis (*STIP* 7–8, 13, 21 and 34–5). As Wendt puts it: 'We cannot study everything at once' (*STIP* 14 and 244; see also 36). According to Onuf, starting points are unavoidable, but they are not natural (CM 7). He points out that we are always already within our constructions, that processes of construction are always ongoing, that

---

[196] Kratochwil, 'Constructing a New Orthodoxy?', 82.
[197] See also Wendt, 'On the Via Media', 169.

we are always 'in the middle', so to speak, of what we are aiming to analyse (*WOM* 43; *C* 59). Yet we must create a beginning (*CM* 7). It is impossible to think about the world without doing so. However, the point, and the upshot of my detailed analysis throughout the book, is that these so-called methodological choices are neither predetermined by an independent reality nor neutral with respect to analytic outcome. They are not innocent. The choice of a beginning opens up certain avenues of thinking and closes down others. It is about the creation of non-natural relationships, about politics. Constructivism obscures this political character of constructions and representations of reality. It accepts reality as a limit.

Following a deconstructive line of reasoning the challenge is, however, to make problematic what is portrayed as real. These issues will be taken up in chapter 6, but I want to raise some key points here. Turning 'reality' into a given starting point is a political move. Whether the given 'reality' which we must take into account or must start from concerns the existence of subjects, the norm structure or underlying materiality, the starting point already encompasses the possibilities of solutions. This is suspect if these starting points are just as made as anything else and acquire their superior standing only in relation to a structure of thinking that constructivism fails to address. Constructivism does not take sufficient note of the problem that '[n]o text opens itself immediately to everyone',[198] not even the text of 'reality'. Moreover, as thinking on the basis of logocentric premises is bound to deconstruct, every concept is 'always dislocating itself because it is never one with itself'.[199] Although constructivism investigates how we construct our world, it stops short of scrutinising what is an inextricable part of it: how we think. The problem is then that constructivism may be said to fail in its own project. At the very least its critical potential is limited.

This failure is as significant as it is difficult to avoid. Derrida recognises that the result of his reasoning is 'what is called "difficult" research' (*OH* 102 [118]) which is reproached with being inaccessible. Yet this difficult research is the only way to avoid closure. As Derrida says, '[w]hatever the answer may be, the question remains. I would even say that this is necessary: it should remain, even beyond all answers' (*OH* 16–17 [22]). Note, however, that this does not imply that there cannot be answers, that we must shy away from practice, which in any event, we never could. On the contrary, Derrida argues for the need to invent new

---

[198] Derrida, *Points*, p. 176 [p. 188].   [199] Derrida, *Archive Fever*, p. 84 [p. 132].

gestures (*OH* 44 [46]), gestures which try to take account of, rather than neutralise, the contradictory demands which make a responsible or just decision both necessary and impossible. In doing so, we must never claim that the law, knowledge or morality – or, I might want to add, reality – require following a certain path. We must recognise our decision for what it is: a decision. Anything else would imply irresponsibility posing as responsibility.

6   The politics of constructivism

Constructivism obscures the politics already involved in representing reality. This is at the heart not only of constructivism's success but also of the celebration and despair it triggers. Those wary of constructivism object to the exclusion of challenging and thought-provoking questions about politics and the political.[1] On the other hand, it is precisely a certain unproblematic acceptance of reality which has made the constructivist 'success story' possible. 'Taking reality into account' is one of the supposed virtues of constructivism. Both the material and the social worlds are construed to have a facticity which constructivist analyses of international relations must, and do, take into account. Wendt's, Kratochwil's and Onuf's approaches take given realities as their starting points, but this also seems to be a key part of the constructivist project more broadly. According to Stefano Guzzini, constructivism acknowledges 'the existence of a phenomenal world, external to thought'.[2] It does not deny 'a reality to the material world',[3] as Emanuel Adler and Michael Barnett put it. Adler also asserts that constructivism opens up 'the objective facts of world politics, which are facts only by human agreement', as new areas for empirical investigation.[4]

In the introduction I claimed that a critique of Wendt's, Kratochwil's and Onuf's work would be relevant to 'constructivism'. Two points can be made without a lengthy exploration as to which 'constructivist' studies would fall prey to the criticisms made here. Firstly, much of

---

[1] See, for example, R. B. J. Walker, 'Alternative, Critical, Political', paper for the International Studies Association conference in Los Angeles, 14–18 March 2000, and Cynthia Weber, 'IR: The Resurrection or New Frontiers of Incorporation', *European Journal of International Relations* 5 (1999), 435–50.
[2] Guzzini, 'Reconstruction', 159.   [3] Adler and Barnett, 'Security Communities', p. 12.
[4] Adler, 'Seizing the Middle Ground', 348.

the 'constructivist' literature approvingly cites these scholars at least as inspiration and therefore is likely to make similar key moves. If they did not, they would not rely on work which promotes a concept of limited construction, relating it to an independently existing reality. Indeed, recognising the existence of such a reality is often made out to be an important feature of constructivism. Secondly, the definitions offered of 'constructivism' in articles evaluating and locating the approach also suggest that the moves I focused on and questioned in relation to Wendt's, Kratochwil's and Onuf's work are part of what makes a constructivist a constructivist. This is important because constructivism has become a phenomenon in IR not merely because a lot of scholars are 'doing' it but also because a lot of scholars, and not always the same ones, are debating it.

Definitions of constructivism frequently stress the dual character of social and material world. Social constructions, in this conceptualisation, must refer back to and hook up with a pre-existing materiality. Adler argues that the material world shapes human interaction and vice versa.[5] Jeffrey Checkel says that 'the environment in which agents/states take action is social as well as material'.[6] Richard Price and Christian Reus-Smit similarly speak of constructivism as 'emphasizing the importance of normative as well as material structures'.[7] These descriptions invoke a duality of the social and the material and thereby claim an existence independent of representations for the material realm. Peter Katzenstein, Robert Keohane and Stephen Krasner stress that constructivists insist 'on the primacy of intersubjective structures that give the material world meaning'.[8] This takes us on to a second key element of constructivism, namely intersubjectivity.[9] John Ruggie highlights the significance of addressing intersubjective rather than merely individual beliefs.[10] According to Adler, constructivism's 'importance and its added value for the study of International Relations lie mainly in its emphasis on the ontological reality of intersubjective knowledge and on the epistemological and methodological implications of this reality'.[11] He devotes an entire section to elucidating intersubjectivity as collectively

---

[5] Adler, 'Seizing the Middle Ground', 322. See also Adler and Barnett, 'Security Communities', pp. 12–13.
[6] Checkel, 'Constructivist Turn', 325.
[7] Price and Reus-Smit, 'Dangerous Liaisons?', 259.
[8] Katzenstein, Keohane and Krasner, '*International Organization*', 679.
[9] On the significance of intersubjectivity, see also Guzzini, 'Reconstruction', 162–4.
[10] Ruggie, *Constructing the World Polity*, p. 20.
[11] Adler, 'Seizing the Middle Ground', 322–3.

shared knowledge which both empowers and constrains actors and also defines social reality.[12] The upshot of Adler's portrayal of constructivism is, as the title of his article suggests, that it has a justifiable claim to the 'middle ground', which he construes as situated between rationalism and poststructuralism.[13] Adler identifies 'seizing the middle ground' as the key to the constructivist project. This assessment is echoed by other scholars. Checkel sees constructivism as situated in the middle ground between rational choice theory and postmodernism, whilst Ted Hopf locates it between the mainstream and critical theory.[14] Similarly, Steve Smith claims that it aims to bridge the gap between rationalist and reflectivist theories and to find a 'via media'.[15]

Thus in defining constructivism scholars make reference to recognising the material world as existing independently of, but interacting with, the social world, the central role of intersubjectivity and the significance of occupying a middle-ground position. These key elements of constructivism, as presented in the debate about the approach and its role in IR theory, are related to key moves I identified and critiqued in the work of the three constructivists: Wendt's positioning in the middle ground, related to a particular notion of identity; Kratochwil's reliance on an unproblematic intersubjectivity, based on normative context; and Onuf's claim to an independently existing material world behind our constructions.[16] Hence, whilst my critique was worked through only in relation to three specific scholars, it crystallised around what are construed as central features of the constructivist project. This suggests that my critique has some bearing beyond the work of the three.

The acknowledgement of materiality and an unproblematic intersubjectivity appear to be crucial to the constructivist enterprise. In fact, these are part of the aspiration to a middle-ground position which itself merits further consideration since it is, as I have already argued in relation to Wendt's work, not an accidental and largely insignificant aspect of constructivism. It is precisely what makes constructivism so seductive. According to Guzzini, constructivism's success is at least partly based on its supposed position in the middle ground.[17] In chapter 2 I showed

---

[12] Adler, 'Seizing the Middle Ground', 327–8.
[13] Adler, 'Seizing the Middle Ground', esp. 321–3.
[14] Hopf, 'Promise of Constructivism', 199; Checkel, 'Constructivist Turn', 327.
[15] Steve Smith, 'New Approaches', pp. 183–8.
[16] Note, however, that Kratochwil is critical of a middle-ground position. See 'Constructing a New Orthodoxy?'.
[17] Guzzini, 'Reconstruction', 147.

that in Wendt's work taking the via media depends on proposing a conception of identity based on social construction which nevertheless remains unitary so as to function as a variable in an explanatory process. In other words, in this approach, identity construction is added to social science practices as Wendt understands them. It does not overturn them.[18] The point is to achieve greater sophistication within the already existing logic of social science.

This aim resonates with the particular function constructivism is attributed, at least by some, in statements about the state of IR theory. Constructivism is portrayed as a critical but at the same time scientifically sound alternative to the mainstream.[19] Adler highlights the ways in which constructivism challenges and indeed improves upon rationalist theories, but at the same time stresses the 'scientific basis' of constructivism which has, he argues, been obscured.[20] In a jointly authored article Katzenstein, Keohane and Krasner, similarly, see constructivism as being within 'the social science enterprise'.[21]

Constructivism is acceptable, and even to some extent welcome, as a critical alternative to the 'mainstream' because it accepts the rules of the scientific game. Occupying the middle ground, in other words, is supposed to enable constructivists to have their cake and eat it, too. Whilst they critically distance themselves from the mainstream, they at the same time receive professional recognition from within it. Constructivism has come to be not only one of the main acceptable ways in which the international world may be studied[22] but also, as Guzzini notes ironically, 'the officially accredited contender to the core of the discipline'.[23] This is reflected in the reception of Wendt's *Social Theory of International Relations* in two key journals. In the *Review of International Studies*, which published a number of reviews as a 'forum' on the book,[24] it has been predicted to gain a status similar to that which Kenneth Waltz's *Theory of International Politics* supposedly had in the 1980s,[25] and in the journal *Millennium* Kratochwil asks whether, and

[18] See also Campbell, 'Epilogue', esp. p. 218.
[19] See, for example, Katzenstein, Keohane and Krasner, '*International Organization*'; Adler, 'Seizing the Middle Ground'.
[20] Adler, 'Seizing the Middle Ground', 320.
[21] Katzenstein, Keohane and Krasner, '*International Organization*', 678.
[22] See Walt, 'International Relations', 38.   [23] Guzzini, 'Reconstruction', 147.
[24] Keohane, 'Ideas Part-Way Down'; Stephen D. Krasner, 'Wars, Hotel Fires, and Plane Crashes', *Review of International Studies* 26 (2000), 131–6; Doty, 'Desire'; Alker, 'On Learning from Wendt'; Steve Smith, 'Wendt's World'.
[25] 'Forum on *Social Theory*', 123; Alker, 'On Learning from Wendt', 141; Steve Smith, 'Wendt's World', 151.

indeed worries that, Wendt is 'constructing a new orthodoxy'.[26] These reactions confirm that Wendt in particular and the constructivist project by association are seen to be at the heart of the discipline. This assessment is, as I laid out more fully in the introduction, supported by constructivism's ubiquity in surveys of the discipline, scholarly debate and even undergraduate textbooks.

Constructivism promises to be critical as well as scientific. It promises to introduce the dimension of shared meaning and thus to promote a new understanding of the social world without abandoning consideration of the material or indeed cherished social science practices. This double orientation towards what are considered opposites is often construed as occupying the middle ground. Some constructivists may be wary of this project[27] but it seems part and parcel of what they are proposing. In the light of my argument, however, constructivism appears to be much less critical, indeed much less different from rationalism,[28] than its marketing platform suggests. It accepts as given a 'reality' from which enquiry must start, a 'reality' which reasonable people would presumably be able to recognise. This is both bewildering in the face of the lack of agreement on what this reality is, either in constructivist scholarship or political debate, and problematic as positing such a 'reality' naturalises what is made. This is not only about how we conceive of the international world, but also about how we conceptualise our relationship to it.

Responsibility in international relations

Constructivist theories appear attractive to the study of international relations because of their supposed ability to take account of reality. They start from what they posit this reality to be. The plight of the Somalis, Bosnians or Kosovars, within an approach that starts from states, becomes a problem for the FRG *qua* German state. German military involvement abroad, within an approach that starts from norms, becomes the result of a reasoning process within a given and unquestioned norm structure. And the use of the military becomes the only feasible alternative in a world limited by material conditions, such as

---

[26] Kratochwil, 'Constructing a New Orthodoxy?', esp. 74–5.
[27] See Kratochwil, 'Constructing a New Orthodoxy?', esp. 75, 97 and 101.
[28] See also Steve Smith, 'Wendt's World', 162.

the possibility of death. In other words, by attempting to start from 'reality' the status quo is privileged as independent, and binding conditions that limit our possibilities are asserted. Although the status quo may be critically questioned, it remains the baseline against which claims and suggestions are measured. If there is no agreed reality, if indeed there cannot be one, this is suspect.

The alternative is not, of course, to forget about reality. Rather, my engagement with Derridean thought led me to claim that portraying something as real, and indeed the assertion of knowledge about what reality is, has immense political power. The valorisation of the real over the represented is, according to Derrida, a feature of Western thought which understands being as presence. The real dominates the relevant dichotomy, which is a hierarchical opposition. In other words, in the context of such thinking, a representation is always less valuable than the thing itself. Thus, whilst Derrida's strategy of deconstruction questions and subverts the opposition real/represented, his analysis of Western thought, of what he calls logocentrism, gives an explanation for why the 'real' has such a powerful hold on our imagination.

Therefore, it is not enough to overturn the dichotomy of real versus represented. Rather it must be displaced. The argument is not, as is sometimes claimed about postmodernism or poststructuralism, that representations are more important than what we consider real or that they can be made anything we wish. My detailed analysis, based on a Derridean move, took 'reality' and its power seriously. Given Derrida's great concern with context (*LI*), it is clear that neither analysts nor actors can just (re)make the world according to their wishes. Precisely because context is boundless (*LI* 3 [20]), it cannot be dominated at will. That which is usually called 'reality' therefore has an important impact.

This does not, however, leave us in the same position as the acknowledgement of reality in constructivism. What is at issue is how to deal appropriately with always already being part of a reality that cannot be described or grasped other than through our interpretations and in relation to our practices, which are at the same time constituting it. Claims to simply take reality into account are troubling because they obscure our involvement in its making. This has serious consequences for how we relate to the international world. Arguably, the conviction that there is a reality which must be acknowledged as a baseline and an ultimate limit makes it possible to defer responsibility to 'the circumstances', as the German government did in relation to military participation in the Kosovo operation: 'We don't have a choice.'[29] This claim may have been persuasive in what was seen to be the immediate circumstances. However, a lot of choices were made nevertheless: the choice of whether only to bomb or also to send ground troops; the choice of whether to grant residence permits to Kosovar refugees in the FRG; the choice of whether to spend resources on fighting or on helping refugees.[30] The claim that there was no choice is significant not as a reflection of an outside reality but as a political contextualisation of actions. If we do not have a choice, we cannot be blamed. We are not responsible. Our conceptualisation of reality is thus pertinent to the problem of responsibility.

According to Derrida, when 'the path is clear and given' (*OH* 41 [43]), we are dealing with a matter of applying knowledge rather than exercising responsibility. In that sense, the debates about German military involvement abroad, despite the rhetoric about responsibility, hardly ever touched upon the issue. The point many made in the debates was precisely that they knew what was required in order to be responsible: participation in international military operations. This way of thinking, according to Derrida, represents an escape from responsibility. Even more, he calls it 'the surest, the most reassuring definition of *responsibility as irresponsibility*' (*OH* 71–2 [70–1]). Yet, interestingly, the claim that there was no choice was made in a situation in which two unpalatable courses of action seemed to be available: staying out and ignoring the atrocities believed to be inflicted on Albanian Kosovars by Serbian security forces, or interfering and thereby harming other innocent civilians in Kosovo and Serbia. Thus, decision-makers were faced with the aporia of the undecidable. The undecidable is not just the oscillation between contradictory and imperative rules or between two decisions; 'it is the experience of that which, though heterogeneous, foreign to the order of the calculable and the rule, is still obliged . . . to give itself up to the impossible decision, while taking account of law and rules' (FoL 963/962). A decision which does not involve this aporia is not free but rather part of a calculable process, merely an application. Where we experience the undecidable, a decision must be made but the decision does not resolve

<hr/>

[29] Chancellor Gerhard Schröder quoted in Josef Joffe, 'Wir haben keine andere Wahl', *SZ*, 24 Mar. 1999, 4.
[30] See, for example, Jürgen Hogrefe and Alexander Szandar, 'Die Spaltung liegt in der Luft', *Der Spiegel*, 26 Apr. 1999, 22–5; Heribert Prantl, 'Es gibt nichts Gutes, außer man tut es', *SZ*, 5 Apr. 1999, 4; Heribert Prantl, 'Im Gesetz, aber nicht in Kraft', 6 Apr. 1999, 8; UNHCR Evaluation and Policy Analysis Unit, *Kosovo Refugee Crisis*, chapter 6, section 438.

the undecidable. It remains caught up in it. For responsibility to be possible, experiencing this aporia of the undecidable is necessary (*LI* 116 [210]; *OH* 41 [43]).

It may be recalled that in 1995 Joschka Fischer, of the Green opposition, drew attention to a crucial contradiction, the impossibility of preventing Auschwitz without war, which could not be overcome. He recommended that his party stand up for, rather than try to resolve, the contradictory demands which the Bosnian conflict, he thought, entailed.[31] Thereby he acknowledged a 'double contradictory imperative' and hence a situation in which responsibility was called for. Derrida speaks of 'the responsibility to think, speak, and act in compliance with this double contradictory imperative' (*OH* 79 [77]). The aim is not to resolve the contradiction in favour of one over the other demand, but to encompass both within new practices.

By the time the Kosovo crisis was leading to an international response, Fischer had become foreign minister. Although he said that he was trying not to break with his ideals and, in particular, was aiming to disrupt 'the logic of war',[32] Fischer ended up not only authorising what was portrayed as the first proper combat mission of the Bundeswehr. He even claimed that he had 'tried everything',[33] that he had had no choice. He not only made a decision in the condition of the aporia of the undecidable but, having made it, disputed the double contradictory imperative to which it had responded. Thus, he resolved the double contradictory imperative in favour of one of the demands, a course of action he previously had rejected. Instead of acknowledging that the decision was just that, a decision, he insisted that the path had been clear and given. Fischer now represented the situation as one in which a free decision was impossible. This, as Derrida points out, leaves only the possibility of 'irresponsibly, and in good conscience', applying or implementing a programme (*OH* 41 [43]).

Thus Fischer attempted to disown the responsibility for the decision. This, however, cannot work as the 'undecidable remains caught, lodged, at least as a ghost – but an essential ghost – in every decision, in every event of decision. Its ghostliness deconstructs from within any assurance of presence, any certitude or any supposed criteriology that would assure us of the justice of a decision' (FoL 965/964). A decision in a

---

[31] 'Das wäre blutiger Zynismus', *Der Spiegel*, 34/49, 21 Aug. 1995, 27–9, here 29.
[32] Quoted in 'Aus freier Überzeugung', *Der Spiegel*, 16/53, 19 Apr. 1999, 22–32, here 24.
[33] Kurt Kister, 'Metamorphosen eines Ernstfalles', *SZ*, 1–2 Apr. 1999, 3; Manfred Ertel et al., 'Das Gespenst von Vietnam', *Der Spiegel*, 14/53, 5 Apr. 1999, 150–64, here 164.

situation in which responsibility is called for involves the experience of aporia, of the impossible. Responsibility, in Derrida's sense, does not involve the feel-good factor which German participation in international military operations as taking international responsibility was expected to deliver. As the responsible decision remains caught up in contradictory demands there is no point in time when we could feel pleased. There is always already an imperative demand which cannot be satisfied. Thus, living with responsibility, in Derrida's conceptualisation, is painful. The question of responsibility only ever arises where we experience the limit of our ability to control, the limit of our knowledge, the limit of our ability to satisfy contradictory ethical demands.

Hence, when it comes to responsibility, nothing is self-evident. Derrida asks: 'And responsible before whom? Before what memory? For what promise?' (*OH* 13 [19]). In relation to German military involvement abroad, responsibility became significant as a responsibility for the horrors of the past. This translated into the assertion of a responsibility for those suffering today. In addition to solidarity with friends and partners, the case for sending the military to Somalia, Bosnia or Kosovo was about helping those in need, those whose lives were threatened by starvation and violence. Derrida points out the significance of 'the *heading of the other*, before which we must respond, and which we must *remember*, *of which* we must *remind ourselves*, the heading of the other being perhaps the first condition of an identity or identification that is not an ego-centrism destructive of oneself and the other' (*OH* 15 [20–1]). This is to some extent the problem of international politics in which international military operations were caught up: how to respond to others and their needs without either losing oneself or further endangering both the other and oneself.

Derrida claims that it is necessary to invent new gestures, gestures which encompass rather than aim to resolve the contradictory demands which are part of a responsible decision (*OH* 44 [46]). In view of the impossibility of a fully responsible decision, the invention of 'new gestures' represents a difficult option. It is nevertheless one which must be attempted if we do not want to settle for the irresponsible implementation of rules and programmes. Fischer, who earlier acknowledged the contradictory ethico-political situation that makes such gestures both necessary and possible, was unable to break out of the application of a programme. However, it is necessary to recognise the need of inventing new gestures and to recognise that the execution of military intervention as a pregiven response to 'humanitarian' crisis situations is not responsible. The point is that the kind of thinking in evidence in the debates, and unchallenged by constructivist analyses, makes it impossible even to recognise the significance of new gestures, much less to open up the space to invent them. It makes possible the illusion of responsibility and hence good conscience, which, according to Derrida, must be avoided 'at all cost.'[34]

Constructivism, reality, International Relations

The claim to be able to take responsibility, as well as the failure to invent practices which would encompass the contradictory demands of responsibility, are related to starting from a given 'reality'. It is not only politicians, but also constructivists, who appeal to reality in order to support their positions. The treatment of reality in constructivism and in politics are not two separate issues but rather two manifestations of the same problem. The rhetoric of reality gives a special status to what is being claimed, a status which is unfounded. Moreover, it privileges ways of thinking based on the availability of reality as an adjudicator. Positions that assert the existence of a background reality validate themselves with appeals to that reality. Alternative positions that question the relevance of reality conceived of as separate from representations fail to acquire the same authority. They are bound to look insecure, weak and unscientific.

In assessments of current IR theory, constructivism, which starts from a given reality, is thought to provide scientific knowledge about it. Crucially, this is opposed to modes of thinking which are characterised as 'unscientific' and which, as a consequence, may legitimately be ignored. Katzenstein, Keohane and Krasner stress that postmodernism 'falls clearly outside the social science enterprise' and, as a consequence, such work does not get published in *International Organization*, but that this is not true of constructivism.[35] Indeed, Krasner praises Wendt for putting 'to rest the notion that constructivism is necessarily postmodern, devoid of any objective referent',[36] and Keohane seems grateful to him for convincingly showing that 'one does not have to swallow the contaminated epistemological water of postmodernism in order to enjoy

---

[34] Derrida, *Aporias*, p. 19 [p. 316].
[35] Katzenstein, Keohane and Krasner, *'International Organization'*, 678.
[36] Krasner, 'Wars, Hotel Fires, and Plane Crashes', 131.

the heady ontological wine of constructivism'.[37] Hence, the trouble with Derridean thought, if held up against 'constructivism', is its failure to provide what passes for scientific knowledge in IR, the failure to provide security. Roxanne Lynn Doty has remarked that Wendt's starting points reveal a desire to secure the discipline of IR.[38] Indeed, the preference for security may go some way towards explaining why, considering the above portrayals of the theoretical landscape in IR, it is constructivism and not poststructuralism which is seen to have such impact on the discipline.

This brings us back to what Nalini Persram criticises as a 'strategic use' of constructivism.[39] According to Persram, representing constructivism as on one end of the spectrum of possible ways of studying international relations with rationalism on the other makes the engagement with (other) critical approaches seem unnecessary. As constructivism may be seen to satisfy the need for a critical stance, it may become a licence to ignore and exclude other critical approaches, namely poststructuralism, whether or not particular constructivists may intend, support or condone this move.[40] Thus, the constructivist 'success story' has the potential to marginalise other ways of thinking.

In the context of Derrida's thinking, even if an answer is given, the question does and should remain (*OH* 16–17 [22]). This results in 'what is called "difficult" research, that which resists the stereotypes of the image or narration, which does not submit to the norms of the culture' (*OH* 102 [118]). Because such research interferes with well-established patterns of thought, it is often portrayed as 'obscure' or 'unreadable' (*OH* 102 [118]). Such research, at the same time, does not yield clear guidelines for political behaviour. The aim is not to outline a 'path' or 'programme' (cf. *OH* 41 [43]). This 'failure' to provide security of thought or action is, however, one of the important implications of Derridean thought: for it is only this 'insecurity' which makes responsibility possible. Where a certain 'reality' would delimit the realm of the possible, it would at the same time bound our responsibility. In Derrida's words, '[w]hen the path is clear and given, when a certain knowledge opens up the way in advance, the decision is already made, it might as well be said that there is none to make: irresponsibly, and in good conscience, one simply applies or implements a program' (*OH* 41 [43]). According to Derrida, and this is crucial to what is at stake here,

---

[37] Keohane, 'Ideas Part-Way Down', 129.   [38] Doty, 'Desire', 139.
[39] Persram, 'Coda', p. 164.   [40] See also Steve Smith, 'Wendt's World', 163.

good conscience as subjective certainty is incompatible with the absolute risk that every promise, every engagement, and every responsible
decision – if there are such – must run. To protect the decision by
knowledge, by some theoretical assurance, or by the certainty of being
right, of being on the side of science, of consciousness or of reason, is
to transform the experience into the deployment of a program, into the
technical application of a rule or a norm, or into the subsumption of a
determined 'case'.[41]

There can be no security of knowledge when it comes to responsibility.
Hence, one must, at least, 'stop talking with authority about moral or
political responsibility' (*OH* 41 [43]). Responsibility is only possible and
called for when knowledge fails to provide an answer and when the
decision has not already been made. Positing starting points as *a priori*
given, however, means that a decision has been made before a specific
situation arises. The problem, whatever it will be, is already one for
state agents with stable identities, for people reasoning with each other
within a given norm structure, or of constructing a world from given
raw material, because this is the reality with which the analysis starts.

The claim to be able to deal appropriately with the reality of matters
is powerful not only in politics but also, it appears from the debates, in
academia. Constructivism implicitly or explicitly makes such a claim by
positing some given, intersubjectively accessible 'reality' as a starting
point. The existence and character of this reality is rendered unproblematic. This book has demonstrated that both the act of construction,
and the representation of it in constructivism – which is always already
implicated in the act of construction itself – is political, more political
than is admitted. The idea of social construction implies that what is
made is something common, shared, intersubjective – something which
reasonable people can agree on. As a consequence, whilst construction
is recognised as a mechanism of world making, its political implications are not acknowledged. From the constructivist perspective, 'social'
construction certainly does not seem a terribly controversial practice.[42]
R. B. J. Walker clearly highlights the problem with this when he asks why
such construction should be described as social rather than political.[43]
In other words, the representation of construction in constructivism is
depoliticised.

---

[41] Derrida, *Aporias*, p. 19 [p. 316].
[42] Ian Clark makes a similar point from a different perspective: *Globalization and International Relations Theory* (Oxford University Press, 1999), p. 30.
[43] Walker, 'Alternative, Critical, Political', III.iv.

Thus, constructivism limits the space for critical thinking. It operates on the possibility of a secure origin. If we can start with 'reality as it is', we need not worry about the politics of asserting a particular reality. We need not, and indeed cannot, ask about what has already been foreclosed, who has already lost when we claim the authority to speak about reality as if it was obvious. We cannot explore what already happens within that claim. Constructivism does not allow us to think beyond what it asserts reality to be. Although reality may change in the future, through different practice, in the here and now it simply is. Starting from reality is represented as apolitical, or rather non-political. For politicians this might be just a rhetorical manoeuvre. For scholars I fear it is a matter of faith, namely the faith in the possibility to separate the real and the represented. It is this separation of the represented and the real which makes it possible for constructivism to exclude political questions despite analysing construction, and for the debate in IR to exclude certain kinds of thinking.

Through this move 'reality' comes to constitute the boundary to what we can think and, as a consequence, do. The point, however, is not to simply accept this boundary but to recognise it as a limit which, although always already there, is one of our vocabulary, our representations, our imagination rather than a limit which is imposed on us by an outside force. It is therefore necessary to make problematic what is portrayed as real. According to Derrida, deconstruction concerns the 'limits *declared* to be insurmountable'.[44] Attempting to think and act beyond the boundaries which seem impossible to transgress is part of the way in which deconstruction constitutes a political intervention in the world.

We invest considerable energy in persuading ourselves that our claims are in tune with reality. The security of thought which would derive from being able to do so is seductive. Constructivism aims to provide it. The illusion of being able to simply reflect an independent reality has implications for how we relate to the international world, not merely for how we analyse it. Following Derrida, we will only ever be responsible before the other when we are fundamentally insecure as to the ethics of our decision. A new politics cannot be invented without experiencing tension and indeed aporia. This is why 'one must avoid good conscience at all cost'.[45] By positing 'reality' as a starting point, constructivism seems to chase the elusive confirmation that its claims are right and indeed that to some extent reality requires us to carry on as we are.

---

[44] Derrida, *Archive Fever*, p. 4 [p. 15].   [45] Derrida, *Aporias*, p. 19 [p. 316].

This might alleviate our conscience but, whilst we expend our energy in this way, we fail to go beyond restating the ethico-political dilemmas of international relations and responding to them in tried and tested, but ultimately unsatisfactory ways. We fall prey to the trick of language which makes our inability to conceive of ways to respond to suffering without creating more of the same look like an unavoidable feature of reality. Precisely because 'reality' appears to lock us in, appears to be an insurmountable boundary, inventing new gestures which might enable us to respond to the demands of responsibility towards others, however imperfectly, requires all our creative energy. Making problematic what appears to us as real is only the first step, but it is a necessary one. By looking to constructivism as the future, IR has given up on this possibility before considering it and risks so successfully separating the real from the represented that it becomes, or rather remains, marginal to international relations.

Bibliography

Abenheim, Donald, *Reforging the Iron Cross: The Search for Tradition in the West German Armed Forces*, Princeton University Press, 1988.

Adler, Emanuel, 'Seizing the Middle Ground: Constructivism in World Politics', *European Journal of International Relations* 3 (1997), 319–63.

Adler, Emanuel and Michael Barnett (eds.), *Security Communities*, Cambridge University Press, 1998.

   'Security Communities in Theoretical Perspective', in Adler and Barnett, *Security Communities*, pp. 3–28.

Alker, Hayward E., *Rediscoveries and Reformulations: Humanistic Methodologies for International Studies*, Cambridge University Press, 1996.

   'On Learning from Wendt', *Review of International Studies* 26 (2000), 141–50.

Austin, J. L., *How to Do Things with Words: The William James Lectures Delivered at Harvard University in 1955*, 2nd edn, Oxford: Clarendon Press, 1975.

Banchoff, Thomas, 'German Policy Towards the European Union: The Effects of Historical Memory', *German Politics* 6 (1997), 60–76.

Barnett, Michael N., 'Identity and Alliances in the Middle East', in Katzenstein, *Culture of National Security*, pp. 400–47.

Barnett, Michael and Alexander Wendt, 'Systemic Sources of Dependent Militarization', in Brian L. Job (ed.), *The Insecurity Dilemma: National Security of Third World States*, Boulder and London: Lynne Rienner Publishers, 1992, pp. 97–119.

Bartelson, Jens, 'Second Natures: Is the State Identical with Itself?', *European Journal of International Relations* 4 (1998), 295–326.

Baylis, John and Steve Smith (eds.), *The Globalization of World Politics*, Oxford University Press, 1997.

Berger, Peter L. and Thomas Luckmann, *The Social Construction of Reality*, London: Allen Lane The Penguin Press, 1966.

Berger, Stefan, *The Search for Normality: National Identity and Historical Consciousness in Germany Since 1800*, Providence, RI, and Oxford: Berghahn Books, 1997.

264

Berger, Thomas U., 'Norms, Identity, and National Security in Germany and Japan', in Katzenstein, *Culture of National Security*, pp. 317–56.

'The Past in the Present: Historical Memory and German National Security Policy', *German Politics* 6 (1997), 39–59.

Berndt, Michael, *Deutsche Militärpolitik in der 'neuen Weltunordnung'. Zwischen nationalen Interessen und globalen Entwicklungen*, Münster: Agenda Verlag, 1997.

Bertram, Christoph, 'The Power and the Past: Germany's New International Loneliness', in Arnulf Baring (ed.), *Germany's New Position in Europe: Problems and Perspectives*, Oxford and Providence, RI: Berg Publishers, 1994, pp. 91–105.

Bhaskar, Roy, *The Possibility of Naturalism: A Philosophical Critique of the Contemporary Human Sciences*, Brighton: Harvester Press, 1979.

Bitterlich, Joachim, 'La politique communautaire et occidentale de Bonn: un examen de passage pour l'Allemagne unie?', *Politique Etrangère* 56 (1991), 833–47.

Blumer, Herbert, *Symbolic Interactionism: Perspective and Method*, Englewood Cliffs, NJ: Prentice-Hall, 1969.

Borkenhagen, Franz. H. U., *Außenpolitische Interessen Deutschlands. Rolle und Aufgaben der Bundeswehr*, Bonn and Berlin: Bouvier Verlag, 1997.

Boysen, Sigurd, 'Sicherheitspolitik und Bundeswehr', *Österreichische Militärische Zeitschrift* 1 (1991), 30–5.

Brunner, Stefan, *Deutsche Soldaten im Ausland. Fortsetzung der Außenpolitik mit militärischen Mitteln?*, Munich: Verlag C. H. Beck, 1993.

Burch, Kurt and Robert A. Denemark (eds.), *Constituting International Political Economy*, Boulder and London: Lynne Rienner Publishers, 1997.

Calic, Marie-Janine, 'German Perspectives', in Alex Danchev and Thomas Halverson (eds.), *International Perspectives on the Yugoslav Conflict*, Houndmills and London: Macmillan, 1996, pp. 52–75.

Campbell, David, 'Political Prosaics, Transversal Politics, and the Anarchical World', in Michael J. Shapiro and Hayward R. Alker (eds.), *Challenging Boundaries*, Minneapolis: University of Minnesota Press, 1996, pp. 7–31.

'Epilogue: The Disciplinary Politics of Theorizing Identity', in David Campbell, *Writing Security: United States Foreign Policy and the Politics of Identity*, revised edn, Manchester University Press, 1998, pp. 207–27.

National Deconstruction: Violence, Identity, and Justice in Bosnia, Minneapolis and London: University of Minnesota Press, 1998.

Checkel, Jeffrey T., 'International Norms and Domestic Politics: Bridging the Rationalist–Constructivist Divide', *European Journal of International Relations* 3 (1997), 473–95.

'The Constructivist Turn in International Relations Theory', *World Politics* 50 (1998), 324–48.

Clark, Ian, *Globalization and International Relations Theory*, Oxford University Press, 1999.

Clemens, Clay, 'Opportunity or Obligation? Redefining Germany's Military Role Outside of NATO', *Armed Forces and Society* 19 (1993), 231–51.

Cooper, Alice H., 'When Just Causes Conflict with Acceptable Means: The German Peace Movement and Military Intervention in Bosnia', *German Politics and Society* 15 (1997), 99–118.

Cornell, Drucilla, *The Philosophy of the Limit*, New York and London: Routledge, 1992.

Culler, Jonathan, *On Deconstruction: Theory and Criticism After Structuralism*, London: Routledge, 1983.

Derrida, Jacques, *De la grammatologie*, Paris: Les Editions de Minuit, 1967.

L'écriture et la différence, Paris: Editions du Seuil, 1967.

Marges de la philosophie, Paris: Les Editions de Minuit, 1972.

Positions: entretiens avec Henri Ronse, Julia Kristeva, Jean-Louis Houdebine, Guy Scarpetta, Paris: Les Editions de Minuit, 1972.

Writing and Difference, translated with introduction and additional notes by Alan Bass, London: Routledge, 1978.

Spurs: Nietzsche's styles/Eperons: les styles de Nietzsche, English translation by Barbara Harlow, Chicago and London: University of Chicago Press, 1979.

Margins of Philosophy, translated, with additional notes, by Alan Bass, University of Chicago Press, 1982.

Positions, translated and annotated by Alan Bass, London: Athlone Press, 1987.

Limited Inc, Evanston, IL: Northwestern University Press, 1988.

Limited Inc, présentation et traductions par Elisabeth Weber, Paris: Galilée, 1990.

L'autre cap, Paris: Les Editions de Minuit, 1991.

'Force de loi: le "fondement mystique de l'autorité" '/'Force of Law: The "Mystical Foundation of Authority" ', translated by Mary Quaintance, *Cardozo Law Review* 11 (1990), 919–1035.

The Other Heading: Reflections on Today's Europe, translated by Pascale-Anne Brault and Michael B. Naas, Bloomington and Indianapolis: Indiana University Press, 1992.

Points de suspension: entretiens, choisis et présentés par Elisabeth Weber, Paris: Galilée, 1992.

Aporias, translated by Thomas Dutoit, Stanford University Press, 1993.

'Apories: mourir – s'attendre aux "limites de la vérité" ', in *Le passage des frontières: autour du travail de Jacques Derrida*, Paris: Galilée, 1994.

Le monolinguisme de l'autre, ou la prothèse d'origine, Paris: Galilée, 1995.

Mal d'archive: une impression freudienne, Paris: Galilée, 1995.

Points . . . Interviews, 1974–1994, edited by Elisabeth Weber, translated by Peggy Kamuf and others, Stanford University Press, 1995.

Archive Fever: A Freudian Impression, translated by Eric Prenowitz, Chicago and London: University of Chicago Press, 1996.

Monolingualism of the Other; or, The Prothesis of Origin, translated by Patrick Mensah, Stanford University Press, 1998.

Of Grammatology, translated by Gayatri Chakravorty Spivak, corrected edn, Baltimore and London: Johns Hopkins University Press, 1998.

Dessler, David, 'Constructivism Within a Positivist Social Science', *Review of International Studies* 25 (1999), 123–37.

Dorff, Robert H., 'Normal Actor or Reluctant Power? The Future of German Security Policy', *European Security* 6 (1997), 56–69.

Doty, Roxanne Lynn, *Imperial Encounters: The Politics of Representation in North–South Relations*, Minneapolis and London: University of Minnesota Press, 1996.

'Desire All the Way Down', *Review of International Studies* 26 (2000), 137–9.

Edkins, Jenny, 'Legality with a Vengeance: Famines and Humanitarian Relief in "Complex Emergencies"', *Millennium: Journal of International Studies* 25 (1996), 547–75.

Poststructuralism and International Relations: Bringing the Political Back In, Boulder and London: Lynne Rienner Publishers, 1999.

Edkins, Jenny and Véronique Pin-Fat, 'The Subject of the Political', in Edkins, Persram and Pin-Fat, *Sovereignty and Subjectivity*, pp. 1–18.

Edkins, Jenny, Nalini Persram and Véronique Pin-Fat (eds.), *Sovereignty and Subjectivity*, Boulder and London: Lynne Rienner Publishers, 1999.

Eley, Geoff, 'Nazism, Politics and the Image of the Past: Thoughts on the West German *Historikerstreit* 1986–1987', *Past and Present* 121 (1988), 171–208.

Evans, Richard J., *Rereading German History: From Unification to Reunification 1800–1996*, London and New York: Routledge, 1997.

Falk, Richard, Friedrich Kratochwil and Saul H. Mendlovitz (eds.), *International Law: A Contemporary Perspective*, Boulder and London: Westview Press, 1985.

Fierke, K. M., 'Multiple Identities. Interfacing Games: The Social Construction of Western Action in Bosnia', *European Journal of International Relations* 2 (1996), 467–97.

Changing Games, Changing Strategies: Critical Investigations in Security, Manchester University Press, 1998.

Fierke, Karin M. and Knud Erik Jørgensen (eds.), *Constructing International Relations: The Next Generation*, Armonk, NY, and London: M. E. Sharpe, 2001.

'Introduction', in Fierke and Jørgensen, *Constructing International Relations*, pp. 3–10.

Finnemore, Martha, *National Interests in International Society*, Ithaca and London: Cornell University Press, 1996.

Finnemore, Martha and Kathryn Sikkink, 'International Norms Dynamics and Political Change', *International Organization* 52 (1998), 887–917.

Fischer, Joschka, 'Die Katastrophe in Bosnien und die Konsequenzen für unsere Partei', reprinted in *Blätter für deutsche und internationale Politik* 40 (1995), 1141–52.

'Forum on *Social Theory of International Politics*', *Review of International Studies* 26 (2000), 123–4.

Franzke, Hans-Georg, 'Art. 24 II als Rechtsgrundlage für den Außeneinsatz der Bundeswehr?', *Neue Juristische Wochenschrift* 45 (1992), 3075–7.

Garton Ash, Timothy, *In Europe's Name: Germany and the Divided Continent*, London: Vintage, 1993.

Gasché, Rodolphe, *The Tain of the Mirror: Derrida and the Philosophy of Reflection*, Cambridge, MA and London: Harvard University Press, 1986.

Genscher, Hans-Dietrich, *Erinnerungen*, Munich: Goldmann, 1997.

Giddens, Anthony, *Central Problems in Social Theory: Action, Structure and Contradiction in Social Analysis*, London: Macmillan, 1979.

    The Constitution of Society: Outline of the Theory of Structuration, Cambridge: Polity Press, 1984.

Glotz, Peter, 'Der ungerechte Krieg', *Der Spiegel*, 9/45, 25 Feb. 1991, 38–9.

    'Neue deutsche Ideologic', *Der Spiegel*, 40/45, 30 Sep. 1991, 62–5.

Gordon, Philip H., *France, Germany, and the Western Alliance*, Boulder: Westview Press, 1995.

Grässlin, Jürgen, *Lizenz zum Töten? Wie die Bundeswehr zur internationalen Eingreiftruppe gemacht wird*, Munich: Knaur, 1997.

Gutjahr, Lothar, *German Foreign and Defence Policy After Unification*, London and New York: Pinter Publishers, 1994.

Guzzini, Stefano, 'A Reconstruction of Constructivism in International Relations', *European Journal of International Relations* 6 (2000), 147–82.

Habermas, Jürgen, 'A Kind of Settlement of Damages: The Apologetic Tendencies in German History Writing', in *Forever Under the Shadow of Hitler? Original Documents of the Historikerstreit, the Controversy Concerning the Singularity of the Holocaust*, translated by James Knowlton and Truett Cates, Atlantic Highlands, NJ: Humanities Press, 1993, pp. 34–44 (reprinted from *Die Zeit*, 11 Jul. 1986).

    The Past as Future, interviewed by Michael Haller, translated and edited by Max Pensky, Lincoln and London: University of Nebraska Press, 1994.

Hanrieder, Wolfram F., *Germany, America, Europe: Forty Years of German Foreign Policy*, New Haven and London: Yale University Press, 1989.

Hasenclever, Andreas, Peter Mayer and Volker Rittberger, *Theories of International Regimes*, Cambridge University Press, 1997.

Hellmann, Gunther, 'Die Westdeutschen, die Stationierungstruppen und die Vereinigung. Ein Lehrstück über "verantwortliche Machtpolitik"?', in Gunther Hellmann (ed.), *Alliierte Präsenz und deutsche Einheit. Die politischen Folgen militärischer Macht*, Baden-Baden: Nomos Verlagsgesellschaft, 1994, pp. 91–125.

    'Goodbye Bismarck? The Foreign Policy of Contemporary Germany', *Mershon International Studies Review* 40 (1996), 1–39.

Hennes, Michael, 'Der Krieg und die deutsche Politik', *Gewerkschaftliche Monatshefte* 44 (1993), 190–200.

Hodge, Carl Cavanagh, 'Germany and the Limits of Soft Security', *European Security* 7 (1998), 110–30.

Hoffmann, Oskar, *Deutsche Blauhelme bei UN-Missionen. Politische Hintergründe und rechtliche Aspekte*, Munich: Verlag Bonn Aktuell, 1993.

Hopf, Ted, 'The Promise of Constructivism in International Relations Theory', *International Security* 23 (1998), 171–200.

'Constructivism All the Way Down', *International Politics* 37 (2000), 369–78.

Horsley, William, 'United Germany's Seven Cardinal Sins: A Critique of German Foreign Policy', *Millennium: Journal of International Studies* 21 (1992), 225–41.

Hyde-Price, Adrian, '"Of Dragons and Snakes": Contemporary German Security Policy', in Gordon Smith, William E. Paterson and Stephen Padgett (eds.), *Developments in German Politics II*, Houndmills, Basingstoke and London: Macmillan, 1996, pp. 173–91.

Inacker, Michael J., *Unter Ausschluß der Öffentlichkeit? Die Deutschen in der Golfallianz*, Bonn and Berlin: Bouvier Verlag, 1991.

Inayatullah, Naeem and David L. Blaney, 'Knowing Encounters: Beyond Parochialism in International Relations Theory', in Lapid and Kratochwil, *Return of Culture and Identity in IR Theory*, pp. 65–84.

Jaeger, Hans-Martin, 'Konstruktionsfehler des Konstruktivismus in den Internationalen Beziehungen', *Zeitschrift für Internationale Beziehungen* 3 (1996), 313–40.

Jepperson, Ronald L., Alexander Wendt and Peter J. Katzenstein, 'Norms, Identity, and Culture in National Security', in Katzenstein, *Culture of National Security*, pp. 33–75.

Johnson, Barbara, 'Translator's Introduction', in Jacques Derrida, *Dissemination*, translated, with introduction and additional notes, by Barbara Johnson, University of Chicago Press, 1981, pp. vii–xxxiii.

Jørgensen, Knud Erik (ed.), *The Aarhus–Norsminde Papers: Constructivism, International Relations and European Studies*, Aarhus University, 1997.

'Four Levels and a Discipline', in Fierke and Jørgensen, *Constructing International Relations*, pp. 36–53.

Kaiser, Karl and Klaus Becher, *Deutschland und der Irak-Konflikt. Internationale Sicherheitsverantwortung Deutschlands und Europas nach der deutschen Vereinigung*, Bonn: Europa Union Verlag, 1992.

Katzenstein, Peter J., *Policy and Politics in West Germany: The Growth of a Semi-Sovereign State*, Philadelphia: Temple University Press, 1987.

(ed.), *The Culture of National Security: Norms and Identity in World Politics*, New York: Columbia University Press, 1996.

Katzenstein, Peter J., Robert O. Keohane and Stephen Krasner, '*International Organization* and the Study of World Politics', *International Organization* 52 (1998), 645–85.

Keck, Otto, 'Rationales kommunikatives Handeln in den internationalen Beziehungen. Ist eine Verbindung von Rational-Choice-Theorie und Habermas' Theorie des kommunikativen Handelns möglich?', *Zeitschrift für Internationale Beziehungen* 2 (1995), 5–48.

'Zur sozialen Konstruktion des Rational-Choice-Ansatzes. Einige Klarstellungen zur Rationalismus-Konstruktivismus-Debatte', *Zeitschrift für Internationale Beziehungen* 4 (1997), 139–51.

Kegley, Charles W. jr and Eugene R. Wittkopf, *World Politics: Trend and Transformation*, 7th edn, New York: St. Martin's, 1999.

Kelleher, Catherine and Cathleen Fisher, 'Germany', in Douglas J. Murray and Paul R. Viotti (eds.), *The Defense Policies of Nations: A Comparative Study*, 3rd edn, Baltimore and London: Johns Hopkins University Press, 1994, pp. 160–89.

Keohane, Robert O., 'International Institutions: Two Approaches', in Robert O. Keohane, *International Institutions and State Power: Essays in International Relations Theory*, Boulder: Westview Press, 1989, pp. 158–79.

'Ideas Part-Way Down', *Review of International Studies* 26 (2000), 125–30.

Khan, Daniel-Erasmus and Markus Zöckler, 'Germans to the Front? Or Le malade imaginaire', *European Journal of International Law* 3 (1992), 163–77.

Kielinger, Thomas, 'The Gulf War and the Consequences from the German Point of View', *Aussenpolitik* 42/2 (1991), 241–50.

Kinkel, Klaus, 'Verantwortung, Realismus, Zukunftssicherung', *FAZ*, 19 Mar. 1993, 8.

'Peacekeeping Missions: Germany Can Now Play Its Part', *NATO Review* 42/5 (1994), 3–7.

Klose, Hans-Ulrich, 'Die Deutschen und der Krieg am Golf', *FAZ*, 25 Jan. 1991, 6.

Klotz, Audie, *Norms in International Relations: The Struggle Against Apartheid*, Ithaca and London: Cornell University Press, 1995.

'Norms Reconstituting Interests: Global Racial Equality and US Sanctions Against South Africa', *International Organization* 49 (1995), 451–78.

Knutsen, Torbjørn L., *A History of International Relations Theory*, 2nd edn, Manchester University Press, 1997.

Koslowski, Rey and Friedrich V. Kratochwil, 'Understanding Change in International Politics: The Soviet Empire's Demise and the International System', *International Organization* 48 (1994), 215–47.

Krasner, Stephen D., 'Wars, Hotel Fires, and Plane Crashes', *Review of International Studies* 26 (2000), 131–6.

Kratochwil, Friedrich V., *International Order and Foreign Policy*, Boulder: Westview Press, 1978.

'The Humean Perspective on International Relations', *World Order Studies Program*, Occasional Paper No. 9, 1981.

'On the Notion of Interest in International Relations', *International Organization* 30 (1982), 1–30.

'Is International Law "Proper" Law?', *Archiv für Rechts- und Sozialphilosophie* 69 (1983), 13–46.

'Errors Have Their Advantage', *International Organization* 38 (1984), 305–20.

'The Force of Prescriptions', *International Organization* 38 (1984), 685–708.

'Thrasymmachos Revisited: On the Relevance of Norms for International Relations', *Journal of International Affairs* 37 (1984), 343–56.

'The Role of Domestic Courts as Agencies of the International Legal Order', in Falk, Kratochwil and Mendlovitz, *International Law*, pp. 236–63.

'Of Law and Human Action: A Jurisprudential Plea for a World Order Perspective in International Legal Studies', in Falk, Kratochwil and Mendlovitz, *International Law*, pp. 639–51.

'Of Systems, Boundaries, and Territoriality: An Inquiry into the Formation of the State System', *World Politics* 34 (1986), 27–52.

'Norms and Values: Rethinking the Domestic Analogy', *Ethics and International Affairs* 1 (1987), 135–59.

'Rules, Norms, Values and the Limits of "Rationality"', *Archiv für Rechts- und Sozialphilosophie* 73 (1987), 301–29.

'The Protagorean Quest: Community, Justice, and the "Oughts" and "Musts" of International Politics', *International Journal* 43 (1988), 205–40.

'Regimes, Interpretation and the "Science" of Politics: A Reappraisal', *Millennium: Journal of International Studies* 17 (1988), 263–84.

'The Challenge of Security in a Changing World', *Journal of International Affairs* 43 (1989), 119–41.

Rules, Norms, and Decisions: On the Conditions of Practical and Legal Reasoning in International Relations and Domestic Affairs, Cambridge University Press, 1989.

'International Order and Individual Liberty: A Critical Examination of "Realism" as a Theory of International Politics', *Constitutional Political Economy* 3 (1992), 29–50.

'Contract and Regimes: Do Issue Specificity and Variations of Formality Matter?', in Volker Rittberger (ed.), *Regime Theory and International Relations*, Oxford: Clarendon Press, 1993, pp. 73–93.

'The Embarrassment of Changes: Neo-Realism as the Science of Realpolitik Without Politics', *Review of International Studies* 19 (1993), 63–80.

'Norms Versus Numbers: Multilateralism and the Rationalist and Reflexivist Approaches to Institutions – a Unilateral Plea for Communicative Rationality', in John Gerard Ruggie (ed.), *Multilateralism Matters: The Theory and Praxis of an Institutional Form*, New York: Columbia University Press, 1993, pp. 443–74.

'Changing Relations Between State, Market and Society, and the Problem of Knowledge', *Pacific Focus* 9 (1994), 43–59.

'Citizenship: On the Border of Order', *Alternatives* 19 (1994), 485–506; also published in Lapid and Kratochwil, *Return of Culture and Identity in IR Theory*, pp. 181–97.

'The Limits of Contract', *European Journal of International Law* 5 (1994), 465–91.

'Sovereignty as *Dominium*: Is There a Right of Humanitarian Intervention?', in Lyons and Mastanduno, *Beyond Westphalia?*, pp. 21–42.

'Is the Ship of Culture at Sea or Returning?', in Lapid and Kratochwil, *Return of Culture and Identity in IR Theory*, pp. 201–22.

'Politics, Norms and Peaceful Change', *Review of International Studies* 24 (1998), 193–218.

'Constructing a New Orthodoxy? Wendt's "Social Theory of International Politics" and the Constructivist Challenge', *Millennium: Journal of International Studies* 29 (2000), 73–101.

'Constructivism as an Approach to Interdisciplinary Study', in Fierke and Jørgensen, *Constructing International Relations*, pp. 13–35.

Kratochwil, Friedrich, Paul Rohrlich and Harpreet Mahajan, *Peace and Sovereignty: Reflections on Conflict over Territory*, Lanham, MD: University Press of America, 1985.

Kratochwil, Friedrich and John Gerard Ruggie, 'International Organization: A State of the Art on the Art of the State', *International Organization* 40 (1986), 753–75.

Kubálková, Vendulka, Nicholas Onuf and Paul Kowert (eds.), *International Relations in a Constructed World*, Armonk, NY and London: M. E. Sharpe, 1998.

'Constructing Constructivism', in Kubálková, Onuf and Kowert, *International Relations in a Constructed World*, pp. 3–21.

Lamers, Karl, 'Was die Friedensmissionen lehren', *Die politische Meinung* 39 (1994), 51–7.

Lantis, Jeffrey S., 'Rising to the Challenge: German Security Policy in the Post-Cold War Era', *German Politics and Society* 14 (1996), 19–35.

Lapid, Yosef and Friedrich Kratochwil (eds.), *The Return of Culture and Identity in IR Theory*, Boulder and London: Lynne Rienner Publishers, 1996.

'Revisiting the "National": Toward an Identity Agenda in Neorealism?', in Lapid and Kratochwil, *Return of Culture and Identity in IR Theory*, pp. 105–26.

Leicht, Robert, 'Mit Volldampf in den Verfassungsstreit', *Die Zeit*, 24 Jul. 1992, 3.

Linnenkamp, Hilmar, 'The Security Policy of the New Germany', in Stares, *New Germany and New Europe*, pp. 93–125.

Livingston, Robert Gerald, 'United Germany: Bigger and Better', *Foreign Policy* 87 (1992), 157–74.

Lutz, Dieter S. (ed.), *Deutsche Soldaten weltweit. Blauhelme, Eingreiftruppen, 'out of area' – Der Streit um unsere sicherheitspolitische Zukunft*, Reinbek: Rowohlt, 1993.

Lyons, Gene M. and Michael Mastanduno (eds.), *Beyond Westphalia? State Sovereignty and International Intervention*, Baltimore and London: Johns Hopkins University Press, 1995.

Markovits, Andrei S. and Simon Reich, *The German Predicament: Memory and Power in the New Europe*, Ithaca and London: Cornell University Press, 1997.

Maull, Hanns W., 'Zivilmacht Bundesrepublik Deutschland. Vierzehn Thesen für eine neue deutsche Außenpolitik', *Europa-Archiv* 47 (1992), 269–78.

'Allemagne et Japon: deux pays à suivre', *Politique Etrangère* 60 (1995), 477–96.

'A German Perspective', in Michael Brenner (ed.), *Multilateralism and Western Strategy*, London: Macmillan, 1995, pp. 42–76.

'Germany in the Yugoslav Crisis', *Survival* 37 (1995/6), 99–130.

McKenzie, Mary M., 'Competing Conceptions of Normality in the Post-Cold War Era: Germany, Europe, and Foreign Policy Change', *German Politics and Society* 14 (1996), 1–18.

Mead, George H., *Mind, Self and Society: From the Standpoint of a Social Behaviourist*, University of Chicago Press, [1934] 1965.

Meiers, Franz-Josef, 'Germany: The Reluctant Power', *Survival* 37 (1995), 82–103.

Mercer, Jonathan, 'Anarchy and Identity', *International Organization* 49 (1995), 229–52.

Müller, Harald, 'German Foreign Policy After Unification', in Stares, *New Germany and New Europe*, pp. 126–73.
  'Internationale Beziehungen als kommunikatives Handeln. Zur Kritik der utilitaristischen Handlungstheorien', *Zeitschrift für Internationale Beziehungen* 1 (1994), 15–44.
  'Military Intervention for European Security: The German Debate', in Lawrence Freedman (ed.), *Military Intervention in European Conflicts*, Oxford: Blackwell Publishers, 1994, pp. 125–41.
  'Spielen hilft nicht immer. Die Grenzen des Rational-Choice-Ansatzes und der Platz der Theorie kommunikativen Handelns in der Analyse internationaler Beziehungen', *Zeitschrift für Internationale Beziehungen* 2 (1995), 371–91.

Müller, Michael, 'Vom Dissensrisiko zur Ordnung der internationalen Staatenwelt. Zum Projekt einer normative gehaltvollen Theorie', *Zeitschrift für Internationale Beziehungen* 3 (1996), 367–79.

Mutz, Reinhard, 'Die Bundeswehr steht am Ende ihrer Geschichte als Friedensarmee', *FR*, 16 Jul. 1993, 10.

Naumann, Klaus, *Die Bundeswehr in einer Welt im Umbruch*, Berlin: Siedler Verlag, 1994.

Neumann, Iver B., 'Self and Other in International Relations', *European Journal of International Relations* 2 (1996), 139–74.

Neumann, Iver B. and Ole Wæver (eds.), *The Future of International Relations: Masters in the Making?*, London and New York: Routledge, 1997.

Nolte, Georg, 'Bundeswehreinsätze in kollektiven Sicherheitssystemen. Zum Urteil des Bundesverfassungsgerichts vom 12. Juli 1994', *Zeitschrift für ausländisches öffentliches und Völkerrecht* 54 (1994), 652–85.

Onuf, Nicholas Greenwood, 'International Law-in-Action and the Numbers Game: A Comment', *International Studies Quarterly* 14 (1970), 325–33.
  'The Principle of Nonintervention, the United Nations, and the International System', *International Organization* 25 (1971), 209–27.
  'Law and Lawyers in International Crises', *International Organization* 29 (1975), 1035–53.
  'International Legal Order as an Idea', *American Journal of International Law* 73 (1979), 244–66.
  (ed.), *Law-Making in the Global Community*, Durham, NC: Carolina Academic Press, 1982.

'Global Law-Making and Legal Thought', in Onuf, *Law-Making in the Global Community*, pp. 1–81.

'International Codification: Interpreting the Last Half-Century', in Falk, Kratochwil and Mendlovitz, *International Law*, pp. 264–79.

World of Our Making: Rules and Rule in Social Theory and International Relations, Columbia: University of South Carolina Press, 1989.

'Sovereignty: Outline of a Conceptual History', *Alternatives* 16 (1991), 425–46.

'The Constitution of International Society', *European Journal of International Law* 5 (1994), 1–19.

'Imagined Republics', *Alternatives* 19 (1994), 315–37.

'Intervention for the Common Good', in Lyons and Mastanduno, *Beyond Westphalia?*, pp. 43–58.

'Levels', *European Journal of International Relations* 1 (1995), 35–58.

'A Constructivist Manifesto', in Burch and Denemark, *Constituting International Political Economy*, pp. 7–17.

'Hegemony's Hegemony in IPE', in Burch and Denemark, *Constituting International Political Economy*, pp. 91–110.

'Constructivism: A User's Manual', in Kubálková, Onuf and Kowert, *International Relations in a Constructed World*, pp. 58–78.

'Everyday Ethics in International Relations', *Millennium: Journal of International Studies* 27 (1998), 669–93.

The Republican Legacy in International Thought, Cambridge University Press, 1998.

'Speaking of Policy', in Vendulka Kubálková (ed.), *Foreign Policy in a Constructed World*, Armonk, NY: M. E. Sharpe, 2001, pp. 77–95.

'The Politics of Constructivism', in Fierke and Jørgensen, *Constructing International Relations*, pp. 236–54.

Onuf, Nicholas G. and Thomas J. Johnson, 'Peace in the Liberal World: Does Democracy Matter?', in Charles W. Kegley jr (ed.), *Controversies in International Relations Theory: Realism and the Neorealist Challenge*, New York: St. Martin's Press, 1995, pp. 179–99.

Onuf, Nicholas Greenwood and Frank Klink, 'Anarchy, Authority, Rules', *International Studies Quarterly* 33 (1989), 149–73.

Onuf, Nicholas Greenwood and V. S. Peterson, 'Human Rights from an International Regimes Perspective', *Journal of International Affairs* 37 (1984), 329–42.

Palan, Ronen, 'A World of Their Making: An Evaluation of the Constructivist Critique in International Relations', *Review of International Studies* 26 (2000), 575–98.

Pasic, Sujata Chakrabarti, 'Culturing International Relations Theory: A Call for Extension', in Lapid and Kratochwil, *Return of Culture and Identity in IR Theory*, pp. 85–104.

Paterson, William E., 'Beyond Semi-Sovereignty: The New Germany in the New Europe', *German Politics* 5 (1996), 167–84.

274

Persram, Nalini, 'Coda: Sovereignty, Subjectivity, Strategy', in Edkins, Persram and Pin-Fat, *Sovereignty and Subjectivity*, pp. 163–75.

Peters, Susanne, 'Germany's Security Policy After Unification: Taking the Wrong Models', *European Security* 6 (1997), 18–47.

Philippi, Nina, *Bundeswehr-Auslandseinsätze als außen- und sicherheitspolitisches Problem des geeinten Deutschland*, Frankfurt am Main: Peter Lang, 1997.

Price, Richard and Christian Reus-Smit, 'Dangerous Liaisons? Critical International Theory and Constructivism', *European Journal of International Relations* 4 (1998), 259–94.

Ringmar, Erik, 'Alexander Wendt: A Social Scientist Struggling with History', in Neumann and Wæver, *Future of International Relations*, pp. 269–89.

Risse-Kappen, Thomas, 'Democratic Peace – Warlike Democracies? A Social Constructivist Interpretation of the Liberal Argument', *European Journal of International Relations* 1 (1995), 491–517.

'Reden ist nicht billig. Zur Debatte um Kommunikation und Rationalität', *Zeitschrift für Internationale Beziehungen* 2 (1995), 171–84.

'Collective Identity in a Democratic Community: The Case of NATO', in Katzenstein, *Culture of National Security*, pp. 357–99.

Ruggie, John Gerard, *Constructing the World Polity: Essays on International Institutionalization*, London and New York: Routledge, 1998.

'What Makes the World Hang Together? Neo-Utilitarianism and the Social Constructivist Challenge', *International Organization* 52 (1998), 855–85.

Rühe, Volker, 'Es geht nicht um Eroberungskriege, es geht um Hilfe', *FAZ*, 10 Sep. 1993, 12.

Sauder, Axel, *Souveränität und Integration. Französische und deutsche Konzeptionen europäischer Sicherheit nach dem Ende des Kalten Krieges (1990–1993)*, Baden-Baden: Nomos Verlagsgesellschaft, 1995.

Scharping, Rudolf, 'Deutsche Außenpolitik muß berechenbar sein', *Internationale Politik* 50 (1995), 38–44.

Schlör, Wolfgang F., 'German Security Policy: An Examination of the Trends in German Security Policy in a New European and Global Context', *Adelphi Paper* 277 (1993).

Schmalz-Bruns, Rainer, 'Die Theorie Kommunikativen Handelns – eine Flaschenpost? Anmerkungen zur jüngsten Debatte in den internationalen Beziehungen', *Zeitschrift für Internationale Beziehungen* 2 (1995), 347–70.

Schneider, Gerald, 'Rational Choice und kommunikatives Handeln. Eine Replik auf Harald Müller', *Zeitschrift für Internationale Beziehungen* 1 (1994), 357–66.

Schöllgen, Gregor, 'Geschichte als Argument. Was kann und muß die deutsche Großmacht auf dem Weg ins 21. Jahrhundert tun?', *Internationale Politik* 52 (1997), 1–7.

Searle, John R., *Speech Acts: An Essay in the Philosophy of Language*, Cambridge University Press, 1969.

Shapiro, Ian and Alexander Wendt, 'The Difference That Realism Makes: Social Science and the Politics of Consent', *Politics and Society* 20 (1992), 197–223.

Smith, Michael E., 'Sending the Bundeswehr to the Balkans: The Domestic Politics of Reflexive Multilateralism', *German Politics and Society* 14 (1996), 49–67.

Smith, Steve, 'The Forty Years' Detour: The Resurgence of Normative Theory in International Relations', *Millennium: Journal of International Studies* 21 (1992), 489–506.

'Positivism and Beyond', in Steve Smith, Ken Booth and Marysia Zalewski (eds.), *International Theory: Positivism and Beyond*, Cambridge University Press, 1996, pp. 11–44.

'New Approaches to International Theory', in Baylis and Smith, *Globalization of World Politics*, pp. 165–90.

'The Discipline of International Relations: Still an American Social Science?', *British Journal of Politics and International Relations* 2 (2000), 374–402.

'Wendt's World', *Review of International Studies* 26 (2000), 151–63.

Stares, Paul (ed.), *The New Germany and the New Europe*, Washington, DC: Brookings Institution, 1992.

Staten, Henry, *Wittgenstein and Derrida*, Oxford: Basil Blackwell, 1985.

Stephan, Cora, 'An der deutschen Heimatfront', *Der Spiegel*, 10/45, 4 Mar. 1991, 238–45.

van Orden, Geoffrey, 'The *Bundeswehr* in Transition', *Survival* 33 (1991), 352–70.

Varcoe, Ian, 'Identity and the Limits of Comparison: Bauman's Reception in Germany', *Theory, Culture and Society* 15 (1998), 57–72.

Viotti, Paul R. and Mark V. Kauppi, *International Relations Theory: Realism, Pluralism, Globalism and Beyond*, 3rd edn, Boston: Allyn and Bacon, 1999.

Voigt, Karsten, 'German Interest in Multilateralism', *Aussenpolitik* 47/2 (1996), 107–16.

von Prittwitz, Volker, 'Verständigung über die Verständigung. Anmerkungen und Ergänzungen zur Debatte über Rationalität und Kommunikation in den Internationalen Beziehungen', *Zeitschrift für Internationale Beziehungen* 3 (1996), 133–47.

Wæver, Ole, 'Figures of International Thought: Introducing Persons Instead of Paradigms', in Neumann and Wæver, *Future of International Relations*, pp. 1–37.

Walker, R. B. J., 'Alternative, Critical, Political', paper for the International Studies Association conference in Los Angeles, 14–18 March 2000.

Walt, Stephen M., 'International Relations: One World, Many Theories', *Foreign Policy* 110 (1998), 29–46.

Waltz, Kenneth N., *Theory of International Politics*, New York: McGraw-Hill, 1979.

Weber, Cynthia, 'IR: The Resurrection or New Frontiers of Incorporation', *European Journal of International Relations* 5 (1999), 435–50.

Weldes, Jutta, 'Constructing National Interests', *European Journal of International Relations* 2 (1996), 275–318.

Constructing National Interests: The United States and the Cuban Missile Crisis, Minneapolis and London: University of Minnesota Press, 1999.

Weldes, Jutta, Mark Laffey, Hugh Gusterson and Raymond Duvall (eds.), *Cultures of Insecurity: States, Communities, and the Production of Danger*, Minneapolis and London: University of Minnesota Press, 1999.

'Introduction: Constructing Insecurity', in Weldes et al., *Cultures of Insecurity*, pp. 1–33.

Wendt, Alexander E., 'The Agent–Structure Problem in International Relations Theory', *International Organization* 41 (1987), 335–70.

'Bridging the Theory/Meta-Theory Gap in International Relations', *Review of International Studies* 17 (1991), 383–92.

'Anarchy Is What States Make of It: The Social Construction of Power Politics', *International Organization* 46 (1992), 391–425.

'Levels of Analysis vs. Agents and Structures: Part III', *Review of International Studies* 18 (1992), 181–5.

'Collective Identity Formation and the International State', *American Political Science Review* 88 (1994), 384–96.

'Constructing International Politics', *International Security* 20 (1995), 71–81.

'Identity and Structural Change in International Politics', in Lapid and Kratochwil, *Return of Culture and Identity in IR Theory*, pp. 47–64.

'On Constitution and Causation in International Relations', *Review of International Studies* special issue 24 (1998), 101–17.

Social Theory of International Politics, Cambridge University Press, 1999.

'On the Via Media: A Response to the Critics', *Review of International Studies* 26 (2000), 165–80.

Wendt, Alexander and Michael Barnett, 'Dependent State Formation and Third World Militarization', *Review of International Studies* 19 (1993), 321–47.

Wendt, Alexander and Raymond Duvall, 'Institutions and International Order', in Ernst-Otto Czempiel and James N. Rosenau (eds.), *Global Changes and Theoretical Challenges: Approaches to World Politics for the 1990s*, Lexington, MA: Lexington Books, 1989, pp. 51–73.

Wendt, Alexander and Daniel Friedheim, 'Hierarchy Under Anarchy: Informal Empire and the East German State', *International Organization* 49 (1995), 689–721; also published in Thomas J. Biersteker and Cynthia Weber (eds.), *State Sovereignty as Social Construct*, Cambridge University Press, 1996, pp. 240–77.

Wiegandt, Manfred H., 'Germany's International Integration: The Rulings of the German Federal Constitutional Court on the Maastricht Treaty and the Out-of-Area Deployment of German Troops', *American University Journal of International Law and Policy* 10 (1995), 889–916.

Williams, Michael C. and Keith Krause, 'Preface: Towards Critical Security Studies', in Keith Krause and Michael C. Williams (eds.), *Critical Security Studies: Concepts and Cases*, London: UCL Press, 1997, pp. vii–xxi.

Wind, Marlene, 'Nicholas G. Onuf: The Rules of Anarchy', in Neumann and Wæver, *Future of International Relations*, pp. 236–68.

Wittgenstein, Ludwig, *Philosophical Investigations*, translated by G. E. M. Anscombe, Oxford: Basil Blackwell, 1974.

Zangl, Bernhard and Michael Zürn, 'Argumentatives Handeln bei internationalen Verhandlungen. Moderate Anmerkungen zur post-realistischen Debatte', *Zeitschrift für Internationale Beziehungen* 3 (1996), 341–66.

Zehfuss, Maja, 'Sprachlosigkeit schränkt ein. Zur Bedeutung von Sprache in konstruktivistischen Theorien', *Zeitschrift für Internationale Beziehungen* 5 (1998), 109–37.

'Constructivisms in International Relations: Wendt, Onuf, and Kratochwil', in Fierke and Jørgensen, *Constructing International Relations*, pp. 54–75.

'Constructivism and Identity: A Dangerous Liaison', *European Journal of International Relations* 7 (2001), 315–48.

Documents

Basic Law for the Federal Republic of Germany, promulgated by the Parliamentary Council on 23 May 1949 (version in effect since 15 November 1994), official translation, Bonn: Press and Information Office of the Federal Government, 1995.

Bundesminister der Verteidigung, *Weißbuch 1985. Zur Lage und Entwicklung der Bundeswehr*, Bonn, 1985.

Die Bundeswehr der Zukunft – Bundeswehrplan '94, Bonn, 1993.

Bundesministerium der Verteidigung, 'Militärpolitische und militärstrategische Grundlagen und konzeptionelle Grundrichtung der Neugestaltung der Bundeswehr', reprinted in *FR*, 20 Feb. 1992, 21.

Weißbuch 1994. Weißbuch zur Sicherheit der Bundesrepublik Deutschland und zur Lage und Zukunft der Bundeswehr, Bonn, 1994.

official website of the Federal Ministry of Defence, http://www.bundeswehr.de/sicherheitspolitik/uno-missionen/einsaetze.htm (site last updated 14 September 1998).

Bundesverfassungsgericht, 'Urteil des Zweiten Senats vom 8. April 1993 aufgrund der mündlichen Verhandlung vom 7. April 1993', 8 Apr. 1993, E88, 173–85.

'Urteil des Zweiten Senats vom 12. Juli 1994 aufgrund der mündlichen Verhandlung vom 19. und 20. April 1994', 12 Jul. 1994, E90, 286–394.

Deutscher Bundestag, *Drucksache*, 5/2873, 1968.

Drucksache, 12/28, 11 Jan. 1991.

Drucksache, 12/2896, 23 Jun. 1992.

Drucksache, 12/3014, 2 Jul. 1992.

Drucksache, 12/3055, 21 Jul. 1992.

Drucksache, 12/4107, 13 Jan. 1993.

Drucksache, 12/4135, 15 Jan. 1993.

Drucksache, 12/4535, 10 Mar. 1993.

Drucksache, 12/4710, 6 Apr. 1993.

Drucksache, 12/4711, 5 Apr. 1993.
Drucksache, 12/4755, 20 Apr. 1993.
Drucksache, 13/1802, 26 Jun. 1995.
Plenarprotokoll, 11/228, Berlin, 4 Oct. 1990, 18015–83.
Plenarprotokoll, 11/235, Bonn, 15 Nov. 1990, 18819–59.
Plenarprotokoll, 12/2, Bonn, 14 Jan. 1991, 21–43.
Plenarprotokoll, 12/3, Bonn, 17 Jan. 1991, 45–55.
Plenarprotokoll, 12/5, Bonn, 30 Jan. 1991, 67–93.
Plenarprotokoll, 12/101, Bonn, 22 Jul. 1992, 8607–59.
Plenarprotokoll, 12/132, Bonn, 15 Jan. 1993, 11463–559.
Plenarprotokoll, 12/150, Bonn, 26 Mar. 1993, 12865–924.
Plenarprotokoll, 12/151, Bonn, 21 Apr. 1993, 12925–13002.
Plenarprotokoll, 12/219, Bonn, 14 Apr. 1994, 18907–19039.
Plenarprotokoll, 12/240, Bonn, 22 Jul. 1994, 21165–218.
Plenarprotokoll, 13/48, Bonn, 30 Jun. 1995, 3953–4044.
Plenarprotokoll, 13/76, Bonn, 6 Dec. 1995, 6631–708.
Plenarprotokoll, 14/31, Bonn, 26 Mar. 1999, 2561–618.
Genscher, Hans-Dietrich, address of the foreign minister at the 45th General Assembly of the United Nations on 26 Sep. 1990 in New York, in Presse- und Informationsamt der Bundesregierung, *Bulletin*, 115, 27 Sep. 1990, 1201–6.
address of the foreign minister at the 46th General Assembly of the United Nations on 25 Sep. 1991 in New York, in Presse- und Informationsamt der Bundesregierung, *Bulletin*, 104, 26 Sep. 1991, 825–30.
Grundgesetz für die Bundesrepublik Deutschland, 51st revised edn (15 September 1993), Munich: C. H. Beck'sche Verlagsbuchhandlung, 1993.
Kinkel, Klaus, address of the foreign minister at the 47th General Assembly of the United Nations on 23 Sep. 1992 in New York, in Presse- und Informationsamt der Bundesregierung, *Bulletin*, 101, 25 Sep. 1992, 949–53.
'Die transatlantische Partnerschaft als Fundament der Außenpolitik', in Presse- und Informationsamt der Bundesregierung, *Bulletin*, 36, 8 May 1993, 311–13.
'Kernfragen deutscher Außenpolitik', in Presse- und Informationsamt der Bundesregierung, *Bulletin*, 82, 16 Oct. 1995, 800–3.
Kohl, Helmut, 'Ein geeintes Deutschland als Gewinn für Stabilität und Sicherheit in Europa', in Presse- und Informationsamt der Bundesregierung, *Bulletin*, 68, 29 May 1990, 585–9.
message on the day of German unification on 3 Oct. 1990 to all governments in the world, in Presse- und Informationsamt der Bundesregierung, *Bulletin*, 118, 5 Oct. 1990, 1227–8.
'Die Rolle Deutschlands in Europa', in Presse- und Informationsamt der Bundesregierung, *Bulletin*, 33, 22 Mar. 1991, 241–7.
statement of the Federal Government in the Bundestag on 6 Nov. 1991, in Presse- und Informationsamt der Bundesregierung, *Bulletin*, 124, 7 Nov. 1991, 985–90.

'Ziele und Prioritäten der Innen- und Außenpolitik', in Presse- und Informationsamt der Bundesregierung, *Bulletin*, 84, 25 Jul. 1992, 809–12.

'Europäische Sicherheit und die Rolle Deutschlands', in Presse- und Informationsamt der Bundesregierung, *Bulletin*, 15, 16 Feb. 1994, 133–7.

'The North Atlantic Treaty', Washington, DC, 4 Apr. 1949. http://www.nato.int/docu/basictxt/treaty.htm.

North Atlantic Treaty Organization, 'New Strategic Concept', http://www.nato.int/docu/comm/c911107a.htm (accessed 27 Nov. 1998).

Rühe, Volker, 'Gestaltung euro-atlantischer Politik – eine "Grand Strategy" für eine neue Zeit', in Presse- und Informationsamt der Bundesregierung, *Bulletin*, 27, 1 Apr. 1993, 229–33.

United Nations High Commissioner for Refugees Evaluation and Policy Analysis Unit, *The Kosovo Refugee Crisis: An Independent Evaluation of UNHCR's Emergency Preparedness and Response*, pre-publication edn, Geneva: February, 2000.

'Vertrag über die abschließende Regelung in bezug auf Deutschland', reprinted in *Grundgesetz für die Bundesrepublik Deutschland*, pp. 107–14.

Index

absence, 197, 198, 199, 200, 202, 213, 224, 238
Adenauer, Konrad, 65–6
Adler, Emanuel, 7, 8, 250, 251–2, 253
Adriatic Sea, 71, 115, 143
  see also embargo
agency, 20, 88, 152, 155
agent–structure relationship, 12, 45–6,
  90–1
alliance, *see* NATO
altercasting, 46, 47, 55, 79
altruism, 40, 57
AMF, 63–4
analogy, 122, 134, 136, 148
anarchy, 4, 14, 39–40, 42, 207
Annan, Kofi, 75
anthropomorphism, of states, 89, 90, 92
aporia, 230, 231, 232, 256–7, 258, 262
  see also undecidable
appeasement, 122, 123
appraisal, 16, 18, 97, 116
Aristotle, 149
assertive, 20, 153–4, 161, 162, 170, 171,
  173, 178, 191–2
Austin, J. L., 17, 100, 182, 212, 223, 224–5
Austria, 51, 107, 113
AWACS, 29–30, 61, 67–8, 113, 115, 125,
  178–80, 241
  see also Operation Deny Flight

Bahrain, 50
Balkans, 71, 75, 76, 78, 143, 177, 179, 208
  as historically sensitive, 30, 129, 136, 216
  see also Croatia; Kohl doctrine;
    Montenegro; Serbia
Barnett, Michael, 250
Basic Law, 26, 104–5, 123, 135, 139, 209,
  218, 226
  ambiguity of, 52, 166

Art. 24, 24, 101–4, 114–15, 117, 158–9,
  162, 174, 192
Art. 79, 104, 112, 163
Art. 87, 24, 44, 84, 101–7, 110, 112,
  114–15, 117, 158–9, 162, 168
change of, 52–3, 111–12, 176–7, 244
clarification of, 69, 161–3, 164
interpretations of, 24, 48, 101–4, 110, 118,
  164–5, 172–3
necessity of change of, 70, 71–2, 167–8,
  171–2, 217
problems of change of, 24, 80, 124,
  158–60, 162–3
testing limits of, 29, 166–7, 169
violation of, 30, 166, 167
see also constitutionality; legality, of
  military involvement abroad; NATO
  territory
Becher, Klaus, 64, 110
Beck, Marielouise, 143
beginning, 151–2, 157, 247, 248
being, 198, 255
Bergdoll, Udo, 74
Berger, Peter L., 43, 48
Berger, Stefan, 27, 32
Berger, Thomas U., 25, 26
Berndt, Michael, 79
Biehle, Alfred, 182
Blumer, Herbert, 12
boundaries,
  of IR, 151, 189
  of the possible, 35, 37, 156, 183, 262, 263;
    see also limit
  of self, 15, 56, 57, 89
  of thinking, 36–7
Boutros Ghali, Boutros, 78–9, 81
Bülow, Andreas von, 64
Bush, George, 111

Index

Calic, Marie-Janine, 30–1
Cambodia, 29, 50, 52, 107, 109, 165, 182, 228
Campbell, David, 7, 90, 221
Carr, E. H., 149
causality, 92, 155
  of ideas, 90
  of identity, 57, 83, 92
  and science, 13, 91
Checkel, Jeffrey, 5, 251, 252
Cheney, Richard, 72
civilian power, 188–9
Claes, Willy, 73–4
Cold War, 59, 88, 102, 105, 123, 130, 137, 212
combat mission, 32, 61, 180, 183, 243
  readiness to take part in, 52, 71, 159, 162, 168
commissive, 20, 153–4, 171, 173–4, 185, 191–2
common foreign and security policy, 66
common sense, 35–6, 87, 91, 194, 208, 222, 236, 246
  and rationality, 16, 141
commonplace, *see* topos
communication, 18–19, 49, 99, 226
  critique of conception of, 35, 198, 199, 206, 223–4, 229
  and intersubjectivity, 97, 141
  and norms, 16–17, 100, 120, 132, 149, 222
communicative action, 16, 49, 141
community, international, 69, 122, 148
  demands of, 71, 74, 174–5
  as relevant to definition of FRG's identity, 65, 179, 208, 214
  significance of, 67, 68
conscience, good, 231, 232, 235, 257, 259, 260–1, 262
consensus on security policy, 24, 68, 105–6, 179
constitution, *see* Basic Law
constitution, mutual, 12, 45–6, 90, 91, 157
constitutional argument, 24, 26, 30, 47, 63, 100, 104
constitutional court, 29, 68, 113–14, 163–4, 166–7, 242
  cases, 67–8, 178–9
  consequences of ruling, 70, 118, 128, 192, 233, 243
  ruling, 24, 30, 114, 167, 169–70
constitutionality, 68, 80, 109–10, 165, 167, 168, 179
  see also Basic Law; constitutional argument; constitutional court

constructivist turn, 2
context, 200, 226, 227, 228, 244, 247
  as based on rules and norms, 16, 19, 20, 96, 98
  of framework, 220
  historical, 84, 101, 115, 142
  independent from, 89
  as indeterminate, 200–1, 206, 224, 225–6, 255
  intersubjective, 16, 18, 96, 104, 140
  and knowledge, 22
  necessity of, 17, 187, 224–5
  normative, 100, 133, 135–6, 137, 138, 142, 148, 252
  of norms, 34, 111
  relevant, 85, 127, 246
  significance of, 61, 62, 137
  as unavoidable, 157
convention, 20–1, 154
conversation of gestures, 48
Cooper, Alice H., 31, 123
cooperation, 15, 57, 59, 60, 67, 89, 212
Cornell, Drucilla, 244
Costa Rica, 216
coup de force, 142, 230, 236
Croatia, 31, 76, 132, 148
CSCE, 54, 59, 66
Culler, Jonathan, 202, 211
culture, 211, 219, 260
  of anarchy, *see* security environment
  definition of, 43
  Kantian, 57, 77, 83
  of restraint, 125, 130

Dayton Accords, 31
de Charette, Hervé, 78
death, 193–4, 237, 243–4, 255
debate, rationalist–constructivist, 2, 3–6
  see also rationalism
Debate, Third, 92
decision, free, 230–1, 256, 257
deconstruction, 10, 202–6, 223, 229, 246–7, 248, 255, 257
  as political, 205–6, 262
  styles of, 202–3
deed, 20, 21, 151–2, 153, 155, 156, 190, 195
defence, definition of, 103
deployment, definition of, 102–3, 107, 109
depoliticisation, 197, 206, 219–20, 223, 231, 247, 261
dichotomy, 144, 197, 214, 217, 218, 236, 255
différance, 35, 199–200, 201, 214, 217, 223
difference, 144, 199, 204, 215, 217
  see also identity and difference

Index

CAMBRIDGE STUDIES IN INTERNATIONAL RELATIONS